Our Revolution

Our Revolution

A FUTURE TO BELIEVE IN

———————•———————

BERNIE SANDERS

St. Martin's Paperbacks

Photo research and editing provided by Liz Seramur of Selected Shots Photo Research, Inc.

OUR REVOLUTION

For information address St. Martin's Press, 175 Fifth Avenue, New York, NY 10010.

ISBN: 978-1-250-16045-4

Our books may be purchased in bulk for promotional, educational, or business use. Please contact your local bookseller or the Macmillan Corporate and Premium Sales Department at 1-800-221-7945, extension 5442, or by e-mail at MacmillanSpecialMarkets@macmillan.com.

Printed in the United States of America

St. Martin's Press edition / November 2016
St. Martin's Griffin edition / August 2017
St. Martin's Paperbacks edition / January 2018

St. Martin's Paperbacks are published by St. Martin's Press, 175 Fifth Avenue, New York, NY 10010.

10 9 8 7 6 5 4 3 2 1

This book is dedicated to my parents, Eli and Dorothy Sanders, and to my entire family—my wife, Jane, my brother, Larry, my children, Levi, Heather, Carina, and Dave, and their spouses, Raine, Marc, Blake, and Liza, and my grandchildren, Sunnee, Cole, Ryleigh, Grayson, Ella, Tess, and Dylan. Their love and support have always sustained me.

This book is also dedicated to the hundreds of thousands of volunteers who worked so hard, in so many ways, to make our campaign a success. You have made me optimistic about the future of our country. Don't give up. The struggle must continue.

CONTENTS

INTRODUCTION TO THE PAPERBACK

This book was w... ...came president. I wasn't completely s... proved significantly u... people continued to h... new wealth and inco...

During his camp... American people th... working class of thi... ment. It turned out n... A lot of people beli...

There is a lot o... country, and Trum... has changed this ... ple have been left... could provide a d... proud member of ... tory. But over th... have shut down a... have disappeare... and disastrous t... automation. Bu...

When... Apr... establishmen... something r... senator from... nition. Our ... nization, an... Party establ... ning agains... the country... dency for E... cratic pres... 2008.

When ... 2016, it tu... big-time. ... consequen... country— ... way, chan...

We rec... tion t... and cauc... two states ...

formin... real ch... always... when ... stand ...

Tha... is abo... ment i... mover... rights... enviro... rious ...

Tha... I er... future... be oth... sands ... groun... countr... gay ac... sive ... we are... low de... orient...

In ... people... to cast... some ... and v... back t... need a...

In ... ing w... ours ... the co... up aga... gether...

in A... natio... aire... prou... PAC... we r... tribu... dona... majo...

D... the e... long ... com... port... econ... rend... tem, ... care ... crisi... sive ... a for... much...

In... ideas... that ... agen... gover... camp...

Th... our a... force...

In Washington, D.C., I marched with low-wage workers who told the world that they cannot survive on the starvation minimum wage that currently exists. That we need to raise the minimum wage to a living wage. Their message and their fight is reverberating all across the country.

This book describes the history-making campaign that we ran. But more important, it looks to the future. It lays out a new path for America based on principles of economic, social, racial, and environmental justice. On behalf of our children and grandchildren, it is a path that must be followed and a fight that must be won.

The struggle continues.

PART
ONE

Running for President

HOW DO WE TURN OUT
THE WAY WE DO?

BROOKLYN

I grew up in a three-and-a-half-room rent-controlled apartment. My older brother, Larry, and I spent years sleeping on couches in the living room. During the 2016 New York State primary, in order to remind New Yorkers that I had grown up in Brooklyn, we held a rally on the street where I was raised, East Twenty-sixth Street. Fifty-six years after I left, I had a chance to visit the apartment where I spent my first eighteen years. Somehow, it had shrunk. God, it was small. The kitchen/dining room was tiny. It was hard to imagine our family of four having dinner there every night together. And the whole building looked dingier than I remembered. And so many apartments on one floor.

One of my first memories was being on the sidewalk outside of the apartment house where we lived on Kings Highway in the Flatbush section of Brooklyn. There was a military parade. It was the end of World War II. I was four years old.

That war, Hitler, and the Holocaust surely played a major role in shaping the direction of my life. I remember the photos of my father's family in Poland—killed by the Nazis. I remember a telephone call in the middle

Mom, Larry, and me. I'm the little guy. (Author Collection)

of the night, which never happened in our apartment, telling my father the good news that a cousin of his was still alive and in a displaced persons camp. I remember crying whenever I saw photos in a book about the destruction of the Jews. I remember seeing people in the neighborhood with tattooed numbers on their arms—survivors of concentration camps. I remember the excitement in the community at the establishment of the State of Israel in 1948.

No question about it. Being Jewish. The loss of family, including children my own age, in the Holocaust. The rise to power of a right-wing lunatic in a free election in Germany. A war that killed 50 million people, including more than one-third of all Jews on the planet. All of this had an indelible impact upon my life and thinking.

My brother, Larry, six years older than me, introduced me to politics and a whole lot else. He has played an enormously important role in my life, and I am forever grateful for his love, counsel, and overall wisdom. For the last fifty years he has lived in Oxford, England, where he raised his family and worked as a social worker. Ten years ago he was elected to the Oxfordshire County Council as a candidate of the Green Party, and he was reelected for a second term. He is now active in efforts to maintain a strong National

Health Service system in the UK.

My mother taught Larry how to read when he was very young, and he has been a voracious reader for his entire life. Larry first read to me when I was four or five. We would stay in bed late on Saturday mornings going through stacks of comic books. When we were kids he was my mentor and, as older brothers occasionally are, my tormentor. He was very smart, always knew the answers that I didn't—and he let me know it.

My older brother, Larry, and me. (Author Collection)

Being an older brother is not easy. Occasionally, when you want to go out and spend time with your friends, you have to take care of your kid brother and drag him along. Not fun. On Saturdays, if my parents were

Larry and me at the Democratic Convention. (Jane O'Meara Sanders)

away, Larry would also have to prepare lunch for me. I thought his cooking was great. His spaghetti with ketchup and his My-T-Fine chocolate pudding were outstanding.

My parents were not much into reading books, and there were few of them in the house. While we borrowed books from the local library, it was Larry who first brought books into our home and onto a bookshelf. More important, it was Larry who helped me understand what some of those books were about. He was a good teacher, and opened my eyes to so much.

While my parents were not particularly political, they always voted Democratic, as did virtually the entire Jewish neighborhood in which we lived. Larry brought politics into the house when, as a student at Brooklyn College, he joined the Young Democrats and campaigned for Adlai Stevenson in 1956.

During my presidential campaign I was delighted that Larry and his wife, Janet, and son, Jacob, were able to join me at some of our events. I was even prouder when, as a delegate from Democrats Abroad at the Democratic Convention, he cast, with tears in his eyes, his one vote for my nomination.

Was my family "poor"? No. Did we (as the economists say) have much discretionary income? Absolutely not.

My dad was a paint salesman with the Keystone Paint and Varnish Company. He came to this country from Poland at the age of seventeen without a nickel in his pocket. He was always employed and made enough money to provide for his wife, Dorothy, and his two sons, but not much more than that.

Money (or more appropriately, lack of money) was always a point of contention in the house. There were arguments and more arguments between my parents. Painful arguments. Bitter arguments. Arguments that seared through a little boy's brain, never to be forgotten.

"Bernard. Go out and get some groceries. Here's what we need. Here's the list," my mother said. And, dutiful son of twelve, I went out and bought the groceries. But I went to the wrong store. I went to the small shop a few blocks away, rather than the Waldbaum's grocery store on Nostrand Avenue. I paid more than I should have. When I returned and my mother realized what I had done, the screaming was horrible. Money was hard to come by. Not to be wasted.

When I was thirteen, I wanted a leather jacket. It was the fashion. Everyone had one and I was tired of my brother's hand-me-down coat. "Okay," said Mom. "Let's get you a leather jacket." This became the shopping trip from hell. It's probably why sixty-two years later—ask my wife if I'm lying—I still hate shopping and why I want to escape if I am in a department store for more than a half hour.

On that day my mother took me to at least a dozen stores in search of the lowest price on a leather jacket. We started off at several stores at the Kings Highway shopping district. Then we got on the subway to the large department stores in downtown Brooklyn and Manhattan. There was no leather jacket in New York City that I didn't try on.

Well, you guessed it: We ended up buying the jacket from the first store we had visited on Kings Highway much earlier in the day. It's funny to think about that now. It wasn't funny then.

How much money your family had determined the quality of your baseball glove, which brand of sneakers you wore, and what kind of car your father drove. It also, of course, determined whether you lived in a rent-controlled apartment house (as most of my friends did) or a "private house." Not until I was much older did I learn that most people did not refer to the average house on a street as a "private house." But that distinction was very clear where I lived. Those of us who lived in apartment houses were working class and those who lived in "private houses" were middle class. It was one of the early class distinctions that I remember.

I spent much of my childhood playing out on the street or in schoolyards. The street was our world, and we never left home without a pink Spalding rubber ball. Unlike today, there was no adult supervision. None at all. We organized all the games by ourselves.

We played hour after hour after hour. On the street we played hide-and-seek, punchball, hockey, two-hand touch football, and stickball—with time-outs when cars passed by and strict rules as to what happened when the ball got stuck under a parked car. We pitched marbles into sewer grates. If your marble went down the hole in the middle, you got ten marbles back.

We played wall ball against the sides of the buildings. We played box ball on the sidewalk, curb ball against the curbs, and stoopball against the stoops. We played regular handball and Chinese handball. We flipped baseball cards. We raced. In the school yard of PS 197, where I went to elementary school a few blocks from where I lived, we played softball and basketball until we were so tired we could barely drag ourselves home. For nourishment, we chipped in to buy a large bottle of soda.

What I learned playing on the streets and playgrounds of Brooklyn was not just how to become a decent ballplayer and athlete. I learned a profound lesson about democracy and self-rule. From playing punchball and stickball? Yes.

There were no adults on the streets or playgrounds where we spent much of our lives. Nobody supervised us. Nobody coached us. Nobody refereed our games.

We were on our own. Everything was organized and determined by the kids them- selves. The group worked out our disagreements, made all the decisions, and learned to live with them.

"What game should we play? . . .Hey. That's a great idea, let's do it."

"Can I borrow your baseball

With my brother and father.

(Author Collection)

glove? . . . Who brought the bat and ball? . . . Was he safe or was he out? . . . Was the ball foul or was it fair?"

There was no debate about who played on which side. Everyone knew who was the best, second-best, and third-best basketball player when we chose up teams. That's the way it was.

In three-man basketball, the team that lost went to the sidelines and a new team replaced them to challenge the winners. Those were the rules.

And it all worked out.

It was, as I think about it now, an amazingly demo- cratic and self-sustaining community which taught me lessons about working with people that I've never for- gotten.

The other thing I've never forgotten was the relation- ship that the kids on the block, and the entire community, had with the Brooklyn Dodgers. Sometimes, as I travel about, I am asked which baseball team I rooted for when I was growing up. Are you kidding? There was only one team. And they were family.

Gil Hodges at first, Jackie Robinson or Junior Gilliam at second, Pee Wee Reese (my favorite player) at shortstop, Billy Cox at third, Gene Hermanski in left field, the Duke in center, Carl Furillo in right, Roy Campanella behind the plate. On the mound we had Preacher Roe, Don Newcombe, Carl Erskine, Johnny Podres, Clem Labine, Joe Black, Sandy Koufax—among many others. Those names are indelibly planted on my mind. Sixty years have come and gone, and I remember those mythical figures like it was yesterday.

It would have been unthinkable for anyone on the block not to know the names of the players, their batting averages, and the win-loss record of the pitchers. We knew who they were playing on a given day, where they were playing, who was pitching, and how many games out of first place they might be. We also knew as much information about their personal lives as the baseball cards we flipped and traded provided. Most of our contact with the Dodgers came through the radio and TV play-by-play commentary of Red Barber and Vin Scully, who were as familiar to us as the players.

Ebbets Field, where the Dodgers played, was a half-hour subway ride away, and we would go to the ball games a few Saturdays or Sundays a season, sometimes for a doubleheader. Usually, we got the 60-cent bleacher seats, sometimes the $1.25 seats way up the first-base line. On occasion, we would wait outside the players' entrance to get autographs. I still remember seeing a tired Jackie Robinson walking out of the ballpark.

The Dodgers brought joy and despair to our world. What kid who grew up in Brooklyn does not still remember the end of the 1951 season, and the collapse of the Dodgers, who gave up a thirteen-game lead to the hated New York Giants. And then the playoffs. And Ralph Branca. And Bobby Thomson's home run, the shot heard 'round the world.

But better times came in 1955. Finally, finally, the Dodgers beat the Yankees and won the World Series. Johnny Podres the hero. Mass hysteria in Brooklyn.

You do not have to be a sociologist to understand the impact that the Dodgers had on the people of Brooklyn, race relations, and our sense of community. As kids we all knew, of course, that Jackie Robinson, Don Newcombe, and Roy Campanella were black. But what was far more important to us was that they were great ballplayers. We were not bleeding-heart liberals. We just wanted the Dodgers to win. Of course they were part of our family.

There was a saying that went around Brooklyn during the time that the Dodgers were about to leave for Los Angeles. It went like this: The three worst people in modern history were Adolf Hitler, Joseph Stalin, and Walter O'Malley, but not necessarily in that order. The departure of the Dodgers, orchestrated by O'Malley, the team owner, was devastating to the borough and to the city. It left a gaping hole.

Frankly, as a nonpolitical teenager, I found it very difficult to understand how the Dodgers *could* be moved. This team was the *Brooklyn* Dodgers. You know—like the *Brooklyn* Bridge. Like *Brooklyn* College. Like the *borough* of Brooklyn. How could you take something away that was an essential part of the life of the people and that meant so much to them? O'Malley's devastating decision to rip the Dodgers out of Brooklyn in order to pursue greater profits on the West Coast was, I suspect, one of my first observations regarding the deficiencies of capitalism.

But my childhood experiences were not just on the streets of Brooklyn.

I will never forget one summer when I was thirteen years old and my parents sent me to the Ten Mile River Scout Camp in Narrowsburg, New York. It was an inexpensive way for kids to get out of the city during the summer. My first summer at the camp was supposed to be four weeks. I came home after two. I was homesick. The next year I was supposed to be there two weeks. I stayed four. I had a great time. The last time I went I stayed for six weeks and cried when I had to come back to the city.

As a kid, I had been in the Cub Scouts, where my mom was a den mother, and later was part of Troop 356 in the Boy Scouts. Our troop went on occasional hikes and cookouts, but it was nothing like summer camp.

Boy Scout camp was an extraordinary experience for me. For the first time in my life I was exposed to the outdoors and a rural way of life: living in a lean-to without a front door, spending nights in a sleeping bag on a straw-filled "mattress," hiking, camping, observing beautiful starry nights for the first time in my life, learning about Indian lore, swimming in the lake, canoeing, having communal meals in a giant mess hall, singing folk songs.

My yearbook picture at James Madison High School. (James Madison High School Yearbook)

One day, my bunkmate and I were sitting on our beds reading comic books. A rather large black snake slithered across the upper bunk bed on my friend's side of the cabin. The snake was heading down toward his shoulder. We ran like hell.

Quite the experience for a boy from Brooklyn.

Going to Boy Scout camp changed my life. It turned out that I really liked country living, and I never forgot that. I doubt very much that I would have ended up in Vermont, one of the most rural states in the country, if I hadn't gone to Scout camp.

High school for me, James Madison High School, was not as much fun as my days in elementary school. The school was much larger and, unlike PS 197, where I had known almost all the kids for my whole life, there were a lot of new faces. I was a good student in high school, but not a great one. The social studies interested me more than math and science.

I ran for senior class president. I remember pacing up and down the bedroom floor as I worked with my mother on the speech I was going to give in the school

Running track in high school. (Lou Howart/James Madison High School Newspaper)

auditorium. My main campaign platform called for the high school to adopt a South Korean war orphan. I lost that election. The fellow who won, however, eventually took my idea: Our school "adopted" that child.

One of the first great disappointments in my young life was not making the James Madison High School basketball team, consistently one of the better teams in the city, under the legendary leadership of its longtime coach, Jamie Moskowitz.

How happy I was to have made the junior varsity team in my freshman year. I came home with a beautiful uniform, number 10. If truth be told, I even slept in that silky uniform. But then disaster struck. At a practice early in the season I was told by the coach that I was cut. No junior varsity team, no varsity team in the future, no beautiful uniform. A crushing experience.

I don't remember exactly why, but I then went out for the track and cross-country teams. As a kid, I always had good endurance and could run forever. Track and cross-country were not as sexy as basketball. No large crowds at the meets, not as much attention. But it turned out to be an exciting and meaningful experience for me. I enjoyed it very much and was pretty good at it.

There were long subway rides from Brooklyn to Van Cortlandt Park in the Bronx for the cross-country events. There were the many hundreds of runners at the starting line and, then, after the starter's gun went off, the mad dash into the woods for the two-and-a-half-mile run. There was the smell of the fall leaves on the ground through the deep breaths of a body pushing hard. There was the final kick down the long straightaway to the finish line, passing runners who were even more tired than me. Great experiences that I have never forgotten.

I was a good runner, not just in cross-country but in the mile and half-mile events. I ran the mile in 4:37, fast enough for third place in the New York City indoor mile championship. I also won a number of borough and local meets. Running track and cross-country turned out to be important to my life. Training hard, not quitting even when you were dead tired, gave me a discipline that has stayed with me for the rest of my life.

CHICAGO

It was around midnight at LaGuardia Airport. I was nineteen years of age and on my very first plane trip, taking the cheapest flight available to Chicago. I said goodbye to my dad. Scared and apprehensive, I was leaving home and heading to the University of Chicago.

My mother had died a few months before. I wanted out of Brooklyn and Brooklyn College, where I had attended my freshman year. I had a friend who was already at the university, so I applied and was accepted. The school apparently had some slots to fill in their sophomore class, even for a student who was below their quite high academic standards. The plane landed at three A.M. and I made my way from Midway Airport to the Hyde Park neighborhood on Chicago's South Side.

Attending the University of Chicago was an eye-opening experience for me. It changed my life and, for better or worse, helped shape me into the person I am today. But it was also a very difficult time.

My dad had dropped out of school at the age of sixteen in Poland. Having lived through the Depression, he worried a lot about money and making a living. He preferred that I not go to college, but get a steady job after high school. My mother was a housewife who graduated high school in New York City, but never went further in her education. Most of our friends and neighbors were from a similar background.

At the University of Chicago, most of my fellow

students were children of college graduates. Their parents were successful professionals or businesspeople. I felt very out of place, and a bit over my head. At times it was quite lonely.

While I struggled personally, the University of Chicago opened up opportunities for me that I had never experienced before. I enjoyed many of my teachers, but my intellectual interests were taking me outside of the classroom and into subject matters that were not necessarily part of the curriculum. In Harper Library, the university had one of the great libraries in the country. I spent a lot of time there—deep down in "the stacks."

While I was often unprepared for class and exams, and earning rather unspectacular grades, I was reading up on all kinds of subjects. I studied history, sociology, psychology, economics, and politics. I read about aspects of American history and life that I had never been exposed to before. I learned that America was not always "the land of the free and the home of the brave" and that our country was not always on the right side of history. I also read many biographies.

I was blown away by the number of magazines and periodicals there were in the large and beautiful reading room on campus. Who knew that so many publications existed? And on every conceivable subject, and from all over the world! I would often come to the reading room intending to study for a classroom assignment but end up spending the evening absorbed in one magazine or another in the Periodical Room. It was there that I was first exposed to *The Nation*, *Monthly Review*, *The Progressive* magazine, and other progressive publications. My political views were developing.

I also began to read critically. When I was in high school, if you wanted to win an argument, it was enough to point out that "it said so in the newspaper." Well, I was learning, to my amazement, that different publications had different points of view, and that what appeared in a newspaper was not necessarily true.

But I was not only reading. I was running. During my first year at the university, I went out for the cross-country and track teams and did pretty well. While the University of Chicago was by no means a big-time athletic school, its facilities were far superior to anything that I had ever seen. There were beautiful indoor and outdoor tracks, and I was amazed that you could throw your sweaty track clothes into a hamper and they would be returned to you all cleaned and folded the next day. While on the track team, I ran the half-mile in under two minutes, my best performance ever.

Ironically, while I took interesting classes and spent long hours buried in the library stacks on campus, much of my learning during my years in Chicago took place off campus—through organizations that I joined and activities in which I participated. While at the university, I became a member of the Young People's Socialist League (YPSL), the Student Peace Union (SPU), and the Congress of Racial Equality (CORE).

Through these organizations, I learned to look at politics in a new way. It wasn't just that racism, war, poverty, and other social evils must be opposed. It was that there was a cause-and-effect dynamic and an interconnectedness between all aspects of society. Things didn't just happen by accident. There was a relationship between wealth, power, and the perpetuation of capitalism.

How did the general population get the information they needed to make political decisions? Well, the media was controlled by large corporations. How did politicians get elected? Well, big-money interests played a role in that as well. Who benefited from low wages and poor working conditions? Was racism just about irrational prejudice or was there an economic benefit in keeping the races divided? Who made the decision to go into a particular war, and who profited from that war? Was the good life really about earning more and more money so that we could consume more and more products?

During that period, I met some great people, including community activists who were involved in civil rights, labor, and peace issues. I even got involved in my first political campaign, working, successfully, for the reelection of alderman Leon Despres, an independent member of the Chicago City Council who was opposed by Mayor Daley's Democratic organization. In that campaign I got a glimpse of what a powerful political machine, one based on patronage, could do. At that time I also got a part-time job with a union headquartered in Chicago, the United Packinghouse Workers of America.

The early 1960s, when I was at the University of Chicago, were turbulent years for the civil rights movement. People my age in organizations like the Student Nonviolent Coordinating Committee (SNCC) were being arrested and getting their heads broken in Mississippi, Alabama, and throughout the South as they struggled for desegregation and voting rights. I joined the CORE chapter on campus, and eventually became vice president. A fellow student, Bruce Rappaport, was the president.

While providing a bit of financial support for the civil rights movement in the South, our chapter of CORE began to focus on racism in Chicago. The University of Chicago was and is located in a largely African-American community. It turned out that the university was a major landlord in the area, and it also turned out that the university owned segregated housing.

Our CORE chapter sent white couples and black couples into the university-owned housing, pretending to

The photograph of me that drew so much attention during the campaign. (Danny Lyon/*Chicago Sun-Times*)

be looking for an apartment to rent. A black couple would find that there were just no apartments available. A few hours later, a white couple would find a choice of apartments in the same building. After unsuccessful negotiations with the university to desegregate their housing, our CORE chapter staged a sit-in demonstration in the administration building. It was one of the first student civil rights sit-ins in the North.

During that same period, working with a citywide organization, I got arrested during a demonstration to desegregate the Chicago public school system—a struggle that went on for years and later involved Dr. Martin Luther King Jr. The Chicago schools were bad in general; they were worse in the black neighborhoods. Instead of allowing black children in overcrowded schools to go to white ones, the school department established mobile classrooms to perpetuate the segregation. Hundreds of Chicagoans protested. During our demonstration, the police demarcated a line that couldn't be crossed. If you crossed that line, you would be arrested. Several of us crossed that line, and we were thrown into paddy wagons. I spent the night in jail. In the morning we were bailed out by the NAACP.

As part of my civil rights activities, I was also involved in a movement to protest police brutality. In that capacity, I made an unwelcome acquaintance with the Chicago Police Department when some local police followed me in their squad car and took down leaflets I had been posting announcing a public meeting on police violence. They referred to me, in language that became familiar during that period, as an "outside agitator." A few years later, during the Democratic Convention of 1968, the entire world saw the Chicago police in action during the infamous police riots. Their brutality didn't surprise me.

In August 1963, a number of my fellow University of Chicago students and I took a long bus ride to participate in the March on Washington for Jobs and Freedom, led by Dr. Martin Luther King Jr. For me, it was an unforgettable experience, led by one of the great leaders in the history of our country.

Dr. Martin Luther King Jr. was a man of enormous courage who followed the path that his conscience and intelligence dictated. Yes, he was an important civil rights leader who, against enormous obstacles, helped desegregate the South and pass the Voting Rights Act of 1965. But, incredibly, he was more than that. He understood that if real justice in this country was to be established, for people of every race, we had to create an economy that worked for all and not just the few. As he often reminded the country, desegregating a restaurant meant nothing if a black worker didn't have the money to pay for the meal being served.

Against very strong opposition from his financial backers and "liberal" supporters, King spoke out against the war in Vietnam. How could he be consistent in his belief in nonviolence if he didn't oppose that war and its horrific brutality? How could he continue his demand for a change in national priorities if he didn't speak out against a bloated military budget while the poor were going hungry and the sick were without health care?

King, taking on the entire establishment, plunged ahead into uncharted territory and media hostility. He demanded that the issues of poverty and income and wealth inequality be addressed. He refused to be just a great black civil rights leader. Instead, he became a great American leader who was black. Let us not forget: King was assassinated not in a "civil rights" demonstration, but in the fight for decent wages and working conditions for garbage collectors in Memphis, Tennessee. At the time of his death he was also organizing a Poor People's March on Washington for people of all races.

Standing on the National Mall on August 28, 1963, with hundreds of thousands of others, was a day that I will never forget. King's "I Have a Dream" speech still rings in my mind. His life's work continues to inspire me.

In June 1964, I married a classmate of mine at the University of Chicago, Deborah Shiling. My father had died the previous year and left my brother and me a bit of money. Deborah and I bought eighty-five acres of woodland in Middlesex, Vermont, for $2,500. We worked hard to convert an old maple sugar house on the property to a livable cabin. There was no electricity or running water, but we did build a nice outhouse. We bathed in a cold stream in the middle of the woods. *Really* cold!

After our graduation from the University of Chicago, Deborah and I traveled to England, Greece, and Israel. In England, we visited Summerhill, the radical school started by A. S. Neill back in 1921. Summerhill was based on the very democratic and sane principle that the school should serve the needs of the children, not the other way around. To as great a degree as possible, children learned what they wanted and how they wanted, and had a democratic voice in how the school was run. Neill's belief, way ahead of its time, was that we must keep children's intellectual and emotional spirits alive, not crush them as so many schools did.

In Greece, we spent time in Athens, where we did the tourist thing and were thrilled by the Parthenon, other ancient monuments, and Greek food. Having read some of Nikos Kazantzakis's novels, we also took a trip to Crete, where, in the rural areas, we observed a way of life that seemed unchanged from a century before.

In Israel, we spent time working on several kibbutzim. It was a unique experience and a very different type of culture than I was used to. I enjoyed picking grapefruits, netting fish on the "fish farm," and doing other agricultural work. Mostly, however, it was the structure of the community that impressed me. People there were living their democratic values. The kibbutz was owned by the people who lived there, the "bosses" were elected by the workers, and the overall decisions for the community were made democratically. I recall being impressed by how young-looking and alive the older people there were. Democracy, it seemed, was good for one's health.

VERMONT

In 1968, I moved to Vermont, more or less full-time. Deborah and I had divorced and I was then living with Susan Mott. We had met when we were both working at a Head Start program in New York City. On March 21, 1969, Levi Noah Sanders, our son, was born in St. Johnsbury, Vermont.

One of the more interesting jobs that I had during that period was doing research at the State of Vermont Tax Department in the waning days of the administration of Governor Phil Hoff. This was my introduction to tax policy. Hoff had been the first Democratic governor elected in Vermont in a hundred years. He was also one of the most progressive elected officials in the country. Years later, I had the privilege of getting to know Phil and his wife, Joan, quite well.

During those years, I worked as a journalist for several Vermont papers. In the St. Albans area of northern Vermont I wrote for a weekly newspaper and learned a lot by simply going out, stopping people, and doing "man on the street" interviews. I found that the views of ordinary people, for better or worse, did not necessarily jibe with those of the establishment. I was surprised by the kind of support that George Wallace was generating.

During that period, I also became part of the construction crew for John Rogers of Barre, Vermont. John, whose family was part Native American and went back generations in Vermont, was an excellent carpenter and builder. He taught me a lot about building homes and farm silos. He also exposed me to the Vermont way of life, something I was just beginning to absorb.

Not only was John knowledgeable about construction matters, but he also knew every inch of central Vermont. Like most Vermonters, he loved the outdoors. In the warm weather he and his family explored the area in cars, trucks, and on motorcycles. In the winter, they were out on snowmobiles. Years later, I had the opportunity of seeing the incredible winter beauty of Vermont by traveling through forests on a snowmobile.

John and I grew up in very different worlds. That resulted in great discussions in his truck as we traveled to work sites.

Hanging out at the University of Vermont library in the seventies. (Author Collection)

In 1969, Susan, Levi, and I lived in a small house we had bought in the town of Stannard, Vermont. Stannard, with a population of fewer than two hundred people, is located in Vermont's Northeast Kingdom, one of the poorest, most rugged and beautiful parts of the state. There are no stores, no schools, no post offices, no paved roads in Stannard—and in the winter the main dirt road going over the mountain to Lyndonville is closed because of snow and ice.

I learned a lot living in Stannard. I learned about the beauty of walking on quiet dirt roads, seeing deer in the fields, and finding paths that led to the remains of old farmhouses that had not been occupied for decades. I learned about the friendships established when you live in an isolated community—five miles from the nearest store or gas station. People need people, and that developed a different type of community than I had previously known.

I learned about surviving in cold weather and trying to keep our baby warm when the temperature was twenty below zero and the cold air leaked in through poorly insulated walls. I learned very quickly why people put plastic over their windows. Not pretty, but it keeps the cold air out. I learned about getting by when the pipes freeze and you have no running water, and how you have to haul large plastic water jugs so that you can stay clean, wash the dishes, and flush the toilet. I learned about starting a car after a cold, cold night when the tires were actually frozen to the ground.

One day, I was visiting a neighbor who was the town's road commissioner, the guy responsible for plowing the roads after it snowed. This was no minor position. If the roads were not open, people couldn't get to work, reach a doctor, go to school. My eyes nearly popped out of my head when I saw him put a car battery into the stove in his kitchen. Was he totally crazy? Not really. The pilot light in the oven kept the battery warm overnight, which enabled him to start up the town plow in the morning, no matter what the weather had been.

TWO

MY POLITICAL LIFE
IN VERMONT

I think it's fair to say that my political life has taken a very different path from that of any other member of Congress. It's not just that I am the longest-serving Independent in its history. It's not just that my first visits to Washington, D.C., were all for civil rights and antiwar demonstrations. It's not just that I was never inside the Capitol until *after* I ran for Congress.

It's that I started way, way outside of establishment politics.

Jim Rader is my oldest friend. I have known him since my days at the University of Chicago, and we renewed our acquaintance after Chicago when we bumped into each other at a meeting in Vermont in the late sixties.

In late 1971, Jim mentioned to me that he was going to a meeting of the Liberty Union Party, a small third party in Vermont. Winston Prouty, Vermont's U.S. senator, had died in September and a special election was being held to elect his successor. Robert Stafford, Vermont's lone congressman at the time, was giving up his position in the House to run for Prouty's seat—which meant that there were two seats up for grabs. "Would you be interested in going to the meeting?" Jim asked. "The party will be discussing the issues to be covered in the campaign and will nominate its candidates." "Why not," I answered. A fateful decision.

The Liberty Union meeting was held in a room at Goddard College in central Vermont. By definition, the forty or fifty people there were opinionated. There was a lot of discussion. Not being shy, I added my two cents' worth. I recall talking about economics, education, the war in Vietnam, and a few other subjects.

At a certain point in the meeting, nominations were in order. Who would be the Liberty Union candidates for the U.S. Senate and for the U.S. House? There were not a whole lot of takers. Doris Lake, one of the founders of the party with her husband, Peter Diamondstone, was nominated for the House. And *I* was nominated for the Senate. Yes, the Senate! Welcome to grassroots politics. Welcome to Vermont politics.

Needless to say, my campaign had no money, no organization, and very few in the party had the vaguest idea of how to run for office. But we did the best we could with what we had, and we learned as we went along. Among other issues, our campaign focused on economic justice, opposition to the war in Vietnam, and women's rights.

As I think back, I realize that my campaign was not only a great learning experience and a lot of fun, but it laid the foundation for everything I have done politically since. During that campaign I did as much research as I could into the major issues facing the country, something I very much enjoyed doing, and spoke my mind about them. I didn't worry about who I offended. I didn't worry about how I looked. (A few years ago, I was named by some publication as the worst-dressed member of the U.S. Senate. Trust me. Compared with how I looked then, I am Mr. GQ today.)

Vermont is a small state. But there were radio stations and newspapers prepared to do interviews in most of the larger towns, and we took advantage of every opportunity we could find to get the word out. I remember the first radio interview I did. It was on WVMT in Colchester, one of the largest stations in the state. The interviewer was Jack Barry, a well-known fixture of Vermont media. And I was nervous, very nervous.

The people who listened to that show may or may not have agreed with what I said, but what they probably remember was a constant thumping sound on their radios. I was so nervous that my knee kept shaking and banging up against the table. The sound engineer kept waving his arms for me to stop, but there it was. My first radio interview—*thump, thump, thump.*

As the campaign proceeded, I did better and became more focused. It was difficult at the beginning, but I became more and more comfortable standing on street corners handing out literature. I discovered that I liked talking to strangers about politics.

I also did reasonably well in the debates. I was running against Republican congressman Robert Stafford, the odds-on favorite to win. It may be hard to believe now, given the complexion of contemporary Vermont politics, but in 1971 no Democrat had ever been elected to the United States Senate. Randy Major, a state representative, was giving it a try.

During that campaign I got my first personal glimpse of the nature of the media's political coverage. Randy, a very strong underdog in that race, came up with an imaginative way to capture attention. It was winter in Vermont, and he said he would "ski around the state to meet the voters." And that ploy worked. Throughout the campaign the media was talking about the skiing candidate. Here I was, pontificating about the major issues facing humanity, and the TV cameras were focused on the blisters on Randy's feet.

Needless to say, neither Randy's skiing nor my pontificating made much difference. In January 1972, Bob Stafford won the special election by 31 points. Spending less than a thousand dollars, I came in third, with only 2 percent of the vote. The Republican candidate for the House, Richard Mallary, also won a landslide victory.

An aside here about the Vermont Republican Party of the 1970s. It was different, in almost every way, from the national Republican Party of today. Was Bob Stafford a fiscal conservative? Yes, he was. But he was also pro-choice, and was a strong advocate for the environment and education.

Remarkably, in the last years of his life, when he was living in retirement in Rutland, Vermont, this eighty-seven-year-old lifelong Republican and former military officer came out strongly for gay rights. There was a very bitter debate in Vermont in 2000 as to whether our state should be the first in the nation to pass "civil union" legislation. Stafford strongly supported it, which paved the way for other Republican support and made passage easier.

But Stafford was not alone as a moderate Vermont Republican. He was preceded by U.S. senator George Aiken, a liberal Republican who served in the Senate for thirty-four years. Stafford was later followed to the Senate by Republican Jim Jeffords, another moderate. Many people still remember that in 2001 it was Senator Jim Jeffords who left the Republican Party because of its growing right-wing tilt, became an Independent, and shifted control of the Senate to the Democrats.

Not content with the 2 percent of the vote that I

received in the special election, I ran for governor, again on the Liberty Union ticket, in the general election six months later in 1972. This time I received 1 percent of the vote. I was on the move, just in the wrong direction. During that campaign I became involved, for the first time in my life, in a presidential campaign. Dr. Benjamin Spock, the world-renowned pediatrician, was running for president on the People's Party ticket and was supported by the Liberty Union Party. I campaigned with Spock when he visited Vermont.

The year 1974 was the Liberty Union Party's high point. Michael Parenti, who was ousted from his teaching position at the University of Vermont because of his opposition to the war in Vietnam, ran an excellent campaign for Congress and received 7 percent of the vote. Martha Abbott and Art DeLoy, our candidates for governor and lieutenant governor, received 5 percent of the vote. Nancy Kaufman, a young attorney who was the Liberty Union candidate for attorney general, received 6 percent.

In 1974 I ran again for the U.S. Senate. This was a tough race. Senator George Aiken had retired, and it was widely expected that Republican congressman Richard Mallary would replace him. But a young liberal Democratic state's attorney named Patrick Leahy mounted a very strong campaign against him.

One of the never-ending dilemmas facing third-party candidates is that you are often considered a "spoiler." People like your views, they want to vote for you, but they fear that a candidate they really dislike might get elected if they "waste" their vote. That certainly affected the low total that I got. I ended up with 4 percent—less than I expected, but double what I had ever received before! In a major surprise, Leahy won the election. Leahy and I now serve together in the Senate and have been friends for years. Occasionally, we reminisce about the campaign of 1974.

In 1976, I ran for governor again. During that campaign I was invited to participate in a prime-time debate on the largest television station in the state. I did well in that debate, which helped me reach my all-time high, as a Liberty Union candidate, of 6 percent.

That turned out to be my last campaign with the Liberty Union Party. I was proud of what we had accomplished. I was proud that we were able to educate people in Vermont about some of the most important issues facing our state and country, and to give them a progressive perspective outside of the two-party system. I was proud of our often successful efforts in opposing utility rate increases and supporting striking workers. Further, since many of our candidates were women, we played a major role in breaking down sexism in statewide politics. We had done extremely well with the limited resources and people that we had. But it was time for me to move on. I was out of politics.

With politics behind me, I set out to make a living, and began building a reasonably successful small business. With the help of a few coworkers, I wrote, produced, and sold filmstrips for schools on the history of Vermont and other New England states. The market was too small for the big companies, so we more or less had the field to ourselves. The business was a lot of fun. In the process, I improved my writing skills and learned something about photography, marketing, and door-to-door salesmanship. I also met a lot of amazing educators.

In 1979, after discovering that most of the college students I spoke to had never heard of Eugene Victor Debs, I produced a thirty-minute video on his life and ideas. Debs was a great American, but his life and work remain largely unknown. He was a man of extraordinary courage and integrity whose tireless efforts on behalf of workers and the poor laid the groundwork for many of the programs established by FDR during the New Deal.

Debs was the founder of the American Socialist Party and a six-time candidate for president. In 1920 he received nearly a million votes running from a jail cell after being imprisoned for his opposition to World War I. The life of Eugene V. Debs, his vision of a world of peace, justice, democracy, and brotherhood, has always been an inspiration to me. I have a plaque of Debs on a wall in my Washington Senate office.

The Debs video was sold and rented to colleges throughout the country, and we also managed to get it shown on public television in Vermont. In addition, Folkways Records produced the soundtrack of the video on vinyl.

I very much enjoyed the small media business that I was running. I didn't make a lot of money, but I was able to make my own decisions, work my own hours, and learn a lot. I was looking forward to a future of making more videos on aspects of American history that were unfamiliar to the American people.

In 1980 my life as a small businessman came to an end. I was back in politics.

SOCIALISM IN ONE CITY

Richard Sugarman has been one of my closest friends for forty years. He is a professor of religion at the University of Vermont, a philosopher, an author of a number of important books and publications, an expert on baseball statistics, and a Hasidic Jew. He also follows politics closely.

In late fall 1980, Richard had a strange idea. "Run for mayor of Burlington as an Independent," he said. "You can win." He had analyzed the 1976 results of my gubernatorial run. Statewide I won 6 percent of the vote. In Burlington I won 12 percent, and in the working-class wards of the city I carried over 16 percent of the vote. Richard figured that if we focused all of our attention on Burlington we had a shot to win.

We brought a number of our political friends together, many of them former colleagues from the Liberty Union, and talked it out. It would be a tough race. We would be taking on a five-term Democratic incumbent who had not had serious opposition in years, as well as the entire economic and political establishment of the city. As usual, we had no money or organization. We were starting from scratch.

Once the decision to run had been made, the strategy became pretty clear. We would run a campaign based on coalition politics. We would try to bring together, under one umbrella, the many diverse elements of the city that were unhappy with the current city leadership. And there were a lot of them. Over the years, as is often the case in urban politics, the administration had drifted further and further away from the neighborhoods and the working families of the city, and closer and closer to the downtown business community and the moneyed interests.

We reached out to every possible group and organization that we could, and had good results. We brought into the campaign some of the municipal unions that were upset about paltry wage increases and poor labor-relations practices. We attracted tenants and their organizations that were getting very little help from the city as rents skyrocketed. We brought aboard low-income groups that were unhappy with how the city was running the public housing system. We got the support of neighborhood activists who opposed the construction of a highway that would run right through their community.

Environmentalists joined us in opposition to a disastrous high-rise condominium project on the waterfront of Lake Champlain, the city's most precious natural resource. They also joined me in opposition to a major expansion of the hospital that would encroach into a neighborhood. On top of all that, the mayor was proposing a big hike in the city's property tax, something that many homeowners were less than enthusiastic about.

Starting in the low-income and working-class neighborhoods, I knocked on as many doors as possible. And what an extraordinary experience that was. Over the years, during my statewide campaigns, and later, of course, during the presidential race, my campaigns have spent a great deal of money on TV and radio ads—many millions of dollars. I have never forgotten, however, that the most important political work that can be done is making door-to-door contact, speaking directly to your constituents and answering their questions. We need a lot more grassroots politics in America.

The big breakthrough for us came late in the campaign, when we won the endorsement of the Burlington Patrolman's Association. They backed us because I promised to listen to the concerns of cops on the beat and to open serious negotiations with their union. In supporting my candidacy, the police union and its leader, Joe Crepeau, showed enormous courage. If I lost, which most people expected, they would be even deeper in the doghouse with the incumbent mayor.

There was no question that the endorsement of the police union was extremely important. If a leftist populist, a former opponent of the war in Vietnam, could win the support of the conservative men in blue, we were on our way. Further, I did well in a much-publicized mayoral debate, sponsored by neighborhood organizations and organized by my soon-to-be co-workers Phil Fiermonte and Jane Driscoll (now Sanders).

Election Day—March 3, 1981—was a day I will never forget. My political gut was telling me one of two things would happen. Most likely, as the media was predicting, we would once again go down in flames. After all, I had never received more than 6 percent in an election. Why would this campaign be any different? On the other hand, the response we were receiving all over the city was very positive. Maybe, just maybe, we could win a major victory.

The one thing I never anticipated is exactly what happened. The election results were extremely close. We won the working-class wards in the city by two to one. We lost in the wealthier neighborhoods. By the time the last ballot was counted, I had won by fourteen votes. So stunning was the upset that nine years later the state's largest newspaper would still be referring to it as "the story of the decade."

Two weeks after the election, and after we obtained a court order to move the ballots away from City Hall to the safekeeping of the state judiciary, the recount was completed. While my margin dropped from fourteen to ten votes, I was elected mayor of Burlington. I was now the only mayor in the country to have bucked the two-party system, the only socialist mayor in America.

I was inaugurated in April 1981, before a very large crowd at City Hall. Later a reporter asked for a copy of the speech I had given and I handed her my pages of scribbled notes on a yellow legal pad. I was pleased with the speech I had delivered, injecting local issues into the broader national and international context.

One of the immediate crises I faced was purchasing clothing suitable for a mayor. At the time, I didn't own a suit, just one or two corduroy sports jackets and a few

I am inaugurated as mayor of Burlington, April 1981. (Rob Swanson/*Vermont Vanguard Press*)

ties. It wasn't my intention to become the best-dressed mayor in America, or even to wear a tie all that often. I thought, however, that a little sprucing up wouldn't hurt. Overnight my wardrobe doubled in size.

The great challenge that we faced in 1981 was how we would implement our ambitious campaign promises and how we would transform city government. How would we democratize Burlington politics and open the government to all people, regardless of their income? How would we break our dependency on the regressive property tax yet raise the revenue we needed to implement our programs? How would we protect the environment and stop unnecessary road construction and at the same time create a people-oriented waterfront?

How would we bring municipal services to the long-ignored lower-income and working-class neighborhoods? How would we bring women into a city government long dominated by an old boys' network? How would we reach out to the young people of the city, as well as to the seniors? How would we treat city employees fairly, not only through decent wages and working conditions, but by involving them more in the decision-making of their departments? How would we improve the arts in Burlington and make cultural activities available to all people regardless of their income?

Those were a few of the challenges we faced as we took office.

In order to bring new people and new ideas into city government, we created a number of Mayor's Councils: on youth, the arts, women, senior citizens, health care, and tax reform, among other areas of concern.

The early days of my administration were exhilarating, but very tense. In fact, there was a civil war taking place in Burlington city government. Conservative Democrats had controlled Burlington city government for decades, and with their Republican allies were going to do everything possible not to give up their power. The Board of Aldermen (as it was then called) consisted of eight Democrats, three Republicans, and two allies of mine.

At my first official meeting as mayor, the Board of Aldermen fired my secretary, the only person I had been able to hire. They claimed I hadn't hired her in the proper way. It was their way of reminding me who had the power.

Two months later, on the day that the mayor formally announced his choices for positions in the administration, the board rejected all of my appointees. The situation was absurd: I was expected to run the city government with the administrative leaders of the guy I had just defeated in a bitter election, as well as with a group of people who vigorously opposed me and my agenda.

The Democrats' strategy was not complicated: They would tie my hands, make it impossible for me to accomplish anything, then win back the mayor's office by claiming that I had been ineffective.

And what was our strategy in response? First, we were going to do everything that a mayor could possibly

Thinking hard at a Burlington City Council meeting.
(Jym Wilson/*Burlington Free Press*)

do without the support of the Board of Aldermen. Second, we were going to expose the local Democrats and Republicans for what they were—obstructionists and political hacks who had very few positive ideas. Last, and most important, we were going to build a third party in the city to defeat them in the next election.

Over the following months, we started a successful Little League program in a low-income neighborhood, a program that still exists today. We began what was to become a citywide tree-planting program that transformed block after block in Burlington and eventually won us national recognition for city beautification.

We began a very popular free summer-concert series that drew thousands of people to a beautiful waterfront park, where they listened to music and watched the sunset over Lake Champlain. We did all this and more, despite opposition from the Board of Aldermen, by scratching together a few bucks here and a few bucks there.

As the year progressed, it became clear that the only way we could fully implement our agenda for the city was by electing a majority of progressives to the Board of Aldermen—which meant the creation of a new political entity. In the beginning we called it the Independent Coalition. Later it was renamed the Progressive Coalition. Over several months, we put together a very impressive slate of candidates who were prepared to challenge Democrats and Republicans in every one of the city's six wards.

This coalition, formed in 1982, became the foundation for progressive third-party politics in Vermont. Not only has it continued in Burlington to this day, electing two progressive mayors after me, it has spread statewide. Today, three out of thirty members of the Vermont State Senate are Progressives, as are seven members of the Vermont House. The Vermont Progressive Party is one of the most successful and long-standing third parties in America.

Our municipal elections are in early March, and it gets very cold in Vermont in the winter. Frankly, it was not always fun knocking on doors in January and February when the temperature was below zero, but that's what we all did. I went out with our candidates as often as possible. The themes of the campaign were clear. First, our candidates were running on our progressive platform. Second, we were taking on Democrats and Republicans who were obstructing the mayor from doing his job.

Voter turnout for the aldermanic elections hit an all-time high in a city that now had an enormous amount of political energy. On Election Night, we won three out of the six wards that we were contesting, and we drove a Republican and a Democrat into runoff elections in two other wards. Not surprisingly, in the runoff election the Democrats and Republicans worked together and we failed to win in those wards.

Nevertheless, that campaign was an enormous success. Instead of having just two members on the Board of Aldermen, we now had five. This gave us veto power. We could block any Democratic-Republican initiative. They had no other choice but to work with us. There was a new balance of power in city government, and we could go forward. And forward we went.

I have to say our accomplishments over the years were significant. In fact, several books have been written about them. I was proud to have been named one of the best mayors in America by *U.S. News & World Report*, and many cities around the country emulated the programs we developed.

We became the first municipality in Vermont to develop progressive alternatives to the property tax. Every day, people flocked to the city in order to work, play, and enjoy our active nightlife; it was right that they contribute to the city services they enjoyed. We established the first municipal Meals and Rooms tax in the state. After a court battle, the utilities were forced to pay for the damage done when they tore up our streets for utility work. We needed new funding to build a strong infrastructure. Following a heated battle with the local cable TV company, and an effort on our part to create a municipally owned system, we managed to get substantial revenue from the company and reduced rates for seniors and residents of low-income housing.

We addressed the inequities in the city's relationship to our large, tax-exempt institutions. We managed to get a substantial increase in payments in lieu of taxes from the University of Vermont and the Fletcher Allen Hospital for police and fire services. The hospital also began to play a more active role in the health care needs of people in our lower-income communities. We also developed a plan that brought in more revenue from our municipally owned airport in South Burlington.

It turned out that our expansion of cultural activities was extremely popular. We started a jazz festival, a blues festival, a reggae festival, and a country music festival. We also started a First Night celebration on December 31 that was attended by thousands of people, who enjoyed a wide variety of cultural activities in downtown Burlington. Most of these events continue today.

One of my favorite evenings was a poetry reading in Burlington City Hall where Allen Ginsberg, the brilliant poet of the Beat Generation, joined Burlington schoolkids in reading poetry. Noam Chomsky, perhaps the best-known progressive writer in America, spoke to a full house in City Hall. Studs Terkel, the great writer, visited us during a workers' rights celebration. I spoke on a panel, along with Abbie Hoffman and David Dellinger, two heroes of the '60s, in what turned out to be a very amusing evening. Ella Fitzgerald, the iconic singer, performed at a jazz festival. Burlington was becoming one of the most exciting small cities in the country.

In the midst of all of those new activities, we never forgot about the traditional responsibilities of city government. I kept my word to the city's police officers; I expanded and improved the police department and raised pay. We upgraded the very expensive and lifesaving trucks and apparatus used by the fire department. We created a much more efficient public works department, and implemented a major street and sidewalk repaving program. We purchased an entirely new fleet of snow-removal vehicles, and created a more effective snow-removal plan—in Vermont, snow removal is serious business.

We instituted the largest environmental improvement

program in the state's history: a $52 million city-state-federal project to rebuild our sewer system, upgrade our wastewater plants, and stop the pollution of Lake Champlain. We shut down the environmentally unsound landfill, and killed a proposed trash-burning plant that would have been both an environmental and fiscal catastrophe. We also passed a bond for our municipally owned electric department to start us on the path of energy efficiency.

After a whole lot of debate, we initiated an extensive waterfront beautification plan. The plan for expensive condos on the waterfront was replaced with a people-oriented waterfront consisting of public parks, a nine-mile bike path, and a community boathouse. Today, Burlington's is one of the most beautiful and well-utilized waterfronts in the country.

We also developed some of the most innovative affordable housing concepts in the country. Against opposition from some members of the local real estate industry, we became the first city in America to fund community land trust housing. Through the Burlington Community Land Trust, working-class people were able to purchase their own homes at a lower cost than was available on the commercial market. The housing remains affordable in perpetuity because the owners must agree not to resell the property at market rates, accepting only a reasonable and limited return on their investment.

This community land trust concept has not only spread all across our country, but it has been adopted in other nations as well. The United Nations acknowledged the Burlington Community Land Trust as one of the most creative approaches to affordable housing in the world.

With the help of my soon-to-be wife, Jane O'Meara Driscoll, who became head of our Youth Office, we paid a lot of attention to children and young people. After a major fight with a reluctant school department, we established after-school programs across the city. Kids needed a place to play and do homework after school, and working parents needed to know that their kids were safe. Today, thirty years later, the program is a vital part of the city's educational system.

We also established a teen center, known as 242 Main, which was, within limits, run by the young people themselves. In fact, some of them helped build and design it. No drugs, no smoking, no alcohol. Just the loudest music imaginable. Kids from throughout the city, and other towns, flocked to 242 Main because it allowed them to be themselves. Over the years, we heard from many people about how important that center was in their young lives.

My administration fought for a universal child-care program. The opposition was too strong and we didn't succeed. We did, however, start the largest child-care center in the city. It's still in existence today.

Jane's work with the children and teenagers of Burlington was incredibly innovative and effective. From after-school programs, to a teen center, to a teen newspaper and TV show, to a youth theater program, to the creation of a Little League in a low-income neighborhood, to a child-care center, Jane helped transform the city's relationship to our young people.

And for us, it was the beginning of a working relationship that has now gone on for thirty-five years.

Our city government was not just about bricks and mortar, waterfront development, and snow removal. We were also about baseball. In 1983, working with a citizens' committee, we managed to bring minor league baseball back to Burlington after a hiatus of thirty years. The AA team, affiliated with the Cincinnati Reds, was an enormous success both financially and on the field.

The team won three straight Eastern League championships and was one of the great minor league teams of their time. At least half a dozen players on the Vermont Reds eventually became major leaguers.

How many cities of forty thousand, which is the population of Burlington, have a foreign policy? Well, we did. During my tenure as mayor we made the point that excessive spending on the military and unnecessary wars meant fewer resources to address the needs of ordinary people. Somewhere in the Reagan Library, or wherever these things are kept, there is a letter from the mayor of Burlington opposing the U.S. funding of contras in Nicaragua. The letter stated, "Stop the war against the people of Nicaragua. Use our tax dollars to feed the hungry and house the homeless. Stop killing the innocent people of Nicaragua."

As mayor of Burlington, I helped establish two sister-city programs. One was with the town of Puerto Cabezas in Nicaragua. The other was with the city of Yaroslavl in what was then the Soviet Union. Both programs continue today.

In 1983 the *Burlington Free Press*, the city's daily newspaper and voice of the business community, urged the Democratic and Republican parties to join forces around one candidate in order to defeat my reelection bid. That didn't happen. I won reelection with 52 percent of the vote. The Democratic candidate, Judith Stephany, got 31 percent while the Republican, Jim Gilson, won 17 percent.

Interestingly, during my tenure as mayor voter turnout soared. In 1979, before the progressive movement was active in Burlington, 7,000 people voted in the mayoral election. In 1981, when I was first elected, participation went up to 9,300. In 1983, when I was reelected mayor, 13,320 people voted—almost twice as many as in 1979. The citizens of Burlington had seen a local government working in their interests, and they came out in large numbers to support it. In the low-income and working-class wards, I won close to 70 percent of the vote in a three-way race. And our aldermanic candidates there won landslide victories as well.

In 1987 the Democrats and Republicans in the city took the advice that the *Burlington Free Press* had offered four years before. They combined their parties for the mayoral campaign and rallied around one candidate, a Democrat on the city council. Needless to say, taking on the combined parties wasn't easy, but we ended up winning that election, 54 percent to 46 percent.

In July 2016, *The New York Times* described Burlington as a city "with breakthrough technology now spawning a wave of technology pioneers." Burlington has one of the lowest unemployment rates in the country and a strong public school system. It is extremely environmentally conscious. It has been aggressive in energy efficiency and now receives all of its energy from sustainable sources. In recent years, Burlington has welcomed immigrants from around the world, and has been a national leader in the struggle for LGBT rights. I am proud to live in Burlington, Vermont. (As you may have noticed.)

In 1986, during my third term as mayor, I ran for governor of Vermont and, in a three-way race, received 14 percent of the vote. This was a tough campaign. I was running against a liberal incumbent, Madeleine Kunin, the first woman governor in the history of the state of Vermont. That campaign differentiated what it meant to be a "liberal" as opposed to a "progressive." Kunin and I mostly agreed on social issues. Our differences were on economic ones—where I stood more strongly with the workers of Vermont.

Two years later, in 1988, I ran for Vermont's lone seat in the U.S. Congress. When that campaign began I was considered to be the "spoiler," someone who would take away votes from the Democrat and allow the Republican to win. It turned out differently. The Republican, Lieutenant Governor Peter Smith, did win, with 41 percent of the vote. But I came in second with 38 percent, while the Democrat was far behind at 19 percent. I felt very good about the campaign I had run. I focused on important issues facing our country and had a much stronger presence in the southern part of the state, where I was not particularly well known, than had been the case in 1986.

GOING TO WASHINGTON

Two years later, in 1990, I became the first congressman in forty years to be elected to the United States Congress from outside the two-party system. I defeated

Election Night 1990. We win. We're on our way to Congress.

(Author Collection)

Congressman Smith by 16 points. Two years before, Smith and I had run an issue-oriented, cordial campaign. This time was different. Smith apparently listened to some Washington consultants and ran a very negative campaign. There was one TV ad in which he compared me to Fidel Castro. It didn't work. The people of Vermont dislike negative ads, and his strategy backfired. The vote for the Democratic candidate was negligible. On Election Night there was a huge celebration in Burlington. We were on our way to Washington.

My first weeks in Congress were rather difficult and dramatic. The Democratic leadership didn't know what to do with the first Independent elected to the House in forty years. Despite earlier assurances that I would be welcomed into the House Democratic Caucus, that turned out not to be the case. Some conservative Democratic members balked, and I found myself in no-man's-land—neither in nor out of the caucus. Also, it was

A young couple comes to the Congress in 1990. (*USA Today/Gannett*)

unclear what committee assignments I would have and where I would physically sit in the committees.

Finally, after several painful weeks, an agreement was worked out. I was accepted into the Democratic Caucus and got assigned to the House Banking Committee and the House Government Operations Committee, where I served under the very able leadership of Congressmen Henry B. Gonzalez and John Conyers.

On top of all the caucus nonsense I was experiencing during my first weeks in Congress, there was a more important reality. The United States was about to go to war. President George H. W. Bush was determined to send in our military to drive the Iraqi army out of Kuwait, which Saddam Hussein had invaded in August 1990. Almost all Republicans supported the war effort, as did a number of Democrats. I didn't. I had campaigned against going to war, and did everything I could to stop it.

I feared not only the immediate impact of the war, in terms of the death and destruction it would bring, but what it portended for the future. Would war, and more and more wars, be the norm in solving international conflicts in the future? The entire world was united against a small country with a weak army. Surely, I reasoned, there must be a way other than war to achieve our goals and get Iraq out of Kuwait. On January 15, 1991, in one of my first speeches in Congress, this is what I said on the floor of the House:

> Mr. Speaker, let me begin by saying that I think we all agree in this body, and throughout this country, and throughout virtually the entire world, that Saddam Hussein is an evil person, and that what he has done in Kuwait is illegal, immoral, and brutal. It seems to me, however, that the challenge of our time is not simply to begin a war

which will result in the deaths of tens of thousands of people—young Americans, innocent women and children in Iraq—but the real challenge of our time is to see how we can stop aggression, how we can stop evil in a new way, in a nonviolent way.

If ever there has been a time in the history of the world when the entire world is united against one small country, this is that time. It seems to me a terrible failing, and very ominous for the future, if we cannot resolve this crisis, if we cannot defeat Saddam Hussein in a nonviolent way. If we are not successful now, then I think all that this world has to look forward to in the future for our children is war, and more war, and more war.

In March 2003, buoyed by the "success" of the first Gulf War, President George W. Bush decided to invade Iraq and topple Saddam Hussein. Once again, as was the case in the first Gulf War, virtually all Republicans supported the war, as did a number of Democrats. The results: hundreds of thousands dead, millions displaced from their homes, massive instability in the region, and the growth of a number of fanatical terrorist organizations that continue to threaten the lives and safety of the American people and our allies. Today the fighting continues.

During my first year in Congress I managed, with a few other members, to form the House Progressive Caucus, which today is one of the largest caucuses in Congress. The Progressive Caucus, currently led by Congressmen Keith Ellison and Raul Grijalva, has been in the vanguard in the fight for economic and social justice since its inception.

Over the years, as a member of the House, I played an active role in fighting the deregulation of Wall Street and opposing corporate welfare and an unfair tax system. I was also on the picket lines against disastrous trade deals like the North American Free Trade Agreement (NAFTA) and Permanent Normal Trade Relations (PNTR) with China. In my sixteen years in Congress I am proud to have compiled one of the strongest voting records there on behalf of workers' rights, seniors, women, children, the LGBT community, and the environment.

One of my longtime fights has been against the greed of the pharmaceutical industry, which charges our people, by far, the highest prices in the world for prescription drugs. In 1999, I became the first member of Congress to take constituents over the Canadian border to purchase low-cost prescription drugs. With tears in their eyes, working-class women, struggling against breast cancer, were able to purchase the same brandname medicine they were using in Vermont for onetenth of the price in Montreal. After my trip, many other members of Congress did the same thing. Over the years, millions of Americans have purchased affordable prescription drugs in Canada.

In 2006, Republican senator Jim Jeffords retired. On the day he made his announcement, I issued a public statement that I intended to run for his seat. I was very grateful that, on that day, Senate Democratic Leader Harry Reid, whom I had never met, announced that he was supporting me. Senator Chuck Schumer of New York also endorsed me. Their endorsements helped tamp down possible Democratic opposition in Vermont.

During that campaign, a young senator from Illinois, Barack Obama, came to Vermont to campaign for me. We had hoped to fill the fifteen-hundred-seat chapel at the University of Vermont. Instead, about three thousand people showed up. Because of the resulting crunch, Obama and I had to go out onto the steps of the chapel and give impromptu speeches there before we returned inside.

My Republican opponent in the race for the Senate seat was the wealthiest person in the state, a businessman named Richie Tarrant. This was a rather extraordinary campaign for Vermont. Not only was it extremely negative, with ad after ad portraying me as an enemy of humanity, but it was also very expensive. Tarrant spent more money per vote in 2006 than any Senate candidate had in American history up to that point. His money ended up not mattering very much. I defeated him with a vote of 65 to 32 percent. I was now on my way to the U.S. Senate.

THE U.S. SENATE

The U.S. Senate is a very, very different place from the House of Representatives, where I spent sixteen years as Vermont's lone congressman. There are 435 members of the House and most members serve, as I had, on just two large committees. During my years in the House I was a member of the House Banking Committee, later renamed the House Financial Services Committee. I also was a member of the Government Operations Committee, later renamed the Oversight and Government Reform Committee. Both panels had more than fifty members.

The U.S. Senate has only one hundred members and, by definition, each member plays a larger policy role than a member of the House. When I was elected in 2006, the Democrats, by two votes, took control of the U.S. Senate. Senator Harry Reid, the new majority leader, was extremely kind to me and appointed me to most of the committees I wanted.

I had requested of Senator Ted Kennedy, the longtime

leader of the Senate Health, Education, Labor and Pensions Committee, the opportunity to serve with him on that very important committee. I was very appreciative that he consented. My interest in environmental issues was long-standing, and I was fortunate to be appointed to the two major environmental committees, the Committee on Energy and Natural Resources and the Committee on Environment and Public Works. The Environment Committee was led by an old friend of mine from California, Barbara Boxer. As a strong advocate for veterans, I also was delighted to be appointed to the U.S. Senate Committee on Veterans' Affairs, as well as to the Budget Committee, which gave me an important say in the development of national priorities.

As a member of the Senate, I am proud to have passed some major legislation. Majority Leader Harry Reid, Congressman Jim Clyburn of South Carolina, and I succeeded in putting $11 billion into community health centers throughout the country, as part of the Affordable Care Act. This enabled some 6 million more Americans, regardless of their income, to access primary health care, dental care, low-cost prescription drugs, and mental health counseling. We also substantially increased funding for the National Health Service Corps, which brought thousands of doctors, dentists, and nurses into medically underserved areas throughout the country.

In Vermont, almost 25 percent of our people now receive their primary health care through community health centers, a higher percentage than in any other state. I've always believed that, within a broken and dysfunctional health care system, the lack of primary care for so many is one of our most serious problems. People should be able to get to a doctor or dentist when they need to. We have made some progress in that area. More needs to be done.

As part of the 2009 stimulus package, working with Senator Bob Menendez of New Jersey, we passed funding for the Energy Efficiency and Conservation Block Grant Program. This legislation, strongly supported by the U.S. Conference of Mayors, has been one of the government's major efforts to combat climate change. It provided billions of dollars for communities all across the country to move toward energy efficiency and sustainable energy. In Vermont, a number of schools throughout the state were able to use that money to place solar panels on their rooftops. This not only cut carbon emissions, but saved schools money on their electric bills.

As a staunch defender of Social Security, I helped lead the fight against Republicans, and some Democrats, who wanted to cut this program—which is life and death for so many seniors and people with disabilities. Working with seniors' organizations, I helped create the Defending Social Security Caucus. The other senators in the caucus and I took on the Bowles-Simpson Commission, billionaire Pete Peterson and his organization, and a whole lot of other groups that wanted to cut Social Security in one way or another. In the end, barely, we managed to prevail—and Social Security was not touched.

Times are changing. I am proud that much of the discussion with regard to Social Security now deals with how we can *expand* the program, not cut it. More and more members of Congress understand that seniors cannot live on $11,000 or $12,000 a year and that we need to lift the cap on taxable income and raise benefits.

In 2013, I became chairman of the U.S. Senate Committee on Veterans' Affairs. In that capacity, I worked closely with virtually all of the veterans' organizations in developing comprehensive legislation that significantly addressed the problems facing the men and women who put their lives on the line to defend our country. I was tired of hearing about how much we all loved and respected veterans. It was time to *do* something.

The legislation I introduced was, according to the veterans' organizations, the most comprehensive piece of legislation offered for them in many decades. Sadly, despite the strong support of the American Legion, the Veterans of Foreign Wars (VFW), the Disabled American Veterans (DAV), and other organizations, my legislation only received fifty-six votes on the floor of the Senate—all of the Democrats, but only two Republicans. We needed sixty votes. It turned out that Republicans loved veterans very much, except when it came to funding their needs.

If I was to be successful in winning important veterans' legislation, I would have to go back to the drawing board and bring additional Republicans on board. My unlikely ally in that effort was Senator John McCain of Arizona. John and I and our staffs spent hours yelling at each other over the provisions in the bill, but finally reached a $15 billion compromise that significantly improved veterans' health care. It also provided some new benefits for veterans. The bill carried in the Senate with an almost unanimous vote and became law when President Obama signed it in a ceremony with hundreds of veterans in attendance.

I've always had a good relationship with President Obama. He is incredibly smart and I admire him greatly for his focus, discipline, and determination. But we have had our strong disagreements. Obama has continued U.S. support for unfettered free trade agreements—including the Trans-Pacific Partnership (TPP). I think those trade policies have been a disaster for American workers, and I have opposed all of them.

On December 10, 2010, I took the floor of the Senate in opposition to another one of Obama's policies—the extension of some of Bush's tax breaks for the wealthiest Americans. I began that speech at 10:30 A.M.; it ended eight and a half hours later. It was the longest filibuster on the Senate floor in many years. I did the filibuster to call attention to and oppose a very bad tax agreement between President Obama and the Republican leadership. At a time of massive wealth and income inequality, and a huge national debt, it was absurd that hundreds of billions of dollars in tax breaks would continue going to millionaires and billionaires.

This speech received a great deal of attention—especially online. The Senate Web site crashed because of the huge number of people trying to watch it. C-SPAN 2 also had an exceptional viewing audience. According to *The New York Times*, my speech was the most tweeted event in the world that day. There were front-page stories in newspapers around the country, and the speech was covered widely in the international media.

In one day, the number of people who signed up as "friends" on my Facebook page doubled the previous total. Visits to my Web site went sky-high. Some journalists even claimed that Obama held an unscheduled, impromptu press conference that day with former president Bill Clinton, who defended the tax deal, in order to divert media attention from what I was doing on the Senate floor.

A few months later, Nation Books published the entire speech as a book. My ideas were beginning to generate more interest.

THREE

THINKING ABOUT RUNNING

The writer Jonathan Tasini did an interview with me for *Playboy* magazine that was published in October 2013. He is a good writer, and the interview went well. At the end of our discussion Jonathan said, "Many of your hard-core supporters are urging you to run for president in 2016. Are you considering it?" And then he followed up by asking, "Are you absolutely ruling out running for president, a hundred percent?"

My response was "Absolutely? A hundred percent? Cross my heart? Is there a stack of Bibles somewhere? Look, maybe it's only ninety-nine percent. I care a lot about working families. I care a lot about the collapse of the American middle class. I care a lot about the enormous wealth and income disparity in our country. I care a lot that poverty in America is near an all-time high but hardly anyone talks about it. I realize running for president would be a way to shine a spotlight on these issues that are too often in the shadows today. But I am at least ninety-nine percent sure I won't."

How did I go from being 99 percent sure that I would not run for president in October 2013 to standing before a crowd of five thousand on May 26, 2015, in Burlington, Vermont, declaring my candidacy? There were four basic reasons.

First. Did it make sense that Hillary Clinton, the centrist candidate of the Democratic establishment, be anointed as the Democratic nominee and be allowed to run without opposition? Was that good for democracy? Was that good for the Democratic Party? Was it good for the progressive movement?

At that time, very early in the campaign season, it was also assumed that Jeb Bush, the son of President George H. W. Bush and the brother of President George W. Bush, would be the likely Republican candidate for president. What was going on in our country? Was there really going to be an election between the son and brother of former presidents and the wife of a former president? Talk about oligarchy! Talk about political dynasties!

That was not what I wanted to see. That was not what most Americans wanted to see.

Hillary Rodham Clinton and I were not best friends, but I had known her for twenty-five years, liked her, and respected her. I first met her in 1993 when she became First Lady and I was a member of Congress. I got to know her better when we served together in the Senate from 2006 to 2008.

During the Clinton administration I was impressed by her willingness to break the mold of what a First Lady was supposed to do. She became the administration's leader on health care reform, one of the major and most controversial issues of the day. In that role she took a lot of abuse, much of it unjustified. Above and beyond the normal criticism that goes with differences of opinion in any policy debate, it was clear that many of the Republican attacks against her were sexist. She was a woman; she was the First Lady. Why was she leading the effort to transform our nation's entire health care system? Weren't there other more ladylike things for her to do?

Throughout my entire political life, I have been an advocate for a Medicare for All, single-payer program. That approach is simpler, more comprehensive, and far more cost-effective than the reforms advocated by mainstream politicians, including Hillary Clinton. My view is, and has always been, that health care is a *right* of all people, and that the United States should join the rest of the industrialized world in guaranteeing that right.

The approach taken by the Clinton administration, led by Hillary Clinton, was very different. Their plan called for combining the private health care system with a significantly increased government presence. The result was something that was *enormously* complicated, which was one of the reasons that led to its downfall.

While there may not have been many Americans or members of Congress who fully understood the health care system that the Clinton administration was advocating, one thing was very sure: Hillary Clinton did. She was not some kind of figurehead in leading the administration's health care effort. For better or worse, she helped design the plan, and knew it inside out. She was deeply in the weeds in a plan that was overgrown with weeds.

In December 1993, Hillary gave a speech on health care reform to the Dartmouth Medical School in Hanover, New Hampshire. I was invited to attend the speech and, given that Hanover is across the river from Vermont, was able to hitch a ride with the First Lady on the Air Force Two plane that took her there. On the plane trip, she and I had a pleasant discussion about health care and other issues.

What impressed me most about Clinton's speech at Dartmouth was not *what* she said; I disagreed with a lot that was in the Clinton health care reform package. It was *how* she said it. For over an hour, *without notes,* she went through detail after detail of that enormously complicated plan. She knew that plan backward and forward. She also answered questions flawlessly. Twenty-five years later, I still marvel at that performance.

Further, ask Barack Obama about her abilities as a debater. In 2008, she and Obama went up against each other in some twenty-five debates. I think the president would be the first to admit that she won most of them. No one should doubt Hillary Clinton's intelligence.

While I respected her, and liked her as a person, we had very strong differences of opinion not only with regard to policy, but in our basic political approaches.

Hillary Clinton was a key player in the centrist Democratic establishment, which had, over the years, been forged by her husband, Bill Clinton. In fact, Bill Clinton had been the head of the Democratic Leadership Council (DLC), a conservative Democratic organization funded by big-money interests, which was described by Jesse Jackson as "Democrats for the Leisure Class."

The Clinton approach was to try to merge the interests of Wall Street and corporate America with the needs of the American middle class—an impossible task. While the Clinton administration can boast of some positive accomplishments, and I supported Bill Clinton in his two campaigns, there were some major policy failures during his presidency directly related to his alliances with big-money interests. These failures caused a lot of pain for many Americans.

These were policies that Hillary Clinton supported.

The Clinton administration worked closely with Wall Street and Republicans to repeal the Glass-Steagall Act and deregulate the major financial institutions in the country. This initiative, pushed by Clinton's secretary of the treasury, Robert Rubin, a top Wall Street executive, unleashed the greed of the major financial institutions and their contempt for the law. It allowed large commercial banks to merge with investment banks and insurance companies. In my view, and in the view of many financial experts, that decision led to the 2008 Wall Street crash and the worst economic downturn since the Great Depression of 1929. A Democratic president should not be in bed with Wall Street.

It was not only Wall Street deregulation that the Clinton administration pushed. They also worked with corporate America, and against the trade union movement and a majority of Democrats, in pushing through NAFTA, a disastrous trade agreement that not only cost us hundreds of thousands of jobs but laid the groundwork for future free trade deals that were equally disastrous.

On social issues, Clinton, in 1996, signed the homophobic Defense of Marriage Act (DOMA). Hillary Clinton defended that decision for years and was very late in getting on board with marriage equality. The Clinton administration, with Hillary's support, also pushed "welfare reform" and mass incarceration policies.

My disagreements with the Clintons' centrist approach were based not only on policy, as important as that was, but on politics—how you bring about real change in the country. What kind of party should the Democratic Party be? The Clintons, over the years, received huge amounts of money in campaign contributions and speaking fees from powerful financial interests and corporate America. Whether it was on the campaign trail or in their private lives, they spent an enormous amount of time raising money from the wealthy and the powerful. In fact, in some circles they became known as Clinton, Inc.

To me, a very basic political principle is that you cannot take on the establishment when you take their money. It is simply not credible to believe that candidates who receive significant amounts of financial support from some of the most powerful special interests in the world would make decisions that would negatively impact the bottom lines of these donors. The only way to bring about real change is to mobilize millions of people at the grassroots level *against* the establishment, *against* the big-money interests.

I also worried about Hillary Clinton's approach to foreign policy. As a senator, she had supported President Bush and voted for the war in Iraq, one of the worst foreign policy blunders in the history of the United States. As secretary of state, she had supported a number of initiatives, including policies in Libya and Syria, which were too hawkish from my point of view. While very few debate the right of Israel to exist in peace and security, I thought she did not pay enough attention to the suffering of the Palestinian people.

For me, the bottom line was that this country was facing enormous crises: the continued decline of the middle class, a grotesque level of income and wealth inequality, high rates of real unemployment, a disastrous trade policy, an inadequate educational system, and a collapsing infrastructure. On top of all that, we needed bold action to combat climate change and make certain that this planet was healthy and habitable for our children and grandchildren.

Politically, we were facing a corrupt campaign finance system where billionaires were able to buy elections, more and more people were becoming demoralized, and low-income and young people were not voting.

Did I believe that the same old same old establishment politics and establishment economics, as represented by Hillary Clinton, could effectively address these crises? No. I didn't.

A presidential campaign is a unique opportunity to raise issues and force debate on perspectives that are often ignored by the establishment and the media. Should

that once-in-four-years opportunity be ignored? Should
Hillary Clinton be allowed to get the Democratic nomination without having to defend her views against a progressive perspective? The answer was *no*. There were
too many issues out there that *had* to see the light of day,
and it would be wrong to squander the opportunity that
is available in a presidential campaign.

Second. If I didn't run, who else would? Elizabeth
Warren, the U.S. senator from Massachusetts, is a good
friend of mine and an outstanding member of Congress.
Years before she became a senator, when she taught at
Harvard Law School, she joined me for town meetings
in Vermont, where she did a remarkable job in convey-
ing complicated economic concepts in a language that
everyone could understand. She is a strong and progressive leader in the Senate, opposing Wall Street malfea-
sance and tackling many other formidable issues.

There was a lot of discussion within liberal circles
and in the media regarding the possibility of Elizabeth
running for president. In fact, there was even a well-
funded and well-publicized effort to draft Senator
Warren that included paid organizers in various states
around the country. A widely circulated letter from the
"Ready for Warren" campaign captured what many
Americans were feeling about the need for opposition
to Hillary Clinton.

> *"We Are Ready for Warren"*
> *We are Americans of all stripes calling for a
> leader who's fighting on our side for a change.*
>
> *We are progressives ready to support someone
> who isn't afraid to take on powerful interests like
> the Wall Street banks that crashed our economy.*
>
> *We are students in New Hampshire worried
> about how we'll make it after racking up thou-
> sands of dollars in debt to get an education.*

Moms in Iowa struggling to raise families while costs go up each day but paychecks don't keep pace.

We aren't wealthy or well-connected. We don't have any lobbyists. What we are is a movement of individuals working together who believe that folks like us should have a greater say in the direction of our country.

It was clear that millions of Americans wanted to see a serious primary campaign in which a progressive vision would be matched against Secretary Clinton's more moderate views. Liberal organizations like Democracy for America (DFA) and MoveOn.org were mobilizing grassroots support for a candidate they could back in the nomination process.

In her public utterances Senator Warren and her staff were clear and consistent in stating that she would not run. In the private conversations that we had, she also gave no indication that she intended to run for president.

What other possible candidates were out there who could credibly run a progressive campaign against Clinton? Martin O'Malley, the former governor of Maryland and mayor of Baltimore, was making it clear that he was interested in running. While he was an intelligent and effective governor, it didn't seem likely that he could capture much progressive support. Nor could my friend and the former U.S. senator from Virginia, Jim Webb. Former Rhode Island governor and senator Lincoln Chafee also indicated an interest in running.

Was there a better potential progressive candidate out there than me? Probably not. I was a U.S. senator, a former congressman, and a former mayor. I had won my last election with 71 percent of the vote. I had real policy achievements and years of political experience. I had met with foreign government leaders throughout the world. While I was far from a household name nationally, I was known by millions of people. My Senate Facebook was one of the most popular in Congress, with more than a million "friends," and I had given more than a few speeches around the country.

But to put things in perspective, the American people were not exactly clamoring for a Sanders candidacy, even among the most progressive circles in the country. As the *Rutland Herald* reported in April 2014, "In an online survey of more than 100,000 MoveOn.org members taken earlier this year, Sanders was the third most popular choice among named candidates, with 6 percent, following Clinton with 32 percent, and Warren, with 15 percent." And that was among progressives!

Third. I did not have to make a definitive decision right away. There was plenty of time to "test the waters" and determine if there really was the kind of interest and support necessary to run a serious campaign. What did I have to lose by letting people know that I was "thinking" about running? Jane, and those politically close to me, reasoned that, at worst, "floating a balloon" would give me the opportunity to get some public attention on issues I felt strongly about: income and wealth inequality, the declining middle class, climate change, a corrupt campaign finance system, etc. The national media is much more interested in what a possible presidential candidate has to say than it is in the words of a plain old senator. If we found that our efforts were generating excitement, support, and commitment, we could go forward and begin the campaign. If not, we could pull the plug and not run. What was wrong with that?

At a speech I gave in New Hampshire in October 2014, someone in the audience said, "Senator, I am a lifelong Democrat—an avid Democrat—but I think that the current environment is so bad that our Democrats who are running for president will not talk about these issues. They've bought into the system enough that they are part of the system. If you don't run for president, we won't be discussing these on a national level the way we should be doing it. Will you do that for us?"

Seven Days, a Vermont publication, reported:

> *To that, the previously quiet audience burst into applause and someone standing in the back of the hall let out a loud whoop. "I've been going around the country and talking to a lot of working-class audiences, and people are angry," an unsmiling Sanders responded. "People know that the deck is stacked against them. People want real change. They want these issues not only discussed—they want policies to represent them and not just the 1 percent. So for that reason, in fact, I am giving thought—I'm giving thought," he continued. "I haven't made that decision yet. But if I do it, I want to do it well. Not just for me, but for you."*

Fourth. I had talked for years about the need to take my politics outside of Vermont and outside of Capitol Hill. Over and over again I had expressed the view that Vermont was not some kind of isolated fortress for progressive ideas and that, if properly presented, there was a nationwide audience that would be receptive to the views we held. I was especially curious as to how these ideas would play in other rural states, states that Democrats often did poorly in.

In Vermont we win support not just from "activists"— our ideas resonate with ordinary working-class and middle-class voters. Would that be true elsewhere? Could we break through in parts of the country that rarely hear a progressive perspective, but are saturated with Fox News, Rush Limbaugh, and other right-wing propaganda? How would I, or anyone else, ever know if we didn't try?

Further, as chairman of the Senate Committee on Veterans' Affairs and a member of the Health, Education, Labor and Pensions Committee, getting around the country would give me an opportunity to see, with my own eyes, some of the issues that we discussed abstractly every day in committee or on the floor of the Senate. I could visit, in a nonpolitical capacity, VA facilities and those people on the front lines in education, health care, housing, and other areas I had long been concerned about. What was the problem with traveling to parts of the country I had never seen, and learning from people I would otherwise never meet?

If I expressed interest in running for president, a question that would be asked of me immediately was whether I would be running as an Independent or within the Democratic primary process. Given the fact that I was the longest-serving Independent in the history of the U.S. Congress, it would not have been an unreasonable question. The truth is that there were pluses and minuses to both approaches. The honest answer to that question would have been "Let's hear what our supporters have to say." What did they think? It wasn't a decision we could make in a political vacuum.

TESTING THE WATERS

In presidential politics, you really hit the campaign trail before you hit the campaign trail. It's called "testing the waters," determining whether there is the kind of support in the real world that you'll need to run a successful campaign.

Well before I was formally a candidate for president, when I was still just thinking about it, my longtime

Vermont friend and coworker Phil Fiermonte and I did some traveling around the country. We wanted to get a sense of what kind of support there was for our ideas and whether running for president made any sense. I know, I know, that's what candidates who intend to run for office *always* say. But in our case it was true. If there was real support, if it looked like we could run a credible campaign, we would do it. If not, no big deal. I was proud of being a senator from Vermont. There are worse jobs in the world.

As is the Vermont way, our trips were pretty low-key. No entourage. No advance people. No communications director. No security. Just Phil and me flying in coach, renting cars, and showing up for meetings—trying to get a sense of the potential support that might exist.

I have always believed that the Democratic Party must be a fifty-state party. This was an idea forcefully articulated by my fellow Vermonter, former governor Howard Dean, when he was chairman of the DNC, and he was right. The Democrats do well in the East. They do well in the West. They do well in a number of Midwestern states. But there were entire regions of the country, including the Deep South and rural America, where the party was extremely weak, had almost no organization, and was unable to run serious candidates for statewide office.

While it is not likely that Democrats will start winning statewide elections tomorrow in Alabama, South Carolina, Kansas, Wyoming, or Utah, they will *never* win if they don't plant a flag and start organizing. My own state of Vermont is a good example. Forty-five years ago, Vermont was one of the most Republican states in the country. Today, as a result of a lot of hard work by many people, it is one of the most progressive.

It is inconceivable that a serious national party would surrender dozens of states in this country to right-wing

Republicans, including some of the poorest states in the country. But that is exactly what the Democrats are doing. Democratic Party leaders have got to start getting around the country, not just to raise money in affluent blue-state communities, but to talk to low-income and working-class people in poor counties in red states.

If I ran for president, I was determined to visit areas that Democrats often ignore and spread the progressive message. To the degree possible, our campaign would be a fifty-state effort. Our goal would be not just winning over Democratic voters and visiting Democratic strongholds. It would be to appeal to those who had given up on the political process, those who had not yet become involved, and those who were unfamiliar with the progressive ideology. This would be a very different type of campaign.

As part of that goal, on my very first "exploratory" swing, Phil and I headed south to some of the most conservative areas in the country. In mid-October 2013, Vermont's democratic-socialist senator, one of the most progressive members of Congress, was heading to Mississippi, Alabama, Georgia, and South Carolina. I wanted to get a sense of what was going on there. What could we learn?

It has always been my view that health care must be a right of all people. In Mississippi I learned why that must happen as soon as possible. In my position as a member of the Senate Health, Education, Labor and Pensions Committee, I met with a group of African-American health care workers in the Jackson-Hinds Comprehensive Health Center in Jackson, Mississippi. They described the dismal health care conditions for poor people in that state and how there were entire counties there that had *no* doctors. Think about it. In the United States of America, entire counties that have *no* doctors.

In Mississippi, it also turned out that many people, despite being poor, were ineligible for Medicaid because of stringent and unfair state requirements. My Republican colleagues in Congress tell me, over and over again, that we have the "greatest" health care system in the world. Really? In Mississippi, and in many other areas of the country, there are counties in low-income areas where thousands of people have no health insurance at all and, for those who do, there is no access to medical care at all. That system doesn't sound so "great" to me.

As chairman of the Senate Committee on Veterans' Affairs, I also had the opportunity to visit the VA hospital in Jackson.

The following year, in August 2014, I returned to Mississippi. On that trip, we held an unforgettable meeting in Jackson at the International Brotherhood of Electrical Workers (IBEW) Local 480 union hall. I was excited by the idea of meeting with trade unionists in Mississippi, but had my doubts as to how many people would actually show up to meet with the socialist senator from Vermont.

We were very pleasantly surprised. The doors opened and people kept coming. We ended up filling the hall with several hundred attendees—almost all working class. Approximately two-thirds were white, one-third black. There were also a number of black members from the state legislature at the meeting, as well as the chairman of the state Democratic Party. People were happy to attend, because it was very unusual for a non-Republican U.S. senator to visit Mississippi. After all, the state was deep red. There was no money to raise. Why would a Democratic senator visit?

I was introduced by the local union president, John Smith. He and his wife could not have been more gracious, and I still have the denim IBEW jacket, made in America, they gave me. I spoke for a while and then asked a question to the audience that had been on my mind for a long time. "How does it happen that in one of the poorest states in this country, Mississippi, voters keep electing right-wing Republicans who have contempt for working people and who push policies that benefit the rich at the expense of nearly everyone else?" The answer that I got back was "Race, race, race." The white population in Mississippi was overwhelmingly Republican. In 2012, Obama received, unbelievably, only 10 percent of the white vote.

For two hours, that was the issue we discussed. How do we get white working-class Americans to stop voting against their own best interests? What kind of efforts do we have to make to bring people together, black and white, around economic issues? Republicans have cultivated, into a fine art, the ability to divide people up by race, gender, nationality, or sexual orientation. That's what they do. That is the essence of their politics. They get one group to fight another group while their wealthy friends and campaign contributors get richer and laugh all the way to the bank.

At a time when so many Americans, in Mississippi and around the country, are hurting financially, how do we overcome those divisions and bring people together? This is not just a challenge in places like the South. It is a challenge that progressives face throughout the country. We lose when we are divided. We win when we are united.

At that meeting, I heard from white workers on that subject. I heard from black workers and black members of the state legislature. The meeting was intense. I came away with an extraordinary amount of respect for the white workers there, who were prepared to stand up for justice and solidarity, not racism. I had equal respect for the black workers, who after years of political and economic discrimination kept their heads high and continued the struggle. In the environment in which they all lived, none of this was easy.

The small town of Philadelphia, Mississippi, has a unique place in American history. In June 1964, in the midst of the civil rights struggle over desegregation and voting rights, three civil rights workers—James Chaney, Andrew Goodman, and Michael Schwerner—were brutally murdered there by members of the Ku Klux Klan. The killings outraged the nation.

Then, in 1980, just coincidentally, no doubt, Ronald Reagan selected Philadelphia, Mississippi, as his first campaign stop after winning the Republican nomination. On August 3, 1980, Reagan stated in Philadelphia: "I believe in states' rights. . . . I believe we have distorted the balance of our government today by giving powers that were never intended to be given in the Constitution to that federal establishment." He went on to promise to "restore to states and local governments the power that properly belongs to them." In other words, racism and discrimination would be protected in the South if Reagan was elected. That was the Republicans' "Southern strategy." It worked.

What was going on in Philadelphia, Mississippi, now, fifty years after the murders and thirty-four years after the Reagan visit? I was interested in finding out. In Vermont, I do a lot of town meetings in high schools. I love speaking to young people. Why not do something similar in Philadelphia, Mississippi? My office contacted the principal of the local high school, Jason Gentry, and he was kind enough to allow us to hold a town meeting in the school.

I was escorted into the school auditorium by the black chief of police and spoke to an integrated student body. I was probably the first U.S. senator most of the students had ever seen. The meeting went well, with a good question-and-answer period. Most strikingly, after the meeting a number of the faculty stayed around for an informal discussion. What I learned was that many of the students came from very poor families, most of them worked long hours after school to help provide for their families and hunger was a serious issue. Some families just did not have enough food.

During that first trip through the South, I had the opportunity to give a keynote address to the South Carolina Progressive Network. The turnout was high, followed by a good discussion. The event was held at the historic and beautiful Penn Center in Beaufort, South Carolina, founded in 1862 and one of the first schools in the South for freed slaves. It was also the location where Dr. Martin Luther King Jr. held retreats for his organization, the Southern Christian Leadership Conference. Penn Center remains an important part of African-American culture in the community there.

In Vermont, California, Massachusetts, and many other states, it is no big deal to be a "progressive." You believe in social, racial, and economic justice. You want to combat climate change. You support gay marriage. And that's what most of your friends, neighbors, and co-workers also believe. You're part of the crowd.

In South Carolina and other conservative states, it is very different. In South Carolina, there are two Republican senators, a Republican governor, and a very Republican state legislature. In fact, in 2014, because of a resignation, two U.S. Senate seats in the state were up for election. Unbelievably, the Democrats were unable to put up one serious candidate. To be a progressive in South Carolina and other conservative states means to be in the minority, sometimes a weak minority. It takes a lot of courage to maintain progressive views in that kind of political climate, and I applaud those who do.

At the South Carolina Progressive Network event in Beaufort I met some wonderful people, including

Gloria Tinubu, an African-American economist who intended to run for Congress. She had run two years earlier and did reasonably well—with virtually no support from the national Democratic Party. Gloria and I became friends, and I was happy to help her campaign. Gloria, running in a very red state, is exactly the type of candidate Democrats need to support if we're going to turn red states blue.

During that trip to the South in mid-October 2014 we also had a breakfast town meeting with trade unionists and the general public in Atlanta, Georgia. The meeting was organized by South Forward and a local chapter of the Communications Workers of America (CWA). Here's how Cole Stangler of *In These Times* described it:

> *It's early on Friday morning and the union hall is packed with people waiting to see Bernie Sanders. Mostly gray-haired retirees fill the first few rows while unionists, college students and activists, including some veterans of the Occupy movement, are scattered toward the back of the modestly-sized room. They're here for a town hall meeting that's been billed "The Fight for Economic Justice."*
>
> *When the Vermont Senator arrives a bit later than advertised, the crowd at Communications Workers of America Local 3204's headquarters in Atlanta greets the 72-year-old independent with a raucous standing ovation. Sanders may be a thousand miles away from his New England constituency, but here he's the "People's Senator," as a couple of folks declare during the question and answer portion of the meeting.*

I was pleasantly surprised that two hundred people showed up in Atlanta. There was a great deal of energy and excitement in the room. People wanted cell phone photos. I was beginning to get used to the concept of the "selfie."

The lesson I learned from that first trip was that even in the most conservative part of America, the Deep South, there were many people, black and white, who were sick and tired of the economic and political status quo. They understood that the rich were getting richer while most everyone else was getting poorer. They were anxious to come out to meetings to hear an alternative vision of where America should be going. They were prepared to fight back, and the word "socialism" didn't frighten them. We were off to a good start. If this was conservative America, what would the rest of the country look like?

On February 9, 2016, New Hampshire would hold the first primary in the country as part of the Democratic presidential nominating process. It would take place one week after the Democratic caucus in Iowa, where the very first votes are cast. We may not have known much about running a national campaign, but we did know that New Hampshire and Iowa were enormously important and that, if I chose to run, we would have to focus a lot of attention on those two states.

During this period, we began reaching out to Iowa and New Hampshire. Who did we know in those states? Where could I speak? Who should we contact in the local media? What kind of volunteer support could we put together?

Obviously, New Hampshire was going to be an easier task for us. It is Vermont's sister-state, and we share a long border. We had some friends there, and my son Levi was a resident. Also, importantly, some Vermont television and newspapers get into the state, and a number of people there knew who I was. Over the years, I had given speeches in New Hampshire on several occasions.

Iowa was going to be much more difficult. I had been there only once in my life, and we knew virtually no one there. As was to be the case in many other states, in Iowa we were starting from scratch.

In mid-April 2014, I was invited to speak at the Institute of Politics at St. Anselm College in Manchester, New Hampshire. The Institute, led by Neil Levesque, plays an important role in New Hampshire's primary process. Almost all presidential candidates speak there. As I waited to step onstage, it was interesting to see the photos and posters of candidates past and present on the Institute's walls. Some of those candidates made it through the New Hampshire primary and all the way to the White House. Others are a blip on the memory. That's politics.

New Hampshire is across the Connecticut River from Vermont, and Manchester is about three hours away from my home in Burlington. On April 12, Jane, some staff members, and I drove there from Burlington. My son Levi met us there.

The room where candidates speak at St. Anselm is not particularly large; it seats maybe two hundred people. I spoke to a standing-room-only crowd. I was surprised to learn that it was one of the largest turnouts in recent years. Speaking at the Institute of Politics not only gave me the opportunity to address hundreds of people in New Hampshire, it gave me a national television audience, as C-SPAN covered it as part of their "Road to the White House" series.

WMUR, the largest television station in New Hampshire, also covered the speech. They reported:

> *During the event, Sanders said the middle class is disappearing, poverty is up and had strong words about health care in the United States.*
>
> *"There is something profoundly wrong when,*

in this great nation, we are the only major coun-
try on earth that does not guarantee health care
coverage as a right of citizenship," he said.

Sanders said he is considering a bid for presi-
dent in 2016. He said he hasn't decided if he would
run as an Independent or a Democrat. He said he
doesn't shy away from a platform built on a so-
cialist agenda.

"To create a society in which all people have a
fair shot rather than just a nation that is domi-
nated by big-money interests is something that I
will fight for," he said.

Sanders said his decision on a run for the White
House will not be affected by former secretary of
state Hillary Clinton's presidential candidacy
decision.

An aside: I am more than aware that C-SPAN has a
relatively small viewing audience compared with the
major networks. But I have always been a big fan of
C-SPAN, both as a senator and as a presidential candidate. C-SPAN plays an enormously important and positive role in the political life of our country, because
it portrays political reality as it is, without spin, commentary, or prejudice. It covers the proceedings in
Congress, day after day, including important committee hearings. Nothing dramatic. Just what goes on. In
terms of campaigns, it covers speeches and rallies and
gives candidates the opportunity to communicate with
the American people in a way that sound bites and brief
interviews do not allow.

In late June, I visited New Hampshire again, speaking at a town meeting in Warner in the afternoon and a
county Democratic dinner in Milford in the evening.
What do you do on a hot day in New Hampshire when
you have hours to kill before the next event? You go

swimming in a nearby river. That's what we always did on the campaign trail in Vermont—why not do the same in New Hampshire? That's an advantage of campaigning in a rural area. Always bring your bathing suit.

In September, I was invited by Mark MacKenzie, the New Hampshire AFL-CIO president, to keynote their Labor Day breakfast. The meeting was attended by many Democratic state officials, including the governor and senator. The midterm elections were two months away and the turnout for the breakfast was large. The response I received was very positive, which was noted by the local media. This was not insignificant. To win in New Hampshire, we would need strong labor support. We were off to a good start there.

In late April 2014, Phil and I made another trip to the South. In North Carolina we attended a meeting of some very brave people. These were workers in the fast-food industry, employed at McDonald's, Burger King, Wendy's, and other fast-food restaurants, who were earning $8 or $9 an hour with limited benefits. There were maybe fifty people in the room when I spoke, mostly African-American, with some whites and Latinos as well.

Together, they were learning from union organizers about how to work together and fight for a living wage—$15 an hour—and the right to form a union in the fast-food places where they worked. Talk about courage and standing up to the system. Talk about grassroots organizing. Talk about making real change. In many of the speeches that I gave during the campaign, I discussed how *real* change never comes from the top on down. It always comes from the bottom on up, when ordinary people stand up and fight back. That is exactly what these workers were doing.

Some of the workers there were parents who had brought their young kids to the meeting. They knew, I knew, that it was impossible to raise children on $8 or $9 an hour. Their efforts, and the efforts of many thousands of others engaged in the "Fight for $15" struggle, are paying off. All across the country, city and state governments are responding to the pressure and raising the minimum wage to a living wage. That's what we have to do at the federal level. That's what I talked about at every speech I gave.

As would often be the case throughout the campaign, meeting courageous people like these workers inspired me and filled me with optimism for the future.

During that same trip we held a town meeting at North Carolina State University in Raleigh. A young student there named Ben Stockdale, active in the Young Democrats, did an excellent job of organizing and, to my surprise, some 225 people showed up. The panel of young people who spoke before I did discussed environmental issues, women's issues, student debt, and the needs of the LGBT community. In our town meetings, the panel discussions we had before I spoke were an important part of what we were trying to accomplish. While speakers may have focused on different topics, it was important to see the commonality of interests and the need for everyone to work together. At North Carolina State University, it was very moving to hear young people who were so articulate and passionate.

In August 2014, Phil and I traveled to the South again. We went back to North Carolina, where we attended a meeting with trade union leaders at the AFL-CIO headquarters in Raleigh. This was the conservative South, but we learned that there were serious and progressive people there, black and white, actively organizing for a better future for working people. When a discussion took place about the presidential campaign, I heard support in the room. Some, however, believed that if I ran it should be done outside the Democratic Party, with the goal of building a new political movement. While this was a minority opinion, it surfaced frequently. A number of people we ran into felt that the Democratic Party was just too conservative and corrupt, and could not be reformed.

After the meeting with the AFL-CIO leadership, we attended a town meeting in a local church that we had organized and had a standing-room-only crowd of over two hundred people. Once again, our panel consisted of people from different walks of life. We had a young college student, a trade unionist, and a local representative of the Democratic Party. Our goal was to build coalitions and bring people together, and we were making some progress.

Also in August, I received the Patriot Award from the American Legion, the largest veterans' organization in the country. In receiving the award I spoke to an audience of 2,500 American Legion representatives from across the country in Charlotte, North Carolina. This is the most prestigious award the American Legion presents and, as the former chairman of the U.S. Senate Committee on Veterans' Affairs, I was honored to receive it. National Commander Daniel M. Dellinger said that the award was being presented for my "unwavering dedication to our nation and its veterans."

The American Legion is, by and large, a conservative organization. Many of their members vote Republican. It showed real courage on their part to give that award to one of the most progressive members of the U.S. Senate.

Throughout my political career, and especially as chairman of the Veterans' Committee, I have been a strong advocate for veterans and their families. It has always seemed to me that if men and women are prepared to put their lives on the line to defend this country, we have a moral obligation to do everything we can to protect them and their families when they return to civilian life. This means a strong and well-run VA, the best quality health care we can provide, and prompt payment of benefits they've earned.

Some may see it as incongruous for a strong progressive to be a fierce advocate for veterans' rights. I don't, and never have. I opposed the war in Vietnam when I was a young man. I opposed the first Gulf War and the war in Iraq as a member of Congress. I will continue to do everything that I can to make sure the United States does not get entangled in wars that we should not be fighting. But I will never blame the men and women who do the fighting for getting us into those wars. If you don't like the wars we get involved in, hold the president and Congress responsible. Don't blame the veterans.

During that Southern trip, Phil and I traveled to South Carolina. In Columbia, we met with a very impressive organizer with the Service Employees International Union (SEIU), the union pushing the "Fight for $15" campaign. We talked about low-income workers and voter participation. The woman had recently checked out voter registration information in the area. It turned out that of the five hundred workers she was attempting to organize, most of whom were black, only a handful were registered to vote.

While I was there I also met with a young black man who worked at McDonald's. He and I chatted for a while. He informed me that, to him and his friends, politics was totally irrelevant to their lives. It was not something they cared about or even talked about.

Frankly, this lack of political consciousness is exactly what the ruling class of this country wants. The Koch brothers spend hundreds of millions to elect candidates who represent the rich and the powerful. They understand the importance of politics. Meanwhile, people who work for low wages, have no health insurance, and live in inadequate housing don't see a connection between the reality of their lives and what government does or does not do. Showing people that connection is a very big part of what a progressive political movement has to do. How can we bring about real social change in this country if people in need are not involved in the political process? We need a political revolution. We need to get people involved. We need to get people voting.

While in South Carolina I spoke at a rather poorly attended health care rally on the grounds of the state Capitol. Like most other Republican states, South Carolina had rejected the Medicaid expansion provided by the Affordable Care Act. The result was that hundreds of thousands of low-income South Carolinians, black and white, were not receiving the health insurance they were eligible for, despite the fact that it was national legislation and paid for by the federal government. Some of those people will unnecessarily die. Others will become sicker than they should have become. This type of reactionary governmental action in South Carolina and elsewhere could only take place in a political environment where public consciousness is extremely low, where people feel powerless and don't vote.

While at the rally, I had the good luck to meet Virginia Sanders, a no-nonsense black woman in her seventies. We hit it off right away. Virginia had been involved in the civil rights movement, had lived in the area forever and, it seemed, knew every person in South Carolina. The next morning Phil and I got a historical tour as we drove off the beaten path around Columbia with this remarkable woman. I knew that if I ran for president, Virginia would be exactly the kind of person I'd want on my staff. Eight months later she was on board.

One of the challenges of a campaign is good scheduling. Don't arrange for the candidate to be in two places at the same time. Make sure the candidate has enough time to go from one event to the other. Schedule events at a time when people are likely to attend. And, in South Carolina, don't have a public meeting in Columbia on the opening of the University of South Carolina's football season. Unfortunately, that's exactly what we did. Being unfamiliar with the culture of the area, we had not realized that football games at the university were something like supercharged national holidays. Schools shut down. Huge traffic jams occur. The game is the sole topic of conversation.

Despite that mistake, we had a successful town meeting at a senior citizen housing complex in Columbia. Some two hundred people showed up, many of them seniors. I stressed the fact that instead of cutting Social Security, as many Republicans wanted to do, we should *expand* the program. Erin McKee, the president of the South Carolina AFL-CIO, spoke at the meeting, as did a low-wage fast-food worker. (Erin later became an active supporter of our campaign.)

It goes without saying that fund-raising is an important part of any national campaign. As a U.S. senator and former congressman I had done my fair share of raising money. In contemplating a campaign for the White House, there was one thing I was absolutely certain of. I was not going to spend large amounts of time raising money from wealthy individuals, as most politicians, Democrats and Republicans, do. I much preferred spending my time doing free public meetings, and talking to ordinary people.

Raising money from the rich is not only debilitating, it's time-consuming. While it is certainly not true for all, many wealthy contributors are arrogant and self-centered and demand a lot of time and access for the money they donate. Instead of just sending you a check, they want to talk, talk, and talk about their needs or the issues that concern them. This process drains the energy right out of you.

A year later, when I was a full-time candidate, I was truly amazed by the amount of time Hillary Clinton was spending raising money at the homes of wealthy people, talking to fifty or a hundred very rich folks. It was really incredible. But it was not just Hillary Clinton. It is what most politicians do, and what a corrupt campaign finance system is all about. Today, politics is largely about raising tons of money, hiring consultants and pollsters, and spending a fortune on television advertising. That is why we urgently need *real* campaign finance reform and why we should move to public funding of elections.

But, like every other candidate, we needed money. How could we raise some and not lose our focus on turning out large numbers of people?

The solution was simple. While most of our meetings were admission-free, we would do a few low-donor events and see what happened. In June 2014, I had been invited to speak at the University of Chicago. While there, my fund-raiser, Ben Eisenberg, a native of the Chicago area, put together an event at a large bar in Evanston, Illinois. The admission price was $25. The logistics were terrible—the audience was gathered in several weirdly shaped rooms, and I could hardly see many of the people I was speaking to. The sound system barely worked, and the crowd was raucous and loud. Nonetheless, the meeting was a success. Hundreds of people showed up. They had a great time. And we raised some money. Conclusion: On occasion it would be possible to bring out good crowds at the same time as we raised some campaign funds.

As one of the Senate leaders in the fight to protect

the U.S. Postal Service, I was invited to speak before six thousand workers at the National Association of Letter Carriers—the largest postal union in the country. The postal service has been, for years, under intense political attack by Republicans, who ultimately want to privatize all or some of it. The workers were aware of my efforts in support of their needs. The response was very positive.

Ed Garvey of Madison, Wisconsin, is a dear friend of mine. He has had an extraordinary career as a labor lawyer and received a great deal of national attention as the founder and executive director of the National Football League Players Association. In that capacity, he educated the public that while professional football players do make good salaries, their careers are mostly short and their bodies are often damaged.

Ed is a progressive leader in Wisconsin and had run a strong campaign for governor there. Years earlier, he had come to Vermont to help me as we struggled to protect jobs and wages against a union-busting rail company that had taken over a Vermont railroad.

Ed and Betty Garvey, John Nichols, Mary Bottari, and other Wisconsin progressives had put together a terrific event that I loved very much and attended as often as I could. It was called the Fighting Bob Fest, named after Bob La Follette, the great Wisconsin governor and U.S. senator from the early part of the twentieth century. The event took place at the Sauk County Fairgrounds in Baraboo, Wisconsin, was attended by thousands of people from throughout the state, and involved dozens of progressive organizations. On September 13, 2014, I looked forward to speaking at the event. While in the Midwest, we were also going to visit Iowa. A problem arose, however. A good problem.

If one of my goals in "testing the waters" for a presidential run was to attract national media attention, that strategy was working. After twenty-five years in Congress, often as a leading voice on some of the most important issues facing the country, I was invited for the first time to be on *Meet the Press*. Chuck Todd had recently taken over as host, and he asked me to be on the show, which was recorded at the NBC studio in Washington. The problem was that I was supposed to be in Baraboo at the same time. How do you appear in Washington, D.C., and Baraboo, Wisconsin, almost simultaneously? The answer is simple, but expensive. You charter a private plane. For $13,000, we were able to make it to Wisconsin right on time. It was the first time we had chartered a plane, but it would not be the last.

The event in Wisconsin was a lot of fun. It was a beautiful fall day, and some four thousand people showed up. My old friend Jim Hightower, the talented and humorous writer from Texas, was there, as well as other national and state leaders. I had a great time renewing acquaintances with my many friends from Wisconsin and the Midwest. After Wisconsin, it was on to Iowa.

IOWA, NEW HAMPSHIRE, AND BEYOND

The state of Iowa plays a unique and outsized role in American presidential politics. It is the first state in the country, followed closely by New Hampshire, to vote in the nominating process. It is the state that, through its caucus, provides the first indication of how well a candidate might do overall and how serious his/her campaign is. For many campaigns, Iowa is "make or break." Some campaigns, like Barack Obama's, gain momentum from their showings there. Others do poorly and never recover.

Back in September 2011, I made my first visit to Iowa

to speak at the Tom Harkin Steak Fry, one of the major annual Democratic political events in the country. Tom was one of the most progressive members of the Senate, a good friend of mine, and I very much appreciated the invitation. While the weather for this outdoor event was not cooperative, and the crowd not as large as expected, I had a great time and my remarks were well received. I liked the people I met there. They were down-to-earth, unpretentious, and very much like the people of Vermont. I was especially impressed by how many trade unionists and working-class people were in attendance.

In the early part of our exploratory campaign Phil and I made several trips to Iowa. On one of our first trips, in May 2014, I spoke to several hundred people at the Clinton County Democratic Party Hall of Fame dinner in Goose Lake. Coming from a rural state, I felt very comfortable in the tiny town that we were in—which had a very small old bank that looked like it might have been robbed by Jesse James.

In other early trips to Iowa, we made the acquaintance of a grassroots organization called Citizens for Community Improvement (CCI), led by Hugh Espey, an excellent organizer. This organization brings together people from all walks of life—farmers, trade unionists, educators, environmentalists, seniors—to address the major issues facing Iowa and the country. They're organizers, educators, and lobbyists for the public. When we later articulated the concept of the political revolution and the need for citizens to come together in grassroots organizations to take back our government from the 1 percent, groups like CCI were exactly what I had in mind.

In addition to smaller meetings with CCI activists, in mid-September we held a number of town meetings around the state. We met in Dubuque and in Waterloo. We also held a town meeting at the Grace United Methodist church in Des Moines sponsored by the CCI Action Fund. The crowd of 450 spilled out into the streets. For an undeclared candidate in Iowa, so long before the caucus, this was an excellent turnout of highly energized people. During that meeting, as I was to do at most meetings, I asked the audience whether or not they thought I should run for president and whether they would be willing to play a role in the campaign. Some 75 percent voiced support for a campaign. While it wasn't unanimous, the vast majority thought I should run as a Democrat.

On October 5, 2014, I returned to Iowa as the keynote speaker at the Johnson County Democratic Party barbecue in Iowa City. Senator Debbie Stabenow of Michigan was there as well. At this gathering of Iowa Democrats, a few weeks before the important midterm elections, something became very clear to me: The energy, even amongst these strong and dedicated Democrats, just wasn't there for the local candidates. Something was missing. Bruce Braley, a congressman from Iowa, was running for the U.S. Senate to replace my friend Tom Harkin. Bruce is a very decent guy, but his remarks, which consisted of tepid Democratic centrist rhetoric, were just not resonating with people in the room. It was obvious that the people there wanted something more. A few weeks later in New Hampshire I noticed the same phenomenon. On Election Day, Bruce lost his race to Joni Ernst.

At that meeting, for the very first time, I noticed lapel stickers supporting my candidacy. A lot of people were wearing them. They were distributed by a group called Progressive Democrats of America. While a relatively small national group, the PDA had been enthusiastically supporting my candidacy from the very beginning. In May, I did several events with them in Massachusetts.

While I was busy running around the country, I also held a few meetings in Washington, D.C. I wanted to get a sense of what the "Inside the Beltway" liberal community was thinking in terms of a Sanders run for the presidency. If truth be told, most of them did not have a lot of enthusiasm for it. There was the overwhelming perception that Hillary Clinton was going to be the nominee. Why stir the pot? Why cause unnecessary conflict? That was also the message I got from my Senate colleagues. Almost zero interest. Strange. I was picking up increased excitement and interest around the country, but not much in D.C.

Ten days after Iowa, we were on our way out West. First stop, Las Vegas. Hot, hot, hot. We got out of the plane to a temperature of 106 degrees.

Most people go to Las Vegas to party and to gamble. Not us. We were there to meet with the people who serve the tourists their food, wash their dishes, and make their beds. We had a meeting set up with the Culinary Workers Union Local 226, affiliated with the national UNITE HERE union.

The Culinary Workers Union is one of the great unions in this country, and what they have accomplished is nothing less than revolutionary. At a time when we have lost millions of decent-paying manufacturing jobs, and when more and more of the new jobs being created in our country are low-wage service industry jobs, the Culinary Workers Union has shown the world that people who make beds, serve food, and clean toilets can earn a living wage, have good health care, and live middle-class lives. They did this by taking on the hotels and organizing the workers there into a strong and effective multiracial union of sixty thousand members. The union also plays a major role in Nevada politics.

To those people who tell you that politics doesn't matter, just talk to the chambermaids in Las Vegas, who now earn a decent living, have good health insurance and a pension, and can send their kids to college. They did it. We can do it all across the country. Service industry jobs do not have to be low-wage jobs.

And then it was on to California for a very exciting evening. In Richmond, a working-class community in Contra Costa County, the Richmond Progressive Alliance had taken control of the city council under the leadership of Green Party member Gayle McLaughlin. Chevron, which had a giant oil refinery in the city, didn't like the idea of a progressive government. They didn't want to pay more in taxes. They didn't want to deal with strong environmental standards. They preferred to have a more compliant, more corporately oriented city council, and they put $3 million in campaign contributions into the local election to make that happen. In other words, they were trying to buy the local government.

I was invited by the mayor and the Richmond Progressive Alliance to speak at a meeting in opposition to Chevron, and for the reelection of the progressive city council. It turned out to be one of the largest and loudest audiences that I had spoken to since I began traveling around the country. As the Bill Moyers and Company Web site reported: "After an hour-long speech, [Sanders] had the crowd of around 500 on their feet giving the independent senator from Vermont a standing ovation." Harriet Rowan of the online news service *Richmond Confidential* quoted me as saying, " 'At this profound moment in American history, where the billionaire class wants to get it all . . . we have got to fight back tooth and nail . . . we cannot allow them to take over Richmond . . . we cannot allow them to take over

America.'" By the way, the Progressives won the election. Chevron, with all its money, was defeated.

The next day, we were in Oakland to meet with National Nurses United president RoseAnn DeMoro and her staff. And we were pleased to walk into another major controversy.

Most everybody loves nurses. We recognize that they are the backbone of our health care system. They are there when our babies are born, and they are there when our loved ones die. What I especially loved about the nurses' union was that they not only fought vigorously for the rights of their members but, even more importantly, they fought for their patients. They want high-quality care in hospitals and wherever they work. They also understand that under the current dysfunctional system, with so many uninsured and underinsured, they are unable to do the quality work they want to do and were trained to do. That is why they are strong supporters of a Medicare for All single-payer program.

When I visited with them on October 17, 2014, there was considerable concern about the Ebola crisis, and whether American hospitals were effectively prepared to deal with it. National Nurses United also wanted to make sure that their members had the proper equipment and protective gear to treat Ebola patients. After a rally outside the union's building, I helped lead a march to Kaiser Permanente headquarters. They didn't appear happy to see us.

The next time I returned to Oakland, the union endorsed my candidacy. I didn't have a stronger ally during the course of my campaign. I am always proud to stand with the nurses.

In October 2014, I did two sets of meetings in New Hampshire, focusing on college campuses. Not only was I testing the waters for myself, but I was trying to get some votes for Senator Jeanne Shaheen, who was in a tough reelection fight against former senator Scott Brown of Massachusetts. I learned something very interesting during those visits, something that I did not forget.

The earlier visit, on October 10, was to the University of New Hampshire in Durham and was organized by a group of progressive students. These young people were serious about politics; they knew what they believed in and were fighting for real change. They were motivated, hardworking, and well organized. They felt strongly that big money in politics was threatening our democracy and were part of a national movement to bring about real campaign finance reform. I was delighted to accept an invitation from them to speak on campus. When I got to the auditorium, I found an excellent turnout of some three hundred people, not only students but community members as well. It was a great meeting and a thrill to see such bright young people in action.

Two weeks later in New Hampshire, I had a very different experience. Working with local Democrats, we had scheduled meetings at Keene State College, Dartmouth, and Plymouth State. Unlike the meeting at the University of New Hampshire, these were badly attended. The local Democrats had done a poor job in organizing the events and political interest on campus was very low. In fact, walking around Keene State, I had the distinct impression that not only was Senator Shaheen not going to get many votes on that campus but that, two weeks before the election, most students didn't even know that an election was occurring. That visit was extremely depressing.

The lesson I learned from those visits was that establishment Democratic politicians often have very few roots in their communities and are unable to generate grassroots enthusiasm. In too many cases they lived in their own world, separated from ordinary people. On the other hand, what I also saw was that small numbers of dedicated and motivated people were capable of bringing people together, creating excitement and interest, and having a real impact.

In many ways, what happened in New Hampshire on those two visits became a metaphor for what was to take place a year later during my campaign for the presidency. Time and time again we took on the entire Democratic establishment—governors, senators, and mayors. And time and time again our small, ragtag group of volunteers and staff created the excitement and political interest to defeat them.

A presidential campaign is a national campaign. To win, you have to do well all over the country. In late October, we took our show on the road to California, Nevada, and Texas. On the way back east we stopped in Chicago. This Western swing was the most successful trip we had taken so far as we pondered whether or not to run. More than any other set of meetings, it showed me that our support was growing and that people wanted real change. We were also attracting some great and committed people who were prepared to come on board if I ran.

Marianne Williamson is a bestselling author, well-known lecturer, and community activist in California. She is also the founder of Sister Giant, an organization that provides women the support they need to run for political office. She has an enormous following and is active on social media. On March 28, 2015, I spoke before a very large audience at a Sister Giant conference. Marianne, a dynamic speaker, could not have been more supportive. As she introduced me, the chants became louder and louder: "Run Bernie Run, Run Bernie Run." A large majority in the audience indicated that they were prepared to volunteer in the campaign if I ran.

With volunteers in Laredo, Texas. (Jane)

The next day we had an even more mind-blowing experience. On short notice, the Progressive Democrats of America had organized an event for us in West Hollywood. It was a beautiful Sunday afternoon, and I had my doubts as to how many people would show up. Well, over five hundred people packed the hall of the local musicians' union, one of the largest turnouts we had ever had. The excitement was palpable. Once again, we heard "Run Bernie Run, Run Bernie Run." And all over the hall, people were signing up to volunteer.

Then it was onto a plane to Austin, Texas. And what an unbelievable meeting we held there. As our car was getting closer to our destination, an IBEW union hall, I was becoming more and more annoyed at the traffic. We were moving at a crawl, and I was worried that we would be late. Not to worry. Our meeting was the *cause* of the traffic jam, and *everybody* was going to be late.

There was a fellow on the road trying to direct traffic, and cars were parked all over the place. People were packed into the room, some sitting on windowsills. And what was so beautiful and memorable about that meeting, and something that we would see so often in the future, was the diversity of the people who attended. There were workers, students, seniors, Latinos, blacks, and whites. These were people coming together, with passion, to transform America. This meeting, almost more than any we had held so far, told me that something unusual was going on. I was not well known in Texas, and yet the excitement for a Sanders campaign was sky-high.

I had known Rahm Emanuel when we served together in Congress, and I had dealt with him when he was chief of staff for President Obama. Rahm was part of the corporate wing of the Democratic Party, a prolific fund-raiser, closely aligned with the Clintons. He and I were not best friends.

Rahm left Washington and moved on to become mayor of Chicago. In 2015 he ran for reelection. To everybody's surprise, despite spending a huge amount of money, he was unable to get the 50 percent that he needed to win the Democratic Party nomination for mayor on the first round. His opponent was Jesus "Chuy" Garcia, a strong progressive and a county commissioner. In addition to the mayor's race, there were a number of progressives running for the Board of Aldermen against the Democratic machine.

Fifty years before, when I was a student at the University of Chicago, I got slightly involved in an aldermanic election. I volunteered for a candidate who was in opposition to what was then known as the Daley machine. Now I was back, as a U.S. senator, once again supporting a progressive candidate running against the Chicago Democratic machine. Not much had changed politically in Chicago over fifty years.

I liked Chuy, because he was putting together the kind of coalition that I believed in—black, white, and Latino working people standing together against the big-money interests that controlled the city. In Chicago, while the downtown business interests thrived, the neighborhoods were hurting and schools were being closed. In that primary election I was also supporting Susan Sadlowski Garza, who was running for the Board of Aldermen from a working-class district.

The rally in support of Chuy and Susan took place in a steelworkers' union hall. The place was mobbed, the enthusiasm high. This was the first time that I had gotten to meet Chuy, and I liked him. After his defeat by Emanuel, Chuy Garcia became a great surrogate for me during the campaign. He traveled the country, often speaking to Latino audiences. Chuy and his wife and Jane and I had breakfast together the morning of the Illinois primary. Susan, who ran against a longtime incumbent, won her election by a few votes and is now a member of the Board of Aldermen. I was glad I could help.

ELECTION DAY 2014

Election Day 2014 was a disaster for Democrats all across the country. With voter turnout atrociously low, the Democrats lost control of the U.S. Senate for the first time since 2006, and lost seats in the House as well. Like other Democrats, I had to give up my chairmanship to a Republican. Needless to say, the Democrats in the Senate were sullen. Harry Reid, our majority leader and a friend of mine, was out. Mitch McConnell, the Republican leader, was in.

In the 2014 election, the Republicans won the largest majority in Congress since 1928, and the largest majority of state legislatures since 1928. How could it happen that an obstructionist Republican Party, which was in favor of cutting Social Security, Medicare, and Medicaid, giving huge tax breaks to billionaires, and unwilling to recognize the reality of climate change, could win a landslide victory?

To my mind, understanding Election Day 2014 was not to see it as a victory for the Republican Party. It was a *loss* for the Democratic Party. The Democrats blew it, big-time. Republicans win elections when voter turnout is low and their big-money friends spend a fortune on ugly TV ads. Democrats win elections when ordinary people are excited, involved in the political process, and come out to vote. In 2014, 63 percent of the American people didn't vote, and the turnout was even worse for low-income and young people.

As I saw in Iowa and New Hampshire, there was very little energy or enthusiasm for the Democratic candidates. In my own state of Vermont, where a Democratic governor won reelection in a close race, we had the lowest voter turnout since World War II.

Yes. The economy was better than it had been when President Bush left office. Yes. There had been major troop withdrawal from Iraq. Yes. President Obama was doing a number of things that were right. But, despite that, something was deeply wrong in the country, and people felt it. Millions of workers were falling further and further behind. The gap between the rich and everyone else was growing wider. The political system was increasingly corrupt and the economic and political establishment was far removed from the lives of ordinary Americans.

The election of 2014 was a wake-up call for the Democratic Party. I wondered if they heard it.

REACHING A DECISION

As I suspected would happen, the fact that I was "thinking" of running for president generated a significant increase in the national media coverage that I received. I was no longer just a U.S. senator, I was now a possible future president. I became a regular on cable TV shows, on CNN, MSNBC, and occasionally Fox. I was also appearing on the important Sunday news shows and doing interviews with newspapers all across the country.

My communications director, Michael Briggs, did a great job in maximizing media opportunities. When we were in New York City, for example, we started early on the morning shows and went full blast throughout the day. On November 14, 2014, as an example, I did an early morning interview with Chris Cuomo on CNN, did an editorial board meeting with Bloomberg News, did an interview with *New York Times* columnist Gail Collins, taped an interview on WNET TV, met with my old friend Katrina vanden Heuvel of *The Nation* magazine, and concluded with an appearance on *The Colbert Report*.

In December 2014, Jane and I attended, as we usually did, the White House Christmas Ball. This is an annual opportunity for members of Congress, the administration, and friends to get together in a bipartisan, informal way. Many hundreds of people attend. One of the very weird things about this event is that the president does not address the people there, and he does not socialize. What he does, all night long, is take photos. The guests line up on the first floor, get ushered into a room with the president and Michelle, engage in small talk, and get their picture snapped. While Jane and I were there, I asked the president for a meeting.

A week or so later, I met with the president in the Oval Office. I had known Barack Obama for eight years, and we had served in the Senate together. While I had strong disagreements with him on some issues, we were friends and I respected him very much. On a number of important matters, we had worked closely together. Now, as I was seriously thinking about running for president, I wanted to get his views on some of the issues that I was discussing around the country. I also wanted his take on the recent elections and where he thought Democratic Party politics was going. As usual, I was impressed by his candor and intelligence.

During this period, we began to focus more on Iowa and New Hampshire—the first two states that would be voting. While the Democratic Party's nominating process is, of course, a national process, it is also fifty separate state elections. And, despite their relatively small sizes, Iowa and New Hampshire are two of the most important states. If we did well in those states, we would be off and running. If we did not, we would not be taken seriously as we advanced to other states.

In mid-December we returned to Iowa for a few days. In Des Moines I did interviews at *The Des Moines Register*. *The Des Moines Register* is the largest and most influential newspaper in Iowa, and it takes its responsibilities seriously. It understands the importance of the Iowa caucus and it tries to give all of the candidates, Democratic and Republican, a fair shake. It also conducts polling for the Iowa caucus, which is generally regarded to be of very high quality and receives a lot of national attention. During that trip I also appeared on *Iowa Press*, Iowa's equivalent of *Meet the Press*, a public television show with a veteran moderator, Dean Borg.

Later in the day we headed to Ames, where we held a town meeting. Before that meeting, we did something that I found very helpful, something we had not done before. We invited the various elements of the state's progressive community to join us for brief separate meetings so that we could better understand the issues they were dealing with. Within the course of a few hours we met with some of the leaders of the Latino community, the peace community, the LGBT community, the environmental community, Planned Parenthood, labor, and groups concerned with civil liberties. I found these meetings to be extremely informative; I believe those who attended felt the same way. As the campaign progressed, this is something we did in other states as well.

In late January I was back in New Hampshire. Arnie Arnesen is a well-known political figure in New Hampshire and an old friend of mine. Years before, she had run a strong and progressive campaign for governor of the state, and later became a host on a radio show that I often called in to. Arnie held frequent political gatherings at her home in Concord and was kind enough to hold one there for us.

In early February, for the first time, we ventured to Pennsylvania. In Philadelphia we did a low-donor fundraiser that brought out hundreds of people at $25 a head. The event was held in a large bar. Once again, as we had seen in Evanston, Illinois, I was learning that we could raise a modest amount of money and at the same time have a good-sized event. I was surprised and proud that so many people—working people—were prepared to make a financial contribution to the campaign. The campaign was taking root.

In Philadelphia we also attended a dinner for the House Progressive Caucus, which was chaired by my good friends Congressmen Keith Ellison and Raul Grijalva. A number of members of Congress were there. My speech followed that of Lee Saunders, president of the large union the American Federation of State, County and Municipal Employees (AFSCME). While there I did a number of media interviews. The next day I was in Harrisburg to speak before the Pennsylvania Progressive Summit. I was joined there by some eight hundred people. On the way back from Harrisburg to Washington, Michael Briggs and I drove through Gettysburg,

Pennsylvania. Neither of us had ever visited the Gettysburg battleground. We stopped there, walked around the grounds, saw a movie at the museum, and talked to some of the park employees. As Vermont soldiers had played a very important role in the Union victory at Gettysburg, I visited the statue of General George Stannard, one of Vermont's military leaders, as well as other Vermont monuments.

We also visited the site where Lincoln gave his famous address in 1863. As every schoolchild knows, in his speech Lincoln stated "that we here highly resolve that these dead shall not have died in vain . . . that this nation, under God, shall have a new birth of freedom . . . and that government of the people, by the people, for the people, shall not perish from the earth." As we left Gettysburg, it struck me forcefully that what Lincoln had said in 1863 was as relevant today as it was back then. Especially with the Supreme Court's disastrous 2010 Citizens United decision that opened the floodgates to virtually unlimited corporate spending in campaigns and allowed big money to buy elections, we were still fighting for a government "of the people, by the people, for the people." As a result of that trip to Gettysburg, I often referenced Lincoln, and what he said there on that day in 1863, in my speeches.

In early March 2015, along with many congressional colleagues and President Obama, I visited Selma, Alabama, to commemorate the fiftieth anniversary of the "Bloody Sunday" march across the Pettis Bridge in the fight for voting rights. The event was organized by Congressman John Lewis, who had been one of the leaders of that demonstration fifty years before as a member of the Student Nonviolent Coordinating Committee (SNCC). During that demonstration, Lewis had been brutally beaten and almost killed by Alabama state police.

While in Selma, Jane and I had the opportunity to meet some of the heroes and heroines of that period and of the civil rights movement. These were people who had shown incredible bravery standing up to official state terrorism, and listening to their stories was a moving and inspiring experience. While there we also heard some great gospel, one of my favorite kinds of music. We had a wonderful time.

Naturally, while we were in Selma, there was a lot of discussion about the state of the civil rights movement: where it had come from, how it had evolved, where it was today. Clearly, everyone agreed, huge and incredibly positive changes had taken place since Lewis and other demonstrators were almost killed in the fight for voting rights fifty years before. Today, Lewis was no longer a demonstrator. He was a U.S. congressman from Georgia, serving with dozens of other African-American members of Congress. Fifty years before, African-Americans in Selma didn't have the right to vote. Now, the mayor of Selma was black. Fifty years ago, it was incomprehensible to believe that the United States would ever have an African-American as president. Now, President Obama was serving his second term. These were changes that every American has a right to be proud of.

But there was another reality that those gathered in Selma knew. While the African-American community has made huge advances in politics, and while the United States was much less of a racist society than it had been, there were still enormous economic and social problems facing the black community. The Voting Rights Act that John Lewis, Dr. Martin Luther King Jr., and others had fought so hard to pass had recently been gutted by a Supreme Court decision, and all across the country Republican governors and legislators were rolling back the clock and making it harder for blacks and others to vote.

The unemployment rate, especially among young people, was much, much too high. In some communities the real unemployment rate for recent black high school graduates was 30 to 40 percent. Too many urban schools were nothing more than dropout factories, and too few young African-Americans were making it through college.

The African-American situation with regard to criminal justice was a national disgrace. Jails from coast to coast were filled with African-Americans, many of whom lacked decent education or job skills appropriate for the twenty-first century. Unbelievably, if present trends continued, one out of four black males born today would end up in jail.

During the campaign, I met frequently with members of the Black Lives Matter movement. This loosely knit organization was successfully educating the nation that in many black communities the police were not there protecting the people, but intimidating them. And time and time again, tragically, cell phone video cameras were recording horrific examples of extreme police brutality, the taking of innocent lives by overly aggressive police action. The names of the victims were becoming household names: Sandra Bland, Michael Brown, Rekia Boyd, Eric Garner, Walter Scott, Freddie Gray, Jessica Hernandez, Tamir Rice, Jonathan Ferrell, Oscar Grant, Antonio Zambrano-Montes, Samuel DuBose, Anastasio Hernandez-Rojas, and many others. Each of them died unarmed at the hands of police officers or in police custody.

Yes. There was no question that, as a nation, we had made great advances in civil rights. But there was also no doubt in my mind that much, much more needed to be done.

During the campaign, working with civil rights advocates, we introduced the strongest criminal justice reform any candidate had ever presented.

It was now April 2015. Over the past eighteen months I had visited twelve states, given dozens of speeches, and sat through countless media interviews. I had spoken to many thousands of people and met privately with hundreds more. The time was rapidly approaching when we would have to make a very simple decision. Was there sufficient support for me to run a credible national campaign? Could we put together an effective political organization to mount that campaign?

Bottom line: Do I run for president of the United States?

My mind went back to Burlington, Vermont, and 1981. It all sounded familiar. Nobody then thought that the city's political and economic establishment could be beaten. They were just too powerful. Nobody thought that we could put together the kind of coalition that we did. How can you get police officers, environmentalists, low-income tenants, college students, and city employees to be part of the same movement? Nobody, absolutely nobody, thought we could win that election. But we did. We pulled off the biggest political upset in the modern history of Vermont, and over the next eight years went about the business of putting our ideas into effect and transforming the city.

But clearly, what we were talking about now was not Burlington, Vermont. This was not a small city in a small state. This was the United States of America, a diverse nation of 320 million people in fifty states. In the few national polls in which my name had been included, I'd barely registered. I had virtually no national name recognition, very little money, no political organization, and in most states in the country my staff and I knew absolutely nobody. We would be taking on the entire political establishment. Not one of my Senate colleagues, not one member of Congress, not one governor, not one mayor had told me that he/she would be supportive if I ran. Not one. Were we totally crazy to be even thinking about this?

Maybe. But then I thought about the inspiring people I had met from one end of this country to the other, the many thousands who had come out to our meetings and enthusiastically supported a run. That was real, absolutely real. There was nothing crazy about them. Maybe the Inside the Beltway pundits didn't know they existed, but I had seen them and heard them. They were people who were hurting. People who were tired of the status quo. People who loved this country but knew that we could be much more than we were. People who didn't want Hillary Clinton, but wanted real political change— and were prepared to fight for it. If I didn't run, I would be letting them down.

There was a strong feeling growing within me that if I didn't run, it would be something I would regret for the rest of my life. I was ready to do it.

But wait a minute.

A decision of this magnitude was not going to be made based on political calculations or on my feelings alone. There were a whole lot of very personal matters that had to be considered as well. If I ran, the campaign would have a huge impact upon my family—my wife, Jane; my kids, Levi, Heather, Dave, and Carina, and their families, including my seven grandchildren. It would also impact the staff at my Senate office, who would have to pick up the extra work that my absence would entail.

Let me be honest. Jane was not enthusiastic about the idea of a presidential campaign—never was. She is smart and a realist. She knew that if I ran it would obviously mean that our family life would be radically altered. As Vermont's senator, I am back in the state almost every weekend. As a presidential candidate, I would almost always be on the road and away from home. It would also mean that we would be living in a world of stress, seven days a week.

She also worried about how, if against all odds we actually won, we could survive politically against the unprecedented hostility that was sure to come from Wall Street, the corporate world and their media, the Republican Party, and many Democrats. What we were trying to do was unprecedented in American history. We were taking on the *entire* political and economic establishment. If we won, what would happen the day after the election?

Jane and I also knew what modern politics is about and the kind of ugly personal attacks, lies, and distortions that we and the entire family would inevitably have to endure. In Vermont, where there is much less political ugliness than is the case nationally, we had already experienced it. What would it be like at the national level when we'd face well-funded adversaries who paid operatives whose sole function was to destroy their opponents? It was just one more factor to take into consideration.

While we were closing in on the decision of whether or not to make the run, Jane and I had breakfast at a Denny's restaurant in South Burlington, Vermont. We often went there on weekends—their blueberry pancakes are especially good. While we were there that Sunday morning, a man came over to our table and movingly thanked me for the work that my office had done for him in gaining his veterans' benefits. Our efforts had changed his life. He urged me to run for president. Jane started crying. She now knew what we had to do.

In early April, we invited Tad Devine, a national

media and political consultant who had worked on two of my Vermont campaigns, to come to our home in Burlington to describe what a presidential campaign would entail. I am not much into national political consultants, and Tad is the only one I have ever worked with. Unlike Jane and me, Tad actually knew what a national campaign was about. He had been involved in Al Gore's run for the presidency in 2000, as well as a number of other presidential campaigns.

Tad went down the checklist of what a campaign would mean. He talked about the tens of millions that would have to be raised, the scheduling requirements, staffing, security issues, how best to relate to national and state media, and the kind of paid media program that he thought we would need. He also believed that we would have to very heavily focus on Iowa and New Hampshire. If we made the decision to go forward, he was prepared be part of the team.

In the following weeks Jane and I talked to Levi, Heather, Carina, and Dave to get their feelings about a possible campaign. Without exception, they were on board and wanted to help out in any way they could. In fact, they were pretty excited.

On April 30, 2015, I strolled to an area outside the Capitol and informally told the Beltway media that I would soon be filing papers to establish a presidential campaign exploratory committee. Quietly, we decided that we would formally begin the campaign on May 26 in Burlington.

FOUR

HOW DO YOU RUN A PRESIDENTIAL CAMPAIGN?

The great anxiety that I had when I was contemplating running for president was that if I ran a poor campaign, if we were unable to get our message out effectively, if we failed to get a significant number of votes, if the actual campaign *itself* malfunctioned, we would be doing a disservice to the shared vision of the progressive movement. If our campaign was unsuccessful, the message left to history would be that our *ideas* were rejected and that nobody supported our agenda. More than anything else, that is what I feared.

Well, how do you run an effective national campaign? How do you make sure you don't fall flat on your face and call it quits two months after you begin, which is not uncommon? We hadn't a clue.

Vermont is a small state of 630,000 people. In my reelection campaign for the Senate in 2012 I received 207,000 votes—71 percent of the total vote. We knew how to run good campaigns in Vermont and how to win there. We knew nothing about national campaigns and how to compete effectively in fifty states and a bunch of territories. We were about to learn a lot, and quickly.

The one thing I did know was that if we were going

to be successful we had to remain true to ourselves. We would not be slick, or cute, or poll-driven. We knew whom we were fighting for, and whom we were fighting against. We could lose the election, but we wouldn't lose our soul.

Campaigns are about organizational capabilities, fund-raising, press relations, advertising, and a million other details. But what I always knew in my heart is that the most important part of any successful campaign is the *message*. What do you believe? What are you prepared to fight for?

THE MESSAGE

For me, that was the easy part. I knew what the message would be; no consultant, no pollster had to tell me. It was the same message I had been delivering my entire life.

We had to listen to and express to the public the real pain of the people: the working families of our country, the elderly, the children, the sick, the poor, and the young. These are the people who don't make campaign contributions, who don't know how to manipulate the system, and who are almost always ignored by government. We had to tell the truth about what was really going on in the country, a truth hardly addressed by corporate media. We had to forcefully take on the arrogance and greed of the ruling class, a small group of powerful people who wanted it all.

Further—and uniquely in modern campaigns—we had to put together a strong grassroots movement in which people understood that of course it was important that we elect a progressive president, but it was equally important that we create a political revolution by involving millions of new people in the process, people who were prepared to stand up and fight back against a corrupt political and economic system. In other words, this was not going to be a typical campaign. It was not just about electing a candidate. It was the building of a movement. It was the understanding that no president alone could or should do it all. The working families and the young people of this country had to be involved.

Our campaign was also determined to think big, not small. We were prepared to raise the issues that most other campaigns would not go near, issues that were far removed from ordinary American political discourse. I have always believed that asking the right questions was far more important than giving the right answers. And this campaign *would* ask the right questions.

In that regard, I was very much helped and guided by Pope Francis and the role he was playing throughout the world. To my mind, Pope Francis was distinguishing himself as one of the great moral and religious leaders not only of our time, but of modern history. He was opening up the entire world to new perspectives. His focus on the "dispossessed"—the poor, the elderly, and the unemployed, who were being cast aside by country after country—was awakening the conscience of the entire planet. His call for a "moral economy," an economy that addressed the needs of ordinary people and not just capitalist profiteers, was also inspiring millions.

I had the opportunity to hear the pope when he spoke at both the White House and the Congress during his visit to Washington. In April 2016, I was invited to attend a conference in the Vatican on the need to create a moral economy. I had to take time off the campaign trail to go to Italy, but it was an opportunity that I didn't want to miss. While there, I was able to briefly meet with the pope and some impressive leaders of the Catholic Church.

Pope Francis's mission had helped inspire me to think big. For decades now, especially with the ascendancy of right-wing Republicanism and the growing conservatism of the Democratic Party, Congress had been thinking smaller and smaller. Too often, the debate in Washington centered on questions like: Which program for the poor should be cut? Should we lower spending on Medicaid or food stamps? Should we slash education or affordable housing? Or, conversely, how much should we give in tax breaks to wealthy people who don't need them? How many more billions should we put into military spending?

The great challenges of our time were being ignored. Big ideas, from the progressive perspective at least, were not being discussed.

Our campaign would change that. Among other approaches, we would inject the radical concept of "morality" into the campaign. Further, we would look at what other countries around the world were doing to protect their working families and ask, "Why isn't the wealthiest nation on earth, the United States of America, doing the same?"

Once you think about it for a minute, you realize that this is not a very complicated approach. It is simple, straightforward, honest—and it reaches people. It changes the entire nature of the discussion.

Is it *moral* that, when millions of seniors are unable to afford the medicine they need, the top one-tenth of 1 percent owns as much wealth as the bottom 90 percent? Is it *moral* that, when we have the highest rates of childhood poverty of almost any major country in the world, the twenty wealthiest people in the country have more wealth than the bottom half of America—160 million people? Is it *moral* that, when our citizens are working longer hours for lower wages, 52 percent of all new income generated today is going to the top 1 percent?

And let's take a hard look at what's going on in the rest of the world. My Republican colleagues in the Senate often talk about "American exceptionalism." Well, they're right, but not for the reasons they think. It turns out that the United States is exceptional in being far, far behind many other nations in addressing the basic needs of working families. Why is the United States the only major country on earth not to guarantee health care to all people as a right? If the United Kingdom, France, Germany, Scandinavia, and Canada can do it, why can't we?

Why do our people work the longest hours of almost any people in the industrialized world, despite the explosion of technology and huge increases in worker productivity? Why do we have much shorter vacation time than any other major country?

Why is the United States one of the very few countries in the world, including the vast majority of poor countries, not to provide paid family and medical leave? Why do working-class women in this country have to separate themselves from their newborn babies and return to work just one or two weeks after giving birth?

At a time when almost everyone understands that human development is largely shaped during the first four years of life, why do we have one of the most dysfunctional and ineffective child care systems in the world?

Why does the United States have more people in jail than any other country? Why are we spending $80 billion a year to lock up 2.2 million Americans—disproportionately African-American, Latino, and Native American?

Why is higher education in America far more expensive than in any other country? How does it happen that Germany, Scandinavia, and other countries can provide free tuition at their colleges while hundreds of thousands of young Americans cannot afford to get a higher education because of the cost?

These were just *some* of the questions we intended to ask.

I was comfortable with our message. The next question was: How do we get the word out?

RALLIES

From day one, I knew that rallies and public meetings would be an essential component of the campaign. Why? Mostly, I must confess, because I love doing them, and always have. As Vermont's congressman and senator, I am quite sure that I have held far more official congressional town meetings—many, many hundreds of them over the years—than any other elected officeholder in the history of our state. We hold them in the state's largest cities (Burlington, Rutland, Colchester, Brattleboro, Bennington, and Montpelier) and in towns with populations of two hundred or less. Usually, somewhere between one and three hundred people come out for the meetings—pretty good turnouts for a small, rural state.

In addition, during my election races in Vermont, rallies are always the cornerstone of the campaign. Sometimes we do three or four in a day, going from town to town. The format is pretty simple. We meet in a school, church, or town hall. The event begins with a performance by local musicians. We serve hamburgers and hot dogs or some other simple fare. A few local supporters on a panel then get up and speak briefly about issues of concern to the community and why they are supporting me. I speak for a half hour or so, take questions from the audience, and move on. And that's it.

I love town meetings and rallies for a simple reason: It gives me an opportunity to interact with ordinary people and to find out what's on their minds. I am able to communicate with them directly, without the filter of the media. Moms and dads are there with their kids. People of all ages and backgrounds show up. These public events energize me. It is what democracy is all about. I have a poster of Norman Rockwell's painting of a Vermont town meeting right on the wall of the front entrance to my Burlington office.

We were going to make rallies and town meetings the central part of our presidential campaign, however, not just because I loved doing them or because I believed that's what democracy was all about. We were going to do a large number of rallies and town meetings because they generated excitement and energy and would win us votes. It was good politics.

Today, much of what elections are about is the raising of outrageous sums of money, hiring consultants, polling, and doing television ads. In fact, many candidates spend more time raising money than doing anything else. In large states like California, television advertising is pretty much all that a statewide campaign is about. There is very little face-to-face contact with the voters. A candidate is just another product being sold.

On top of that, because of Citizens United, there are campaigns where "independent expenditures" play a more important role than does the actual candidate. As insane as this may sound, outside special interests can have more influence in developing positive and negative themes, raising money, and putting ads on the air than the real-life candidate. In a campaign like that, the average voter is really voting for the unknown donors behind the "independent expenditures," not the person on the ballot.

Our campaign, to say the least, was going to be

different. We were not going to have independently
financed super PACs telling people what I believed or
didn't believe, or demonizing my opponents. I was going to be the person expressing my views and, to as great
a degree as possible, I would be stating those views before real people. I wanted to put energy, spontaneity, and
messiness back into the political process, not just a well-
choreographed set of productions or "listening tours"
carefully made for TV.

One of the goals of our campaign was to "bring people together," not just metaphorically but in the flesh.
The pundits and the establishment may not have thought
so, but I have always felt that the ideas I was espousing
were not radical or fringe. They were mainstream, the
views that millions held.

The truth is that when people come into a room, or a
gymnasium or an arena, and they look around them and
see all the other people in that venue sharing those same
views, they come away strengthened and energized.
They are not alone. They are part of something bigger
than themselves. They are part of a movement. This
is especially true when the audience is of diverse
backgrounds, which became increasingly true as our
campaign progressed. A rally of thousands of people
standing together—blacks, whites, Latinos, Native
Americans, Asian-Americans, young and old, gay and
straight, people who immigrated here and those born
here. This is something unforgettable and extraordinarily powerful. It is not something that a television ad
can accomplish.

Further, in the smaller states, rallies became a key
part of our get-out-the-vote effort. If you go to a small
town and five hundred people come out, everyone in
the town will know that you were there. That is especially true if you visit, as we did, rural or remote areas
where most politicians never go.

I love meeting with kids. They are our future. (Arun Chaudhary, Revolution Messaging)

In New Hampshire, for example, we held sixty-eight public meetings and spoke to 41,810 people. In winning that state handily, I received 151,584 votes. While there is no doubt that some people attended our meetings more than once, that means that approximately one out of four people who voted for me actually heard me in person. That is what grassroots democracy is all about. I love it.

In Iowa, we held 101 meetings, with 73,415 people attending. The total number of votes cast was about 171,000. In the Iowa caucus we won about half the delegates and believe that we may have won a small majority of the votes cast. In California, in an effort that was unprecedented in modern history, we spoke to 274,951 people at forty-six rallies throughout the state.

There was probably nobody in Congress who had more experience with town meetings and rallies than I did. We were going to learn soon, however, that rallies and public events for our presidential campaign were a little bit different from what we were used to in Vermont.

STAFFING

It is a political truism that you can't run a good campaign without a good staff. And here we had a particular problem that other campaigns did not. If you are a liberal, moderate, or conservative Democrat, if you are a traditional candidate, there are many excellent and experienced political operatives around the country whom you can hire, who have experience in those worlds. There are consulting firms, Democratic and Republican, that get involved in campaigns every two years. Some of them are excellent and staffed by highly skilled and experienced professionals.

But what if you are a democratic socialist, running a kind of campaign that no one else has ever attempted to run? What models do you build upon? Whom do you hire?

First, we attempted to get the best ideas we could from staff that had been involved in recent progressive

Saying hello to people after a rally. (Arun Chaudhary, Revolution Messaging)

campaigns. While our campaign would be different, there was no sense in reinventing the wheel. Three campaigns that we got good advice from were those of Jesse Jackson, Dennis Kucinich, and Barack Obama.

I had supported Jesse Jackson for president in 1988, and I have always believed that his campaign was enormously important in breaking down barriers and opening up new political space in our country. His concept of the "Rainbow Coalition" played a transformative role in American politics. Frankly, Barack Obama would not have been elected president without the groundbreaking work of Jackson's campaigns. Further, not only was Jackson a brilliant and charismatic campaigner, which I saw firsthand when I campaigned with him in Vermont, but he ran a smart, guerrilla-type campaign that did remarkably well given the limited financial resources he had. We got useful advice from some of the veterans who had worked with him, and from time to time I would chat with Reverend Jackson on the phone. His son Jonathan also spoke at a number of our rallies.

Dennis Kucinich is an old friend of mine. We met each other back in the eighties when he was mayor of Cleveland and I was mayor of Burlington. We were two of the most progressive mayors in the country at that time. Later we worked closely together when we both served in the U.S. House. Throughout his political career, Dennis has always shown an enormous amount of courage and never forgot the poor background he came from.

Dennis ran for president in 2004 and 2008. The fact that he never received a whole lot of votes in his campaigns understates the impact that he has had on contemporary politics. During his campaigns for president, Dennis created a strong grassroots movement and forced the debate in the Democratic primary process into a direction it never would have gone without him. Before the campaign began, Jane and I had the opportunity to meet with him and his wife, Elizabeth, and to tap their brains as to what we could learn from his two campaigns. They were very helpful in discussing issues related to fund-raising, staffing, and transportation.

Howard Dean, a fellow Vermonter, ran in the Democratic primary in 2004. His campaign developed a number of important political breakthroughs that we learned from and utilized. He was the first candidate to successfully fund-raise online, and his concept of "meet-ups" or house parties was a very innovative concept that we built upon.

In 2008 a young U.S. senator from Illinois, Barack Obama, ran one of the most brilliant campaigns in the modern history of our country. While he was more conservative than Jackson, Kucinich, or myself, there was much to be learned from Obama's campaign. He utilized social media for communication and fund-raising in a way that no one had before. He held large and effective rallies across the country, and he tapped into the cultural energy of some of the most creative people in America, a greatly underutilized resource. As we prepared, we spoke to many people who had been involved in Obama's campaigns. Not only did we learn a lot from them, such as how to best campaign in Iowa, we eventually brought more than a few on board.

A nontraditional, unprecedented type of campaign required a nontraditional campaign manager. That turned out to be Jeff Weaver, the owner of a small comic book store in Virginia who had never been involved in a national campaign.

I met Jeff thirty years ago when, as a young man, he came into my campaign office to volunteer on my 1986 gubernatorial campaign. He came to us with very good qualifications. Not only was he a former Marine, he had been thrown out of Boston University for his civil rights activism. That worked for me.

Jeff was born and raised in northern Vermont and eventually graduated from the University of Vermont. In 1988, during my congressional campaign, we didn't have a lot of money. We made up for it with hard work and long hours on the campaign trail. Jeff drove me around the state in his car from morning to night, often seven days a week. I am confident that I am the only congressional candidate in history to have, as his official campaign car, a Yugo. It was an unforgettable car which, when it went above 55, started rattling.

In 1990, when we won the congressional race, Jeff went with me to Washington. He is a hard worker and extremely smart. Over the years he advanced his way up in the office and eventually became my chief of staff. In 2006, he managed my campaign for the Senate, and when we won he moved over there with me. Over the years Jeff married, had three great kids, and picked up a law degree from Georgetown.

Unlike every political observer in the world, Jeff believed from day one that we had a real chance to win the election, and he ran the campaign on that basis. Jeff was at the center of our campaign wheel's many spokes. He had to coordinate the fund-raising and the budgeting, the hiring and firing of key staff, and the transferring of some of them as new primaries and caucuses came on the horizon. He was involved in the production of paid media and when and where to air the ads, as well as organizing rallies and handling security issues. His legal skills were also helpful when it came to dealing with the DNC and the Democratic establishment. Jeff is a good writer, and on some issues, like criminal justice, where he is particularly knowledgeable, he helped me prepare speeches. He also became a regular on television shows as he became one of the strongest defenders of me and the campaign against the attacks that were coming our way from the Clinton camp.

Running a campaign, especially ours, is an insane experience that one can never be fully prepared for. Jeff did a great job.

Warren Gunnels has been a key policy adviser of mine going back to when I was in the House. He kindly took a leave of absence from the Senate, where he served as my staff director as the ranking member on the Budget Committee, to plunge into the campaign. As Chief Policy Advisor, Warren played an outstanding role in researching and writing speeches and position papers on a wide range of economic issues, from Wall Street to health care to infrastructure. Warren is an extraordinarily hard worker who, no matter what the obstacles, always gets the job done.

Michael Briggs, a former writer for the *Chicago Sun-Times*, has been my communications director since I entered the Senate ten years ago, and has done a great job. Michael is one of the hardest workers I have ever known. He is on call morning, noon, and night, seven days a week, which is how I often work. Michael wanted to go where the action was and when I announced for president, he took a leave from the Senate office to join the campaign full time. He was at my side every moment of the campaign, dealing with national and local media, and arranging my many interview and media appearances.

In every campaign there is one person who is the "go-to guy." For much of our campaign that person was Shannon Jackson, a young man from Vermont who had formerly worked in my Senate office. Shannon was there to coordinate scheduling, flights, food, and all the other essentials that had to be taken care of.

JANE AND THE KIDS

The campaign became a family affair with Jane and the kids playing a very active role. Jane, who served as my chief of staff for a while when I was in the House, knows politics and media very well. In this campaign she not only was a key adviser but became a very visible media surrogate, appearing on many television and radio shows. She also campaigned for me in Alaska and Hawaii, both of which we won. She also showed the country that not everyone in the family is grumpy.

The four kids were as involved as their schedules allowed. My oldest son, Levi, an advocate for low-income people, gave speeches for me in his home state of New Hampshire and played an invaluable role as a researcher who knows his way around the Internet. My daughter Heather, a yoga teacher, somehow got me on the front page of yoga magazines and helped out as we campaigned in Arizona, where she now lives. My son Dave knows a whole lot of people in the arts community, and

My son Levi with me during a political meeting and, at right, Levi speaking as part of the campaign in New Hampshire.

(Erik Borg; mikemunhallphotos.com)

Levi, Nicole, Carina, Jane, Dave, Liza, Heather, and Marc in the spin room after the New Hampshire debate. (Phil Fiermonte)

did a great job in helping to create the "Art of a Political Revolution" and bringing cultural energy into the campaign. My youngest daughter, Carina, did a bit of speaking, set up some of the administrative structures in the campaign, and made sure we were always greeted with family and good food when we made it home. Carina, Dave, and Liza worked together to take care of family and home matters, not an insignificant thing when you're always on the road. They all joined us as we crisscrossed the country, bringing the love and support necessary for us to maintain a nonstop schedule. Everyone on the campaign particularly enjoyed it when the grandkids came.

SOCIAL MEDIA

I am seventy-five years of age. I grew up with newspapers, radio, television, and books. The editorial page and letters to the editor were important to me, and I have written my fair share of op-eds. When I was elected mayor of Burlington in 1981, there were no computers in City Hall and no video to record the city council meetings. There were no e-mails. Hard to believe, but we actually wrote individual letters to constituents.

In my early Vermont campaigns, much of our communication with the media was through press releases that were sent via the postal system. We sent a release out on Monday, it got to the media on Wednesday, and, if we were lucky, it got printed on Thursday.

In case you haven't noticed, the world has changed.

Personally, I am a bit of a Luddite. I'm not all that impressed with every aspect of modern technology. Too much change for the sake of change. And let me make the radical statement that I don't believe that you can say something profound in the 140 characters that make up a tweet.

But I am not dumb. As a congressman and a senator, it didn't take me long to understand the advantages of modern communications technology. It also made sense to hire young people for my office who knew what they were doing. Originally, Jeff Frank set up our Senate office social media. He was joined in 2013 by Kenneth Pennington, who greatly expanded our efforts. Despite representing one of the smallest states in the country, by 2014 my Senate office had a greater presence on Facebook, Twitter, and the other social media than almost any other congressional office. We were also ahead of the curve in the use of e-mail, video, and conference calling.

With regard to the presidential campaign, we knew from the beginning that the Internet and social media would be important tools for us in terms of communication and raising money. We just didn't know *how* important they would be.

We started the establishment of our campaign's digital team by bringing on some of the bright young people we had in our Senate office who were doing social media there. Kenneth Pennington led that effort and was joined by Hector Sigala. We then interviewed a number of people and organizations to broaden what we could accomplish online. We settled on Revolution Messaging, a well-respected company with leaders, like Scott Goodstein, who had worked on Obama's campaign and for progressive organizations.

Revolution jump-started our online fund-raising and advertising efforts. The first day of the campaign, we signed up a hundred thousand people and raised $1.5 million, with Tim Tagaris leading the fund-raising effort at Revolution. Arun Chaudhary led an excellent team, including Hilary Hess, Fred Guerrier, Eric Elofson, and Peter O'Leary, who captured the excitement of the rallies on video so that Hector could spread them far and wide on social media. And we built a community, with millions of people receiving our e-mails, in large part due to online advertisements driven by Keegan Goudiss, another one of the Revolution partners.

From the beginning, we knew it was important to fund this campaign differently than most. We weren't going to be receiving a whole lot of support from wealthy donors and we didn't want a super PAC. In the end, 94 percent of our money came in online, and we not only talked the talk about campaign finance reform, we walked the walk.

But we didn't use the Internet just to raise money. As an example, on July 29, 2015, I was able to speak to more than 110,000 supporters at 3,700 house parties held in every state in the country. What an extraordinary and powerful organizing tool! We were able to live-stream many of the rallies and town meetings that we held. Almost every week we were sending out short videos on some of the most important issues facing the country, and millions of people viewed them and passed them on to their friends. Every single day, messages on issues of the day and events we were holding went out to millions.

When people talk about how well we did with young people, clearly one of the reasons for that was our success with social media. Social media enabled us to talk directly to an entire generation about the most important issues facing their lives and start an online discussion about them. Needless to say, that was far more effective for us than short sound bites on television or the political gossip that I often have to respond to from the corporate media.

Further, as part of our social media success, I learned something that never in a million years would've occurred to me, but is now part of many modern campaigns. As a result of the growth of our social media network, our campaign began running a quite large and lucrative merchandise marketing company. Yes, while we were busy trying to transform the economic and political life of the nation we were also selling T-shirts, sweatshirts, hats, mugs, buttons, bumper stickers, and all kinds of other paraphernalia. In fact, for a while, I believe we were the major source of business for union-made T-shirts in the United States.

But we weren't the only ones making money off campaign products. We had unleashed an entrepreneurial volcano. Who said I was bad for capitalism: In Vermont, a teddy bear company was making Bernie Bears. There was even an action doll, not to mention underwear, many styles of shirts, shopping bags, and a million different kinds of buttons.

When we began the campaign we had high expectations of what we could do through social media, but they paled in terms of what we actually accomplished in terms of communication and fund-raising. We ended up with some 5 million Facebook friends and more than 3 million followers on Twitter.

Through the Internet we received a record-breaking eight million individual campaign contributions from 2.5 million contributors.

I think it's fair to say that we "wrote the book" for progressive politics in terms of showing the potential of social media.

VOLUNTEER COORDINATION

One of the challenges that we faced was that we were taking on virtually the entire Democratic establishment. And I mean the entire Democratic establishment. Before Hillary Clinton even formally announced her intention to seek the Democratic nomination, eight months before the first vote was cast in Iowa, there were four hundred superdelegates lined up to support her. In every state that we contested we had to take on Democratic governors, members of Congress, senators, locally elected officials, and party leaders—and their organizational ability to bring out the vote.

How do you take on the entire political establishment, especially in states where you start off by knowing almost nobody? You build a great volunteer organization. There is and was no question of seasoned politicians knowing how to get people to the polls. But our campaign had something that the Clinton campaign and the establishment didn't have, something that permeated every aspect of our campaign: We had energy, passion, and dedication. By the end of the campaign, through an enormous amount of effort, we were able to bring many hundreds of thousands of volunteers into the fight.

SURROGATES AND ORGANIZATIONAL SUPPORT

I am a United States senator. I am well known. I can attract a crowd at a rally. I can get on TV and radio pretty easily. I can do newspaper interviews. But, in a presidential campaign, I can't be the only one out there in the public eye. We need help in spreading the message of the campaign. We need support from well-known and respected surrogates who can attract attention from the public and the media and give the campaign credibility. We need the support of large progressive organizations.

Easier said than done.

Normally, in a national campaign, much of the surrogate help for a candidate comes from elected officials. A candidate goes into a city or a state and is joined by a governor, a senator, a mayor. Clearly, that wasn't going to be the case for us. Almost all Democratic elected officials had lined up behind Clinton.

Our strategy was to effectively utilize those few elected officials who were prepared to support us, as well as political activists from the world of labor, environmental activism, academia, and social and racial justice. Frankly, our surrogate support started slowly, but as the campaign gained momentum we received more and more backing from some extraordinary people. One of the joys of the campaign was working with them.

The elected officials from Congress who signed on to the campaign were Senator Jeff Merkley, Representative Keith Ellison, Representative Tulsi Gabbard, Representative Raul Grijalva, Representative Marcy Kaptur, and Representative Peter Welch. There are 46 Democrats in the Senate. We had 1. There are 187 Democrats in the House. We had five. In the world of Democratic politics, it took real courage for each of these members to buck the Clinton organization, the party leadership, and the political establishment and join our campaign. Needless to say, some wealthy campaign contributors were not happy with their decisions.

Jeff Merkley, a senator from Oregon, and I worked together over the years on a number of climate change and environmental issues. He is one of the most progressive members of the Senate. I was proud to have him on board.

Representative Tulsi Gabbard of Hawaii joined our campaign in a rather dramatic fashion: She resigned as vice chair of the Democratic National Committee. Tulsi, a veteran of the war in Iraq, is deeply concerned about foreign and military policy. She saw the lives of too many of her comrades destroyed by a war we should never have gotten into, and she wanted policies to make sure that we never got into another such war again.

The most progressive group in the U.S. House is the Progressive Caucus, with seventy-one members. It is also now the largest caucus within the House Democratic Party. When I entered the Congress in 1991, I helped create that organization. I thought it was important that there be a caucus that brought together members to focus on economic, social, racial, and environmental injustice. Today, the House Progressive Caucus is led by Congressmen Keith Ellison and Raul Grijalva. They are both extraordinary members of Congress and are doing a great job chairing the caucus. I was proud when they both decided to join the campaign.

Keith Ellison is one of the few Muslims in the U.S. Congress. During the early rise of Trumpism and the growing expression of anti-Muslim prejudice, I joined Keith and other Muslims for a public meeting in a mosque in Washington. It was a moving experience and a reminder that this is America. We should not be hating people because of their religion.

Our goal throughout the campaign was to reach out to people of all religious faiths and all ethnic backgrounds. We ended up doing very well within the Muslim community, and Muslim votes, in fact, may have been the margin of victory for us in the Michigan primary. As a Jew, I was especially proud to be working with Muslims. Yes: We can come together.

Raul Grijalva is an old friend from Tucson, Arizona, and a leader in both the progressive and Latino communities. One of the most beautiful nights of the campaign was speaking at a rally before about seven thousand people at a baseball stadium in Tucson after having been introduced by Raul. It was one of the most diversely attended events of the campaign. The crowd was largely Latino, but many blacks and whites were there as well.

Representative Marcy Kaptur and I have worked together for twenty-five years, starting when we served in the House together. Marcy represents Toledo, Ohio. She has seen her community devastated by disastrous trade agreements that have resulted in massive job losses. Marcy remains one of the strongest voices in Congress in demanding that we have trade agreements that work for American workers, not just the CEOs of large corporations. She was a key asset in our campaign.

Representative Peter Welch succeeded me in the U.S. House when I won my seat in the Senate. He is a former president of the Vermont State Senate and someone I have known for almost forty years. Over those years he and I have worked together on many Vermont issues. It was comforting to hear Peter's down-home Vermont perspective on the campaign.

Our campaign also attracted some great leaders from the local and state level. Nina Turner, a former state senator from Ohio and one of the most dynamic orators in

In South Carolina with State Representative Terry Alexander.
(Eric Elofson, Revolution Messaging)

America, came on board early and was extremely active throughout the campaign. Nina was a constant and brilliant spokesperson for us on TV and radio, and introduced me at events throughout the country. Talk about courage! Nina took an enormous amount of heat from party officials in Ohio when she withdrew her support for Secretary Clinton and came on board our campaign. Nina's husband, Jeff, a Teamster, was also very helpful.

Chuy Garcia is a county commissioner in Cook County, Chicago. I supported him when he ran against Rahm Emanuel for mayor of Chicago in 2015. In my campaign, he not only helped in Illinois, but traveled throughout the country—especially before Latino audiences. Chuy is a stand-up guy and has become a good friend.

Why would black members of the South Carolina Legislature like Justin Bamberg, Terry Alexander, Joe Neal, and a few others support a white socialist from Vermont who trailed Hillary Clinton by 50 points in the polls in their state? Well, you'll have to ask them, but that's what they did. In a conservative state like South Carolina, they showed enormous courage in doing so—and I am deeply grateful to them. Truthfully, the problems and politics of the South are not something that I was familiar with when I began the campaign. I learned a lot, and these guys helped teach me.

CELEBRITY SUPPORT

For better or worse, well-known Hollywood personalities and other celebrities can and do play an important role in politics. And we had many of them actively involved in our campaign, including some very dedicated people who have spent much of their lives as political activists. There are many celebrities who simply enjoy the glow of fame and fortune. The people who participated in our campaign, however, used their name recognition and popularity to educate America about issues dear to their hearts and vitally important for the future of our country: poverty, racism, climate change and the environment, immigration reform, voter suppression, peace, and many other issues.

It was a great thrill to be on the stage at the legendary Apollo Theater in Harlem in a panel discussion with the singer Harry Belafonte, who has been involved in progressive politics from his youth. I also had the opportunity to meet with him and his wife earlier, where he told me about some of the great work that he continues to do, at age ninety.

Cornel West is a man of courage and brilliance. He is a prolific writer, an extraordinary orator, and a friend of mine. It is always a bit intimidating to get up on a

What a thrill! At the Apollo Theater in Harlem with Harry
Belafonte. (Aristotle Torres, www.aristotle.nyc)

stage after being introduced by Cornel. Dr. West was an
important part of the campaign from coast to coast.

One of America's most acclaimed actresses, Susan
Sarandon, introduced me at rallies across the country,
and did events on her own. Jane and I had met Susan
years before when she acted in the film *Sweet Hearts
Dance* in Vermont. Susan took heat from some of her
Hollywood friends for supporting me. Her sincerity and
down-to-earthness came across to the thousands of people she spoke to.

Rosario Dawson, a passionate defender of the needs
of low-income people, was onstage with me when we
spoke to 18,000 people at a park in the South Bronx, one
of the poorest communities in the country. Rosario
played an important role throughout the campaign.

Sarah Silverman is a brilliant comedienne and was
funny as hell when she introduced me to a crowd of
25,000 in Los Angeles. She created an amazing video

Cornel West and I had a lot of fun on the trail. (Hilary Hess, Revolution Messaging)

supporting my candidacy that millions saw online, thanks to her extensive social media network.

I am a big fan of Spike Lee and his movies. He created some fantastic videos and radio ads for the campaign, did an interview and photo shoot with me for the New York edition of *The Hollywood Reporter*, gave opening remarks at events, and even attended the Brooklyn debate.

Danny DeVito introduced me at rallies on several occasions, and got a better response than I did. Danny is one of my favorite actors and a real progressive.

Everybody knows Danny Glover's movies. What many do not know is that Danny is a lifelong activist who has been involved in the struggle for racial, economic, and social justice for decades. Danny was very involved in the campaign and spoke at some of our larger rallies. He brought my old friend and fellow mayor, Gus Newport, to one of them and we all had an

Shooting a video at Brooklyn College with Mark Ruffalo on environmental issues. (Fred Guerrier, Revolution Messaging)

excellent discussion over dinner—a rare opportunity in fast-paced days.

Mark Ruffalo is not only "The Hulk." He is a strong environmentalist. We got together in Brooklyn to have an unscripted, in-depth discussion about environmental issues—with cameras just capturing it all. Millions saw it via social media.

Shailene Woodley is a young actress actively involved in the environmental movement and the fight for Native American rights. Her voice was loud and clear throughout our campaign.

I have known Vermont's own Ben Cohen and Jerry Greenfield (Ben and Jerry) for decades. Not only did they create an outstanding ice cream and become leaders in the businesses-for-social-responsibility movement, they are heavily involved in the fight for campaign finance reform and other progressive causes. Both of them campaigned for and with me throughout the country.

Jane had seen Dick Van Dyke, the TV and movie star, in an interview talking about how the United States was moving toward an oligarchic society. He sounded like our kind of guy. He came aboard the campaign, did a number of events with me, and at ninety was incredibly spry.

Killer Mike, the rapper, is a brilliant artist who helped us reach out to young people—black, white, and Latino—throughout the country in a way that I could not have without him. He introduced me to a large audience in his hometown of Atlanta, Georgia, and worked hard for us in numerous venues throughout the country.

Jim Hightower is someone I have known for decades. He is a former Texas commissioner of agriculture, a bestselling author, and one of the great political humorists in the country. In Texas and throughout the country, Jim played an active role in the campaign.

Actress Mimi Kennedy came on board very early, delivering petitions to have me run for president even before I announced. She generously hosted one of our very few fund-raisers in the backyard of her home in California.

Seth MacFarlane, an actor and producer, was also one of the first to come on board, and provided a big boost with the younger generation. Frances Fisher, George Lopez, Stephen Bishop, Justin Long, Josh Fox, Kendrick Sampson, and Tim Robbins all came on early and stayed active as well. They spoke at rallies, came up with innovative ways to reach out to their audiences, and made a significant difference in the campaign.

These are just a few of the men and women—actors, actresses, singers, dancers, rappers, artists—who played an active role in my campaign. These well-known Americans were willing, sometimes against a great deal of peer pressure, to stick their necks out for the political revolution. I am grateful for what they did and look forward to working with them in the future.

FIGHTING FOR ORGANIZATIONAL SUPPORT

From day one of the campaign, we knew that it was important to win the backing of progressive organizations with large memberships. Despite the fact that I was one of the most progressive members of Congress, with a far stronger record than Secretary Clinton, that turned out to be a difficult task.

Hillary and Bill Clinton had developed close personal ties with many of the leaders of these organizations over the years, and the Clinton campaign was able to win many of them over. During the fight for endorsements, I noticed an interesting process. In those organizations that held open and democratic grassroots elections regarding the endorsement process, we usually did very well. In those organizations where endorsements were determined by executive boards, we usually lost. In general, we did well with the rank and file, not so well with the Inside the Beltway leadership.

We knew our campaign was taking off when we won the strong support of Democracy for America (DFA) and MoveOn.org. These are two of the largest online grassroots organizations in the country. They both have millions of members. These two organizations opened up the endorsement process to their members, and in both cases we won landslide victories—over 70 percent of the vote. Both groups played an aggressive and positive role in the campaign.

We also won the support of some great national unions. The National Nurses United, led by the dynamic RoseAnn DeMoro, was the first national union to support us. They joined not just because they are a progressive union, but because of my support for a Medicare for All single-payer health care system. These nurses, who take their lifesaving jobs very seriously, understood that they were unable to fully do the jobs they were trained to do within a dysfunctional health system that denied care to millions. They wanted real health care reform. They wanted Bernie Sanders for president. And they played an active role in many, many states.

The Communications Workers of America (CWA), led by Chris Shelton, also came on board early. They knew my record well and knew that in my twenty-five years in Congress I had one of the strongest pro-union voting records of any member. They also knew that over the years I had worked with them on a number of telecommunications issues. In fact, on more than one occasion I had walked the picket lines with CWA members, in Vermont and elsewhere.

I have been one of the strongest supporters in Congress of the United States Postal Service, and have worked with the postal unions for years against Republican efforts to privatize it. In fact, a couple of years ago, a few of us in the Senate managed to prevent the shutdown of thousands of rural post offices. I was honored to have been invited to speak to the American Postal Workers Union (APWU), led by Mark Dimondstein. The support I received at their meeting in Las Vegas was strong and I was proud to receive their endorsement soon after.

Our infrastructure—roads, bridges, rail, public transit, water systems, and wastewater plants—is crumbling, and nobody knows that better than the workers who are employed in those systems and their unions. One of the most important parts of my agenda was creating millions of new jobs by rebuilding our infrastructure. I was delighted that two of the major transportation unions

We had great rank-and-file union support! (Notice the haircut.) (Fred Guerrier, Revolution Messaging)

in the country—the Amalgamated Transit Union and the International Longshore and Warehouse Union—came on board the campaign in support of that agenda.

As we fought to get union support, Larry Cohen, the former president of the CWA, did an incredible job in organizing grassroots support for a Labor for Bernie coalition. Hillary Clinton had the support of a number of union leaders; we were getting the support of the rank and file. On several occasions I was on a telephone conference call with thousands of grassroots trade union activists.

In the spring, we won an important victory by getting the national AFL-CIO to postpone their endorsement. Despite the fact that it was assumed by almost everyone that the AFL-CIO, representing 12.5 million workers, would endorse Secretary Clinton early on, our backers on the executive committee were able to win a postponement until after the nominating process was completed. This was important because it meant that the significant resources of the national AFL-CIO, in terms of money and volunteer efforts, would not be utilized to benefit the Clinton campaign.

PAID MEDIA

In my Vermont campaigns we almost always did paid media—television, radio, and print—close to home. We relied on local media people we had known for years. The exception to that was in 1996, when I anticipated a rough reelection campaign to the U.S. Congress. In 1994, during the Gingrich Republican landslide, I had run the worst campaign of my life and won by only 2 points. We knew we would have trouble in 1996, and we needed expertise that we didn't have in Vermont.

Tad Devine was recommended to me by Congressman Peter DeFazio, a friend of mine. Devine was a nationally known Democratic media consultant, and had done great work for candidates all across the country. He did our media work in 1996 and returned to Vermont in 2006 to help us with my U.S. Senate campaign.

Tad is actually the only national political media person I know. I had used him on two occasions in Vermont, so it was only natural that I turned to him again for the presidential race. He brought with him a number of other people from his firm, including Mark Longabaugh, Julian Mulvey, and Scott Turner, who were also extremely helpful. Mark, a strong environmentalist, not only helped us do general political work, but played an important role in reaching out for us to the environmental community.

While we put an enormous amount of resources and energy into rallies, social media, and grassroots organizing, there's no question that paid media and television advertising played an important role in the campaign, and that we put a lot of money into that effort.

Political experts can argue about how important TV and radio campaign ads are in the changing media world in which we live. But no one denies that large parts of our population, for better or worse, continue to receive much of the information about the world in which they live from television. Media ads remain very important and, as much as I would have liked to, they were a political tool that we couldn't ignore.

I'm proud of the quality of the ads that we ran. Some of them were pointed, but they weren't negative. We never once mentioned the name of Hillary Clinton in any paid media that we did. Don't take my word for it, but many objective observers commented that some of our ads were the best-produced of the entire campaign. One beautiful ad that received a lot of national attention was called "America," which included the music to the Simon and Garfunkel song of that title. Over lunch in the Capitol, many months before, Jane and I had talked to Paul Simon about allowing us to use one of his songs. He agreed. Art Garfunkel also came on board, and the ad was produced.

Brent Burdowski of the Washington paper *The Hill* wrote:

> The new television ad that was released by the Sen. Bernie Sanders (I-Vt.) campaign, based on Simon and Garfunkel's song "America," is the most brilliant and appropriate campaign ad of the year so far, and may be the most important campaign ad since President Reagan's "Morning in America" ad. The ad perfectly captures the vision and spirit of the Sanders campaign and the mood of an America today that is the stuff of diverse people yearning to come together for

*common dreams and aspirations, at a time when
many voters are hurting and hungering for a better life. The ad brings together music and video
behind the Sanders message in a way that is fun
to watch and memorable in substance and tone.*

FUND-RAISING

The *message* is key to any serious campaign, but the
message doesn't matter much if nobody hears it.

There are fifty states in the country, and we would
eventually need staff for all of them if we were going to
win primaries and caucuses. Rallies are great, but you
have to pay for the venues that you use, and there are
sound system, lighting, security, and other rally costs.
There are many, many people who want to volunteer in
a campaign, but to effectively mobilize them paid coor-
dinators are needed. Television and radio ads may be
old-fashioned, but they remain vital to a modern campaign. Somebody was going to have to produce the ads
and put them on the air—an expensive proposition. Social media is an exploding medium, but the people who
produce it need a paycheck.

How could we pay for all of this? Well, we were going to have to raise a lot of money.

When I ran for governor in 1986 and lost, I was
outspent. When I ran for Congress in 1988 and lost, I
was outspent. When I ran for Congress again in 1990
and won, I was outspent. In 2006, when I was elected as
Vermont's senator, I was outspent.

Raising money is the ugliest part of modern American politics, and I personally hate to do it. As a result
of Citizens United, a bad fund-raising process became
much worse. Nowadays, a serious run for the presidency
requires somewhere around $1 billion. As I've said

many times, I'm going to do everything I can to bring about real campaign finance reform, overturn Citizens United, and move to public funding of elections. But that wasn't going to happen in this campaign. We needed money now. We would have to do some serious fund-raising.

Over the years, the easiest and most effective way for me to raise money was to take an old-fashioned approach. I would write long letters to my list of supporters, analyzing the current situation and describing to them what I hoped to accomplish. We printed up the letters by the tens of thousands, took them to the post office, mailed them, and waited for the return envelopes to come back. In more recent years we also used e-mail and the Internet to raise funds, and that also worked well, bringing in large numbers of small contributions.

All in all, when I was running in Vermont, we were able to raise a reasonable sum of money for a statewide race from small individual contributions. In addition, we received help from labor unions, environmental groups, senior groups, and other organizations sympathetic to my politics. Sometimes, although rarely, I would get on the phone and ask wealthy people for money.

Our approach for raising funds for a statewide campaign in the small state of Vermont worked well for our needs. Now, however, we were playing in a different league, and needed to raise far more money.

As we contemplated the run for president, several things became clear in terms of fund-raising. First, I was not going to do what every other presidential candidate was doing, and that was to establish a super PAC. Super PACs, which allow for unlimited contributions from wealthy people, are the exact manifestation of everything that is wrong with politics today. The idea of establishing one was tempting, and easy to do, but I wasn't going to do it.

Second, I was not going to spend large amounts of time on the phone begging money from wealthy individuals or organizations. Not only was this time-consuming, it was extraordinarily demoralizing. It would take the spirit right out of what I wanted to do.

Third, I was not going to do "high-dollar" fundraisers where small numbers of people made large contributions. This was going to be a people's campaign, and I was going to spend my time and energy talking to ordinary human beings. To the degree that we did fund-raisers—and we did a few—they would be "low-dollar" events. People were welcome to contribute more, but a $25 donation would be more than enough to get you right in the door.

So, how would we raise the kind of money we would need to run a serious national campaign? The answer was pretty simple. We would encourage, in every way we could, large numbers of people to make small contributions. This would be an essential part of what the political revolution was all about. We would show the world that, yes, it was possible to run a serious national campaign without being dependent on wealthy people, Wall Street, corporate interests, and their super PACs. Consistent with my view that real change never takes place from the top on down, but always from the bottom on up, that's how we would raise our campaign funds.

And that is exactly what we did, with a success that we could never have imagined.

Through our online efforts, our campaign ended up raising the astronomical sum of $232 million. That money came through some 8 million individual contributions from 2.5 million people. The average donation was $27. This is an unprecedented accomplishment in the history of American politics, and I am enormously grateful to all those people who helped make it happen.

FIVE

THE CAMPAIGN BEGINS

May 26, 2015, Burlington, Vermont. Today is the day. The formal announcement. I am running for president of the United States.

Jane and I and the few others we had on board had argued as to whether or not we should do the opening campaign event inside or outside, at lunchtime or in the early evening. In my previous campaigns for Congress and the U.S. Senate, we did the events indoors at a large local church. They worked well. Hundreds of Vermonters attended.

But this was different. We were running for the White House. Larger crowd. A lot of media to accommodate. A much bigger deal.

Fortunately, Jane prevailed. We decided to do the event outside, in the very beautiful waterfront park on Lake Champlain that I had helped to create when I was mayor thirty years before. The park had a wide grassy area that could accommodate (we hoped) a large crowd, and as a backdrop we had the beautiful Adirondack Mountains behind the lake. We would hold the event after work, with the hope that more people would be able to attend. And we prayed for good weather. We didn't have much of a rain plan.

We lucked out. It was a perfect Vermont spring day. People started arriving early, and they kept on coming. To our utter amazement, over five thousand people showed up—men, women, and a lot of children. The local newspaper live-streamed the event and seven thousand more people were "there" in that way. According to the local media, it was the largest political gathering in the modern history of the state.

The event attracted a decent amount of national media, too. All of the major networks and cable television stations were there, as well as virtually all of the national newspapers. Ed Schultz of MSNBC broadcast the event live. Needless to say, the event was heavily covered by the Vermont media.

In the past, when I had announced my candidacy for office in Vermont, or given any kind of important speech, it was usually an informal affair. I would walk through the crowd, shake hands, and chat; that's the way we are in Vermont. But today was different. Too many people. Too much media. Too much opportunity for something to go wrong. On this day, I was driven to right behind the stage, and that's where I waited for the introductory remarks to end.

It was an emotional day for me, because many of the Vermonters in attendance were people I knew, some for many years. They were friends, neighbors, and people I had worked with, in one way or another, for decades as a mayor, congressman, or senator. My entire family—Jane, Levi and Raine, Heather and Marc, Carina and Blake, Dave and Liza, and Nicole and Keegan—were up on the stage with me, as were my seven grandchildren: Sunnee, Cole, Ryleigh, Grayson, Ella, Tess, and Dylan.

We were, all together, beginning a very strange venture. We had no idea as to how it would end or where it would lead us. But, in my beautiful state of Vermont, we were starting off with an enormous amount of love.

After great music by my favorite Vermont band, Mango Jam, I was introduced by friends I had worked closely with in Vermont over the years—people who knew me well. Ben Cohen and Jerry Greenfield of Ben & Jerry's; Donna Bailey of the Addison County Parent/Child Center; Bill McKibben, one of the leading environmentalists in the world; Brenda Torpy, the head of the Champlain Valley Housing Trust; Mike O'Day, a local labor leader; and Jenny Nelson, a Vermont leader on agricultural issues.

In his introductory remarks, Ben Cohen was very kind: "Bernie is the real thing. He's not about reading the polls and seeing what he has to say to get elected. The guy's been saying and doing the same stuff for the last thirty years. If it weren't so inspiring, he'd be boring. He's about leading with his heart and his soul and using his brain for what's best for the little guy."

Bill McKibben, who lives forty miles down the road in Ripton, Vermont, said, "What you see is what you get, and nowhere is that more true than in his staunch defense of the environment. . . . We need to let this nation know that Bernie is loved in every corner of this great state—in Newport in the north to Bennington and Brattleboro in the south. There's no leader who Vermonters have ever respected and voted for quite the way that they respect Bernie, because they know he always means what he says and he always stands for what he believes."

Then it was my turn, with family and friends at my side, to give the following remarks.

TODAY WE BEGIN
A POLITICAL REVOLUTION

Thank you very much for being here, and for all the support you have given me over the years: as the mayor of this great city, as Vermont's only congressman and now as a U.S. senator. Thanks also to my longtime friends and fellow Vermonters: Bill McKibben, Brenda Torpy, Donna Bailey, Mike O'Day, and Ben and Jerry for all that you do—and for your generous remarks. Thanks also to Jenny Nelson for moderating this event and for your leadership in Vermont agriculture.

I also want to thank my family: my wife, Jane; my brother, Larry; my children, Levi, Heather, Carina, and Dave, for their love and support; and my beautiful seven grandchildren—Sunnee, Cole, Ryleigh, Grayson, Ella, Tess, and Dylan—who provide so much joy in my life. Today, here in our small state—a state that has led the nation in so many ways—I am proud to announce my candidacy for president of the United States of America.

Today, with your support and the support of millions of people throughout this country, we begin a political revolution to transform our country economically, politically, socially, and environmentally.

Today we stand here and say loudly and clearly that "Enough is enough. This great nation and its government belong to all of the people, and not to a handful of billionaires, their super PACs, and their lobbyists."

Brothers and sisters: Now is NOT the time for thinking small. Now is NOT the time for the same old same old establishment politics and stale Inside the Beltway ideas.

Now IS the time for millions of working families to come together, to revitalize American democracy, to end the collapse of the American middle class, and to make certain that our children and grandchildren are able to enjoy a quality of life that brings them health, prosperity, security, and joy—and that once again makes the United States the leader in the world in the fight for economic and social justice, for environmental sanity, and for a world of peace.

My fellow Americans: This country faces more serious problems today than at any time since the Great Depression, and, if you include the planetary crisis of climate change, it may well be that the challenges we face now are more dire than at any time in our modern history.

Here is my promise to you for this campaign. Not only will I fight to protect the working families of this country, but we're going to build a movement of millions of Americans who are prepared to stand up and fight back. We're going to take this campaign directly to the people, in town meetings and door-to-door conversations, on street corners and in social media—and that's berniesanders.com, by the way. This week we will be in New Hampshire, Iowa, and Minnesota— and that's just the start of a vigorous grassroots campaign.

Let's be clear. This campaign is not about Bernie Sanders. It is not about Hillary Clinton. It is not about Jeb Bush or anyone else. This campaign is about the needs of the American people, and the ideas and proposals that effectively address those needs. As someone who has never run a

Announcing my campaign in Burlington. (Nathaniel Brooks/ *The New York Times*/Redux)

negative political ad in his life, my campaign will be driven by issues and serious debate—not political gossip, not reckless personal attacks or character assassination. This is what I believe the American people want and deserve. I hope other candidates agree, and I hope the media allows that to happen. Politics in a democratic society should not be treated like a baseball game, a game show, or a soap opera. The times are too serious for that.

Let me take a minute to touch on some of the issues that I will be focusing on in the coming months, and then give you an outline of an Agenda for America which will, in fact, deal with these problems and lead us to a better future.

Income and Wealth Inequality. Today we live in a nation which is the wealthiest nation in the history of the world, but that reality means very little for most of us, because almost all of that wealth is owned and controlled by a tiny handful of individuals. In America we now have more income and wealth inequality than any other major country on earth, and the gap between the very rich and everyone else is wider than at any time since the 1920s. The issue of wealth and income inequality is the great moral issue of our time, it is the great economic issue of our time, and it is the great political issue of our time. And we will address it.

Let me be very clear. There is something profoundly wrong when the top one-tenth of 1 percent owns almost as much wealth as the bottom 90 percent, and when 99 percent of all new income goes to the top 1 percent. There is something profoundly wrong when, in recent years, we have seen a proliferation of millionaires and billionaires at the same time as millions of Americans work longer hours for lower wages and we have the highest rate of childhood poverty of any major country on earth. There is something profoundly wrong when one family owns more wealth than the bottom 130 million Americans. This grotesque level of inequality is immoral. It is bad economics. It is unsustainable. This type of rigged economy is not what America is supposed to be about. This has got to change, and as your president, together we will change it.

Economics. But it is not just income and wealth inequality. It is the tragic reality that for the last forty years the great middle class of our country—once the envy of the world—has been disappearing. Despite exploding technology and increased worker productivity, median family income is almost $5,000 less than it was in 1999. In Vermont and throughout this country it is not uncommon for people to be working two or three jobs just to cobble together enough income to survive on and some health care benefits.

The truth is that real unemployment is not the 5.4 percent you read in newspapers. It is close to 11 percent if you include those workers who have given up looking for jobs or who are working part-time when they want to work full-time. Youth unemployment is over 17 percent and African-American youth unemployment is much higher than that. Today, shamefully, we have forty-five million people living in poverty, many of whom are working at low-wage jobs. These are the people who struggle every day to find the money to feed their kids, to pay their electric bills, and to put gas in the car to get to work. This campaign is about those people and our struggling middle class. It is about creating an economy that works for all, and not just the 1 percent.

Citizens United. My fellow Americans: Let me be as blunt as I can and tell you what you already know. As a result of the disastrous Supreme Court decision on Citizens United, the American political system has been totally corrupted, and the foundations of American democracy are being undermined. What the Supreme Court essentially said was that it was not good enough for the billionaire class to own much of our economy—they could now own the U.S. government as well. And that is precisely what they are trying to do.

American democracy is not about billionaires being able to buy candidates and elections. It is not about the Koch brothers, Sheldon Adelson, and other incredibly wealthy individuals spending billions of dollars to elect candidates who will make the rich richer and everyone else poorer. According to media reports the Koch brothers alone—one family—will spend more money in this election cycle than either the Democratic or Republican parties. This is not democracy. This is oligarchy. In Vermont and at our town meetings we know what American democracy is supposed to be about. It is one person, one vote—with every citizen having an equal say—and no voter suppression. And that's the kind of American political system we have to fight for and will fight for in this campaign.

Climate Change. When we talk about our responsibilities as human beings and as parents, there is nothing more important than leaving this country and the entire planet in a way that is habitable for our kids and grandchildren. The debate is over. The scientific community has spoken in a virtually unanimous voice. Climate change is real. It is caused by human activity and it is already causing devastating problems in the United States and around the world.

The scientists are telling us that if we do not boldly transform our energy system away from fossil fuels and into energy efficiency and sustainable energies, this planet could be five to ten degrees Fahrenheit warmer by the end of this century. This is catastrophic. It will mean more drought, more famine, more rising sea level, more floods, more ocean acidification, more extreme weather disturbances, more disease, and more human suffering. We must not, we cannot, and we will not allow that to happen.

It is no secret that there is massive discontent with politics in America today. In the midterm election in November, 63 percent of Americans did not vote, including 80 percent of young people. Poll after poll tells us that our citizens no longer have confidence in our political institutions and, given the power of big money in the political process, they have serious doubts about how much their vote actually matters and whether politicians have any clue as to what is going on in their lives.

Combating this political alienation, this cynicism and this legitimate anger will not be easy; that's for sure. But that is exactly what, together, we have to do if we are going to turn this country around—and that is what this campaign is all about.

And to bring people together we need a simple and straightforward progressive agenda which speaks to the needs of our people, and which provides us with a vision of a very different America. And what is that agenda?

Jobs, Jobs, Jobs. It begins with jobs. If we are truly serious about reversing the decline of the middle class we need a major federal jobs program which puts millions of Americans back to work at decent-paying jobs. At a time when our roads, bridges, water systems, rail, and airports are decaying, the most effective way to rapidly create meaningful jobs is to rebuild our crumbling infrastructure. That's why I've introduced legislation which would invest $1 trillion over five years to modernize our country's physical infrastructure. This legislation would create and maintain at least thirteen million good-paying jobs, while making our country more productive, efficient, and safe. And I promise you, as president I will lead that legislation into law.

Trade. I will also continue to oppose our current trade policies. For decades, presidents from both parties have supported trade agreements which have cost us millions of decent-paying jobs as corporate America shuts down plants here and moves to low-wage countries. As president, my trade policies will break that cycle of agreements which enrich the few at the expense of the many . . .

Raising Wages. Let us be honest and acknowledge that millions of Americans are now working for totally inadequate wages. The current federal minimum wage of $7.25 an hour is a starvation wage and must be raised. The minimum wage must become a living wage, which means raising it to $15 an hour over the next few years—which is exactly what Los Angeles recently did, and I applaud them for doing that. Our goal as a nation must be to ensure that no full-time worker lives in poverty. Further, we must establish pay equity for women workers. It's unconscionable that women earn 78 cents on the dollar compared to men who perform the same work. We must also end the scandal in which millions of American employees, often earning less than $30,000 a year, work fifty or sixty hours a week—and earn no overtime. And we need paid sick leave and guaranteed vacation time for all.

Addressing Wealth and Income Inequality. This campaign is going to send a message to the billionaire class. And that is: You can't have it all. You can't get huge tax breaks while children in this country go hungry. You can't continue sending our jobs to China while millions are looking for work. You can't hide your profits in the Cayman Islands and other tax havens while there are massive unmet needs on every corner of this nation. Your greed has got to end. You cannot take advantage of all the benefits of America if you refuse to accept your responsibilities.

That is why we need a tax system which is fair and progressive, which makes wealthy individuals and profitable corporations begin to pay their fair share of taxes.

Reforming Wall Street. It is time to break up the largest financial institutions in the country. Wall Street cannot continue to be an island unto itself, gambling trillions in risky financial instruments while expecting the public to bail it out. If a bank is too big to fail it is too big to exist. We need a banking system which is part of the job-creating productive economy, not a handful of huge banks on Wall Street which engage in reckless and illegal activities.

Campaign Finance Reform. If we are serious about creating jobs, about climate change and the needs of our children and the elderly, we must be deadly serious about campaign finance reform and the need for a constitutional amendment to overturn Citizens United. I have said it before and I'll say it again: I will not nominate any justice to the Supreme Court who has not made it clear that he or she will move to overturn that disastrous decision which is undermining our democracy. Long-term, we need to go further and establish public funding of elections.

Reversing Climate Change. The United States must lead the world in reversing climate change. We can do that if we transform our energy system away from fossil fuels, toward energy efficiency and sustainable energies such as wind, solar, geothermal, and biomass. Millions of homes and buildings need to be weatherized, our transportation system needs to be energy-efficient, and we need a tax on carbon to accelerate the transition away from fossil fuel.

Health Care for All. The United States remains the only major country on earth that does not guarantee health care for all as a right. Despite the modest gains of the Affordable Care Act,

35 million Americans continue to lack health insurance and many more are underinsured. Yet, we continue paying far more per capita for health care than any other nation. The United States must join the rest of the industrialized world and guarantee health care to all as a right by moving toward a Medicare for All single-payer system.

Protecting Our Most Vulnerable. At a time when millions of Americans are struggling to keep their heads above water economically, at a time when senior poverty is increasing, at a time when millions of kids are living in dire poverty, my Republican colleagues, as part of their recently passed budget, are trying to make a terrible situation even worse. If you can believe it, the Republican budget throws 27 million Americans off health insurance, makes drastic cuts in Medicare, throws millions of low-income Americans—including pregnant women—off of nutrition programs, and makes it harder for working-class families to afford college or put their kids in the Head Start program. And then, to add insult to injury, they provide huge tax breaks for the very, very wealthiest families in this country while they raise taxes on working families.

Well, let me tell my Republican colleagues that I respectfully disagree with their approach. Instead of cutting Social Security, we're going to expand Social Security benefits. Instead of cutting Head Start and childcare, we are going to move to a universal pre-K system for all the children of this country. As Franklin Delano Roosevelt reminded us, a nation's greatness is judged

With my family on the day of the announcement. (Stephen Mease Photography)

not by what it provides to the most well-off, but how it treats the people most in need. And that's the kind of nation we must become.

College for All. And when we talk about education, let me be very clear: In a highly competitive global economy, we need the best-educated workforce we can create. It is insane and counterproductive to the best interests of our country that hundreds of thousands of bright young people cannot afford to go to college, and that millions of others leave school with a mountain of debt that burdens them for decades. That must end. That is why, as president, I will fight to make tuition in public colleges and universities free, as well as substantially lower interest rates on student loans.

War and Peace. As everybody knows, we live in a difficult and dangerous world, and there are people out there who want to do us harm. As president, I will defend this nation—but I will do it responsibly. As a member of Congress I voted against the war in Iraq, and that was the right vote. I am vigorously opposed to an endless war in the Middle East—a war which is unwise and unnecessary. We must be vigorous in combating terrorism and defeating ISIS, but we should not have to bear that burden alone. We must be part of an international coalition, led by Muslim nations, that can not only defeat ISIS but begin the process of creating conditions for a lasting peace.

As some of you know, I was born in a faraway land called "Brooklyn, New York." My father came to this country from Poland without a penny in his pocket and without much of an education. My mother graduated high school in New York City. My father worked for almost his entire life as a paint salesman and we were solidly lower middle class. My parents, brother, and I lived in a small rent-controlled apartment. My mother's dream was to move out of that small apartment into a home of our own. She died young and her dream was never fulfilled. As a kid I learned, in many, many ways, what lack of money means to a family. That's a lesson I have never forgotten.

I have seen the promise of America in my own life. My parents would have never dreamed that their son would be a U.S. senator, let alone run for president. But for too many of our fellow

Americans, the dream of progress and opportunity is being denied by the grind of an economy that funnels all the wealth to the top.

And to those who say we cannot restore the dream, I say just look where we are standing. This beautiful place was once an unsightly rail yard that served no public purpose and was an eyesore. As mayor, I worked with the people of Burlington to help turn this waterfront into the beautiful people-oriented public space it is today. We took the fight to the courts, to the legislature, and to the people. And we won.

The lesson to be learned is that when people stand together, and are prepared to fight back, there is nothing that can't be accomplished.

We can live in a country:

- Where every person has health care as a right, not a privilege.
- Where every parent can have quality and affordable child care, and where all of our qualified young people, regardless of income, can go to college.
- Where every senior can live in dignity and security, and not be forced to choose between their medicine or their food.
- Where every veteran who defends this nation gets the quality health care and benefits he or she has earned and receives the respect he or she deserves.
- Where every person, no matter their race, their religion, their disability, or their sexual orientation, realizes the full promise of equality that is our birthright as Americans.

That is the nation we can build together, and I ask you to join me in this campaign to build a future that works for all of us, and not just the few on top.

Thank you, and on this beautiful day on the shore of Lake Champlain, I welcome you aboard.

SIX

ON THE CAMPAIGN TRAIL

The kickoff event in Burlington was a great success, and we were off and running. The turnout of some five thousand supporters was far more than we had ever expected, and the love and enthusiasm I received from my fellow Vermonters was deeply moving to me. It was a day I will never forget.

During the early stages of the campaign, I was often asked by the media, "Do you really think you can win the nomination? Can you really beat Hillary Clinton?" My response was always the same. Yes. I was running to win. I thought we could win. But, in my heart of hearts, I knew how difficult this challenge would be.

What we were trying to do was unprecedented in modern American history. We were not just running an insurgent campaign as an underdog, we were taking aim at the nation's entire political and financial establishment. And we were running against the most powerful political machine in the country.

Let's not forget. The Clinton political organization had won two presidential campaigns for Bill Clinton, and they had run a strong race for Hillary in 2008. They were closely connected with thousands of Democratic Party leaders at the national, state, and local levels, many of whom had worked for Bill as president or Hillary as secretary of state. The Clintons had, by far, the most powerful fund-raising system in the Democratic Party. They had created their own (very good) think tank, the Center for American Progress, and a huge international organization, the Clinton Foundation. They had vast contacts in the corporate world, the financial world, and the foreign policy world.

The conventional wisdom Inside the Beltway and among the talking heads on TV was that Clinton was the anointed candidate, the inevitable candidate. The primary and caucus process was just a matter of going through the motions until she was officially nominated at the Democratic National Convention in Philadelphia in late July 2016.

CNN more or less captured the position we were in on their Web site on May 28, 2015:

> *The obstacles Sanders faces in the presidential primary race, however, are immense. Sanders has no viable countrywide political organization, so he must foment a grassroots uprising. His task is complicated by the fact that although he caucuses with the Democrats in the Senate, he has always been a political independent wary of formal party affiliations. He must take on the Clinton political machine that has retooled after its defeat in 2008. He's a minnow in the money game in a campaign that will be awash in billions of dollars. He's not exactly a polished pol either, with an unrepentant message of class warfare that makes him an unlikely candidate to win over Middle America. And many Democrats are only beginning to learn who*

Sanders actually is. He's a long shot, but has shown some momentum since indicating he would take the plunge into the presidential race late last month. In a new Quinnipiac University poll released on Thursday, Sanders was at 15 percent of Democratic voters nationwide, up from the 5 percent he managed in a CNN national poll last month.

Further, by the time I announced my intention to run for president in late April, Hillary Clinton had already, through an incredibly unfair system supported by the Democratic establishment, received the support of some four hundred superdelegates, about 15 percent of what she needed in order to win the nomination. She had also received tens of millions of dollars from leading financial backers. In addition, she had lined up almost every Democratic governor, mayor, senator, and congressperson who intended to make an endorsement.

Because of the Clintons' long-standing contacts Inside the Beltway, she had also won the support of the leadership of most of the unions, environmental groups, and women's and LGBT groups. Her lock on establishment support was so strong that by the end of the campaign I ended up winning the endorsement of one major newspaper. She won the support of dozens.

That's what we were running against.

In the face of this, our campaign strategy was not complicated. If the campaign was to succeed and gain momentum, we absolutely had to do well in the early states, Iowa and New Hampshire, followed by strong showings in Nevada and South Carolina. If we did poorly in the early states, the media would lose interest, our funding would dry up, and the campaign would be dead in its tracks. In the early stages of the campaign we did not have the luxury of planning out a national fifty-state strategy. It was all or nothing in the early states—especially Iowa and New Hampshire.

As we thought about New Hampshire, the first stop for us on the campaign trail and the second state up in the nominating process, there was good news and bad news. The good news was that I was reasonably well known in the state given its proximity to Vermont. The bad news was that Clinton was popular in New Hampshire and way ahead of us in early polls. In 2008 she had defeated Obama there, resurrecting her campaign after a loss in Iowa. Bill Clinton had also done well in New Hampshire when he was a candidate. In fact, in his 1992 campaign, amidst all of the allegations regarding sexual impropriety that were then plaguing him, he did well enough there to become the "Comeback Kid."

Our plan for New Hampshire was pretty simple. In the last contested Democratic primary there in 2008, when Clinton defeated Obama, 287,000 people voted. My thought was that if we worked really hard, we could hold a hundred town meetings and rallies in the state leading up to the primary in early February. We could accomplish that by spending thirty or forty days campaigning there, doing two or three events a day. If we were able to bring out an average of a hundred people a meeting, which I thought possible, we would be able to bring some ten thousand people to our meetings. And that's pretty good. In 2008 Clinton won New Hampshire with 112,404 votes. If the voter turnout was similar in 2016, it would mean that almost 10 percent of the people I needed to win would have heard from me face-to-face. And those who attended have husbands and wives, brothers and sisters and friends whom they talk to. Word of mouth, after all, is the best form of advertising. If we were able to accomplish that goal, I believed we could do well there.

I spent the night of the kickoff, May 26, 2015, at home

in Burlington and then we hit the road early the following morning. We were off to New Hampshire, to be followed with trips to Iowa and Minnesota.

The first stop was a town meeting at the New England College in Concord, New Hampshire. And we got lost! The GPS got us to exactly the right address on Main Street, but it was the wrong town. Not a great way to begin the campaign. Fifteen minutes late, we found a parking spot and made our way into the building. The turnout was large, about two hundred people, larger than the room could accommodate. It was standing room only. The format for the event was similar to that of many meetings I had held in Vermont. A number of young people on a panel got up and talked about what was going on in their lives. They discussed the student debt they were incurring, their hopes and fears about job opportunities, and their views on social issues. After the panel finished, I spoke and then took questions.

After the meeting ended, I was told that there was a crowd of people outside the building who couldn't get in. My staff found a location, about a block away, where I talked to them using a megaphone. This pattern, of rooms, large and small, not being able to accommodate the crowds that we attracted, repeated itself over and over again during the campaign. It was a problem, but a very good problem.

In the evening, after a house party in Epping, we continued on to Portsmouth, New Hampshire, one of the larger towns in the state. And here was the first real surprise of the campaign. On a hot spring night, in the beautiful and historic South Church in downtown Portsmouth, seven hundred enthusiastic supporters came out to the rally. This was an extraordinary crowd for a small state like New Hampshire this early in the campaign. Tad Devine, who had worked on a number of national campaigns and had observed Obama's 2008 campaign carefully, said that he had never seen anything like it. Other than the fact that the room was extremely hot and my shirt was soaked with sweat, the event went very well. Needless to say, as happened throughout the campaign, excerpts from the speech got around the country to many thousands of people through social media.

No question about it, our first day on the campaign trail was a great success. I was feeling good. As we drove back to the hotel in Portsmouth, I did a quick calculation. My hope had been to speak to ten thousand voters in New Hampshire with thirty to forty days of campaigning. Well, on our very first day, in the three meetings that we held, we had already spoken to a thousand people. Maybe the goal of ten thousand was too conservative. Maybe, over the course of the campaign, we would be speaking to a lot more people. Maybe we could actually win New Hampshire.

Not only were we off to a great start on the campaign trail, our online fund-raising was also doing very well. My staff and I were shocked, and the national media was surprised as well, when in the first twenty-four hours of my candidacy, we raised $1.5 million in small contributions from 35,000 donors. After four days $3 million had come in from 75,000 donors. That's serious money. The media may not pay much attention to the ideas that a candidate espouses, but they do pay attention to your fund-raising capabilities and, no matter how you slice it, 75,000 donors in four days was pretty impressive. As the media noted early on, I was raising more money than most of the Republican establishment candidates, and we were doing it with large numbers of small contributions.

After our day in New Hampshire, we were on an early-morning plane from Boston to Iowa. We had scheduled five events there over a three-day period.

The first event, at St. Ambrose University in Davenport,

was extraordinary. There were seven hundred people in attendance, the largest turnout for any candidate yet during the 2016 campaign season in Iowa. Many of those who attended were students, but many were from the community. It was a great cross section of Iowans.

As I often did, I took questions from the audience. When the question-and-answer period was over, I stayed around and chatted with a number of people who came to the front of the auditorium. One of those people was a recent dental school graduate. During my speech I had remarked about how I met a physician in Vermont who graduated from medical school $300,000 in debt. This young woman gave me a new statistic to shock people with: She was $400,000 in debt. At a time when we have a desperate need for more dentists, how crazy is it to put young people in such a horrendous financial position? Two days later we had another great Iowa rally, this time in Iowa City. We had more than 1,100 people show up, and the enthusiasm was sky-high.

The most interesting and promising event of that campaign swing, however, was in a town called Kensett, Iowa, where three hundred people packed the community center. What was surprising about the turnout there was that, according to the last census, there were only 266 people in the entire town. In other words, in one of the most rural parts of a rural state, there was significant interest in the need for a political revolution. This was not an audience of political activists, of young people, of trade unionists, of academics. This was an audience of working people and farmers who were sick and tired of the political status quo, and they wanted real change in our country.

How did I end up in Kensett? As the *Albert Lea Tribune* reported, "Kurt Meyers, chairman of the Tricounty Democrats, which covers Worth, Mitchell and Howard counties in northern Iowa, called Sanders an 'effective, articulate, passionate fighter for social justice.' He said Sanders came to Kensett at the invitation of Democratic activist Jim Berge of Kensett. Sanders reportedly read a favorable comment in a Washington, D.C., newspaper that quoted Berge. The next day, one of the senator's staff members called Berge to thank him for his remarks, and Berge ultimately invited him to visit the next time he was in Iowa."

I loved the comment that Mr. Meyers made on *The Rachel Maddow Show* in response to Rachel's question as to why so many people showed up. He said, "I think there are naturally people that are going to come to Kensett because Kensett has waited a long time between presidents or presidential candidates coming. There's a story that FDR perhaps came through on the whistle stop in 1936, but only came through town, didn't stop and talk in town. So, you know, that's a long way to wait. And so, you can imagine some people would come just because a presidential candidate is a rare occurrence in Kensett."

That, by the way, is what an insurgent campaign is all about. Campaigning in a town that no presidential candidate had ever visited.

While some people may have come to the meeting out of curiosity, the response that I got told me that most didn't. In fact, that meeting confirmed to me what I had long believed: Rural people are not as conservative as the Democratic leadership has long believed, and their votes should not be conceded to right-wing Republicans. Kensett was the first, but not the last, large turnout that we had in very rural communities throughout the country.

The turnouts in New Hampshire and Iowa were extraordinary—much larger than we had anticipated. But the first indication that this campaign was taking off much faster than any of us had believed possible took place on June 1, 2015, in Minneapolis, Minnesota. As we were driving to our destination, the Minneapolis American Indian Center, we went past a very long line of people who appeared to be snaked out for blocks. I wondered out loud what was going on, and if there was some kind of concert taking place. When we had reached the Minneapolis American Indian Center, I truly was stunned to learn that the crowd was there for us.

The maximum number of people we could get into the hall was about two thousand. There were about three thousand outside who couldn't get in. This was, far and away, the largest turnout for our campaign up to that point. In the airport in Minneapolis, on the way back to Washington, I bumped into the two senators from Minnesota, Amy Klobuchar and Al Franken. We had coffee together while we waited for the plane. They were pretty surprised to learn that five thousand people had just come out to our meeting.

As the *Star Tribune* wrote about the event: "The crowd, with some people standing outside because the hall was full, seemed unconcerned with the conventional wisdom that there is no race on the Democratic side as Hillary Clinton marches toward the nomination with a pile of money, endorsements and party faithful's love of the Clinton name."

From day one of the campaign we realized that the debates with Secretary Clinton would be enormously important. At a time when my name recognition was low, the debates would give me exposure to millions of voters and increased credibility as I contrasted my views with hers. We wanted as many debates as possible and as early as possible. In early June, I wrote a letter to the chair of the Democratic National Committee, Debbie Wasserman Schultz. I urged that as many debates as possible be held and that they begin in the summer.

Straw polls don't mean anything. They are totally unscientific. They reflect the views only of the people who are at a given place at a given time. Nonetheless, we were surprised and delighted when a straw poll taken at the Wisconsin State Democratic Party Convention in early June showed us with 41 percent support, only 8 points behind Secretary Clinton, at 49 percent. Unscientific though it may have been, this was the first poll of any kind showing us within reach of Clinton. John Nichols, a writer from *The Nation* who is from Wisconsin, called the straw poll "another sign of unexpected and significant support" for Sanders. Nichols noted that the most important support that we were receiving was coming from organized labor.

On June 6, I returned to New Hampshire. Once again, the turnout was larger than we had anticipated. At Keene High School, there was a standing-room-only crowd of 1,100 people. In that speech I made a point that I was going to make over and over again. I said that real change in this country could only take place if millions of people got involved in the political process. I stated, "This campaign is not about Bernie Sanders. You can have the best president in the history of the world, but that person will not be able to address the problems that we face unless there is a mass movement, a political revolution in this country. Right now, the only pieces of legislation that get to the floor of the House and Senate are sanctioned by big money, Wall Street, the pharmaceutical industry, et cetera. The only way we win and transform America is when millions of people stand up, as you are doing today, and say, 'Enough is enough.' This country belongs to all of us and not just a handful of billionaires."

One of the dilemmas of being on the campaign trail if you are a sitting member of the U.S. Senate is that you can't be in two places at the same time. That means that there are votes you will miss in Washington because you are in some other part of the country, and it also means not being able to attend events in your own state. The best way that I could reconcile the latter concern was scheduling events in Vermont on the same days that I would be across the Connecticut River in New Hampshire.

On the same day that I spoke in Keene, New Hampshire, I also marched in the Strolling of the Heifers event in Brattleboro, Vermont. This is one of the fun events in Vermont and the biggest parade in the state, organized by my old friend Orly Munzing. It draws some ten thousand people from all over New England, including my son Levi and his three kids from nearby Claremont, New Hampshire. The event focuses attention on dairy, the largest agricultural industry in Vermont. The parade includes cows marching up Brattleboro's main street and a whole lot of floats from local organizations, from the Girl Scouts to the local bank. It is also my one day of the year when I get to milk a cow, not a pretty sight for real dairy farmers.

As the campaign progressed, Hillary Clinton's political vulnerabilities were becoming more and more apparent. She had started several super PACs, which were collecting millions of dollars from Wall Street, not exactly the constituency of working Americans and progressive Democrats, and not what ordinary Americans wanted to see in a candidate. She had voted for the war in Iraq, the worst foreign policy blunder in the modern history of our country. She supported fracking and was a relative latecomer in supporting gay marriage.

She had also supported, in one capacity or another, virtually every one of the disastrous trade agreements that had cost our country millions of decent-paying jobs and contributed to the race to the bottom. On June 14, in an appearance on the CBS news program *Face the Nation,* I challenged Clinton on her trade position and urged her to join progressives in the Senate, like Elizabeth Warren, Sherrod Brown, and myself, in opposition to the Trans-Pacific Partnership, known as the TPP. This was the largest trade agreement in the history of our country and incorporated many of the same elements that made previous trade agreements so destructive for the American working class. In previous comments, Secretary Clinton had referred to the TPP as the "gold standard" for what a trade agreement should be. During the program I stated, "I would hope very much that Secretary Clinton will side with every union in the country, virtually every environmental group, and many religious groups, and say that this TPP policy is a disaster, that it must be defeated, and that we need to regroup and come up with a trade policy that demands that corporate America starts investing in this country rather than in countries all over the world." In early October, I was pleased that Secretary Clinton came out in opposition to the TPP.

While the minority population of Vermont is growing, it remains very much a white state. We have a small African-American population and an even smaller Latino one. One of the challenges I faced early on in the campaign was to familiarize myself with issues that I had not been heavily involved with as Vermont's representative in the House and Senate.

When we began the campaign we had virtually no support or name recognition in the Latino community—and we were running against a candidate who had the backing of virtually the entire Hispanic Caucus in Congress and, over the years, relationships with many leaders of Latino organizations.

One of my campaign's accomplishments that I am

most proud of is that by the end of it we were winning the Latino vote in various parts of the country, and winning the Latino youth vote overwhelmingly. A lot of that success was the result of our campaign bringing on some extremely smart and hardworking Latinos like Arturo Carmona, Erika Andiola, and Cesar Vargas, who not only educated me about the issues of concern to their community, but also did a great job in voter outreach.

On June 19, while campaigning in Nevada, a state with a very heavy Latino population, I gave my first speech on immigration reform. I focused on the need for comprehensive immigration reform and a path toward citizenship. I also highlighted the fact that the vast majority of Latinos in this country are working class and that for their sake, as well as for all working Americans, we had to raise the minimum wage to a living wage and make it easier for workers to join unions.

In late June, a new Fox national poll was released: Clinton 61 percent, Sanders 15 percent, O'Malley 1 percent. We were making progress. We were now only 46 points down. In Iowa we were making more progress. In early July, a Quinnipiac poll came out that had Clinton ahead of us by 52 percent to 33 percent in Iowa. That's a big gap, but a lot better than the 60 percent to 15 percent we were behind in May.

June 30, the end of the quarter, was the day that candidates had to file information about the contributions they received over the previous three months. I used that occasion to issue a statement attacking the disastrous Citizens United Supreme Court decision. I announced that I would only nominate justices to the Supreme Court who publicly acknowledged their intention to overturn that terrible decision. I was glad to see Hillary Clinton make a similar statement a short time later.

I also stated, "It is a national disgrace that billionaires and other extremely wealthy people are able to heavily influence the political process by making huge contributions. The Koch brothers alone will spend more than the Democratic and Republican parties to influence the outcome of next year's elections. That's not democracy, that's oligarchy."

During this period, under the radar, our grassroots efforts were growing rapidly. Two examples come to mind:

On June 26, as a result of the great work done by Larry Cohen, the former president of the Communication Workers of America, we announced that more than a thousand local union leaders and members were backing our campaign. Clinton had been successful in winning the support of a number of national union leaders. We were now gaining support among the rank and file.

On the same day, due to an aggressive social media effort launched by our campaign, 208,000 people signed a petition calling on the Democratic National Committee to host more presidential debates. The DNC was beginning to get the hint that many Democrats were not exactly enamored with its leadership. In an e-mail we sent out I said: "The people of this country are tired of political gossip, personal attacks, and ugly thirty-second TV ads. They want the candidates to engage in serious discussions about the very serious issues facing our country today." Once again, we called for a more robust series of debates, starting in the summer. Unfortunately, but not surprisingly as we later learned, the DNC and chairwoman Debbie Wasserman Schultz were not terribly interested in what we had to say. They had another agenda.

While our early attention was obviously going to be focused on Iowa, New Hampshire, Nevada, and South Carolina, it was important to reach out to other states and let people all across the country know that we needed their support as well.

Over the years, I had visited Wisconsin a number of times. I enjoyed participating in the Fighting Bob Fest, an event that brings thousands of progressives from Wisconsin together for a day of music, education, and agitation. This visit to Wisconsin, on July 1, was very different from any I had previously made. I spoke at the Veterans Memorial Coliseum in Madison, and the Associated Press put the number of people in attendance at ten thousand. This was not only the largest turnout for an event in our campaign, it was the largest turnout so far for any presidential candidate.

In covering the event, CNN reported:

> *Bernie Sanders has been running for president for two months, but Wednesday night in Madison, Wisconsin, his long-shot campaign got real.*
>
> *When Sanders walked on stage at the Veterans Memorial Coliseum, he was greeted by a raucous, howling crowd of 9,600 people, according to Sanders' campaign aides and arena staff.*
>
> *A clearly energized Sanders, who late last year was speaking to crowds of 50 people in Iowa classrooms, appeared taken aback by the reception he received.*
>
> *"Whoa," he said. "In case you haven't noticed, there are a lot of people here."*
>
> *Sanders, who is rising in the primary polls and trails only Hillary Clinton, only mentioned the former secretary of state once in his speech.*
>
> *"This campaign is not about Bernie Sanders, it is not about Hillary Clinton, it is not about anyone else, it is about you," Sanders said to sustained applause.*

As the first half of 2015 ended and we entered the July Fourth weekend, our leadership team—Jeff, Phil, Jane,

Michael, Tad, and I—assessed where we were, and there was a lot of good news. We were holding the largest rallies of any candidate, our social media was humming and communicating with millions of people on an almost daily basis, the money was coming in much better than we had expected, and while we were still very far behind, we were making some progress in closing the gap in national and statewide polls.

The bad news was that while we were doing well in local media markets, we were being more or less shut out of national television news, which is where Americans still get most of their information. It's hard to win an election if you're not on ABC, CBS, NBC, and PBS, and we weren't getting on those network evening news shows very much. In fact, between January 1, 2015, and the end of November 2015, we had received only ten minutes combined on the three major networks. That included all of twenty seconds on ABC. We were getting far less national network news time than other presidential candidates.

Also, our efforts in the African-American community were not going well. Nobody is going to win the Democratic nomination without a significant number of black votes. We were beginning to put reasonable sums of money and staff into our African-American outreach efforts, but Bill and Hillary Clinton were popular and universally known in that community, especially among older people, and it didn't appear that we were making much headway.

Further, we were continuing to get almost no support from establishment politicians, and I mean *none*. Not one Democratic governor, not one big-city mayor, and no more than a handful of members of Congress were supporting my campaign. In state after state we would have to take on the entire Democratic Party machine and their get-out-the-vote apparatus, and that's not easy.

While we obviously were going to focus on the early states, I was determined to take our message to every part of the country, from Maine to California. And that's literally what we did in the summer of 2015. We started in Iowa on the July Fourth weekend. I love July Fourth parades and had the opportunity to march in a few of them in Iowa. We also held a rally in Council Bluffs, which turned into our largest event yet in Iowa, with 2,600 people showing up.

After Iowa, we got on a plane and headed to Portland, Maine, where we had another great event. It seemed like the entire city came out, but it was just 7,500—one of the largest political rallies that Portland had seen in a very long time. After the rally, we had dinner in a crowded local restaurant. The support there was joyous and seemed virtually unanimous. To top it off, the chef was from Burlington. We took a lot of selfies.

From the day that I announced my candidacy, I was determined to run a positive campaign, not one involved in making personal attacks against Hillary Clinton or anyone else. In that regard, however, I went a little too far. For the sake of running a positive campaign I had not been strong enough about articulating the many differences that I had with Clinton on some of the most important issues facing the country. I was determined to change that, and an opportunity arose on July 14, 2015, to make that happen.

On that day, while the Senate was in session and I was in Washington, Secretary Clinton paid a visit to Congress to talk with fellow Democrats. I thought that her visit, which of course attracted widespread media coverage, would be a good time for me to contrast my differences with her. Nothing fancy, just a straightforward presentation of where we disagreed. In reporting what I did, David Espo of the AP wrote:

Former Secretary of State Hillary Rodham Clinton was escorted by fellow Democrats, her way smoothed by uniformed officers and her every pre-planned step tracked by a pack of chroniclers as she made the rounds of private meetings in the Capitol.

It was more than enough for Bernie Sanders, the independent senator from Vermont who is Clinton's closest Democratic presidential rival in the polls. Emerging from one such meeting on Tuesday, Sanders strode, fast-paced and trailed by a couple of aides, to a collection of nearby television cameras.

"Let me welcome Secretary Clinton back to the Senate," he said, although in fact, the greeting could more fairly be described as brisk and bracing, rather than warm.

His rival was behind closed doors with Democratic senators elsewhere in the Capitol when Sanders said that trade deals negotiated over the past two decades have been disastrous. "Secretary Clinton, I believe, has a different view on that issue," he said, although he omitted that as president, her husband had negotiated the North American Free Trade Agreement.

"I strongly opposed the war in Iraq," he added. He didn't mention that Clinton supported it, but said, "Sadly, tragically, much of what I predicted in fact took place."

Moving on to energy, Sanders said he has "helped lead the opposition to the Keystone pipeline." He added dryly, "I think Secretary Clinton has not been clear on her views on that issue," referring to her unwillingness to state a position on the proposal despite repeated requests that she do so.

> *While not exactly unplanned, Sanders' appearance at the microphones was a reminder of the type of opportunistic campaign he is running as an underdog. The cameras were there in anticipation of comments by other lawmakers, but he made use of them.*
>
> *As a result, he got his say—and on a day that Clinton's aides had designed to highlight her role as a front-runner conferring privately with Democrats who may well share the 2016 ballot with her.*

On July 18 we headed to the Southwest, to Phoenix, Arizona, for what turned out to be, up to then, the largest rally of the entire campaign. More than 11,000 showed up at the Phoenix Convention Center, including my daughter Heather and her husband, Marc, who live in Sedona. What made me feel very good about that event was not just the size of the crowd but the growing diversity that we were seeing. It had taken time, but we were now seeing more and more Latinos and blacks at our events. That was especially true in Phoenix.

Throughout the campaign, my advance team did a very good job in arranging small meetings with local people before our rallies. This gave me an opportunity to meet privately with supporters and to hear the concerns of the people who lived in the area. It was an excellent way to learn about local issues and concerns. Before the Phoenix rally I met briefly with five or six young Latinos. Some were teenagers, some a little bit older. All were born and raised in the United States. With tears in their eyes they described to me their fears that, at a moment's notice, someone in their family, their mom or dad, could be deported. For them, immigration reform was very personal. It was an emotional meeting. I haven't forgotten it.

And then we were on to Texas, with large rallies in Dallas and Houston and a speaking appearance before the Texas Democratic Party. At both rallies I spoke at length about the need for criminal justice reform and for ending the absurdity of the United States having more people in jail than any other country on earth. These rallies took place shortly after the horrific death of Sandra Bland, a young black woman who was found dead in her jail cell, sixty miles outside of Houston. The "crime" that got her into that cell? She was pulled over for failure to use her blinker when she was making a turn. A shouting match developed with a very rude and aggressive police officer. She was thrown to the ground, handcuffed, and arrested. She died several days later in jail, all because of a minor traffic violation. But it was not just Sandra Bland. As the Black Lives Matter movement was pointing out, there were too many other victims. People like Michael Brown, Rekia Boyd, Eric Garner, Walter Scott, Freddie Gray, Tamir Rice, and others.

Many Americans, and not just African-Americans and Latinos, are becoming increasingly outraged by police brutality. They are rightfully tired of turning on the television and seeing videos of unarmed blacks being shot and killed by police officers. They want criminal justice reform. They want police department reform. And I agree.

In my remarks I pointed out that as a former mayor and a senator, I had worked with police officers in my city and across the country, and that a police officer's job was enormously difficult. I also expressed the view that the vast majority of police officers are honest and hardworking. But I also made clear that when a police officer breaks the law, that officer must be held accountable. Further, police officers must be trained to understand that lethal force is the last response, not, as is too often the case, the first response. I also promised that, if elected president, I would make sure that all killings that took place when people were in police custody or being arrested would prompt a U.S. Department of Justice investigation.

It was becoming very clear that the people we were bringing into our movement were not people who had been typically involved in Democratic Party politics, or politics of any kind. These were newly engaged people, most often younger people, who were tired of status quo politics and wanted real change in the world in which they were living. In Houston, where eight thousand people attended our rally, I had an interesting discussion with a local Democratic Party leader. He told me, as he looked at the crowd, that he had never seen 95 percent of these people before.

I have been, for many years, deeply concerned about climate change and the environment, and I am proud to have one of the strongest pro-environment voting records in the U.S. Congress. I was very pleased that Bill McKibben, the founder of 350.org and one of the leading anti–global warming advocates in the world, was one of the speakers at my campaign's kickoff event. I was also proud that, along with Senator Barbara Boxer, I had introduced the strongest climate change legislation in the history of the Senate. It was a real disappointment to me, therefore, that despite the fact that my environmental record was far stronger than Secretary Clinton's, I was unable to win the support of most of the major environmental organizations.

On August 1, 2015, a breakthrough occurred. We were endorsed by Friends of the Earth Action, one of the largest and most progressive environmental organizations in the country, with some 2 million members worldwide. Erich Pica, president of Friends of the Earth

Action, stated: "Senator Sanders's bold ideas and real solutions to addressing climate change, inequality, and promoting a transformative economy that prioritizes public health and the environment over corporate profits, have earned him an enthusiastic endorsement from Friends of the Earth Action."

In my remarks accepting the endorsement at a park along the banks of the Merrimack River in Concord, New Hampshire, I indicated my strong support for a tax on carbon, and for massive investments in energy efficiency and sustainable energy. I also challenged Clinton for refusing to take a stand on the Keystone Pipeline, which would transport some of the dirtiest fuel on the planet. You could be for it, you could be against it, but you had to take a stand on one of the most important environmental issues of our time.

In late September, I was glad to learn that Clinton came out in opposition to the environmentally destructive Keystone Pipeline.

The issue of how many Democratic debates would be held, and when and where they would take place, was something that was getting more and more attention. The Republicans had announced a robust debate schedule that allowed their candidates to be showcased before millions of Americans. But that was, obviously, not what the Democratic National Committee had in mind. On August 6, the DNC announced a series of only six debates. It was clear that they wanted to give Hillary Clinton's opponents as little public exposure as possible. I protested, as did Martin O'Malley. In my statement I said, "I look forward to working with the DNC to see if we can significantly expand the proposed debate schedule." Needless to say, that didn't happen.

On August 6, the Republican Party held its first debate

and I crashed it. Well, not exactly, but through social media. My staff urged me to tweet my responses to what I was hearing, and it turned out to be a very successful exercise. I sat on a couch at our headquarters, watched TV, and commented on what I was seeing and hearing. As the debate ended I wrote, "It's over. Not one word about income inequality, climate change, Citizens United or student debt. That's why the Rs are so out of touch." That got 31,414 retweets and 35,899 "likes," by far the #1 tweet of the night.

If this was going to be a truly national campaign, we had to head out West, which is what we did in early August with a swing through Washington, Oregon, and California. That trip was one of the most exciting and memorable parts of the entire campaign.

When we advertised our rallies through social media, we requested that people RSVP so that we could get some understanding of how many people might be showing up. As we hit the West Coast, the situation became absolutely nuts because of the incredible number of RSVPs we were receiving. Time and time again we had to change our venue in order to accommodate the anticipated crowd. My staff had to work overtime in order to find arenas that could simply hold the crowds we thought were coming.

In Seattle, our first West Coast stop, we did our event at the Hec Edmundson Pavilion at the University of Washington, which holds 12,000 people. The lines to get in were never-ending, and the arena filled up quickly. Before I went into the arena to speak, I spoke to a crowd of 3,000 outside who were unable to get in. The 15,000 people who showed up for a rally in Seattle was our all-time record high for the campaign, but that record didn't last long. It was topped the very next night.

In Seattle, I made the point about how important grassroots activism was in bringing about real change.

As a result of a strong grassroots progressive movement in Seattle, the City Council there raised the minimum wage to $15 an hour, the first major city in the country to go that high. I praised the City Council and talked about legislation I had introduced to make $15 an hour the national minimum wage by 2020. I said, "You did it for Seattle. We're now going to do it for the entire country."

On August 9, we were in Portland, Oregon, at the Moda Center, where the Portland Trail Blazers of the NBA play, a beautiful three-tier arena. We filled it up and then some. That event drew 28,000 people.

The Oregonian did a good job describing the event: "Vermont Sen. Bernie Sanders's insurgent campaign for president received a big boost Sunday when as many as 28,000 showed up for a high-decibel rally at the Moda Center. The crowd packed the basketball arena—with a capacity of up to 19,000—and thousands more couldn't get inside and listened in on loudspeakers. A Moda Center official, Michael Lewellen, estimated the crowd at the free event totaled 28,000."

The article concluded, " 'I've never heard anybody say anything like that before,' said Michaila Konig Taylor, a 25-year-old Bellingham, Wash. resident. 'I'm not personally involved with politics, but he changed my mind because he addressed the issues I actually care about.' "

In one sentence, Ms. Taylor described exactly what our campaign was all about: addressing the real issues that ordinary Americans cared about.

The next night we were at the Los Angeles Memorial Sports Arena, where 27,500 people attended. The "clutch" we did before the rally included some of the very creative members of the Los Angeles arts community—writers, actors, directors, musicians. We tapped their brains as to how, in whatever way, conventional or not, we could expand the campaign's horizon. There are a lot of smart and creative people in Los Angeles, not the least of whom is the brilliant comedienne Sarah Silverman. Sarah, who was to be very helpful throughout the campaign, introduced me by stating: "I give you, if we're all very smart and a little bit lucky, the next president of the United States."

In three days we drew more than 70,000 people to our rallies.

And here is an important point, which I believe differentiated our campaign from the others: At our rallies I did exactly what the consultants tell you not to do. In each of the speeches, before tens of thousands of people, I spoke for at least an hour and discussed, in some detail, what I believed to be the major crises facing our country. I didn't begin with prepared jokes or some other routine, and I didn't shape my remarks around a sound bite for TV. I just laid it out as best I could.

And here is what was remarkable. At all of these rallies, where we were filling up large arenas, people were not walking out during a long speech, they were not (I think) getting bored. They were listening. If there is a lesson I learned from this experience, it was that Americans are hungry for an understanding of what is going on in our country and how we can improve it.

Needless to say, during the course of a long campaign, one receives many compliments. The compliment I remember most came from a young man at one of these rallies, after I had completed my speech. He said, "Thank you, Bernie. You treat us as if we were intelligent human beings."

It is an unbelievable and humbling experience to walk out on a stage and see 25,000 or 30,000 people filling up an arena to hear you speak. The moment not only fills you with awe, but with incredible optimism for the future. There was a microcosm of America in front of me. Black and white, Latino, Asian-American, Native American, men and women, gay and straight, young and old. People who were tired of status quo politics and status quo economics. People who dreamed of a better America. People who wanted real change. To say that those experiences "moved" me would be a major understatement. They were some of the most memorable moments of my life, and I am deeply grateful to all who came.

While we were in California, we picked up our first endorsement from a major national union, the National Nurses United and its 185,000 members. What I love about the nurses' union is not just that they are one of the most progressive unions in the country. It's not just that, as a union that is 90 percent women, they showed enormous courage in supporting me over Hillary Clinton. It is that they are involved in politics because, as nurses, they know they cannot do the job they are trained to do, keeping people healthy, unless we transform this country. That is why they are strong supporters of a Medicare for All national health-care program, and other efforts that help low-income and working families.

Time and time again I have heard from nurses as to how they cannot, as health care workers, do what has to be done for their patients when so many of them have no health insurance or are underinsured. The nurses also know what poverty and pollution do to human health. In explaining to the *Guardian* why they endorsed me, RoseAnn DeMoro, the union president, hit the nail on the head when she stated: "Nurses are an interesting group. They are not political scientists. They want to be nurses. But nurses see the fallout of all the bad decisions, because everything ultimately equates to health. If you are talking about income inequality, they see it. Health concerns and disparity among classes, joblessness—every social problem basically ends up presenting itself in a health care setting."

RoseAnn and the National Nurses Union played a great role in our campaign, and I thank them for that and for what they do every day to keep us healthy.

During the summer I received a most interesting invitation.

I am one of the most progressive members of the U.S. Senate. Liberty University, a fundamentalist Christian school, is one of the most conservative schools of higher education in America. It was founded by Jerry Falwell, the leader of the Christian Coalition and, before his death, one of the leaders of the American conservative movement. The president is now his son, Dr. Jerry Falwell Jr.

It was not unusual for politicians and elected officials to speak at Liberty University. Over the years, many had. In fact, my Senate colleague Ted Cruz had virtually kicked off his campaign for the Republican presidential nomination at a speech to the student body there. Many public officials had spoken there, but *none* with my politics. Virtually all of the previous speakers had been conservatives, most very conservative.

My instinct was to accept the invitation. The idea of going there appealed to me for several reasons. First, I always enjoy speaking to young people. Second, the thought of speaking to a group of people who looked at the world very, very differently than I did was intriguing and challenging. Was it possible to find some areas of common ground? Wouldn't it be useful to give these students a perspective that many of them may never have heard? Jane agreed with me, but not everyone in the campaign was on board. There were some who felt that going there could cause a rift with our supporters in the women's community and the LGBT community. Why, some supporters might ask, would we visit a university that had such a horrendous attitude on women's rights and gay rights, among many other views that I and our supporters rejected?

After the officials at Liberty University assured my campaign that I would be treated fairly and respectfully, and that there was no intention to embarrass me or "set me up," we agreed to accept the invitation. It would, I was sure, be an interesting day. Now all I had to do was to write the speech, which was not an easy task and not completed until the wee hours of the morning before I gave it. Here are excerpts from the speech that I gave before 12,000 students at Liberty University on September 14, 2015:

> *Thank you, President Falwell and David. Thank you very much for inviting my wife, Jane, and me to be with you this morning. We appreciate the invitation very much.*
>
> *And let me start off by acknowledging what I think all of you already know. And that is the views that many here at Liberty University have and I, on a number of important issues, are very, very different. I believe in a woman's right to choose. . . .*
>
> *And the right of a woman to control her own body.*
>
> *I believe in gay rights and gay marriage.*
>
> *Those are my views, and it is no secret. But I came here today because I believe from the bottom of my heart that it is vitally important for those of us who hold different views to be able to engage in a civil discourse.*
>
> *Too often in our country—and I think both sides bear responsibility for this—there is too*

much shouting at each other. There is too much making fun of each other.

Now, Liberty University is a religious school, obviously.

And all of you are proud of that.

You are a school which, as all of us in our own way, tries to understand the meaning of morality. What does it mean to live a moral life? And you try to understand, in this very complicated modern world that we live in, what the words of the Bible mean in today's society.

You are a school which tries to teach its students how to behave with decency and with honesty and how you can best relate to your fellow human beings, and I applaud you for trying to achieve those goals.

Let me take a moment, or a few moments, to tell you what motivates me in the work that I do as a public servant, as a senator from the state of Vermont. And let me tell you that it goes without saying, I am far, far from being a perfect human being, but I am motivated by a vision, which exists in all of the great religions, in Christianity, in Judaism, in Islam and Buddhism, and other religions.

And that vision is so beautifully and clearly stated in Matthew 7:12, and it states: "So in everything, do to others what you would have them do to you, for this sums up the law and the prophets." That is the golden rule. Do unto others, what you would have them do to you. That is the golden rule, and it is not very complicated.

Let me be frank, as I said a moment ago. I understand that the issues of abortion and gay marriage are issues that you feel very strongly about. We disagree on those issues. I get that, but

let me respectfully suggest that there are other is-
sues out there that are of enormous consequence
to our country and in fact to the entire world that
maybe, just maybe, we do not disagree on and
maybe, just maybe, we can try to work together to
resolve them.

Amos 5:24: "But let justice roll on like a river,
righteousness like a never-failing stream." Justice
treating others the way we want to be treated,
treating all people, no matter their race, their
color, their stature in life, with respect and with
dignity.

Now, here is my point. Some of you may agree
with me, and some of you may not, but in my view,
it would be hard for anyone in this room today to
make the case that the United States of America,
our great country, a country which all of us love,
it would be hard to make the case that we are a
just society, or anything resembling a just society
today.

In the United States of America today, there is
massive injustice in terms of income and wealth
inequality. Injustice is rampant. We live, and I
hope all of you know this, in the wealthiest coun-
try in the history of the world.

But most Americans don't know that. Because
almost all of that wealth and income is going to
the top 1 percent.

You know, that is the truth. We are living in a
time—and I warn all of you if you would, put this
in the context of the Bible, not me, in the context
of the Bible—we are living in a time where a
handful of people have wealth beyond compre-
hension. And I'm talking about tens of billions of
dollars, enough to support their families for thou-
sands of years. With huge yachts, and jet planes,

and tens of billions. More money than they would ever know what to do with.

But at that very same moment, there are millions of people in our country, let alone the rest of the world, who are struggling to feed their families. They are struggling to put a roof over their heads, and some of them are sleeping out on the streets. They are struggling to find money in order to go to a doctor when they are sick.

Now, when we talk about morality, and when we talk about justice, we have to, in my view, understand that there is no justice when so few have so much and so many have so little.

There is no justice, and I want you to hear this clearly, when the top one-tenth of 1 percent—not 1 percent, the top one-tenth of 1 percent—today in America owns almost as much wealth as the bottom 90 percent. And in your hearts, you will have to determine the morality of that, and the justice of that.

In my view, there is no justice, when here in Virginia and Vermont and all over this country, millions of people are working long hours for abysmally low wages of $7.25 an hour, of $8 an hour, of $9 an hour, working hard, but unable to bring in enough money to adequately feed their kids.

And yet, at that same time, 52 percent of all new income generated is going to the top 1 percent. You have got to think about the morality of that, the justice of that, and whether or not that is what we want to see in our country.

I concluded my remarks by making reference to Pope Francis, and discussing the profound issue of morality within the context of massive levels of wealth and inequality in this country and around the world.

I agree with Pope Francis when he says, and I quote, "The current financial crisis originated in a profound human crisis, the denial of the primacy of the human person," and this is what he writes: "We have created new idols. The worship of the ancient golden calf has returned in a new and ruthless guise in the idolatry of money and the dictatorship of an impersonal economy lacking a truly human purpose," end of quote.

And the pope also writes, "There is a need for financial reform along ethical lines that would produce in its turn an economic reform to benefit everyone. Money has to serve, not to rule."

Now, those are pretty profound words, which I hope we will all think about. In the pope's view, and I agree with him, we are living in a nation and in a world, and the Bible speaks to this issue, in a nation and in a world which worships not love of brothers and sisters, not love of the poor and the sick, but worships the acquisition of money and great wealth. I do not believe that is the country we should be living in.

Money and wealth should serve the people. The people should not have to serve money and wealth.

Throughout human history, there has been endless discussion. It is part of who we are as human beings, people who think and ask questions, endless discussion and debate about the meaning of justice and about the meaning of morality. And I know that here at Liberty University, those are the kinds of discussions you have every day, and those are the kinds of discussions you should be having and the kinds of discussions we should be having all over America.

I would hope, and I conclude with this thought, I would hope very much that as part of that discussion and part of that learning process, some of you will conclude that if we are honest in striving to be a moral and just society, it is imperative that we have the courage to stand with the poor, to stand with working people and when necessary, take on very powerful and wealthy people whose greed, in my view, is doing this country enormous harm.

After the speech, Dr. Falwell and his family invited Jane and me to lunch. He and his family and staff were very cordial and we had a pleasant conversation. Did I win any votes at Liberty University or change many opinions? Probably not. Did I give 12,000 young people a perspective that they may not have heard before? Yes.

I do write my own speeches. (Arun Chaudhary, Revolution Messaging)

Did I open up a few hearts and minds to look at the world a little bit differently? Probably.

Was it a good idea to have gone to Liberty University? I think so.

In mid-September, my campaign issued a very forceful response to an ugly and dishonest attack that came from the Clinton super PAC run by David Brock, the former right-wing journalist. Brock had attempted to link me to the former Venezuelan president Hugo Chavez. My "crime" had been that I had worked with former congressman Joe Kennedy and his nonprofit Citizens Energy Corporation to bring inexpensive Venezuelan heating oil into Vermont to help low-income people get through our cold winter. It was a very sleazy attack. Our response: explain to our supporters what the Clinton super PAC had done, and raise money off of it.

In just forty-eight hours, as a direct response to that ugly attack, our donors contributed $1.2 million into the campaign, with an average contribution of $23. In an e-mail thanking our contributors I stated: "I hope that sends a very clear message that the American people are sick and tired of politics as usual and negative campaigning." Erin Hill, the executive director of Act Blue, the long-established organization that administered our online fund-raising, stated: "We've never seen an immediate donor response like what the Sanders campaign received on Tuesday. At one point, it drove 180 contributions through our platform per minute."

The point here was not just the money. Our supporters wanted real change in the way politics was done in America, and their actions made it very clear that they were not going to tolerate unfair and unfounded negative attacks from Clinton surrogates or anyone else.

As late September approached and we reached the

filing period for the Federal Election Commission (FEC) at the end of the third quarter of 2015, it was time for another leadership team assessment to determine how well we were doing. The answer was: very well. What had once seemed to us an impossible dream now seemed like, just maybe, a possibility. Perhaps, perhaps, perhaps we *could* pull off the biggest political upset in the modern history of the United States.

When we began the campaign in late May, a CNN national poll had Secretary Clinton leading us 60 percent to 10 percent. We were behind by 50 points. By late September, a Fox poll had Clinton at 44 percent, Joe Biden at 18 percent, and me at 30 percent. Nationally, we had closed the gap to 14 points, with Biden in the race.

In the United States, of course, we don't have national elections. We have elections that are determined state by state, and here we were making real progress as well. In early May, before we had formally announced, a Bloomberg poll in New Hampshire had us down 62 percent to 18 percent and poll after poll continued to have us trailing. Then, on August 7, headlines on the front page of the *Boston Herald* announced a new poll in New Hampshire. For the first time in the campaign, anywhere, there was a poll showing Bernie Sanders in the lead. Their poll had us leading Clinton 44 percent to 37 percent. It turned out this poll was not a fluke. In the coming weeks other polls also showed us in the lead. Unbelievably, we were now winning in the New Hampshire primary.

In Iowa, we were also making good progress. We were not doing as well there as we were in New Hampshire, but we were steadily moving forward. In late May, at the time I announced my candidacy for president, we were trailing Secretary Clinton 57 percent to 16 percent.

By the end of September, we had cut the gap to 5 points, trailing her 33 percent to 28 percent.

In terms of excitement and energy, there was no question as to who was in first place. Our rallies all over the country were the largest of any candidate's, and our grassroots efforts were truly unbelievable. Almost every day I would read something, or hear something, about an activity taking place in one part of the country or another, and let me tell you, it wasn't our campaign organizing them. They were occurring spontaneously at the grassroots level. There were marches and musical activities. People were writing music, designing T-shirts and posters, and doing all kinds of incredible artwork. Others were on the phone or knocking on doors in their communities. It was extraordinary, and it was a beautiful thing to behold.

You can't run a serious national campaign without serious money, and we were doing that, too. In fact, we were rewriting the playbook with regard to campaign finance. Never before in history had a campaign received as many individual campaign contributions as we were receiving. Never. At a time when most campaigns were being supported by super PACs and wealthy individuals, we were raising tens of millions in small individual contributions. In the third quarter of 2015, we shocked the pundits and, I suspect, the Clinton campaign by raising $25 million. This was almost as much as Clinton had raised during that period. We had now raised individual contributions from 1.3 million people since the beginning of the campaign. Obama did a fantastic job in raising money in small individual contributions in 2008. We were doing even better.

And people were noticing, in a very significant way, the differences between the way our campaign functioned and the way Clinton's worked. Zaid Jilani, on August 10, 2015, wrote in *Alternet*, under the headline "Bernie Sanders Speaks to 28,000 People in Portland, While Hillary Hosts $2,700-a-Head Fund-raiser":

> *Yesterday, Democratic presidential candidate Bernie Sanders spoke to 28,000 people in Portland, Oregon—the largest rally of 2015 of any candidate. Sanders hit the usual marks—decrying income inequality, money in politics, climate change, and mass incarceration. What's interesting is that Hillary Clinton also came to Portland last week. But instead of doing a public event, she held a fund-raiser at the home of Democratic Party consultants Win McCormack and Carol Butler. Access was granted only to donors willing to give the minimum donation of $2,700. The contrast in Portland is a microcosm of the two types of campaigns Sanders and Clinton are running. The former is counting on a grassroots network of hundreds of thousands of people donating small amounts of money and making up the difference with volunteer hours. The latter is a more conventional politician: court Big Money donors and flood the airwaves with television commercials to win the election. In six months, we'll start to see which succeeds.*

Whether it was the West Coast or the East Coast, the giant rallies continued. In Boston, on October 3, we drew more than 20,000 enthusiastic supporters to the Boston Convention and Exhibition Center, and there were some 4,000 outside in an overflow area. It was the largest political rally in Boston in years. When I took the stage there I said, "We are running a people's campaign, and while the millionaires and billionaires have something we don't have, we have something they don't have. Look around this room."

In early October, after four months on the campaign trail, we finally began receiving support from members of Congress. Representatives Raul Grijalva of Arizona and Keith Ellison of Minnesota came on board. They were the first members of Congress to buck the political establishment, and I was very appreciative. For us, this was a very big deal not just because they were both excellent and well-respected congressmen, but because they were the co-chairs of the House Progressive Caucus. Keith and Raul became great surrogates and both of them played important roles throughout the campaign.

During the course of the campaign, Hillary Clinton attacked me on the issue of gun control. This was an unfair attack but one that I didn't handle well. It was an attack that also had significant political implications with regard to the rural vote and the general election.

In 1988, when I first ran for Congress, I supported a ban on the sale of assault weapons. In a very rural state like Vermont, a state that has virtually no gun control, that was not a particularly popular position, but one that I thought was right. Strongly opposed by gun organizations in the state, I lost that election by 3 percentage points. Two years later, maintaining my same view, I won the election by 16 points. In 1992 I was fiercely opposed by the gun groups in the state, who produced a bumper sticker that said "Bye Bye Bernie." They wanted to get rid of me instead of assault weapons. I won that election by a wide margin. As a result of my support over the years for commonsense gun-safety legislation, I have earned a D-minus rating from the NRA. To suggest, as

Clinton did, that I was somehow sympathetic to the gun lobby was absurd.

The issue of guns is an extremely volatile one, and one in which I believe, coming from a rural state where guns are very much part of our way of life, I can play a constructive role. But politically, it is a very, very tough and divisive issue with a very real cultural divide. And there is not a simple political solution.

The overwhelming majority of Americans are appalled by the level of gun violence in this country, where 300,000 people have died in the last decade as a result of guns. They are especially outraged by the hundreds of mass shootings we have seen in recent years, including the horror that took place at the Sandy Hook Elementary School in Connecticut.

The difficulty is that the political divide now is very wide. Led by the NRA, which has become more and more irresponsible in recent years, there are those who think they have a constitutional right to have a nuclear launch pad in their backyards. On the other hand, there are many who believe that we should eliminate every gun in America. While most Americans disagree with both of these extreme views, the division over guns is becoming wider and wider and more and more ugly.

On October 5, 2015, after yet another mass shooting, I issued the following statement:

> Like the rest of the nation, I am appalled by gun violence in our country and the mass shootings in our churches and colleges. While there is no simple fix, that does not mean we should do nothing. The status quo is not working and people on both sides of the issue cannot simply continue shouting at each other. Nobody wants more mass killings and serious people are going to have to engage in serious discussion.

In my view, there are very concrete steps we can take to lessen the number of tragedies and to make those that happen less lethal, including ideas supported by a majority of gun owners:

- *We must strengthen and better enforce the instant background check system.*
- *We must close the gun-show loophole, which allows unlicensed dealers to sell guns to people who otherwise would not be able to get them.*
- *We must make "straw man" purchases a federal crime.*
- *We must ban semiautomatic assault weapons, which are designed strictly for killing human beings.*
- *We must recognize that our mental health system is seriously broken. While there has been much talk about mental health parity in our healthcare system, we are not even close to achieving it. It's past time for a serious discussion about identifying, intervening, and treating mental illness and ensuring access to care.*

THE DEBATE

As someone who has been interested and involved in politics for most of my adult life, I have of course paid attention to presidential debates and have watched many of them. If the truth be told, I can even remember the Kennedy-Nixon debate of 1960.

But now, as I watched a CNN commercial advertising the Democratic debate on October 13, 2015, in Las Vegas, I noticed something very strange. That was my picture up there. I was going to be in the debate, and there would be millions of people watching it. It all seemed a bit surreal.

As a candidate in a number of elections in Vermont, I had participated in many debates. Sometimes I debated one person, and sometimes I debated as many as seven or eight people. Sometimes the candidates would stand at podiums, and sometimes they'd be seated at a table. Sometimes the debates were on statewide TV, and sometimes they were in schools with almost no media and relatively few people in attendance. I, of course, always "prepared" for a debate, which meant that I would spend an hour or so going over what I wanted to say and work on my opening remarks. That, more or less, was my preparation. Sometimes I did very well in debates, often I did okay. On occasion, as in the first debate when I was running for reelection as mayor, I did poorly. I had been so busy with my job that I almost forgot that I had a debate.

Needless to say, what I was getting involved in now was a little bit different from my previous debates in Vermont. I was running for president of the United States, and I was running against Hillary Clinton, who was a very experienced and effective debater. In 2008 she had debated Barack Obama many times and won most of them. In the first debate, I was also up against former Maryland governor Martin O'Malley, former Virginia senator Jim Webb, and former governor and senator of Rhode Island Lincoln Chafee.

This time, I needed more than an hour to prepare.

Obviously, before the debate took place there were debates about the debate. Who would the moderator be and who else would be asking questions? How long would the debate be? How long would the opening statements be? Who would stand where? How much time would there be for rebuttal? What topics were going to be discussed? Would it be mostly domestic issues or foreign policy, or what?

Generally speaking, most of those issues were resolved to everybody's mutual satisfaction.

If I had my druthers, I would love to participate in a Lincoln-Douglas-type debate today. The people are entitled to serious answers to serious questions, which can't be done in thirty seconds or a minute. The voters also have the right to know the basic philosophical assumptions and priorities that a candidate holds, which also takes a bit of time to express. Unfortunately, that type of debate is not going to take place in modern American politics and on modern American television. So we do the best we can and prepare for the debates of today.

Michaeleen Crowell, Warren Gunnels, Caryn Compton, and Edward Chapman joined Tad, Mark, Jane, Jeff, Levi, Dave, and Carina and played active rolls in preparing me. Together, led by Tad, they did an excellent job in anticipating what the questions would be. The challenge was that while we had a pretty good idea of the questions that might be asked, we had to be prepared for *anything*. The range of potential questions, dealing with foreign and domestic issues, was enormous. For a debate, it wasn't necessary to have extensive knowledge about every issue under the sun, but you did have to know enough to provide a credible answer to anything that was asked.

Further, you had to anticipate the kinds of attacks and charges that would be coming from your opponents. How would they try to attack you? How would they try to get you off balance? During the practice sessions (and this wasn't easy) I had to get into the mind-set of responding seriously to the attacks coming from Michaeleen (playing Hillary Clinton) when it was really just Michaeleen, who in her day job was my friend and chief of staff.

Then, on top of everything that *I* had to prepare for, the campaign had to make certain that we had an effective "spinning operation." That means that during and after the debate we had to convince the media and the public that, hands down, no matter what I said or did, it was all quite brilliant, always factually correct, and that I was far and away the clear winner. This operation included a sophisticated tweet system that highlighted my extraordinary strengths in the debate and my opponents' unbelievable weaknesses. Needless to say, all the other candidates were thinking about the exact same things.

Oh, yes. In addition, my staff reminded me that it would be great if I could mention our Web site, berniesanders.com, and make a request for contributions. A debate is an opportunity to raise a lot of campaign contributions.

In Nevada, we did the practice runs at the hotel where we were staying outside of Las Vegas. Tad Devine did a brutally good job in playing the moderator and asking me very sharp questions that went after my vulnerabilities. The more we went at it, the more nervous I became. There were some questions to which I was just not responding well.

On Tuesday night, October 13, after going through all kinds of security, getting made up, and becoming increasingly nervous in the green room, I walked out on the stage with the other candidates. The debate began.

Perhaps the most memorable moment of the night was a response that I made to a question from Anderson Cooper. When he asked me about Secretary Clinton's e-mail problem, I said, "Let me say something that may not be great politics. But I think the Secretary is right. And that is that the American people are sick and tired of hearing about your damn e-mails. And let me say something about the media as well. I go around the country, talk to a whole lot of people. The middle class of this country is collapsing. We have twenty-seven million people living in poverty. We have massive wealth and income inequality. Our trade policies have cost us millions of decent jobs. The American people want to know whether we're going to have a democracy or an oligarchy as a result of Citizens United. Enough of the e-mails. Let's talk about the real issues facing America." The answer certainly struck a chord in the audience, which rose in a standing ovation and prolonged applause. Interestingly, but not surprisingly, the media combined the two remarks about the e-mails and chose to omit coverage about the issues.

One of the most fascinating and telling aspects of this debate and those that followed was the answer to the question "Who won?" And what we learned was that "victory" was very much in the eyes of the beholder. People see what they want to see. For a lot of the establishment media and the Inside-the-Beltway pundits, Hillary Clinton "won." As usual, she was composed, she was knowledgeable, and, most important, she "looked presidential." But there was another world out there that did not look at things quite the way the pundits did. They were less concerned about whether a candidate "looked presidential," and more concerned about whether or not that candidate was going to take on the big-money interests controlling our country, and address the issues that impacted their lives. Among those people, I did pretty well.

More than one hour after the debate ended, we were winning the unscientific online polls overwhelmingly. In a *Time* magazine poll, 68 percent of respondents thought I had won. Clinton was in second place at 16 percent. A *U.S. News & World Report* online poll had 84 percent of the people voting for me, and *Slate* readers had me at 74 percent.

Further, as the online polling indicated, what was becoming increasingly obvious was that there was a very wide generational divide in the electorate. We were winning the younger generation, people under forty who were learning about us online, by very large numbers. Clinton was easily winning the older voters, who got much of their news from mainstream media and knew relatively little about our campaign.

Social media was playing a vitally important role. It was not just bringing in millions of small donations, it became the fabric that united the campaign, that brought us together, that shared our message. One example of the power of our social media were the four thousand debate-watch parties we organized on the night of that first debate in homes, union halls, theaters, on college campuses, and at locations in every state in the country. It was an extraordinary event that was unprecedented in any presidential campaign.

What we were accomplishing with social media was the ability to go outside of the corporate interpretation of events, bring our supporters together, and communicate directly with millions of people. This was very much the political revolution in action. It was also, to a very significant degree, why we were doing so well with younger people.

One of the very serious and ongoing problems that our campaign faced from day one was our inability to effectively connect with seniors. Poll after poll showed us doing extremely well with voters under forty, but we were getting trounced by Clinton among older Americans. At our rallies and town meetings, it was also obvious that relatively few seniors were showing up. Why was this happening? What could we do about it?

The campaign staff came up with several explanations as to why this was occurring. First, older Democrats

Lemonade for Bernie: another small donor contribution.

(Arun Chaudhary, Revolution Messaging)

remembered the Clinton years fondly, and Bill and Hillary were popular with them. Hillary was especially popular with older women, who very much wanted to see a woman become president. Second, older people who lived through McCarthyism and the "evil empire" of the old Soviet Union often had negative impressions of the word "socialism." To the degree that they heard that I was a socialist, that wasn't helping.

The third explanation that we came up with was one that we could do very little about, and one that also hurt John McCain when he ran for president. While younger people had few problems with the fact that I was seventy-four years old, it appeared that older voters did. Older people, some of whom had health problems or the general fatigue issues that age can bring, were asking themselves: "How can this guy become president, the hardest and most stressful job in the country, at seventy-five and keep going strong until he completes his first term at seventy-nine?" The fact that my health and stamina were excellent may not have been enough to convince them that I had the energy for the job.

The last obstacle that we had with seniors, which was also not going to be easily resolved, was that many older people did not use social media—Facebook, Twitter, Reddit, etc. We were much more effective in getting our message out through social media than through the mainstream media and network news that many seniors got their information from.

The poor response we were getting from seniors, for whatever the reasons, was disappointing. I had one of the strongest records in Congress on senior issues. I not only had helped lead the effort in defending Social Security against Republican attacks, but I had introduced legislation expanding benefits. In Vermont, seniors were always part of my core constituency. Somehow, we had to figure out a way to communicate better with senior citizens.

While we were preparing for the debate, another major political development was brewing. More and more attention was being paid to the possibility that Joe Biden might jump into the race.

Joe Biden is a friend of mine. While we have our differences of opinion, I believe that he has been a very effective vice president and an excellent representative for the administration. As our campaign gained momentum and the Clinton machine sputtered, there was growing speculation that Joe might enter the race. He was talking with union leaders, he was dropping hints about the possibility of running, and there were a growing number of voices urging him to run. The "inevitability" of Hillary as the Democratic nominee was now in doubt, and there were those who were searching for an alternative to Bernie Sanders.

I had mixed feelings about Biden getting into the race. On one hand, what the polls seemed to show was that his candidacy would probably be helpful to us because he would split the more conservative Democratic vote with Clinton. We probably had a better chance to win a three-way race than a two-way contest. On the other hand, our entire campaign effort was now focused on Clinton and we would have to go through some major adjustments to figure out how best to deal with a Biden candidacy.

On October 21, Joe ended the speculation. He announced that he would not be running. A few months earlier he had lost his son Beau, whom he was very close to, and he felt it best for his family that he not run. I chatted with Joe on the day he made his announcement and we met soon after.

Reaching out to young people was one of the strong components of our campaign. We wanted them involved in politics. We wanted them fighting for a new America. On October 28, we held a rally at George Mason University in Virginia, which was live-streamed into 250 student meetings in every state in the country. There were about 1,500 students who attended the event on campus.

The meeting was notable for a couple of reasons. First, I went into some detail about my views on marijuana. What I said is that if we were serious about dealing with the crisis in criminal justice, we had to completely rethink the so-called "War on Drugs." Far too many people had their lives harmed by arrests for marijuana possession, and the nature of drug arrests was most certainly tied to race. In 2014 alone there were 620,000 marijuana possession arrests, and those numbers were disproportionately high within the African-American community. Although about the same proportion of blacks and whites use marijuana, a black person was almost four times more likely than a white person to get arrested for it.

The view that I expressed to the students was that it was absurd that marijuana be listed as a Schedule I drug within the federal Controlled Substance Act, right next to heroin, a killer drug. I proposed taking marijuana completely out of that act. The decision to legalize marijuana was a state decision, and four states had already done that. But regardless of what states did or did not do, possession of marijuana should not be a federal crime.

The other part of that evening was a quite emotional discussion that I had with a Muslim student at the university. During the question-and-answer period a young woman with a headscarf raised her hand and asked me my views about the Islamophobia that was on the rise because of the racism of Donald Trump and some of his followers. I thought her question was so important that I invited her up to the stage. The *International Business Times* described the scene:

> *At a Wednesday evening town hall, a young Muslim woman wearing a purple headscarf asked how the presidential candidate would combat a rising tide of anti-Islam rhetoric in the country.*
>
> *"Let me be very personal if I might. I'm Jewish, my father's family died in concentration camps," Sanders responded during the speech in front of a couple hundred people at George Mason University in Fairfax, Virginia. "I will do everything that I can to rid this country of the ugly stain of racism that has existed for far too many years."*
>
> *Sanders invited the questioner, Remaz Abdelgader, a senior in college who said she wishes to*

become a human rights attorney, to join him on stage and gave her a hug as the crowd watched and cheered, Think Progress *reported. Abdelgader, the daughter of Sudanese asylees, expressed concern over recent anti-Muslim rhetoric from other presidential candidates. Republican presidential candidate Ben Carson said last month that he would not support electing a Muslim president, and later added that he would only support a Muslim candidate if they were to denounce Shariah law.*

"Being an American is such a strong part of my identity, but I want to create a change in this society," she said as she asked Sanders her question. "I'm so tired of listening to this rhetoric saying I can't be president one day, that I should not be in office. It makes me so angry and upset. This is my country."

Abdelgader told Think Progress *after the event that she was pleased with Sanders's answer, adding that she was nearly moved to tears by his gesture.*

"If there's anyone that should be elected to the White House, it's him," she said. "He stands for everybody, whether you're gay or Muslim or black or Christian or Latino. He is for equality. That's why I identify with the next president of the United States: Bernie Sanders."

Two of the areas that I was considered to be "vulnerable" on were foreign policy and the fact that I was a democratic socialist. I decided to address both of those issues head on in a major speech at Georgetown University on November 19.

Hillary Clinton had been secretary of state for four years under President Obama. She had traveled the world, been involved in a number of important foreign policy decisions, and knew many heads of state personally. Therefore, according to the pundits, she was the "expert" on foreign policy. I was, presumably, the novice, and ill-prepared in that area.

Needless to say, that wasn't my view. While it was obvious that Clinton, as a former secretary of state, had more hands-on experience in foreign policy than I did, that did not necessarily make her better qualified in that area. In foreign policy judgment mattered, and on the most important foreign policy issues of our time, my judgment had been better than Hillary Clinton's.

I not only voted against the war in Iraq, I helped lead the opposition to what turned out to be the worst foreign policy blunder in American modern history. In my speech at Georgetown I discussed that war and what I had said on the floor of the House before the vote:

> *I am concerned about the problems of so-called unintended consequences. Who will govern Iraq when Saddam Hussein is removed and what role will the U.S. play in an ensuing civil war that could develop in that country? Will moderate governments in the region who have large Islamic fundamentalist populations be overthrown and replaced by extremists? Will the bloody conflict between Israel and the Palestinian Authority be exacerbated? And these are just a few of the questions that remain unanswered.*

Hillary Clinton, as a U.S. senator from New York, had voted for the war.

Further, against a great deal of political pressure, I had voted against the first Gulf War. I was worried about the precedent that it was setting in using military force and believed that economic sanctions could have driven

Saddam Hussein out of Kuwait. I believed that war was unnecessary.

Yes, I was willing to concede that Hillary Clinton had more foreign policy experience than I did. No, I did not believe that her record made her better prepared than me to conduct U.S. foreign and military policy.

In terms of the issue of democratic socialism, the main point that I made at Georgetown was that we must establish "economic rights" in this country, that in a democratic, civilized society all Americans were entitled to health care, the ability to get a higher education, decent housing, and a decent job at a decent wage.

The New York Times got it right when it said:

> *Senator Bernie Sanders of Vermont aggressively confronted voter concerns about his electability as president on Thursday, making a rare formal address to explain his left-wing ideology of democratic socialism and argue that its principles reflected mainstream American values like fairness and equality.*
>
> *Mr. Sanders, who is hugely popular with liberals but is struggling to attract more voters to his Democratic presidential bid against Hillary Rodham Clinton, made blunt overtures to the party faithful by presenting himself as the heir to the policies and ideals of Franklin Delano Roosevelt and the Rev. Dr. Martin Luther King Jr.*
>
> *Invoking the two men several times, Mr. Sanders said that democratic socialism was reflected in Roosevelt's priorities like Social Security and in Dr. King's call for social and economic justice, contrasting them to "socialist-communist" caricatures of his thinking put forward by Republicans to tar the Democratic field.*
>
> *"I don't believe government should take over*

the grocery store down the street or own the means of production," Mr. Sanders said in an hour-long speech before a friendly audience of college students at Georgetown University in Washington. "But I do believe that the middle class and the working families of this country, who produce the wealth of this country, deserve a decent standard of living and that their incomes should go up, not down."

In mid-November, a new and very interesting development was occurring. National polls were showing that I, not Hillary Clinton, was the stronger candidate against possible Republican nominees. This completely undercut one of the main arguments made by the Clinton organization, which was that Bernie Sanders was unelectable in a general election, and that a vote for me would result in a Republican president.

In a *Wall Street Journal* poll released on November 3, I was defeating Trump by 9 points and Marco Rubio by 5. Throughout the campaign, from late November to the end of my campaign, I defeated Trump in twenty-eight out of thirty national polls, almost always by double digits. In almost all of those polls during that period, I was running much stronger against Trump than Clinton.

In early December, a Public Policy Polling poll in New Hampshire showed the same trend. In that battleground state, we were doing an average of 4 points better than Clinton against the leading Republican candidates. Jeff Weaver, my campaign manager, made the point that we were going to make over and over again. He stated: "The results from New Hampshire, a key general election battleground state, tell us the same thing we've seen in national polls. The fact is that Bernie is the most electable candidate Democrats could nominate."

The Clinton campaign may not have liked it. The Democratic establishment may not have liked it. But it was becoming increasingly clear that I was the strongest candidate if Democrats were to retain the White House.

On February 1, the people of Iowa walked into their caucus locations and cast the first votes of the 2016 Democratic presidential nominating process. We lost, but we won. At the end of a very chaotic night where some delegates were won with the toss of a coin, Clinton received 50 percent of the vote and I received 50 percent of the vote. She received 701 delegates to the state convention, and I received 697. Most of the media correctly perceived the night as a victory for us. From the first day of the campaign, we knew that we would have to do well in the early states to establish credibility and let the world know that we were in this for the long haul. And that's exactly what we did. With the help of a great team led by Robert Becker and Pete D'Allessandro, we had come a very long way in a few months.

As *The New York Times* reported from Iowa:

> *On Monday night, a disappointed-looking Ms. Clinton raised her voice to a near yell as she tried to demonstrate her own conviction. But she offered oddly little direct assuagement to the unsettled working class that still craves her assurance.*
>
> *That task fell instead, as it has throughout the campaign, to Mr. Sanders, Mrs. Clinton's ultra-liberal rival, whose denunciations of greedy plutocrats and an unfair economy are at the center of his message. "Given the enormous crisis facing our country," he said here after voting had concluded, "it is just too late for establishment politicians and establishment economics."*

An analysis of the exit polls done by some of the media organizations yielded some remarkable information. We had done unbelievably well among young people. We had done very poorly among the elderly. According to *The Washington Post,* we had won 84 percent of the vote among voters twenty-nine or younger and 58 percent of the vote from those younger than forty-four. On the other hand, we had won only 26 percent of the vote of people who were sixty-five or older. While we lost the women's vote to Clinton, we did respectably well. She won 53 percent of the women. I won 42 percent. I won 50 percent of the men's vote. She got 44 percent. Also, importantly, I won 69 percent of the Independent vote.

During the evening, with caucus results showing him doing poorly, Martin O'Malley dropped out of the race. I liked O'Malley. He ran a progressive, issue-oriented campaign. It just never caught on.

Now, with Jim Webb and Lincoln Chafee having already dropped out, we were down to a two-person race. And it was off to New Hampshire, where the primary would take place the following week. Our plane landed at five o'clock in the morning and, why not, we held a rally. Damnedest thing I ever saw, but hundreds of New Hampshire and Vermont supporters met us at a parking lot near our hotel in Manchester to welcome us back—at five A.M. I couldn't believe it. After commenting that these people were completely out of their minds, I gave a short speech while standing on the back of a pickup truck. We then drove to our hotel and went to sleep.

An analysis of the Iowa exit polls, as well as other public polls, told us exactly what we had to do to win in New Hampshire and the other states. As I've said, we were doing phenomenally well with young voters, but these are the people least likely to vote. We were doing terribly with older people, who are the most reliable voters. We were also doing well with Independents, people who are not enamored with either political party.

Clearly, if we were going to win the nomination, we had to do everything we could to make sure that young people came out to the polls, we had to improve our standing with seniors, and we had to work as hard as we could to win the support of women. We also, when necessary, had to get Independents to re-register as Democrats so that they could vote in those states that held closed primaries. While this was not a major issue in New Hampshire, we also knew that we were going to have to do much better in introducing ourselves to the African-American and Latino communities and making the case as to why they should vote for me.

Julia Barnes, the former director of the Vermont Democratic Party, was our state director in New Hampshire. Extremely hardworking, Julia put together an excellent staff and volunteer organization. I had the opportunity to visit a number of our offices around the state and was deeply moved by the commitment and energy of our volunteers. Truly incredible.

Our organization in New Hampshire did an extraordinary job in setting up events and bringing people out. It turned out that we brought out *four* times as many people as we had originally anticipated. By the end of the campaign, over 41,000 people had attended our meetings. Incredibly, that meant that one out of the four voters we needed to win over in New Hampshire had been someone who had actually heard me speak in person. That is what grassroots democracy is all about. One of the fun aspects of the New Hampshire campaign was that my son Levi, who lives in the state, was able to introduce me at a number of our meetings.

The thing that got me most nervous during the last week in New Hampshire was that I was in the very unusual position of being the favorite. That made me uncomfortable. All of the recent polls had us in the lead, and some had us winning by as many as 20 points. The Clinton people were letting on that a "victory" for them would be a single-digit defeat.

After a long and hard week, Election Day finally came. We won. It was a blowout. The final tally was 60 percent to 38 percent.

Watching the results come in on Election Night in New Hampshire was an unbelievable experience. We had come such a very long way. Hillary Clinton's concession speech was gracious, and she called to congratulate me. My extended family—four kids and seven grandchildren—aren't able to get together all that often. I was very happy, therefore, that along with Jane, all of them were there. Levi, Heather, Carina, Dave, and their spouses, Raine, Marc, Blake, and Liza, as well as Sunnee, Cole, Ryleigh, Grayson, Ella, Tess, and Dylan, along with Nicole and Keegan, were all on hand for what turned out to be a very big night for us. Our "holding room" for that evening was a gym in the school where we were holding our Election Night celebration. Before I went upstairs to make the victory statement, the media came in for their photos and video, and caught us shooting hoops. I even made a few jump shots.

After winning New Hampshire, we began receiving Secret Service protection. Needless to say, it is a life-changing experience. Previously, when I was home, I enjoyed jumping in my small car and running to the grocery store for milk and eggs. Now I was traveling in an armored vehicle accompanied by a fleet of cars and a number of well-armed agents who made sure I was safe in the bread aisle, and every place else that I went on the campaign trail.

Over the many months they were with us, we got to know the agents well, liked them very much, and never forgot that they were putting their lives on the line to keep us safe. There was always a car in front of the house and an agent in a booth they had built in the back. They inspected our mail, checked out anyone who came by, and made sure that the house was secure at all times. In a very crazy and dangerous world, Jane and I very much appreciated their protection and their professionalism.

We had tied in Iowa and won New Hampshire. Now we were off to South Carolina and Nevada. Very different worlds.

As we took a deep breath after the New Hampshire primary and began moving our operation to Nevada for the caucus there on February 20, we analyzed where we were, and what we had to do to keep the momentum going. It was clear to all of us—Jeff, Jane, Phil, Michael, Tad, and the whole team—that one of the major reasons we had done so well in Iowa and New Hampshire was that we had the time to run strong grassroots campaigns that enabled me to meet personally with a significant percentage of the voters in both states.

Early on, we made the decision that if we had any chance to win the nomination, we had to do well in the first two states. And that meant spending an enormous amount of time in Iowa and New Hampshire. That was our strategy, we carried it out, and by and large, we succeeded. No regrets.

In Iowa and New Hampshire, we were able to overcome lack of name recognition and unfamiliarity with my views through a very aggressive grassroots effort. Over a period of eight months we held 101 rallies and town meetings in Iowa and brought out 73,415 people to our events. The Democratic Party in Iowa reported that, on Election Night, 171,109 people showed up at the caucuses. We received about half that vote. While there were certainly people who came out to more than one event, it appears that I *personally* had spoken to almost as many people who eventually voted for me. That was extraordinary.

In New Hampshire, the situation was pretty much the same. We held sixty-eight meetings there and brought out 41,810. On Election Day I received 151,584 votes. The likelihood is that over 25 percent of the vote we received came from people who had attended one or more of our meetings and met with me personally.

In both Iowa and New Hampshire, we spent a lot of money on paid media. That was important. But to my mind, the major reason we were creating excitement and energy, and the reason we did so well, was that much of our organizational effort was geared to bringing out people to the many, many events we held in every corner of both of those states. Our message was resonating town by town, county by county, as we worked our way through Iowa and New Hampshire.

Now, with the Nevada caucus coming on February 20, followed by the South Carolina primary on February 27, and eleven states coming up on Super Tuesday, March 1, we were running out of runway. It was just impossible to spend the time that I would have liked in each of the states, and to have the kind of grassroots presence we needed. We had made the decision to focus on Iowa and New Hampshire. It was the right decision. Now, however, we were paying the price for that choice.

In every state that would soon be having primaries and caucuses, we had started way, way behind Clinton in the polls and in terms of name recognition. Many of the people in those states still did not know who I was or what I stood for. And now we faced thirteen state elections in the next three weeks. We had a lot of work to do, and not much time to do it.

The voters in the Democratic caucus in Nevada are the most diverse of any state in the country, including a sizable Latino vote. We were frantically trying to get every vote we could—white, black, and Latino.

In terms of statewide politics, Nevada is two worlds: the Las Vegas area and everywhere else. Virtually all of our rallies and meetings were in Las Vegas and Reno, including a beautiful and large outdoor evening rally at the University of Nevada at Reno. As Election Day approached in Nevada, I was feeling more and more confident. The polls had us close to Clinton, and while we had only done seventeen events in the state, it was clear to me that I was becoming better known.

Further, our staff and volunteer phone callers were finding a lot of support throughout the state. In fact, we had identified more than enough support to win, given the expected voter turnout. On Election Day I campaigned in the hotels and casinos, urging the workers there to come out and vote. The support seemed pretty good. In the afternoon, we heard about an exit poll that had us slightly in the lead.

Winning Nevada was very important for us. It would have extended the momentum that we received from the victory in New Hampshire and shown that we could win states with large non-white populations. But that's not the way it turned out. We did well, but not well enough. We lost Nevada 47.3 percent to 52.6 percent. Our postmortem analysis showed that while we did very well with Latino voters, our overall get-out-the-vote effort had not been as effective as it should have been, and many of our supporters had not come out to caucus.

And now it was on to South Carolina for a February 27 primary, followed by Super Tuesday contests in Alabama, Arkansas, Colorado, Georgia, Massachusetts, Minnesota, Oklahoma, Tennessee, Texas, Vermont, and Virginia. We were in the midst of the battle.

The very first South Carolina poll that I was included in, done by NBC News/Marist, had me at 3 percent, 62 points behind Secretary Clinton. The next poll had me at 1 percent, 58 points behind. From day one we knew that South Carolina would be a very, very tough state for us. We always thought it unlikely that we could win there, but we chose not to write it off. We wanted to make a respectable showing, and we invested a lot of money and staff into trying to make that happen. We failed miserably. Clinton won a landslide victory there, defeating us 73 percent to 26 percent. Our outreach effort to the black community was completely unsuccessful. According to exit polls, Clinton won 90 percent of the black vote.

We were now officially "hurting." We had a shot to win in Nevada, and we lost. We thought we could do respectably in South Carolina, and we got decimated there. Now we were heading to some very tough states for us on Super Tuesday, six of which were in the South.

During this point in the campaign, the disadvantages we faced became very apparent. Clinton was far better known than I was, especially among older black voters. She had run eight years before and she had been very active in her husband's two presidential campaigns. She had a strong political organization with experience in the states and had many connections with the Democratic leadership. In the states in which we were now campaigning we might have the support of a few members of the legislature. She had the entire political establishment. And, in state after state, we had to start from scratch in putting together our organization.

During this Super Tuesday period, we did what we could. We got on our chartered plane and flew to as many destinations as possible. On February 27, we did rallies in Austin and Dallas, Texas, and a third rally in

Super Tuesday in Vermont. Guess who we are voting for for president? (Eric Elofson, Revolution Messaging)

Rochester, Minnesota. On February 28, we were in Oklahoma City, Oklahoma, and Fort Collins, Colorado. On February 29, we did events in Minneapolis, Minnesota, and Milton, Massachusetts. On March 1, Super Tuesday, we came home to Vermont to vote and to hold a celebration in the evening.

The event in Vermont was beautiful, and emotional for Jane and me. Almost four thousand people came out to say hello, and for a small state like Vermont, that is a lot of people. And we did celebrate. In my own state, where the people knew me best, we won 86 percent of the vote and Clinton won 13 percent—a 73 percent victory. In the Democratic nominating process, a candidate has to win at least 15 percent of the vote to get any delegates. Vermont was the only state in the entire primary campaign where one candidate got all of the delegates. We shut Clinton out in Vermont.

Needless to say, the results were not quite so good elsewhere. We were defeated very badly in all of the

Southern states. We did well in Massachusetts but ended up losing there—50.1 percent to 48.7 percent. The good news was that we won very strong victories in Colorado, Minnesota, and Oklahoma in addition to Vermont. On Super Tuesday, Clinton took 518 pledged delegates. We won 347.

We were losing, but we were still in the fight. That became very clear on the weekend of March 5 when we had landslide victories in Kansas, Maine, and Nebraska. On the other hand, we lost badly in Louisiana. On March 8, we pulled off one of the major upsets of the entire campaign. Despite polls showing us way, way behind, we won Michigan. That victory showed, for the first time, that we could win a large, industrialized state with a diverse population.

March 15 was a very bad day for us. Despite very close losses in Missouri and Illinois, we lost all five states that were up that day.

March 22 was much better. We won Idaho in landslide proportion, with a victory of 78 percent to 21 percent. If you can believe it, we did even better in Utah, where we won with 79 percent of the vote.

The Arizona primary also took place on that day. We worked very hard in Arizona, and I thought we had a good shot to win there. We didn't, and I still don't know why. One thing I do know was that the voting process in Arizona was an absolute disaster and an embarrassment to American democracy. People in some parts of the state were forced to wait up to five hours to cast a ballot. Nobody can ever really know which candidate was hurt more by this travesty, but I don't think it helped us. Many of Clinton's supporters were older and voted by mail. Most of our supporters came out on Election Day with the obvious expectation that they would be allowed to vote in a reasonable period of time.

On March 26, we won major landslide victories. We

won Alaska with 82 percent of the vote. We won Hawaii with 71 percent. Needless to say, Jane, who had campaigned in both of those states, was pretty excited. Our biggest state victory of the day was the state of Washington, where we received almost 73 percent of the vote. Yes, we were celebrating on the plane on the night of March 26.

What a strange and unprecedented campaign. Hillary Clinton, the candidate whom the pundits had determined was the odds-on favorite, the candidate who had been anointed by the entire establishment, was winning, but at the same time was losing state after state by huge margins.

We were more than aware that we were behind in both the popular vote and the delegate count—especially with the superdelegates who were always being counted by the media, despite not having voted yet. But victories like the ones we were winning strengthened our resolve. We were going to continue this fight. We were going to take it all the way to the Democratic National Convention in Philadelphia. We were not going to give up.

And the good news continued. On April 5, we won the Wisconsin primary with almost 57 percent of the vote, and on April 9 we won the Wyoming caucus with 56 percent.

We had now won seven primaries and caucuses in a row. The Clinton team was not happy. We were ecstatic. According to all the experts, this nominating process was supposed to have ended a long time before, and here we were winning state after state.

Everybody knew that the major showdown yet to come was New York State, which held its primary on April 19. This, as the media pointed out, was going to be a very tough state for us. It was Hillary Clinton's home state, and where she had been elected twice as a

U.S. senator. She was universally known in New York and popular. Further, New York State's election laws were antiquated and reactionary. In a state generally considered to be progressive, the political elite in New York, Democrats and Republicans, had created a system that made it hard for people to vote and where, and as a result, voter turnout was very low.

New York State had a "closed primary," which meant that the 3 million New Yorkers who had registered as Independents could not participate. All of these people were disenfranchised from selecting the Democratic or Republican candidate for president of the United States. Further, one had to change party registration in October 2015—six months in advance—to be eligible to vote in the primary. This was, on the surface, an absurd and undemocratic process. Its major goal was to keep voter turnout low and protect incumbents. This closed-primary process was especially bad for us.

As the longest-serving Independent in the history of the U.S. Congress, I always did well with Independent voters. In this election, they would not be able to vote. Further, many of the young people who were flocking to our campaign had not registered as Democrats, and had certainly not changed their registration six months before. They also would not be able to participate.

On top of all that, we were taking on the political machines of the governor, virtually all the state's members of Congress, and New York's two senators. This was not going to be an easy fight, but we jumped in with both feet. I am very proud of the campaign our team ran.

Our strategy for New York was not complicated. Most of the votes in the New York Democratic primary are in New York City, so we were going to have to spend a lot of time there and do everything we could to bring out our vote. But we were not going to ignore upstate New York. We had to get out there as well.

On March 31, we held a rally in the South Bronx. This is one of the poorest parts of the city, and heavily minority. The crime rate is high. Voter turnout is low. Housing conditions are deplorable. The asthma rate among children is terrible. Nobody could remember the last time that a presidential candidate held a rally in that neighborhood. The police department was worried about a disturbance and they threatened to limit the number of people in attendance. The Secret Service was also nervous.

That evening turned out to be one of the most beautiful events of the entire campaign. More than 18,000 people showed up. Black, white, Latino—virtually all working-class. Rosario Dawson and Spike Lee made the introductory remarks. We were off to a great start in New York.

What I remember most about the New York campaign were the unbelievable turnouts that we were seeing. On April 13, we did a rally at Washington Square Park in lower Manhattan. The official count was 27,032. We were told that it was the largest political event ever at that iconic location. People there were even looking out of windows in the buildings across from the park. A few days later, we held an even larger event in

Talking with CBS's Scott Pelley outside of the apartment house I grew up in. (Arun Chaudhary, Revolution Messaging)

Prospect Park, with 28,356 people showing up. Danny DeVito and Tulsi Gabbard did the introductions. We did low-key or unannounced gatherings throughout the city and large crowds inevitably gathered.

One of the fun events that we did in New York City was on the street where I grew up, East Twenty-sixth Street in Brooklyn. We closed off the street outside of my old apartment house, and a thousand people came. Hillary Clinton may have been New York's senator, but I was the candidate born in Brooklyn and I wanted people to know that.

We did not ignore upstate New York. We did large rallies in Syracuse, Albany, Buffalo, Rochester, Poughkeepsie, and Binghamton. When we were in Poughkeepsie, we dropped into the home where FDR was born and where he is buried, in Hyde Park.

On April 15, we took a slight detour from New York politics. Weeks before, I had been invited to attend a major conference at the Vatican that dealt with the need to create a "moral economy." Despite the pressure of the campaign, I decided to attend, if only for a day. I am a big fan of Pope Francis and strongly support his call for radical changes in international economic priorities.

The Washington Post reported:

> Sen. Bernie Sanders told a Vatican conference Friday that the global market economy has largely failed working people, breaking from the U.S. campaign trail to deliver a talk on his signature issue of income inequality on an international stage. "At a time when so few have so much, and so many have so little, we must reject the foundations of this contemporary economy as immoral and unsustainable," Sanders said.
>
> The address to a prestigious Vatican academy that is nonetheless obscure to most Americans

*puts Sanders in the company of leftist thinkers
and political leaders. Sanders slipped comfortably
into the lexicon of European and South American socialist and leftist politics, including the socialist government models of Scandinavia. He
told the group that failed and crumbling public
schools and annual college tuition priced above
the annual wages of many Americans are marks
of failure.*

While at the Vatican, Jane and I had the opportunity
to briefly chat with the pope, a true honor. We spent the
night in the building where the pope lived. In separate
rooms, as was required.

Defeating Clinton in New York would have been a major
boost to our campaign, but it wasn't to be. We worked
very hard there and ran an excellent campaign, but there
were just too many obstacles in our way. Clinton beat us
there 58 percent to 42 percent. We did very poorly in
New York City. We won almost all of upstate New York.
In the two New York counties that border Vermont,
where people knew me best, we won more than 73 percent
of the vote.

A week later, on April 26, we lost four out of the five
states that were up on that day—Delaware, Pennsylvania, Maryland, and Connecticut. Our only victory was
in Rhode Island. But on May 3, we won a surprise victory
in Indiana and, in the following weeks, we won victories
in West Virginia and Oregon.

Our campaign was many things, but we were not dumb
and we knew how to count. We were more than aware
that we had only 46 percent of the pledged delegates,

virtually no superdelegates, and that the primary and caucus process was grinding toward an end. And every day we were being asked by the media, "Why don't you drop out? You can't win."

At this point our strategy was pretty simple. It had to do with momentum and showing the Democratic Convention who the stronger candidate was against Donald Trump, who by this time we knew would be the Republican nominee. And that all came down to the last day of the state primary and caucus elections, June 7, 2016. On that day, California, New Jersey, New Mexico, South Dakota, North Dakota, and Montana were voting. If we could win big on that day, especially in California, we would be going into the convention with incredible energy that, we believed, would turn into delegate votes. Further, virtually all of the national and state polls were showing us doing much better against Trump than Clinton was doing. If the Democrats wanted to win in November, our hope was that many of the superdelegates would begin to understand that we were the campaign to make that happen.

Jeff, Jane, Tad, Michael, and I reflected on how we could best deal with California, the largest state in the country. The answer became pretty clear: We would barnstorm the state in a way that no other presidential candidate had ever done. I announced that I hoped to have rallies bringing out at least 200,000 people in California between mid-May and early June. That is a lot of people and a lot of work. But we did it.

On May 9, we started off with a giant rally, which brought out 16,000 people in Sacramento. On May 17, we had 11,000 supporters in Carson City, and on May 18, we had almost 10,000 in Vallejo. We followed with 6,700 in Santa Monica, 9,800 in Ventura, and 8,500 in Fresno. We just plowed forward, up and down the state, two or three rallies a day. By the time we were finished campaigning in California on June 7, we had held 40 rallies and brought out more than 227,000 supporters.

One of the more outrageous moments of the entire campaign took place on June 6. The Associated Press aggressively contacted undeclared superdelegates to determine who they would be voting for, and one day before the all-important primary in California and five other states, they announced their belief that Clinton had secured the nomination. The AP had determined that by combining her pledged delegates and those superdelegates who told them they would be voting for Clinton at the convention, she had enough votes to win. The day before the last votes were cast in the Democratic nominating process, the AP decided on their own that the election was effectively over. It's not quite clear to me why they did that, but I believe strongly that their action had a negative impact on voter turnout and hurt us. Why vote if the election is over? Our younger voters were more likely to cast their votes on Election Day rather than voting earlier by absentee ballot, as many Clinton voters did.

In California, for whatever reason, it literally takes weeks before all the votes are counted and the final tally is made official. But on Election Night we knew that we had not won. We had done well, but not good enough. The media announced that we had lost by 14 percent that night. Far from accurate. After the secretary of state announced all the ballots were finally counted, we had cut that margin in half and ended up down by 7 percent. The final results had us with 2,381,714 votes—46 percent of the total. On June 7, Clinton also won contests in New Jersey, New Mexico, and South Dakota. We won in Montana and North Dakota.

The last states had voted, the numbers were in, and it was clear that I would not be the Democratic nominee.

On June 12, I invited a number of our key advisers to our home to discuss the future. (Top photo) Left to right: me, Tulsi Gabbard, Shailene Woodley, Ben Jealous, Raul Grijalva, Dave Driscoll, Justin Bamberg, Terry Alexander, Chuy Garcia, Larry Cohen, Carina Driscoll, Jeff Merkley, and Rich Cassidy. (Bottom photo) Left to right: Jim Hightower, Bill McKibben, Nina Turner, RoseAnn DeMoro, Keith Ellison, Ilya Sheyman, Jerry Greenfield, and Ben Cohen. Also in attendance were Jeff Weaver, Michael Briggs, Phil Fiermonte, Jim Dean, Peter Welch, Shannon Jackson, and Jane Sanders. (Jane)

But we were not giving up the fight yet. If I wasn't going to be the Democratic nominee for president, my goal was to help write the strongest possible Democratic Party platform and, as a senator, do all that I could to see that it was implemented. During the platform-drafting process in St. Louis our campaign had five great representatives who helped begin to draft the most progressive political platform in the history of our country. Our representatives were Cornel West, Keith Ellison, Deborah Parker, Bill McKibben, and Jim Zogby. Warren Gunnels, my policy director, also served on this committee. Thanks to their efforts, we won some major victories on Wall Street reform, expanding Social Security, and ending the death penalty.

The full platform committee met from July 8 to 9 in Orlando. While the 175 committee members debated the draft platform and what amendments should or should not be added, the two campaigns were busy negotiating behind the scenes. David Weinstein, a senior policy adviser in my Senate office who was taking time off to help the campaign, and Warren Gunnels played an active role in the negotiations.

While we didn't get everything we wanted, we did get much of what we were fighting for. It was now the Democratic Party's policy to break up too-big-to-fail banks, pass a twenty-first-century Glass-Steagall Act, make public colleges and universities tuition free for working families, enact a price on carbon and methane, raise the minimum wage to $15 an hour, abolish the death penalty, expand Social Security, close loopholes that allow corporations to avoid paying taxes, create millions of jobs rebuilding our crumbling infrastructure, eliminate super PACs, and pass a constitutional amendment to overturn Citizens United. And these were just some of the key provisions that we got into the platform.

Endorsing Hillary in Portsmouth,
New Hampshire. (Jane)

We also made progress in reaching an agreement with the Clinton campaign on some very important issues of great concern to me. On the evening of June 14, Jeff, Jane, and I met with Secretary Clinton, John Podesta, and Robby Mook for ninety minutes in a Washington hotel room. Out of that meeting came the groundwork, announced some weeks later, for very strong Clinton proposals on making public colleges and universities tuition free, and greatly expanding community health centers.

On July 12, in Portsmouth, New Hampshire, I formally endorsed Hillary Clinton for president. Our campaign had come to an end.

PART

TWO

---

*An Agenda for a New America:
How We Transform Our Country*

ONE

DEFEATING OLIGARCHY

Democracy is about one person, one vote. It's about all of us coming together to determine the future of our country. It is not about a handful of billionaires buying elections, or governors suppressing the vote by denying poor people or people of color the right to vote. Our job is to stand together to defeat the drift toward oligarchy and create a vibrant democracy.

Democracy should be easy. It should be ingrained in the soul of every American. Getting involved, being active in the political process, knowing that your voice matters in helping to shape the future of your community, state, and country should be the essence of our way of life. It should be taught in the schools, discussed at the family dinner table, and celebrated on national holidays.

We should be forever grateful to Jefferson, Adams, Paine, Washington, Madison, Franklin, Hamilton, and all the other revolutionary leaders who founded our country. With incredible courage, they put their lives on the line to create a very different kind of society.

Democracy is the right of a free people to control their destiny. Not kings or queens or czars, but ordinary people who come together in a peaceful manner in order to determine the future of their society. Democracy means that the government belongs to all of us and that it is our inherent right to elect people who will represent our interests. After all, this is what our Declaration of Independence proclaims when it profoundly states: "We hold these truths to be self-evident, that all men are created equal, that they are endowed by their Creator with certain unalienable Rights, that among these are Life, Liberty and the pursuit of Happiness. That to secure these rights, Governments are instituted among Men, deriving their just powers from the consent of the governed." *Their just powers from the consent of the governed.*

What, in our day, does democracy mean? To my mind, it should mean one person, one vote. It should mean an equal opportunity for all who wish to seek public office. It should mean that the wealthy don't have undue influence over the election process. It should mean that voting and participating in the political process is as easy and convenient as possible, and that barriers are not erected to prevent groups of citizens from exercising their right to participate. It should mean that poor people, old people, young people, and people of color are not discriminated against when they want to vote. It should mean that the United States has one of the highest voting turnout rates in the world, not one of the lowest. It should mean that political consciousness is high and that people are aware and well informed about the major challenges our nation is facing.

THE FIGHT FOR A VIBRANT DEMOCRACY

All of us know the rocky and torturous road that American democracy has traveled since the founding of our nation, when colonial revolutionaries took on and defeated the king of England and the enormous power of the British Empire. Determined that the decisions that impacted their lives should be made by the people themselves, and not by an autocratic monarch three thousand miles away across the Atlantic Ocean, the revolutionaries fought to create a new kind of society, a democratic society, unique in the world of its time.

We also know, however, that the Constitution they drafted, while revolutionary in its day, reflected the values and mores of the 1790s: slavery and racism, rigid class lines, and a deeply rooted sexism. We know that since then, amidst bloodshed, struggle, and turmoil, the American people have sought to expand democracy and make it more inclusive. To quote Lincoln at Gettysburg, our goal has been to create "a government of the people, by the people and for the people."

The abolitionists, not just Frederick Douglass and William Lloyd Garrison but the countless thousands who supported their cause, fought to abolish slavery and grant the rights of citizenship to all Americans, regardless of their race. A great war was fought, in part, to insist that this nation treat black Americans as having the same rights as white Americans. That struggle brought us the 14th Amendment to the Constitution, which guaranteed equal protection under the law for all. It brought us the 15th Amendment to the Constitution, which prohibited the use of race in determining which citizens could vote.

And, in more recent years, that's what the demonstrations and sit-ins of the civil rights movement were all about. That's what people were jailed for, were beaten for, and were sometimes killed for. That's what Martin Luther King Jr. and the March on Washington was about. These were determined efforts on the part of millions of Americans, black and white, to demand that our government fulfill the dream of democracy for all. That struggle was successful in pushing Congress to pass the Voting Rights Act of 1965, signed by Lyndon Johnson, to finally assure that all citizens of this country, regardless of race, have the right to vote.

Struggle brought about the 19th Amendment to the Constitution, which prohibited the government from denying women the right to vote. The amendment did not just appear: It was the fruit of the struggle of the suffragettes, led by such figures as Lucretia Mott, Susan B. Anthony, and Elizabeth Cady Stanton in the mid-nineteenth century. In similar fashion, the women's movement of the later twentieth century continued that struggle: It brought about greater rights for women, greater equality for women, more possibilities for women. Women by the millions, along with their male allies, made it clear to all that women in the United States would not be second-class citizens.

Voting is a right, not a privilege. How could we have a real democracy when poor people were denied the right to vote because they couldn't afford to pay a poll tax? Struggle against the dominance of the wealthy and the landed class led to the passage of the 24th Amendment to the Constitution, which prohibited citizens from having to pay in order to vote. All people must have the right to vote, regardless of their economic status. Voting is not just for the wealthy.

How could we send young people off to war, to get killed and maimed fighting for democracy, when they couldn't even vote on whether or not there should be a war? The experience of American soldiers in the Second World War, Korea, and Vietnam led to the adoption of the 26th Amendment to the Constitution, which lowered the voting age to eighteen. All adults must have the right to vote.

THE POWER OF MONEY

We must make our choice. We may have democracy, or we may have wealth concentrated in the hands of a few, but we can't have both.
—SUPREME COURT JUSTICE LOUIS BRANDEIS

Over the last 230 years we have made significant progress in making our country a more democratic and inclusive society. We have made significant progress breaking down barriers of race, gender, class, and age in terms of giving *all* Americans an equal voice in governing their country. In fact, the many struggles to expand the right to vote have been at the very heart of the American experience. They define who we are as a people.

Even though we have far to go to "perfect our democracy," sadly, today, there are people of incredible wealth and power who, instead of moving forward, want to undo the progress we have made and roll back the clock of history. These oligarchs are threatened by what ordinary people can accomplish through the democratic process. In order to protect their vast financial holdings, they utilize their incredible resources to make us a less democratic society.

They want more power for themselves, and less power for ordinary Americans. While they don't announce their intentions on the front pages of newspapers, their goal is clear. They want to move our country toward an oligarchic form of society in which almost all economic and political power rests with a handful of multibillion-aire families. They are not content with controlling most of our economy and owning an outlandish percentage of our national wealth. Now they want to own our government as well. They want to make it virtually impossible for ordinary Americans to make the changes necessary to improve their lives.

Tragically, they are succeeding. Our democracy, the ability of ordinary people to shape their own future, is becoming weaker and weaker every day.

In America today, instead of one person, one vote, and equal voice for all, we are seeing a small group of extraordinarily wealthy people pump billions of dollars into the political process to buy elections for politicians who will be beholden to them. Further, we are seeing a massive and coordinated effort by Republican politicians to suppress democracy by making it harder for minorities, the poor, the elderly, and the young to vote.

As a result of the Supreme Court's disastrous 5–4 Citizens United decision of 2010, pushed by legal organizations funded by powerful special interests and Republican leaders, the wealthiest people in this country, and the largest corporations, can now spend unlimited sums of money on "independent expenditures." The result: A huge amount of advertising from coast to coast—television, radio, and online—is coming from phony front groups owned and controlled by a handful of billionaires. In fact, in many elections, "independent expenditures" now play a more important role than that of the candidates.

In state after state—in races for the U.S. Senate, for the U.S. House, for governors, for state legislatures, for city councils and county commissions, for school boards and judgeships—big-money interests have successfully determined the outcome of elections through their massive expenditures. As I write, a handful of billionaires are spending $100 million to try to win a Senate seat in Ohio—$100 million to win a singie Senate seat in a moderate-sized state. For these billionaires, these expenditures are pocket change and very good investments. For these barons of the fossil fuel industry, Wall Street and banking, defense contracting, the pharmaceutical industry, and more, the policies supported by the candidates they elect will yield a very profitable return on their investments, many times over.

And, by the way, for these oligarchs, Citizens United did not go far enough. Citizens United allows for unlimited *independent* expenditures. A donor can spend as much as he/she wants on a campaign, but cannot coordinate activities with the candidate. This is a very inefficient way to buy elections. It would be much easier and more effective for the donor to control and coordinate the campaign if he/she could just give unlimited amounts of money directly to the candidate.

The oligarchs understand that creating a right-wing judiciary is very important to their goals, and they are spending lavishly to get judges elected or appointed who are sympathetic to their point of view. At the same time, they are fighting in the courts to overturn virtually all existing campaign finance restrictions and regulations, and for their right to make *direct* contributions to the candidates of their choice. If that happens, if billionaires are freed to give unlimited sums of money to candidates, it will mean in no uncertain terms that those candidates become nothing more than the paid employees of their sponsors. That, of course, is exactly what the billionaires want.

The political power of the oligarchs goes well beyond their campaign contributions and ability to influence elections. As a result of their ownership of media, think tanks, university chairs, and political front groups, they influence American public opinion and domestic and foreign policy in ways that few realize.

According to virtually the entire scientific community, climate change is a planetary crisis of extraordinary magnitude that will directly impact the lives of billions of people throughout the world. The scientists believe that we have to move boldly and transform our energy system away from fossil fuels and into energy efficiency and sustainable energy. But that is not what the billionaires who own the fossil fuel industry want. They are far more concerned about their short-term profits than the future of the planet. As a result, they have spent hundreds of millions of dollars creating a "climate denial movement" that has obfuscated and lied about climate change research. They have also used the influence of their massive advertising budget to limit media coverage of this vitally important issue.

When you hear about a report from an "independent nonpartisan think tank" telling us that climate change is just an unproven theory, or why we should give tax breaks to the rich, or why we should not join the rest of the industrialized world in guaranteeing health care for all, are their conclusions influenced by the billionaires and insurance companies who fund those think tanks? Let's not be naive. Of course they are.

Often, in the media, you will hear from spokesmen from organizations called "concerned citizens for this" or "concerned citizens for that." Invariably, these "concerned citizens" want to cut or privatize Social Security, Medicare, the Veterans Administration, the Environmental Protection Agency, or any other entity that protects the interests of working people. Next time you hear from these "concerned citizens," check out which particular group of billionaires funds their activities.

UNDERMINING AMERICAN DEMOCRACY

The Republican Party won a landslide victory in the 2014 midterm elections, amidst historically low voter turnout. They gained control of the U.S. Senate, increased their majority in the House, and won gubernatorial and state legislative races all across the country. Despite the fact that every seat in Congress and one-third of the Senate was up for election, an astounding 63 percent of the American people didn't vote. Even more distressing, 80 percent of young people and the overwhelming majority of low-income Americans didn't vote. Voter turnout in 2014 was the lowest since World War II.

Why don't people vote? Why are they giving up on the political process and our democracy in such huge numbers? The answer is not complicated. People no longer believe that government represents their interests. For the vast majority of Americans, there is a huge disconnect between the reality of their lives and what goes on in Washington or in state capitals. They are choosing not to participate in what, for them, is a charade of democracy.

In the real world, the very rich are getting richer and most everyone else is getting poorer. Is Congress listening? Whose interests is Congress representing? Certainly not those of working families struggling to get by.

In the real world, millions of workers are unable to make it on starvation wages and many of them struggle to put food on the table. Many in the middle class are working longer hours for lower wages. Unless we change the trajectory of our economy, the country's younger generation will be the first in modern history to have a lower standard of living than their parents.

Higher education is the ticket to the middle class, but millions of young people simply can't afford to go to

Percent Voting, By Family Income Bracket, 2012–2014

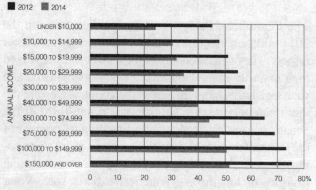

Data Source: U.S. Census Bureau, 2013 and 2015 Demos Calculations

college, while others are leaving school with suffocating debt.

Many families have two wage earners, yet still struggle to find affordable housing or quality child care. Many older workers have seen their manufacturing jobs go to China or Mexico, and find themselves barely surviving on wages far lower than they previously earned. Many seniors and disabled vets are not making it on their $10,000-a-year Social Security, and 43 million people are living in poverty. And on and on it goes.

And what are the members of Congress doing about these issues? I will tell you what they are doing. They are out spending a ridiculous amount of time raising money for their next campaigns. And then, once elected, they are representing the interests of the people who funded those campaigns.

The corrupting influence of big money in our elections and our politics has always been a huge problem in our country. But, today, as a result of Citizens United, as more and more money floods into the electoral system, that problem has reached new and absurd levels.

Let's be clear: Money dominates everything that goes on in Congress. Wall Street, the pharmaceutical industry, the coal and oil companies, agribusiness, and the rest of corporate America spend billions every year not just on campaign contributions, but also on lobbying. In Washington, you get what you pay for. The results: The desires of the rich and powerful are well attended to. The pain of working families is ignored.

We will never have a government that represents ordinary Americans until we pass real campaign finance reform and get big money out of politics. What goes on today is an absolute disgrace. That's not just Bernie Sanders talking. That's what many members of Congress, Democrat or Republican, will tell you privately.

As more and more cash floods the electoral system, candidates have to spend an enormous amount of time and energy raising money just to keep up. On almost any weekday in Washington, D.C., dozens of candidates have fund-raising breakfasts and dinners. That is time they could be spending doing the people's work, but instead they spend it fattening their coffers. And on weekends, many candidates attend destination events at fancy resorts across the country. That is time they could be spending meeting with their constituents back home, but instead they spend it rubbing elbows with the elite who fund their campaigns.

And then there is "dialing for dollars," a totally humiliating experience that often takes place in offices set up by the Democratic and Republican parties and designed for that purpose, with numerous small rooms containing a desk, two chairs, and a telephone. The candidate is given a piece of paper with the names of potential donors, most of whom he/she has never met. To expedite the process, an aide dials the number and keeps notes regarding the progress of each call.

This country and world face enormous crises. And

what are many of our elected officials doing? As part of a corrupt campaign finance system, they are spending an enormous amount of time and energy raising money for their campaigns. Day after day, week after week, month after month.

Today the maximum individual contribution a donor can make to a single candidate is $2,700 during the party primary election, and an additional $2,700 for the general election. Of course, wealthy families can double the amount given to a candidate if each spouse makes the maximum contribution. And then, they can give much larger sums to the political parties, some of which goes to, or is spent on behalf of, their candidates of choice. When all 435 seats in the House and 33 or 34 seats in the Senate are up for election every two years, the total amount a single wealthy family can legally give is truly astounding. And the huge amounts of money these people donate give them disproportionate influence in the political system. It goes against the very ideas of equal voice and one person, one vote.

ENDING VOTER SUPPRESSION

The Supreme Court's decision in Citizens United went a long way toward undermining American democracy, but it's not the only effort that the oligarchs and their political allies are waging in that effort. In 2013, in another disastrous but less-known Supreme Court decision, *Shelby County v. Holder*, the Court gutted key provisions of the 1965 Voting Rights Act. That landmark 1965 legislation required states and local governments that have demonstrated a pattern of discrimination to clear with the federal government any proposed changes to their voting laws.

Of course, Congress passed the Voting Rights Act

law in the first place because many states had implemented laws to keep people—mostly black and poor people—from voting. But, incredibly, the Court found, in a 5–4 decision, that discrimination against voters was no longer a problem, and so the federal government no longer had to protect American citizens and their right to vote.

Literally, within days after that decision was rendered, Republican officials around the country moved aggressively to pass laws designed to make it harder for people to vote—African-Americans, Latinos, poor people, young people, senior citizens: people who would, in large numbers, likely be voting against them. A favorite approach taken by many states is—under the guise of protecting against "voter fraud" that study after study has shown to be virtually nonexistent—to pass legislation requiring all voters to have government-issued photo-identification cards. The patterns are unmistakable. There is a concerted effort to prevent people of color and poor people from voting. Eleven percent of eligible voters do not have a qualifying photo ID, and these voters are disproportionately black, Latino, and poor.

A recent academic paper analyzing the 2014 elections found that "a strict ID law could be expected to depress Latino turnout by 9.3 points, Black turnout by 8.6 points, and Asian American turnout by 12.5 points." After analyzing the data, the scholars found that "Democratic turnout drops by an estimated 8.8 percentage points in general elections when strict photo identification laws are in place," compared with just 3.6 percentage points for Republicans.

At a time when we should be making it easier for people to vote, Republican governors and legislatures acted quickly to do the exact opposite. They restricted early voting, eliminated same-day registration, and aggressively purged voter rolls. Not only did Alabama require photo-identification cards, it closed offices in black communities where people could obtain the cards. The Brennan Center for Justice found that in 2016, fifteen states had new voting restrictions in place for the first time in a presidential election. In a close election, these new laws aimed at further depressing already historically low voter participation could easily sway the outcome of the election. To impact the outcome of an election by making it harder to vote is beyond cynical. It should be illegal.

Further, in many parts of the country, it is more difficult for people in minority communities to cast a ballot on Election Day. In 2012, African-Americans waited twice as long on average to vote as whites. Some voters in minority precincts waited upward of six or seven hours to cast a ballot. How many people who had every intention of participating in our democracy that day simply left, disillusioned, because we made it too difficult for them to vote for the candidate of their choice?

What we are seeing today is, to use Yogi Berra's famous phrase, "Déjà vu all over again." As a nation, we have seen this before. The approach now may take a somewhat different form, but the goal is exactly the same as it was before the Voting Rights Act. Political cowards are doing everything they can to keep people from voting. They are making it harder for people to register and to participate in the political process.

This curtailing of our electoral democracy should offend the conscience of every American. The fight for minority voting rights is a fight for justice. It is inseparable from the struggle for democracy itself.

What should we do? We cannot afford to have our democracy curtailed because of court decisions, partisan discrimination, and blatant gerrymandering.

We can start by demanding that Congress restore the

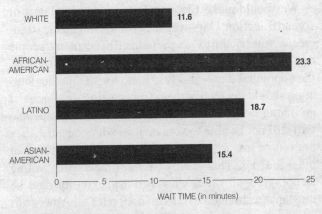

Average Wait Time by Race and Ethnicity Nationwide, Election Day, 2012

WHITE — 11.6
AFRICAN-AMERICAN — 23.3
LATINO — 18.7
ASIAN-AMERICAN — 15.4

WAIT TIME (in minutes)

Data Source: Cooperative Congressional Election Study

"preclearance" requirement under Section 5 of the Voting Rights Act, to again protect minority voters from being disenfranchised and discriminated against in states and counties that have a pattern of doing just that. And we must insist that the Voting Rights Act be expanded in scope so that no American, regardless of skin color or national origin or age, is prevented from voting freely, without hindrance from local authorities.

We need to encourage voter registration, not make it a burden for voters. We should join other countries in making certain that every person is automatically registered to vote when he/she turns eighteen. Every person who moves to a new state should be automatically registered to vote as soon as he/she has a new postal address. The burden of registering voters should be on the state, not the individual voter.

We must put an end to discriminatory practices that disproportionately purge minority and poor voters from voting rolls. We must stop those who pare down voter rolls with the goal of making sure that fewer—not more—Americans vote.

We should make Election Day a federal holiday, or spread Election Day over a two-day weekend, to increase voters' ability to participate. Too many people don't vote because they simply don't have the time on the appointed day—and yes, some forget. Neither situation should disqualify them from casting a ballot. And no matter how we structure election days, some people will still not be able to vote on those days because they are out of town, working, sick, or for any number of other reasons. That is why we must make early voting an option for all voters who need the flexibility. And we must make absentee ballots an option for all Americans who request them—with no tests or conditions that unnecessarily hinder voters from requesting and receiving those ballots.

We must restore voting rights to people who have had them taken away. Today a largely unseen tragedy is taking place throughout the country as a result of our broken criminal justice system, and it is having a profoundly negative impact upon our democracy. Many states take away the right to vote from convicted felons, and do not restore that right even after these people have "paid their debt to society."

This makes no sense whatsoever. We supposedly want those being released from jail to become productive members of society, but we deny them the right to participate in democracy? An estimated 13 percent of African-American men have lost the right to vote due to felony convictions. That is unacceptable. We need to re-enfranchise the more than 2 million African-Americans who have had their right to vote taken away. They are no longer in prison, and deserve to have their rights fully restored.

Moreover, it is incumbent on Congress, on state governments, and on local governments to make sure that there are sufficient polling places and poll workers to prevent long lines from forming at the polls. We spend hundreds of billions of dollars to defend this nation. We can and should spend the money necessary to defend democracy by making sure polling places are adequately staffed, that voting machines function well, and that however voting is tabulated, there are paper ballots that can be counted and audited in cases where the voting is close or contested.

THE KOCH BROTHERS

The Koch brothers—the second-wealthiest family in America, with a net worth of at least $82 billion—are the leading force in the oligarchic movement. Their company, Koch Industries, is the second-largest privately run business in America, with an estimated revenue of $115 billion in 2013. It has its tentacles in many areas of the economy, but makes most of its money in the extraction and refining of oil.

During the first term of the Obama administration, no fewer than eighteen billionaires came together under the Koch brothers' leadership to oppose the president's initiatives and move this country in an extreme right-wing direction. Some of the other billionaires involved were Richard Mellon Scaife, an heir to the Mellon banking and Gulf oil fortunes; Henry and Linda Bradley, defense contractors; John M. Olin, involved in chemicals and munitions; the DeVos family, the founders of the Amway corporation; and the Coors brewing family of Colorado.

In *Dark Money*, her brilliant book on the Kochs, Jane Mayer writes that these billionaire brothers "subsidized networks of seemingly unconnected think tanks and academic programs and spawned advocacy groups to make their arguments in the national political debate. They hired lobbyists to push their interests in Congress and operatives to create synthetic grassroots groups to give their movement political momentum on the ground. In addition, they financed legal groups and judicial junkets to press their cases in the courts. Eventually, they added to this a private political machine that rivaled, and threatened to subsume, the Republican Party. Much of this activism was cloaked in secrecy and presented as philanthropy, leaving almost no money trail that the public could trace. But cumulatively it formed, as one of their operatives boasted in 2015, a *fully integrated network*."

In 2015, the Koch brothers announced that they and their network intended to spend $750 million to support political candidates and promote their policies during the 2016 election cycle. That is more money than either the Democratic National Committee or the Republican National Committee will spend. The Kochs' goal was to make certain that Republicans continue to control the U.S. Senate and U.S. House, as well as win victories in state and local races all across the country. According to more than a few political experts, the Koch family now has more political power than either the Democratic or Republican parties.

Who are the Koch brothers and what do they stand for? The media often describes them as "conservative" or "small-government advocates." The truth is that they are much, much more than that. They are right-wing extremists, with unlimited financial resources, who are leading the most significant effort in modern American history to move this country into an oligarchic form of society and to repeal virtually every major piece of legislation passed in the last seventy-five years that supports the needs of working families.

What are their goals? In 1980, David Koch ran for vice president on the Libertarian Party ticket and helped fund its campaign activities. I understand that 1980 is a long time ago, but there is no evidence to suggest that the Koch brothers' views on the major issues facing our country have substantively changed.

What is frightening is how much success they have had over the years in pushing some of these ideas into the political mainstream. Back in 1980, they were considered "fringe" and "crazy" proposals, and Koch's Libertarian Party received almost no support. Today the views of the Koch brothers are the dominant ideology in the Republican Party, and candidates all over the country publicly defend them.

From their earliest days, the Koch brothers understood that their power rested not in their ideas but in the ability of their money to buy elections. One of the major planks of the Koch brothers' Libertarian Party platform back in 1980 was to "urge the repeal of federal campaign finance laws, and the immediate abolition of the despotic Federal Election Commission." They understood then, and they understand now, that the success was tied to the ability of the superwealthy to buy elections.

Let us give credit where credit is due. The Koch brothers, through their legal front organizations and with the active support of the Republican Party, won the 5–4 Supreme Court decision in the Citizens United case, which went a very long way to implementing that Libertarian Party plank to repeal campaign finance laws. But the Koch brothers are not through yet. They want to go further than Citizens United. They want to eliminate *all* restrictions on campaign spending, and that is precisely what their legal organizations are now working on.

If they are successful, it will mean billionaires could *directly* contribute unlimited sums to the candidates of their choice. It would mean the oligarchs could fully fund and direct the campaigns of their candidates. It would mean that elected officials would essentially become part of the company payroll. That is the political future the Koch brothers and their allies want for America. That is their view of democracy: a nation in which elected officials are bought and paid for by the moneyed interests.

In general, I'm not a great fan of litmus tests for Supreme Court nominees. But during my campaign I made it very clear that I would only appoint nominees who were very public about their willingness to overturn Citizens United. I cannot emphasize this enough: That decision is undermining American democracy and moving us closer and closer to an oligarchy. I was glad that Secretary Clinton took the same position I did.

While ending all campaign finance regulations is one of their major goals, the Koch brothers are interested in many other issues. Their being the second-wealthiest family in America, it should not be surprising they want to pay less in taxes and hate the idea of progressive taxation. But they go way, way further than that. The Libertarian Party platform that David Koch helped draft opposed "all personal and corporate income taxation, including capital gains taxes," and supported "the eventual repeal of all taxation." *All* taxation. The platform even went as far as encouraging the rich and powerful to break the law and stop paying taxes: "As an interim measure, all criminal and civil sanctions against tax evasion should be terminated immediately."

As the owners of a major fossil fuel company, and leading funders of climate change denial groups, they also supported abolishing the Environmental Protection Agency and the Department of Energy. Great idea: Let's just put the fox, a particularly rapacious fox, in charge of the henhouse.

And it gets even better. Here are some more of the ideas David Koch ran on. This is the kind of America they want to create:

- "We favor the abolition of Medicare and Medicaid programs."
- "We oppose any compulsory insurance or tax-supported plan to provide health services, including those which finance abortion services."
- "We favor the repeal of the fraudulent, virtually bankrupt, and increasingly oppressive Social Security system."
- "We propose the abolition of the governmental Postal Service. . . . In addition to being inefficient, [it] encourages governmental surveillance of private correspondence."
- "We support repeal of . . . minimum wage laws."
- "Government schools lead to the indoctrination of children. . . . Government ownership, operation, regulation, and subsidy of schools and colleges should be ended."
- "We condemn compulsory education laws . . . and we call for [their] immediate repeal."
- "We call for the privatization of the public roads and national highway system."
- "We oppose all government welfare, relief projects, and 'aid to the poor' programs."

By any rational standard, these are extreme views. Yet, they are the views of the very people helping bankroll today's Republican Party. So, the next time you see a glitzy ad on television funded by one of the Koch brothers' front groups, professing to care about the issues facing ordinary Americans, please remember what they really stand for and what kind of America the Kochs want.

WHY IT ALL MATTERS

Many people I know are passionately concerned about
health care, the environment, the economy, human rights,
and a host of other very, very important issues. Campaign finance reform, not so much. Let's face it,
campaign finance reform is not exactly a sexy issue.
But what many people don't see or understand is the
direct connection between campaign funding and the
development and implementation of public policy, including the very issues they care deeply about.

Please understand. The wealthy and powerful are not
contributing to candidates and parties for the fun of it.
They want their pound of flesh. If they make a contribution, they want action on their concerns. The more
powerful entities don't even need a member of Congress
to write the legislation they want anymore—they write
it themselves. All they need is someone to introduce it
and shepherd it through the legislative process.

Here are a few examples of what is achieved by money
in politics and a corrupt campaign finance system:

In 2008, the United States suffered the worst economic downturn since the Great Depression, when Wall
Street collapsed. Many experts believe that this horrific
recession was precipitated by the passage of bipartisan
legislation enacted during Bill Clinton's administration
that deregulated Wall Street and the activities of the
largest financial interests in the country.

In order to get that legislation passed, to repeal the
Glass-Steagall Act, which for decades had kept giant
commercial banks, investment banks, and insurance
companies from merging, the financial sector spent
more than $1.2 billion over five years in lobbying and
campaign contributions. They got what they wanted,
and the American people got a terrible recession.

In the United States, uniquely among industrialized

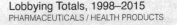

Lobbying Totals, 1998–2015
PHARMACEUTICALS / HEALTH PRODUCTS

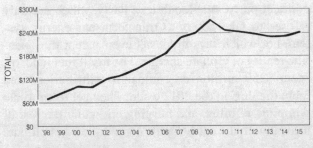

Data Source: Center for Responsive Politics

nations, drug companies can charge any price they want for prescription drugs. As a result, we pay the highest prices in the world, by far, for the medicines we use. The pharmaceutical industry has 1,399 lobbyists working for them at a cost of about $240 million a year. That's more than two and a half times more lobbyists than there are members of Congress. During the 2012 campaign cycle, the pharmaceutical industry contributed over $50 million to members of both parties. Honestly, I cannot remember Big Pharma ever losing a major legislative battle. They win, the American people lose.

The U.S. has a defense budget of some $600 billion a year. This is larger than that of the next seven nations combined. The defense budget is rampant with cost overruns, fraud, and all kinds of unnecessary spending. The military-industrial complex spent about $164 million on campaign contributions and lobbying during the 2012 election cycle. This means they get their weapons systems, but there is less money available for our social needs at home.

The scientific community is absolutely clear that climate change is caused by human activity, primarily by the emissions of carbon dioxide from burning fossil fuels, and that it is the greatest environmental crisis facing our nation and the world. Yet we have a major political party, the Republican Party, which not only refuses to take action to transform our energy system, but which says it doesn't even accept the scientific reality of climate change. The fossil fuel industry spent $250 million on campaign contributions and lobbying during the 2012 cycle. They get to continue pumping, refining, and burning oil, while the rest of us deal with the catastrophic consequences of climate change.

GETTING BIG MONEY OUT OF POLITICS

On November 19, 1863, standing on the bloodstained battlefield of Gettysburg, Pennsylvania, Abraham Lincoln delivered one of the best-remembered speeches in American history. At the conclusion of his Gettysburg Address, Lincoln stated "that we here highly resolve that these dead shall not have died in vain . . . that this nation, under God, shall have a new birth of freedom . . . and that government of the people, by the people, for the people, shall not perish from the earth." In the year 2016, with a political campaign finance system that is corrupt and increasingly controlled by billionaires and special interests, I fear very much that, in fact, "government of the people, by the people, for the people" will perish in the United States of America.

We cannot allow that to happen.

Six years ago, as a result of the Citizens United decision, by a 5–4 vote the U.S. Supreme Court essentially said to the wealthiest people in this country: You already own much of the American economy. Now, we are going to give you the opportunity to purchase the U.S. government, the White House, the U.S. Senate, the U.S. House, governors' seats, legislatures, and state judicial branches as well.

The Citizens United decision hinges on the absurd notion that money is speech, corporations are people, and giving huge piles of undisclosed cash to politicians in exchange for access and influence does not constitute corruption.

During this campaign cycle, billions of dollars from the wealthiest people in this country are already flooding the political process. Super PACs—a direct outgrowth of the Citizens United decision—are enabling the wealthiest people and the largest corporations in this country to contribute unlimited amounts of money.

The situation has become so absurd that super PACs, which theoretically operate independently of the actual candidates, often have more money and more influence over campaigns than the candidates themselves.

As former president Jimmy Carter has said, unlimited money in politics "violates the essence of what made America a great country in its political system. Now, it's just an oligarchy, with unlimited political bribery being the essence of getting the nominations for president or to elect the president. And the same thing applies to governors and U.S. senators and Congress members. So now we've just seen a complete subversion of our political system as a payoff to major contributors, who want and expect and sometimes get favors for themselves after the election's over."

The need for real campaign finance reform is not a progressive issue. It is not a conservative issue. It is an American issue. It is an issue that should concern all Americans—regardless of their political point of view— who wish to preserve the essence of the longest-standing democracy in the world, a government that is supposed to represent all of the people and not just a handful of powerful special interests.

During my campaign for president, I made campaign finance reform one of my highest priorities. I told the American people that, if elected president, I would take the following steps to combat the growth of oligarchy. I am not going to be the next president, but this is the right agenda for the next president to pursue. Real campaign finance reform must happen as soon as possible. Here's what I think it should entail:

First, we must overturn, through a constitutional amendment, the Citizens United decision, as well as the 1976 *Buckley v. Valeo* ruling, which introduced the absurd notion that spending money on behalf of a candidate or a political party is a form of protected speech. Moreover, we must fight to overturn the 2014 *McCutcheon v. FEC* decision, which struck down limits on how much an individual can contribute to a national party and to a candidate's campaign over a two-year period. We must make it clear that Congress and the states have the power to regulate money in elections. I have been a proud sponsor and leading champion of such an amendment in the Senate.

We need to pass legislation to require wealthy individuals and corporations who make large campaign contributions to disclose where their money is going. We must insist on complete transparency regarding the funding of campaigns, including through disclosure of contributions to outside spending groups. There is no reason why the next president can't, through an executive order, require government contractors to disclose political spending intended to influence contracting decisions.

We need to move toward a publicly funded, transparent system of campaign financing that amplifies small donations, along the lines of the Fair Elections Now Act that I have been pleased to cosponsor.

Our vision for American democracy should be a nation in which all people, regardless of their income, can participate in the political process, and can run for office without begging for contributions from the wealthy.

Our vision for the future of this country should be one in which candidates are not telling billionaires at special forums what they can do for them in exchange for large contributions.

Our vision for democracy should be one in which candidates are speaking to the vast majority of our people—working people, the middle class, low-income people, the elderly, the children, the sick, and the poor—and discussing with them their ideas as to how we can improve lives for all of the people in this country.

One of the truly remarkable aspects of my campaign was that we showed the world that a successful national campaign could be run without a super PAC, and without being dependent on big-money contributions. We received some $232 million from 8 million individual contributions, from 2.5 million people, averaging $27 per contribution.

What my campaign showed, and what poll after poll has shown, is that the American people are sick and tired of big money buying elections and democracy being undermined.

The time is now for campaign finance reform—real campaign finance reform.

TWO

THE DECLINE OF THE AMERICAN MIDDLE CLASS

Today in America, more than 43 million Americans—including nearly 20 percent of all children in our country—live in poverty, many in extreme poverty. Almost 28 million Americans have no health insurance, and thousands of those die every year because they don't get to a doctor in time. Millions of bright kids can't afford to go to college without plunging deeply into debt. Millions of seniors and far too many disabled veterans struggle to stay alive on inadequate Social Security checks.

Yet in the midst of all this economic turmoil and pain, there is another reality. The fact is, the wealthiest people and largest corporations in this country have never had it so good. While most Americans are hurting financially and deeply frightened about the future, the very rich are getting much richer, as the majority of new income is now going to the top 1 percent.

The United States is the wealthiest country in the history of the world. But that reality means very little for most Americans, because so much of that wealth is owned and controlled by a tiny handful of individuals.

Share of Total Before-Tax Income
Going to the Top 1% and 0.5%, 1920–2010

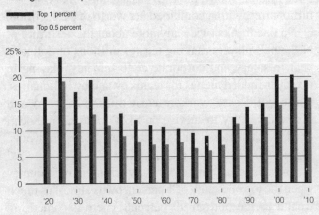

Data Source: Emmanuel Saez, based on IRS data

We now have more income and wealth inequality than any other major country, and the gap between the very rich and everyone else is wider than at any time since the 1920s. To my mind, addressing wealth and income inequality is the great moral issue of our time, it is the great economic issue of our time, and it is the great political issue of our time.

Now, I fully realize that the concept of "distribution of wealth" makes my Republican friends very nervous. The truth is, however, that there has been a massive redistribution of wealth over the last thirty-five years. Unfortunately, that redistribution has gone in precisely the wrong direction, with trillions of dollars leaving the pockets of the middle class and ending up in the bank accounts of the top one-tenth of 1 percent. In 1979, the top one-tenth of 1 percent owned about 7 percent of the wealth in this country. Today it owns 22 percent.

The number of billionaires in the United States has grown tenfold in the past fifteen years. In 2000, the U.S.

had 51 billionaires, with a combined net worth of just $480 billion. Today, the U.S. has a record-breaking 540 billionaires, with a combined net worth of $2.4 trillion.

No one thinks twice anymore about the absurdity of basketball players making tens of millions of dollars a year in salary and corporate endorsements, playing in taxpayer-funded arenas for teams owned by billionaires, while child-care workers earn minimum wage and disabled vets try to survive on $12,000 a year in Social Security payments. That's just the way the system works, we're told. There are no alternatives.

There is something profoundly wrong in our country when the top one-tenth of 1 percent owns almost as much wealth as the bottom 90 percent. There is something profoundly wrong when the twenty wealthiest Americans own more wealth than the bottom 150 million people— almost half of our entire population. There is something profoundly wrong when one family—the Waltons, who founded and own Wal-Mart—has more wealth than the bottom 130 million Americans.

But it is not just a grotesque level of *wealth* disparity that we are experiencing. It is also horrendous inequality in terms of *income,* the amount that we earn every year. Incredibly, in the last several years, 52 percent of all new income being generated in this country is now going to the top 1 percent. In many families, mom works, dad works, and the kids work—and they still struggle to get by. Meanwhile over half of all new income being created goes to the people on top.

When we were kids, we read about "Banana Republics" in Latin America and other oligarchic societies that existed in countries around the world, where a handful of families held almost all of the wealth and power. Fellow Americans, take a look around you. See what's going on in our country today. This obscene level of inequality is immoral. It is bad economics. It is unsustainable. This type of rigged and unfair economy is not what America is supposed to be about. And it's not what America used to be.

In the decades following World War II, our economy expanded on a scale previously unimagined. American industrial might—the same might that helped win the war—was at its peak, providing good-paying and stable employment for millions of Americans. We had factories that actually made things—everything from the cars and trucks we drove, to the tractors and steel beams used in agriculture and construction, to the furniture that filled our homes and offices, to the clothes we wore, and so much more. And the workers in those factories were often unionized, and had good benefits—health insurance, paid sick leave, and vacation time. They negotiated for regular pay raises and had defined-benefit pension plans to ensure that they could retire in dignity. They entered the middle class in droves.

Millions of returning vets went to college on the GI Bill, and graduated with degrees that gave them a pathway into a growing array of middle-class professions. They became the doctors, lawyers, teachers, engineers, and businesspeople who grew the economy and created wealth. They helped usher in great advances in technology and medicine.

The GI Bill, combined with a strong government-backed secondary mortgage system, also opened the door to homeownership for the first time to millions of American families. Owning a home allowed families to build personal wealth, provided greater economic mobility, and gave them an asset that they could borrow against to start businesses or send their kids to college.

It was a time of massive investment in our infrastructure—particularly our transportation infrastructure—creating decent-paying jobs, stimulating local economies, and driving up productivity. President

Eisenhower created an ambitious interstate highway system to connect all of the states in a single, coordinated, and modern road network. San Francisco, Washington, and Los Angeles embarked on building new subway systems, while many other cities expanded existing ones. We built and expanded airports all across the country.

And as the economy grew, it gave rise to a broad middle class that shared in the benefits of that growth. According to the Economic Policy Institute, between 1947 and 1973 real family income for the top quintile (the top 20 percent of earners) grew by 84.8 percent. Meanwhile, the real family income of the broad middle (the three middle quintiles, composed of 60 percent of income earners) grew by 99.4 percent. Perhaps most significantly, real family income for the lowest quintile of earners rose more quickly than any other group's, by 116.1 percent. In other words, the rich were doing well, the middle class was expanding, and fewer people were living in poverty.

Look, I am not suggesting it was a utopian time. There were also great struggles. Women, who'd broken into the workforce in unprecedented numbers to fill domestic labor shortages during the war, largely retreated again as men came home from Europe and the Pacific. And the women who did stay in the labor force were paid just 50 cents for every dollar men were paid for the exact same work. African-Americans, who also made gains during the war, came home to pernicious racism and were shut out of much of the economic gains in the postwar years. They were routinely discriminated against for jobs and mortgages, which contributed to the wealth gap between whites and nonwhites that we see today, and in many states every effort was made to keep them from even voting. Undocumented Latino immigrants waged battle after battle for some shred of dignity and respect as they toiled in the fields.

And it was a time of great labor strife, too. In just the year immediately following the end of the war, 5 million workers in almost every sector of the economy went on strike to protest layoffs and press for long-delayed wage increases and improved working conditions. Rather than siding with the legitimate and pent-up demands of workers, Congress instead passed the Taft-Harley Act in 1947, which greatly restricted and undermined the union movement, allowing states to establish so-called right-to-work laws that are a major reason for the rapid decline of private-sector unions.

No, it was certainly not a utopian time. But, it was a time of enormous economic growth, and while there was income and wealth inequality, the benefits of the economy were far more equitably shared with the working families that made up the broad middle.

That is, until powerful special interests started demanding a bigger and bigger slice of the pie.

They demanded the deregulation of industries, particularly banking, so they could make greater profits. They pushed for free trade deals that decimated our manufacturing base and created a race to the bottom. They made it harder for workers to unionize, and fought increases in the minimum wage. They reduced job-creating investments in our infrastructure. They shredded the social safety net. The political establishment became thoroughly dominated by people for whom unfettered and unstrained free market capitalism was virtually a religion.

They argued that "freedom" was no longer about workers having the right to earn decent incomes and live their lives in dignity and security. No, "freedom" was now about employers having the right to pay their employees

the lowest wages possible without government interference. "Freedom" was about the right of Wall Street
and hedge fund managers to make incredible amounts
of money, without regard for whether their investments
destroyed lives or fouled the environment. "Freedom"
was the ability of billionaires to buy elections and create
a government that worked for them, not the middle class
or working families.

The result of all that: The great American middle
class, once the envy of the world, has been in decline
ever since. And those who remain in the middle class
find themselves struggling to stay there, working longer hours, sometimes at multiple jobs, for lower wages.

In America today the median household income—
the amount the household right in the middle of our
society makes—is almost $1,400 less than it was in
1999, after adjusting for inflation. The real median income of full-time male workers is $2,144 less than it was
forty-three years ago. And the trends seem to be accel-
erating. And over the past decade, a staggering 81 percent
of U.S. households saw "flat" or "falling" incomes.

With wages falling, it should come as no surprise that
Americans are working longer hours. In fact, we work
longer hours than the people of any other major developed country on earth. Japan is renowned as a society
of very hard workers. We now work seventy-one hours
a year more than they do.

Over a hundred years ago, workers in this country
took to the streets to fight for a forty-hour workweek.
Marching under huge banners, they told the world that
they were human beings, not beasts of burden. They
wanted time with their families, time for education, time
for culture. Well, a hundred years have come and gone,
and we are moving backward. Incredibly, according to
statistics from Gallup, the average full-time employee
in America now works about forty-seven hours each and

every week, and nearly 40 percent work at least fifty hours a week.

And many of today's jobs provide little or no vacation or sick time. Last year, 41 percent of workers didn't take a single day of paid vacation, and about half of all low-wage workers don't get any paid vacation at all from their employers. Moreover, 36 percent of private-sector workers don't have access to a single day of paid sick leave.

Today work is all that we are supposed to do. If you get sick, you go to work or you may lose your job. If your kid is in the hospital, you go to work. If your father is dying, you go to work. If you have a baby, you are back on the job in two or three weeks because you don't have paid leave. If you're in a white-collar job, you put in the extra hours because that's what everyone else is doing, and you need to get ahead. You take your cell phone and laptop with you wherever you go.

In Vermont and throughout this country, it is not uncommon for people to be working two or three jobs just to pay the bills and receive some health care benefits. All across the country people are working hard, and going nowhere in a hurry.

When I was in Des Moines, Iowa, I visited a farmers market. I spoke to a young man there who worked with a church group that collected unsold produce for a local emergency food shelf. I was curious about the people who went to the food shelf and asked him what percentage of the people who went there had jobs. His response: Over 90 percent of the people who got help from the food shelf were working, but their wages were too low to adequately feed their families. And that's true all over the country. Millions of Americans are working full-time, but not making enough to survive.

A few years ago I was shopping in a supermarket in Burlington and a woman came up to me. "Bernie," she said, "my husband and I have one child. We would like to have more. But I'm working two jobs and he's working three jobs and we don't think we can be the kind of parents we want to be given the hours that we're working." And that's what I heard all over the country throughout my campaign. Marriages strained, parents not having enough time with their kids. People exhausted and stressed out from overwork.

Meanwhile, many have no job at all. In January 2009, the last month that President George W. Bush was in office, our economy was losing 800,000 jobs a month. The economy has thankfully improved significantly over the last eight years, and President Obama deserves a lot of credit for that. But let's not kid ourselves: Unemployment remains much, much too high.

The government calculates unemployment in a number of ways. The *official* unemployment rate that you read about in the papers every month has been at or below 5 percent since October 2015. Not too bad. Unfortunately, the *real* unemployment rate is about double that number, and is a lot higher in some parts of the country.

The reality is that the *official* unemployment rate that the media loves to talk about doesn't count workers who have given up looking for jobs or who are working part-time when they want to work full-time. And about 20 million Americans find themselves in exactly that position. If you're in a community where there are no jobs, and you are not "actively" looking for work, you are not *officially* unemployed. If you are one of the millions of Americans who are working fewer than thirty hours a week because your employer has figured out a way to avoid providing you with health insurance, you are considered "employed," even if you can't survive on what you earn.

And the employment situation is even worse for

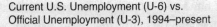

Current U.S. Unemployment (U-6) vs.
Official Unemployment (U-3), 1994–present

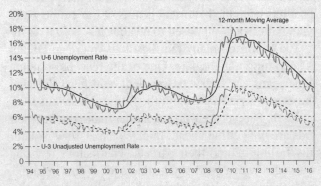

Data Source: U.S. Bureau of Labor Statistics

young Americans. One of the great economic crises that is rarely talked about is the unemployment rate for young people who don't go to college. The truth is that youth unemployment is off the charts. This is true for white high school graduates, and the situation is even worse for young African-Americans, Latinos, and Native Americans—minority youth unemployment is 30 to 40 percent, and in some parts of the country it's much higher than that. And when young people cannot find jobs and earn an income within mainstream society, they often drift away into alternative, and often destructive, behaviors.

Part of the "American Dream" has always been about parents working hard so that their kids can do better than they did. That is what made us an optimistic country, a land unique in the world for the opportunities it provided. That's why people from all over the world, including my father, came here. Things may be tough now, parents reasoned, but they will be better for our kids. That was the case with my family. That was the case with many millions of American families. Dad and mom would work hard and sacrifice. The kids would get a good education, and do better than their parents. That has been the historical genius of our country and what America is supposed to be about.

Today, for too many families, the American Dream is becoming a nightmare. One of the reasons so many Americans are angry, despondent, and fearful is that they are worried sick about the future that awaits their children. Parents are working harder than ever, but their kids are not getting ahead. In many cases, they're actually falling behind their parents. The factory that dad worked at with a good-paying union job is now in China. Will their son, who graduated high school, ever find a decent job? Will their daughter, who dropped out of college, ever be able to pay off her $60,000 student loan while working a low-wage job? Will the kids ever earn enough to be able to purchase homes of their own?

Here's the truth: If we don't turn this economy around, it is likely that, for the first time in the modern history of our country, our kids may have a lower standard of living than their parents. That's the race to the bottom. That's a nation where our people are becoming poorer and poorer. That's something we must not allow to happen.

For many older workers, the economic situation today is truly frightening. Many of them have seen their decent-paying manufacturing jobs go abroad, and they are now working for 50 or 75 percent of what they used to earn. Many have been denied the pensions they were promised after decades of work for a company. Many have had to draw down their life savings to pay daily expenses. Taken together, this is a big reason why more than half of older workers in this country have no savings set aside for retirement. Let me say that again: More than half of older workers have no retirement savings, at all. None.

And the reality is, as I will discuss in greater detail later, it is almost impossible to get by on just Social Security retirement alone. How does one get by on Social Security benefits of $10,000 or $11,000 a year? You do the arithmetic. Rent, food, heat, electric, phone, plus the copayments and deductibles for health care and prescription drugs. Nobody makes it on $10,000 or $11,000 a year, but millions are forced to try.

During the campaign, I had the extraordinary opportunity to visit with people all across the country who are living lives in the shadows, lives that few Americans hear about from the media. These are Americans in inner cities and rural areas. They are black, white, Latino, Native American, and Asian-American. They are the people who struggle every day to find the money to feed their kids, to pay their bills, and to put gas in the car to get to work. In the wealthiest country in the history of the world, they are the disappearing part of the disappearing middle class. I am very grateful that they were willing to share their stories with me.

I held a town meeting at a church in Flint, Michigan, a community devastated by the loss of automobile manufacturing jobs, a loss exacerbated by our failed trade policies. Fifty years ago, Flint was one of the most prosperous cities in America. Working-class people had good jobs with good benefits working for General Motors. Today, years after those jobs disappeared, Flint is one of the poorest cities in America. Poverty, high unemployment, boarded-up buildings, crime, and poor schools is the story of Flint today.

Recently, Flint received international attention when it was revealed that, in order to save money, the city started using water from the highly polluted Flint River. I will never forget a private meeting Jane and I had with Flint residents, who described what happened to their children after they drank the toxic, lead-filled water. In one of the most painful and emotional meetings I have ever attended, we heard from a mother who described her daughter's loss of cognitive abilities because of toxic lead in the water. A once gregarious and bright child now had serious memory loss and was in special education.

Detroit, Michigan, was also built around the thriving auto industry. In fact, on a per capita basis Detroit was the richest city in all of America in 1960. Motor City, USA. But "industrial restructuring" that led to the closure of the auto plants literally gutted the city. Detroit has lost 60 percent of its population since 1950. The downtown is dotted with empty lots where buildings used to stand. Median household income in Detroit is now less than half the national average and its poverty rate is three times the national rate.

I talked to teachers in Detroit who told me how the school system was failing the children and on the verge of fiscal collapse. A few years earlier, I had met with young workers in that same city, who described what it

A private meeting with Flint, Michigan, parents before our Detroit rally. (Hilary Hess, Revolution Messaging)

was like to live on $7.25 an hour working at McDonald's. One young man was working twenty hours a week in one restaurant, getting on a bus to another McDonald's, and then getting on another bus to a third job. In Detroit, I also noticed the lack of grocery stores where people could buy fresh food. Instead, there was an abundance of fast-food restaurants and corner stores where people were charged high prices for poor-quality food.

Baltimore, Maryland, is another once vibrant middle-class city that has been gutted. Since 1970, Maryland has lost more manufacturing jobs than all but four states, and more than a hundred thousand alone in Baltimore.

In Baltimore, I had a very moving meeting with African-American community and church leaders from throughout the country. Not only did they address the effects of dramatic job loss that has nearly wiped out the city's middle class, but they made the extraordinary point that it is *very expensive to be poor.* Poor people actually pay higher prices for food, for financial services, for furniture, and for other basic necessities than do middle-class or wealthy people. Surrounded by a large gaggle of reporters and TV cameras, I walked through the desolate neighborhood where Freddie Gray was killed. What I saw there were boarded-up homes and shops. I was told that in a neighborhood of many thousands of people, there were no bank branches or supermarkets, only payday lenders, corner shops, and liquor stores.

Later in the campaign, I returned to Baltimore for a town meeting with Ben Jealous, the former head of the NAACP, the actor-activist Danny Glover, and others. I learned that there were tens of thousands of heroin addicts in Baltimore, with very little treatment available to them. Surrounded by Secret Service agents—who were a little bit nervous—we took a walk that evening through an area in the middle of the city that consisted of vacant lots and boarded-up homes. We were told that late at night the area came to life—with drug dealers selling their products.

Middle-class decline is not just an urban phenomenon. McDowell County, West Virginia, was once a stable area—never particularly wealthy, but there were jobs. However, when the U.S. Steel Corporation pulled up stakes and the coal mines closed, the bottom fell out in McDowell County. It is now one of the most depressed areas of Appalachia, with high rates of poverty, unemployment, and incarceration. McDowell County has one of the lowest levels of life expectancy in America, and it is still declining. People there are actually dying at a younger age today than the members of their parents' generation did, mostly as a result of drugs, alcohol, suicide—and despair. Yet, I saw incredible courage in the midst of enormous problems. I held an extraordinary town meeting there with hundreds of people, and it was clear they were not giving up. They were fighting for the opportunities they needed to improve their lives.

In Cedar Rapids, Iowa, I walked an informational picket line with workers who were attempting to negotiate a contract with their employer, Ingredion Inc. This is a huge company that processes agricultural crops like corn and potatoes into ingredients for the food and beverage industries. While Ingredion was paying $6 million a year to their CEO, the company wanted to make employees work longer hours for lower wages, cut overtime pay, and offer fewer holidays and vacation days. Even when the jobs remain in this country, it is harder and harder for workers to earn a living wage that affords a middle-class lifestyle. Just another example of workers getting squeezed more and more by corporate greed. Just another example of the rich getting richer while everyone else gets poorer.

Make no mistake, the economic pie keeps getting

bigger. It's just that the poor and the middle class are getting smaller and smaller slices. The decline of the middle class has been dramatic, with painful consequences for millions of Americans.

We must turn that around. We must create an economy that works for all, not just the people on top.

In the following chapter, I'll explain how we can do that.

THREE

ENDING A RIGGED ECONOMY

THE MINIMUM WAGE MUST BECOME A LIVING WAGE

In the wealthiest country in the history of the world, a basic principle of American economic life must be that if you work forty hours or more a week, you do not live in poverty.

Sadly, that is far from reality today.

Millions of Americans work for totally inadequate wages. The current federal minimum wage of $7.25 an hour is a starvation wage. It must be raised. The minimum wage must become a *living* wage—which means raising it to $15 an hour by 2020 and indexing it into the future. And we must also close the loophole that allows employers to pay tipped workers—waiters, waitresses, bartenders, barbers, hairdressers, taxi drivers, car wash assistants, valet parking attendants—a shamefully low $2.13 an hour.

It's been nine years since Congress passed legislation to increase the minimum wage. Since 1968, the minimum wage has lost over 30 percent of its purchasing power due to inflation.

In the year 2016, a job has got to lift workers out of

Percentage of Workers Paid Less than $15 Wage, According to Demographic

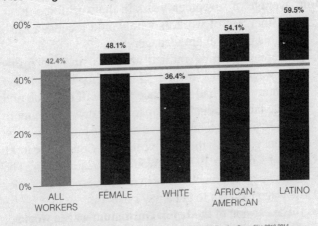

Data Source: NELP calculations from Current Population Survey Merged Outgoing Rotation Group files 2012-2014

poverty, not keep them in it. Raising the minimum wage to $15 an hour would benefit more than 75 million workers and their families. People can't survive on $7.25, and they can't make it on $10 or $12 an hour either.

Raising the minimum wage would give a particularly huge boost to minority workers. Today, more than half of all African-American workers and nearly 60 percent of Hispanic workers earn less than $15 an hour. In addition, according to the most recent statistics, women make up two-thirds of all minimum-wage workers. Increasing the minimum wage to $15 an hour would significantly boost the wages of more than 15 million women.

My Republican colleagues tell us that most minimum-wage workers out there are kids earning some pocket change. This is simply not true, and by perpetuating that lie, my colleagues are keeping tens of millions of working adults in poverty.

The average worker who would benefit from a $15-an-hour minimum wage is thirty-six years old with an average of seventeen years in the workforce. Less than 7 percent of workers who would receive a raise from this proposal are teenagers.

There is nothing radical about raising the minimum wage to $15 an hour. The reality is that if the minimum wage had kept pace with both inflation and average labor productivity since 1968, it would be more than $26 an hour today. Moreover, if the minimum wage had kept pace with the massive income gains of the top 1 percent since the 1970s, it would be $28 an hour. The rich have gotten much richer in recent years. It's time for low-wage workers to get a pay raise, too.

The erosion of the federal minimum wage is a major reason why more than 43 million Americans are living in poverty today. Many of those people actually work, but are still below the federal poverty line. Meanwhile, health care costs are going up, child-care costs are going up, college costs are going up, and housing costs are going up. But wages are not. Low-income workers need a significant boost in what they earn if they are going to live in dignity in today's economy.

Not too long ago, the establishment told us that a $15-an-hour minimum wage was unrealistic and unthinkable. Some thought it was "pie in the sky." But a grassroots movement of low-income working people across the country has refused to take no for an answer. These workers reached out to their communities and their fellow Americans and loudly and clearly stated: We cannot survive on $8 or $9 an hour. The minimum wage has got to be increased, not just to $10.10 an hour, not just to $12 an hour, but to a living wage of $15 an hour.

And the American people heard their pain, and are beginning to respond.

The cities of Seattle, Los Angeles, San Francisco, New York, and Washington, D.C., are all raising the minimum wage to $15 an hour. California and New York, two of the largest states in our country, did the same. As a result of these efforts, over 10 million workers in America will see their wages raised to $15 an hour.

By phasing in a pay raise for tens of millions of workers, we can raise living standards, lift millions of Americans out of poverty, and provide a much-needed boost to our economy.

Today, almost 70 percent of our gross domestic product (GDP) is dependent upon the purchasing power of consumers. If millions of American workers have no discretionary income to purchase goods and services, the economy falters.

On the other hand, when low-wage workers have money in their pockets they spend that money in grocery stores, restaurants, and businesses throughout this country. All of this new demand gives companies a reason to expand and hire more workers. This is a win-win-win situation for our economy. Poverty is reduced. New jobs are created. And we reduce the skyrocketing income inequality that currently exists in this country.

Right-wing Republicans disagree. Backed by billions from the Koch brothers and other corporate interests, the Republican Party now believes that government should do virtually nothing to protect the interests of low-income and working people. Not only do almost all Republicans oppose increasing the minimum wage, many of them want to abolish it altogether. They believe that any floor on wages is an unjust interference in the free market. If an employer in a high-unemployment area can hire someone for $4 an hour, that's just fine with them. In fact, according to their ideology, that's "freedom" at work.

Every time a minimum wage increase is proposed locally or nationally, conservative politicians and their billionaire campaign contributors claim that jobs will be destroyed. Time and time again they have been proven dead wrong.

My state of Vermont currently has the fifth-highest minimum wage in the country, at $9.60 an hour, and the fifth lowest official unemployment rate in the nation, at 3.3 percent. Meanwhile, Louisiana, which currently does not even have a state minimum wage on its books, has the fourth-highest unemployment rate in the country: 6.2 percent.

After San Jose, California, increased its minimum wage to $10 an hour four years ago, fast-food restaurants did not lay off workers—they added workers. In fact, by 2014, employment gains in San Jose exceeded statewide job growth.

San Francisco experienced impressive job gains in the restaurant industry after raising its minimum wage. According to the University of California, Berkeley, after the city increased the minimum wage, restaurants in San Francisco increased employment nearly 18 percent more than nearby counties in the Bay Area that had lower wages.

And in January of 2014, SeaTac, Washington, became the first city in America to raise its minimum wage to $15 an hour—which meant an immediate 63 percent pay increase for low-wage workers. And like clockwork, before this pay raise took effect, business owners warned of massive layoffs.

Scott Ostrander, the owner of Cedarbrook Lodge, said that he would be forced to shut down part of his hotel, eliminate jobs, and reduce the hours of his workforce if SeaTac increased the minimum wage to $15 an hour. But after the minimum wage was raised, Mr.

Ostrander moved ahead with a $16 million hotel expansion and hired more workers.

A restaurateur in SeaTac similarly warned that the higher minimum wage would force him to shut down restaurants. Instead, after the minimum wage was increased, he announced that he would be opening five new restaurants in SeaTac.

Increasing the minimum wage is good for businesses as well as workers, because it reduces employee turnover. When workers earn a living wage they are more likely to stay with their company, reducing the employer's high on-the-job training costs.

The truth is that states that raised the minimum wage in 2014 experienced faster job growth than those that did not. And a higher minimum wage boosts consumer spending. That is why more than two hundred economists and labor experts wrote a letter last year in support of increasing the minimum wage to $15 an hour by 2020. They were right when they said, "The economy overall will benefit from the gains in equality tied to the minimum wage increase and related policy initiatives. Greater equality means working people have more spending power, which in turn supports greater overall demand in the economy. Greater equality also means less money is available to flow into the types of hyperspeculative financial practices that led to the 2008–09 Wall Street crash and subsequent Great Recession."

It's not just that many economists support raising the minimum wage. It's what the American people want. A January 2015 poll by Hart Research Associates shows 63 percent of Americans support raising the minimum wage to $15 an hour.

Increasing the minimum wage to a living wage is not only the right and moral thing to do, it is good fiscal policy. Think about it for a minute. Why do the taxpayers of this country spend billions a year on food stamps, Medicaid, and subsidized housing? The answer is clear. Millions of American workers need these programs because they cannot survive on the starvation wages their employers pay. And that public assistance given to low-wage workers is essentially subsidizing the profits of the companies paying the low wages. The American taxpayer should not be subsidizing large profitable corporations that pay inadequate wages. Those corporations and all businesses should be paying their employees wages that they can live on with dignity.

Republicans in Washington love to talk about "welfare reform." They like to cite examples of low-income people without jobs who are "mooching" off the taxpayers of this country.

In the 1980s, Ronald Reagan focused on a "welfare queen" driving a Cadillac—who, it turned out, simply did not exist. More recently, Republicans and Fox "News" have turned their attention to a young surfer who used the food stamp program to purchase lobster.

But if you listen closely you will never hear much talk about the largest welfare recipient in America: the Walton family, the owners of Wal-Mart. The Walton family is the wealthiest family in the country, with a net worth of more than $130 billion. This one family owns more wealth than the bottom 42 percent of Americans—130 million people. They also receive more welfare than anybody else.

How does it happen that the wealthiest family in America is also the largest welfare recipient in this country? It's really quite simple.

Wal-Mart makes huge profits by paying their workers wages that are so low that the workers not only qualify for, but need, public assistance just to get by. Many Wal-Mart employees rely on Medicaid for health insurance for themselves and their children—paid for by the

It's a big family. Taken on the day of my announcement.
(Alex Pintair, Ambient Photography)

Announcing my campaign for president, May 26, 2015, in Burlington.
(Win McNamee/Getty Images)

The town hall forums were an effective way to talk about the issues. I spoke with Rachel Maddow of MSNBC in November, Anderson Cooper of CNN in February, Chuck Todd of MSNBC in March, and Chris Cuomo of CNN in April. (AP Photo/Chuck Burton; Arun Chaudhary, Revolution Messaging; Arun Chaudhary, Revolution Messaging; Jane O'Meara Sanders)

The bird, me, and thousands in Portland, Oregon. (Natalie Behring/Getty Images)

Preparing for the debate with my grandchildren. (Jane O'Meara Sanders)

Hillary and I have a laugh after the CBS debate. (REUTERS/Jim Young)

The CBS debate, moderated by John Dickerson, with Secretary Clinton and Governor O'Malley. (Chris Usher/CBS via Getty Images)

Coming home to Brooklyn outside the apartment house where I grew up. (Eric Elofson, Revolution Messaging)

PS 197, my elementary school in Brooklyn. I spent a lot of time playing on those grounds. (Jane O'Meara Sanders)

We had fantastic supporters who shared their creative talents, varied experiences, and commitment to build a better future with our campaign, including (*left to right*) Spike Lee, RoseAnn DeMoro, Susan Sarandon, Sarah Silverman, Cornel West, Killer Mike, and Senator Nina Turner. (Jane O'Meara Sanders; Arun Chaudhary, Revolution Messaging; Jane O'Meara Sanders; Jane O'Meara Sanders; Hilary Hess, Revolution Messaging)

July Fourth in Iowa. (Eric Elofson, Revolution Messaging)

At the Iowa State Fair with Gwen Ifill of PBS. (Arun Chaudhary, Revolution Messaging)

Marching in a parade in Iowa. (Eric Elofson, Revolution Messaging)

Jeff, Phil, Jane, and our Iowa guys, Becker and Pete, at Johnny's Steakhouse in the hotel that was our home away from home in Iowa. (Hilary Hess, Revolution Messaging)

Writing new remarks on the bus through Iowa. (Jane O'Meara Sanders)

With my alter ego, Larry David, on *Saturday Night Live*. (Eric Elofson, Revolution Messaging)

(*Top*) With Seth Meyers. (Lloyd Bishop/NBC/NBCU Photo Bank via Getty Images)

(*Above*) Who's the comedian here? I make Stephen Colbert laugh. (Arun Chaudhary, Revolution Messaging)

(*Right*) Clowning around with Jimmy Fallon. (Douglas Gorenstein/NBC/NBCU Photo Bank via Getty Images)

With Jimmy Kimmel. (Randy Holmes/ABC via Getty Images)

On a pickup truck at five A.M. in New Hampshire greeted by hundreds of supporters. (Alex Wong/Getty Images)

The TV announcement is made as Jane, Levi, Dave, Jeff, Phil, and I watch. We won in New Hampshire. (Arun Chaudhary, Revolution Messaging)

My family played a major role in the campaign. (EPA/CJ GUNTHER/Redux)

More than 18,500 people came out in a low-income neighborhood in the South Bronx. A thrilling evening. (Arun Chaudhary, Revolution Messaging)

We traveled to places most politicians don't go. Shannon and I on the west side of Baltimore. (Hilary Hess, Revolution Messaging)

An unlikely speaker at Liberty University. (Chris Dilts, Revolution Messaging)

Jane and I enjoyed the hospitality of many Native American tribes throughout the campaign. (Fred Guerrier, Revolution Messaging)

A rally in Missouri. (Eric Elofson, Revolution Messaging)

This is the future I looked out at every day. (Arun Chaudhary, Revolution Messaging)

Huge rally, gorgeous mountain backdrop in Salt Lake City. (Hilary Hess, Revolution Messaging)

Another huge rally! (Arun Chaudhary, Revolution Messaging)

I probably took more selfies than any other candidate. (Arun Chaudhary, Revolution Messaging)

hese young people are the future of America. (Arun Chaudhary,
evolution Messaging)

A press interview with John Wagner of *The Washington Post.* (Hilary Hess, Revolution Messaging)

An interview by Barbara Walters for her "10 Most Fascinating People of the Year" special. (Heidi Gutman/ABC/Getty Images)

Talking with the "Young Turk" Cenk Uygur. (Arun Chaudhary, Revolution Messaging)

Flying coach in the early part of the campaign. (Jane O'Meara Sanders)

eff, Michael, and me on the Bernie bus. (Jane O'Meara Sanders)

ad, Michael, Jeff, and me strategizing on the plane with Heather, arina, and Dave looking on. (Jane O'Meara Sanders)

Meeting with Tad, Michael, and Jeff in the D.C. campaign office. (Jane O'Meara Sanders)

We are off to another destination... (Arun Chaudhary, Revolution Messaging)

Solidarity forever. (AP Photo/J. David Ake)

taxpayers of this country. To feed their families, many Wal-Mart workers receive food stamps—paid for by the American taxpayers. And to keep a roof over their heads, many Wal-Mart employees live in subsidized housing—paid for by the taxpayers of America.

When you add it all up, it turns out that U.S. taxpayers are subsidizing Wal-Mart's low wages to the tune of at least $6.2 billion each and every year, according to a 2014 report from Americans for Tax Fairness. The Walton family has got to get off of welfare. We need *real* welfare reform. They must pay their workers a living wage.

Raising the minimum wage to $15 an hour would increase the paychecks of nearly a million workers at Wal-Mart alone by almost $5 billion a year. That sounds like a lot of money. But guess what? In 2015, Wal-Mart made more than $15 billion in profits. In other words, if Wal-Mart paid all of its workers at least $15 an hour, it would have still made a profit of over $10 billion. The Walton family could probably survive on that.

Unfortunately, instead of using its profits to raise its employees' starvation wages, Wal-Mart plans to buy back $20 billion of its stock to enrich its executives and shareholders over a two-year period. (And yes: The Walton family is Wal-Mart's largest shareholder, owning more than half of its stock.)

And while Wal-Mart claims it cannot afford to pay its workers $15 an hour, it was able to find enough money to pay its CEO more than $19.4 million in 2015—or more than $9,000 an hour. If Wal-Mart can pay its CEO $9,000 an hour, it can afford to increase the wages of its workers to $15 an hour.

But it's not just Wal-Mart. It is companies all over this country that make excessive profits by paying their workers substandard wages with the full expectation that the taxpayers of this country will step in and subsidize them.

In total, low-wage employers across the country received a subsidy of nearly $153 billion each year from U.S. taxpayers for paying workers inadequate wages from 2009 to 2011, according to a 2015 report from the University of California Berkeley Research Center.

In other words, if employers in this country simply paid workers a living wage, taxpayers would have saved $153 billion a year on Medicaid, food stamps, the earned income tax credit, and other public assistance programs from 2009 to 2011.

I believe that the government has a moral responsibility to provide for the vulnerable—children, the elderly, the sick, and the disabled. But I do not believe that taxpayers should have to expend huge sums of money subsidizing profitable corporations owned by some of the wealthiest people in this country. That's absurd.

In addition to Wal-Mart, one of the major welfare recipients in this country is the fast-food industry and its owners. In fact, taxpayers spend about $7 billion a year subsidizing the low wages of fast-food companies like McDonald's, Burger King, Wendy's, and many others.

I have been proud to stand on picket lines with fast-food workers fighting for decent wages. And I can tell you that these brave workers don't want government assistance. They want to make a living wage, and that is exactly what they have been fighting to achieve.

Not only do these workers want decent wages, they want full-time jobs. The truth is that not only are many of these workers grossly underpaid, but they are unable to find full-time work at forty hours a week because their employers don't want to provide benefits to them.

A few years ago, I was in Detroit talking to fast-food workers. A number of them told me that the only jobs they could find were for twenty hours a week at $7.25 an hour at McDonald's.

It is because of the low wages and outrageous level of exploitation that fast-food workers came together in the "Fight for $15 and a Union" movement. Under the leadership of the Service Employees International Union (SEIU), the largest union in the country, and the three-year-old low-wage employees' organization Good Jobs Nation, a movement was born to improve the lives of fast-food workers.

Workers at McDonald's, Burger King, Wendy's, Popeyes, and other fast-food establishments stood up and fought for justice. They demonstrated, they took to the streets, and even though they do not officially belong to a union, they had the courage to go out on strike in New York City, Detroit, Flint, Chicago, St. Louis, Kansas City, Washington, D.C., and dozens of other cities.

Let's be clear: While millions of workers in the fast-food industry are struggling to survive on totally inadequate wages, that's not the case for everyone. Not everyone in the fast-food industry is poor.

The reality is that the CEOs and owners of these multibillion-dollar corporations are receiving super-sized compensation packages. In fact, out of all of the industries in America, the fast-food industry is by far the most unequal in terms of compensation. In 2012, the CEOs of the largest fast-food companies in America made 1,200 times more than their average workers.

McDonald's, a corporation with over 840,000 mostly low-wage workers, gave its CEO, Steve Easterbrook, a 368 percent pay raise in 2015. Mr. Easterbrook made over $7.9 million in total compensation in 2015, up from $1.69 million in 2014.

Greg Creed, the CEO of Yum! Brands—the owner of Taco Bell, Pizza Hut, Kentucky Fried Chicken, and Long John Silver's—made $7.5 million in total compensation in 2015.

But that's actually pocket change compared with the

fortune of the owner of Burger King. A few years ago, Burger King and the Canadian restaurant chain Tim Hortons were purchased by a private equity firm called 3G Capital. The cofounder of this firm, Jorge Paulo Lemann, has a net worth of more than $31 billion. He is the richest person in Brazil and the nineteenth-wealthiest person in the world.

The owner of Burger King is worth $31 billion. Many of his employees earn just $7.25 an hour.

And while 96 percent of fast-food workers make less than $15 an hour, all Americans should be shocked to learn that more than 85 percent of child-care workers—the people who are providing the intellectual and emotional support for little children, the future of our country—also make less than $15 an hour.

Most people don't know this, but the largest low-wage employer in America is not Wal-Mart, McDonald's, or Burger King. The largest low-wage employer in America is the United States government.

Today nearly 2 million Americans are working at low-wage jobs that are funded by the taxpayers of our country, mainly through government contracts to private-sector employers. That's more than the number of low-wage workers at Wal-Mart and McDonald's combined.

These low-wage employees manufacture uniforms for the U.S. military. They repair our highways, sidewalks, and bridges. They work in gift shops and restaurants at some of our national parks. They serve us breakfast and lunch in cafeterias. They provide care for the elderly, the sick, and the disabled. They are security guards who protect federal buildings and the employees who work there. They are janitors and groundskeepers who clean our office buildings, take out our garbage, and mow our lawns.

In each instance, the companies that hire these work-

CEO-to-Worker Compensation Ratio in Fast Food Compared to Retail, Hospitality Services, and Manufacturing

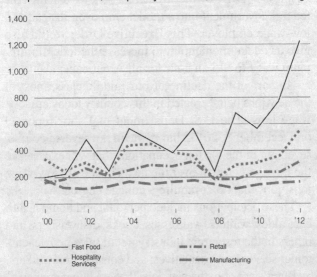

Fast Food ——— Retail ▪—▪—▪
Hospitality Services ▪▪▪▪▪ Manufacturing ▬▬▬

Data Source: Demos analysis of ExecuComp, BLS, and BEA data

ers receive a contract from the federal government, and in too many instances those employers are paying wages that one cannot live on. I have been pleased to work with a grassroots labor group to change that ugly reality. In 2014, as a result of the efforts of a number of us in Congress, I was delighted when the Obama administration signed an executive order requiring federal contract workers to be paid at least $10.10 an hour. But while that was a step in the right direction, much more needs to be done.

In my view, we need a new executive order to increase the minimum wage for federal contract workers to at least $15 an hour, and we need to make sure that federal contracts are awarded to companies that make it easier, not harder, for workers to join unions. I am hopeful that the next president will make signing this

"Good Jobs" executive order one of the first orders of business in 2017. By the stroke of a pen, we can turn the federal government into a model employer, instead of a low-wage employer. This Executive Order would also give us added momentum to increase the federal minimum wage to $15 an hour for all Americans.

As part of the decline of our middle class, most of the new jobs being created in this country today are low-wage jobs. The U.S. Department of Labor reported on December 8, 2015, that if we do not reverse course, seven out of the top ten occupations that will experience the most job growth over the next decade are low-wage jobs, jobs that don't require a college degree.

These occupations include personal and home health care aides; waiters, waitresses, cooks, dishwashers, and others in the restaurant industry; retail sales people; customer service representatives; and construction workers.

But it's not only the new jobs that are being created— it's the lowering of wages for existing jobs. Over the last fifteen years, some 60,000 factories have been shut down in the United States and millions of good-paying jobs have been lost. That's tragic, because many of these jobs were the gold standard for blue-collar workers. But what's equally painful is that many of the manufacturing jobs that remain today are no longer paying decent wages. According to a 2015 study by the National Employment Law Project, almost half of front-line automotive manufacturing jobs in America now pay less than $15 an hour.

While we need to do everything we can to make sure that a majority of the jobs of the future are high-quality jobs, we have also got to make sure that no job in America pays a starvation wage.

Not only would raising the minimum wage to a living wage lift millions of Americans out of poverty and substantially reduce the federal deficit, it would also lead to more social cohesion and a reduction in crime.

One does not have to be a sociologist to understand the connection between poverty, despair, and crime. According to a recent report by the Council of Economic Advisers, "Higher wages for low-skilled workers reduce both property and violent crime, as well as crime among adolescents. The impact of wages on crime is substantial. . . . A 10 percent increase in wages for non-college educated men results in approximately a 10 to 20 percent reduction in crime rates."

In other words, if we are serious about reducing crime, we need to make sure that every worker in America has the opportunity to earn a living wage and has enough money to support a family. People should feel good about the work they do, not ripped off.

There is also a direct correlation between healthy babies and higher wages. Researchers at the University of Iowa, the University of Illinois, and Bentley University have found that every $1 increase in the minimum wage leads to a 2 percent reduction in the risk of a mother having a baby with a low birth weight. Poverty causes stress. Stress causes illness. Decent wages will keep our people healthier.

In terms of wage policy in America, the nation with more income and wealth inequality than any other major country, the bottom line is not complicated. No full-time worker should live in poverty. We must raise the minimum wage to $15 an hour.

EQUAL PAY FOR EQUAL WORK

A living wage should not only be fair; it should be equitable. That is why every man must stand with every woman in the fight for pay equity. Women are sick and tired of making 79 cents for every dollar a man earns. They want the whole damn dollar, and they are right in wanting it.

In 1963, President John F. Kennedy signed into law the Equal Pay Act, requiring employers to provide "equal pay for equal work" regardless of gender. During the signing ceremony of this landmark legislation, President Kennedy said that this bill "affirms our determination that when women enter the labor force they will find equality in their pay envelopes." A year later, the 1964 Civil Rights Act went a step further by prohibiting all wage discrimination on the basis of race, color, religion, gender, or national origin.

But today, despite major advances in civil and political rights over the past fifty years, we still have not come close to achieving pay equity for women in America. Fifty years ago women made up about one-third of our nation's workforce and were paid just 59 cents for every dollar a man earned. Today women make up nearly half of the U.S. workforce. Yet the average woman working full-time in this country still earns just 79 cents for every dollar a man makes. And the gender pay gap is even worse for women of color. African-American women earn just 64 cents for every dollar a white man earns, while the figure for Hispanic women is just 54 cents, and the figure for Native American women only 59 cents.

The reality is that our country still has a very long way to go to truly make gender equality a reality. The gender wage gap is a real and persistent problem that continues to shortchange women and families. Our economy works best when it works for all of us—men and women. As a nation, this is an issue that we must address together.

Today a record-breaking 40 percent of all households

The Gender Pay Gap According to Race and Ethnicity

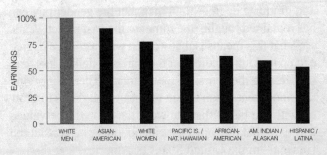

Data Source: The American Association of University Women

with children have a mother who is either the sole or primary breadwinner, up from just 11 percent in 1960. This means that pay equity is not just a women's issue, it is a family issue. When women do not receive equal pay for equal work, families across America have less money to spend on child care, groceries, food, and housing.

Single moms are some of the most courageous people I have ever met. At the same time as they have the responsibility of taking care of their kids, they have to work full-time and make a living. This is tough. This is stressful. They should not be paid less than they deserve.

For millions of families across America, the pay gap between men and women can be the difference between being able to pay the hospital bill or going without needed medical care. It can be the difference between being able to pay the heating bill or going cold in the winter. And it can be the difference between paying the mortgage or losing a home to foreclosure.

We have been told that one of the major reasons for the gender pay gap is that men are much more likely to graduate from college than women, and thus get better-paying jobs. While that was true in the 1960s and 1970s, it is no longer the case, and hasn't been for a while. Since the 1990s, women have received more undergraduate and graduate degrees than men, but the gender pay gap has remained roughly the same for the past fifteen years.

What this means is that women with a college degree end up making hundreds of thousands of dollars less than men during the course of their careers. There is nothing fair about that. I don't want my granddaughters to grow up with the belief that the work they do will be valued less than that of men. That can no longer be considered "normal" in the United States of America.

The reality is that the median earnings of women are lower than those of men in virtually every industry in America. That is true for work primarily done by women, such as teaching, nursing, and administrative jobs. It is also true for jobs done predominately by men, such as truck-driving, management, and software development.

And with some occupations, the gender pay gap is downright obscene. For example, women financial sales agents make 48 percent less than men. Women who are personal financial advisers make 41 percent less than their male colleagues. Even women who enter the legal profession still make just 60 cents for every dollar a man earns doing the same work.

In the twenty-first century, we have also got to stop penalizing women in the workplace for having children. New mothers should receive the same type of respect and remuneration on the job that men receive when they are about to become fathers.

According to one recent study from the University of Massachusetts Amherst, when men have children, their earnings go up by 6 percent. What happens to women? For every child they have, their income goes down by 4 percent. That is absurd.

How do we create a nation in which all people, regardless of gender, get equal pay for equal work?

For starters, we need to pass the Paycheck Fairness Act into law. It is hard to know if you are being paid fairly if you don't know what your coworkers are earning. This legislation would, among other things, prohibit employers from retaliating against employees for discussing wages and salaries with their coworkers. According to a 2014 survey by the Institute for Women's Policy Research, 60 percent of women in the private sector, including two out of three single mothers, report that they are either discouraged or prohibited from talking about wages and salaries with their coworkers. When women are afraid of losing their jobs or being demoted simply for asking their male counterparts how much they earn, employers have a much easier time discriminating against them in the workplace.

But while transparency regarding wages is a good first step, it is not enough. Employers must be required to prove that any differences in wages have nothing to do with gender, race, religion, sexual orientation, or national origin.

In 2007, millions of Americans were shocked to learn that the Supreme Court ruled 5-4 against Lilly Ledbetter in her case against Goodyear, even though she had proof that she'd been paid substantially less than her male colleagues for decades. The conservative Supreme Court ruled against Ms. Ledbetter because she didn't file her lawsuit within 180 days of receiving her first discriminatory paycheck. The Supreme Court apparently didn't care that she didn't even know she was being discriminated against until many years after the fact. And while President Obama signed the Lilly Ledbetter Fair Pay Act in 2009 to correct this injustice in the future, it is nowhere near sufficient.

We need laws that make it unprofitable for companies to engage in pay discrimination. Far too often, when companies do get caught illegally paying women less than men, the fines they receive are little more than a slap on the wrist. For example, in 2015, Home Depot was required to pay a mere $83,400 by the U.S. Department of Labor to forty-six female job applicants at one Home Depot location, who were steered into low-wage cashier jobs, while male applicants received higher-paying jobs as sales associates.

In 2013, Bank of America agreed to pay $39 million to settle a nationwide gender discrimination case filed by female stockbrokers against the bank and its Merrill Lynch brokerage arm who were paid substantially less than their male colleagues. This may seem like a lot of money, but for Bank of America, the second-largest financial institution in the country, it was little more than chicken feed. In fact, that very same year, Bank of America made $11.4 billion in profits. Merrill Lynch has a long history of litigation over its treatment of women and minority employees.

Novartis, a global health care company based in Switzerland, settled a sexual discrimination case in January of 2016 for $8.2 million. It had been filed by more than a dozen female employees who claimed they were denied equal pay and job promotions. Again, that may seem like a lot, but I wonder if this company, with a market cap of $280 billion and annual profits north of $7 billion, will even notice.

On and on it goes. Major corporation after major corporation gets caught for violating pay equity laws. The fines they pay are minimal. Companies that break the law regarding pay equity should not be treated with impunity.

As a nation, we have got to end all forms of discrimination. It is time to guarantee pay equity in America.

MAKING IT EASIER FOR WORKERS
TO JOIN UNIONS

To rebuild the middle class, we must make it easier, not harder, for workers to join unions. The benefits of joining a union are clear:

Union workers earn 27 percent more, on average, than nonunion workers. Over 76 percent of union workers have guaranteed defined-benefit pension plans, while only 16 percent of nonunion workers do. More than 82 percent of workers in unions have paid sick leave, compared with just 62 percent of nonunion workers.

Forty years ago, more than a quarter of all workers belonged to a union. Today that number has gone down to just 11 percent, and in the private sector it is now less than 7 percent. Republican governors across the country have pushed antiunion "right to work" legislation that has drastically cut labor membership in this country.

Historically, unions have enabled workers to earn good wages and work in decent conditions because of collective bargaining. Today, millions of workers are in a "take it or leave it" situation, with no power to influence their wages or benefits.

It is not a coincidence that the decline of the American middle class virtually mirrors the rapid decline in union membership. As workers lose their seats at the negotiating table, the share of national income going to middle-class workers has gone down, while the percentage of income going to the very wealthy has gone up. There is no question that one of the most significant reasons for the forty-year decline in the middle class is that the rights of workers to join together and bargain for better wages, benefits, and working conditions have been severely undermined.

For decades now, there has been a terrible assault on the right to organize, and one of the chief tools employers

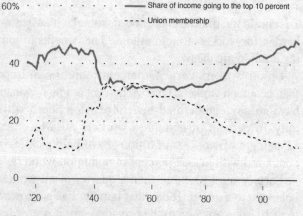

Union Membership and Share of Income Going to the Top 10%

Data Source: U.S. Census Bureau and Piketty and Saez (2013)

use to undermine the formation of unions is intimidation. Today, if an employee is engaged in a union-organizing campaign, that employee has a one-in-five chance of getting fired. Half of all employers threaten to close or relocate their businesses if workers elect to form a union. And, when workers become interested in forming a union, they will almost always be forced to attend closed-door meetings to hear antiunion propaganda. And their supervisors will almost always be forced to attend training sessions on how to attack unions.

As Human Rights Watch has said: "Freedom of association is a right under severe, often buckling pressure when workers in the United States try to exercise it."

Moreover, even when workers, faced with all of these enormous obstacles, are able to form a union, more than half of the victories do not result in a first contract within a year after the election has taken place.

Even as corporate executives routinely negotiate obscenely high compensation packages for themselves, replete with bonuses, options, and many perks, they deny their own employees the ability to bargain for better wages and benefits. The hypocrisy is stunning.

It is time to turn this around.

We must pass legislation that makes it clear that when a majority of workers in a bargaining unit sign valid authorization cards to join a union, they will have a union. Period.

Further, companies must not be allowed to deny or delay a first contract with workers who have voted to join a union. And when companies refuse to negotiate in good faith, there should be arbitration that leads to the completion of the first contract within six months.

We need to send a very loud and a very clear message to corporate America: We will no longer tolerate CEOs who fire workers for exercising their constitutional right to form a union. We will no longer tolerate CEOs who threaten to move plants to China if their workers vote in favor of a union. We will no longer tolerate CEOs and managers who intimidate or threaten pro-union workers.

If we are serious about reducing income and wealth inequality and rebuilding the middle class, we have got to substantially increase the number of union jobs in this country.

REAL FAMILY VALUES

I have four great kids and seven beautiful grandchildren. My wife and I have been married for twenty-seven years. We believe in family values and in strengthening families. But our family values are just a little bit different from Republican ones.

The right has claimed the mantle of "family values" for far too long. When my Republican colleagues use this term they're usually talking about things like opposing contraception, denying a woman's right to choose, opposing gay rights, and supporting abstinence-only education. Let me give a somewhat different perspective on family values—on *real* family values.

When a mother cannot spend time with her newborn child during the first weeks and months of that baby's life, and is forced back to work because her employer doesn't offer paid family leave and she can't afford not to work, that is not a family value. That is an attack on everything that a family is supposed to stand for.

When a husband cannot get time off from work to care for his cancer-stricken wife or gravely ill child, that is not a family value. That is an attack on everything that a family is supposed to stand for.

When a mother is forced to send her sick child to school because her employer doesn't provide sick time and she cannot afford to stay home, that is not a family value. That is an attack on everything that a family is supposed to stand for.

When a husband, wife, and kids, during the course of an entire year, are unable to spend any time together on vacation—that is not a family value. That is an attack on everything that a family is supposed to stand for.

That's wrong. It's a travesty. And it should be an embarrassment to anyone who claims to speak for family values in this country.

So, the next time you hear a politician talking about "family values," you should ask whether he or she supports measures that really help American families— paid family and medical leave, paid sick days, and paid vacation. These initiatives will help families spend more time together, in greater happiness and security. Those are values every family can believe in.

Paid Family and Medical Leave

When it comes to supporting real family values, the United States lags behind every other major country on earth. We are the *only* advanced economy that doesn't guarantee its workers some form of paid family leave, paid sick leave, or paid vacation time. Or, to put that another way: Workers and families in every other major industrialized country get a better deal than we do in the United States.

Here are just a few examples:

- In Canada, parents are guaranteed thirty-five weeks of parental leave at 55 percent of their salary.
- In France, parents are guaranteed at least six months of paid maternity leave at more than $625 a month.
- In Germany, parents are guaranteed one year of paid leave at 67 percent of their salary.
- In Japan, parents are guaranteed six months of paid leave also at 67 percent of their salary.
- In Norway, working parents who have a baby are entitled to forty-nine weeks of paid leave at 100 percent of their wages.

But here in the U.S., workers are not guaranteed any paid leave. Zero. As a result, more than 23 percent of working mothers in America have to go back to work just two weeks after giving birth. Just two weeks to bond with and spend time with their newborn babies. And more than 45 percent of women without college degrees go back to work less than six weeks after giving birth.

Out of 188 countries studied by the Organization for Economic Co-operation and Development (OECD) and the International Labor Organization, the U.S. and Papua

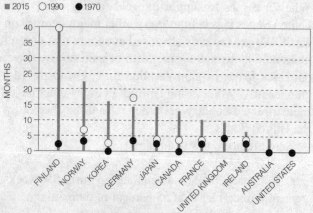

Length of Paid Maternity, Parental, and Home Care Leave
Available to Mothers: 1970, 1990, and 2015

Data Source: OECD Family Database

New Guinea are the only two countries in the world
that don't provide paid maternity leave.

When it comes to having policies that value the contributions of women and that honor and celebrate families, last place is no place for America. It is time to join
the rest of the world by showing the people of this country that we are not just a nation that talks about family
values, but one that is prepared to live up to these ideals by making sure workers in this country have access
to paid family leave, paid sick time, and paid vacations
just like workers in virtually every other country on
earth.

Simply stated, it is an outrage that millions of women
in this country give birth and then are forced back to
work because they don't have the income to stay home
with their newborn babies.

Virtually every psychologist who has studied this issue agrees that the first weeks and months of life are
enormously important to a newborn's emotional and in-

tellectual development. And it's understood that mothers and fathers should spend this time bonding with the new person they have brought into the world.

In some cases, this is even a matter of life or death. The U.S. has the highest infant mortality rate in the industrialized world, and a recent study by researchers at UCLA and McGill University found that enacting paid family leave policies can substantially reduce infant mortality. According to this study, every additional month of paid family leave can reduce the infant mortality rate by 13 percent.

The Family and Medical Leave Act that Congress passed in 1993 is totally inadequate for our twenty-first-century workforce. The FMLA requires some employers to provide workers up to twelve weeks of unpaid leave for personal or family illness, military leave, pregnancy, adoption, or the foster care placement of a child. However, the FMLA only covers employees in companies with fifty or more employees, and it only requires unpaid, rather than paid, leave. Almost 40 percent of all American workers are not even covered by the FMLA, because they work for companies with fewer than fifty employees. And nearly eight out of ten workers in this country who are covered by the FMLA and are theoretically eligible to take time off under this law cannot afford to do so.

In my view, every worker in America should be guaranteed at least twelve weeks of paid family and medical leave—and that is why Congress needs to pass the FAMILY Act, introduced by Senator Kirsten Gillibrand in the Senate and Representative Rosa DeLauro in the House.

This legislation would guarantee employees twelve weeks of paid family and medical leave to take care of a baby; to help a family member who is diagnosed with cancer or has some other serious medical condition; or to take care of themselves if they become seriously ill. Under this bill, workers would be eligible to receive paid family and medical leave benefits equal to 66 percent of their typical monthly wages, capped at a maximum amount of $1,000 per week for high-income workers.

And just like Social Security retirement and disability, paid family and medical leave would be an insurance program that workers pay into with every paycheck, at a price of about $1.61 a week for the typical full-time employee. In my view, that is a pretty good investment in our nation's families and the future economic well-being of our country.

Now, there are some who have criticized this legislation because it would increase taxes on middle-class and working families. These critics claim that working families can't afford to pay for this program.

They have it backward. The reality is that it is too expensive right now for millions of individual workers to take time off when they have a new baby or need to take care of a loved one with a serious medical condition.

Today it would cost the average worker more than $9,300 in lost wages to take twelve weeks of unpaid leave. Most workers simply do not have that kind of money. In fact, according to a December 2015 survey, 63 percent of Americans do not even have $500 in their bank accounts to pay for an unexpected medical emergency or needed car repair.

Just think about it for a moment: How many senior citizens would be living in poverty today if President Franklin Delano Roosevelt had opposed a small payroll tax in the 1930s to fund Social Security?

How many seniors would not have health insurance today if President Lyndon Baines Johnson had opposed a payroll tax increase to fund Medicare in the 1960s?

Fortunately, we don't have to answer these questions today. What FDR correctly understood in terms of Social Security and what LBJ understood in terms of Medicare is the importance of all workers having the legally earned right to a secure retirement and affordable health insurance that could not be easily taken away from them by a future Congress.

The truth is that the economic benefits of paid family and medical leave more than outweigh the very modest costs of this program.

Women who have paid family leave are more likely to stay in the workforce and off federal programs like Medicaid, food stamps, and public housing. Families that have paid leave are much less likely to declare bankruptcy. And children have a greater chance of leading healthy and more productive lives if their parents have paid family leave.

The good news is that California, New Jersey, Rhode Island, Washington, and New York have all passed laws guaranteeing paid family and medical leave to workers.

California and New Jersey guarantee workers six weeks of paid family and medical leave, and in Rhode Island workers are eligible for four weeks of paid leave. Beginning in 2018, New York will become the first state in the nation to offer workers twelve weeks of paid family and medical leave. And all of these programs are funded by a payroll tax similar to the Gillibrand-DeLauro FAMILY Act.

In the year 2016, it is time for all Americans to stand together and say loudly and clearly not only that we are going to make sure every worker receives at least twelve weeks of paid family and medical leave, but that it is paid for in a way that is fair and progressive.

Paid Sick Leave for All

We have also got to make sure that workers in this country have paid sick time. In my view, it is insane that low-wage workers for companies like McDonald's must work when they are sick just because they cannot afford to stay home.

Not only is this bad for the workers who are sick, it is also a public health issue. Who wants to eat food cooked by someone who has the flu or some other contagious illness?

The Healthy Families Act, introduced by Senator Patty Murray, would begin to fix this. This bill would guarantee seven days of paid sick leave per year for American workers. It would benefit 43 million Americans who don't have access to paid sick leave today. And it would also establish a minimum standard for employers who already do offer sick leave.

Congress needs to pass this legislation and the president must sign it into law as soon as possible.

American Workers Need a Vacation

Moreover, when we are talking about a disappearing middle class, we're talking about millions of Americans working longer hours for lower wages. We're talking about millions of Americans who are overworked, underpaid, and under enormous stress. Some are working two or three jobs just trying to care for their families.

What we have are millions of people, working incredibly long hours, some with two or three jobs, just trying to care for themselves and their families.

Today, largely because of the collapse of our middle class and declining wages, Americans are working longer hours than the people of any other major developed country in the G-7, which includes Japan, Germany, Canada, the United Kingdom, France, and Italy.

According to the Organization for Economic Co-operation and Development (OECD), in 2015 Americans worked 419 hours more than the Germans; 308 more than the French; 125 more than Australians; 116 more than the British; 84 more than Canadians; and 71 hours more than the Japanese.

That is why I have introduced legislation to require employers to provide at least ten days of paid vacation to workers in this country every year. This is not a radical idea. It is already being done in almost every country in the world, and it is one more way to demonstrate our commitment to family values.

Today the U.S. is one of only thirteen countries in the world that does not guarantee paid vacation. That puts the U.S. in company with India, Pakistan, and Sierra Leone.

My bill would allow workers to take two weeks of paid vacation so that they can rest and recuperate, travel the country, visit loved ones, or simply spend time at home with their families.

Studies show that nine in ten Americans report that their happiest memories are associated with vacations. And while companies like Costco and Twitter have adopted generous paid vacation policies, aimed at boosting productivity and worker loyalty, nearly one in four American workers gets no paid vacation time, including about half of all low-wage workers. Even worse, 41 percent of workers didn't take one day of vacation in 2015.

Meanwhile, workers in France get an entire month off—paid—every year. The Scandinavian countries guarantee twenty-five days of paid vacation. Germany mandates twenty days, and Japan and Canada both guarantee ten paid vacation days per year.

The United States is the wealthiest country in the history of the world, and the reason we are so prosperous is because the men and women of this country work so hard. They deserve a paid vacation.

And let's be clear: We are not asking for the most generous vacation policy in the world—nothing like what they get in France, Scandinavia, or Germany—but simply a standard befitting a great nation that takes seriously its commitment to family values.

Research shows that vacations reduce stress, strengthen family relationships, increase productivity, and even prevent illness. There is no reason not to pass this bill. It would benefit workers while also helping employers, the economy, and society as a whole.

JOBS, JOBS, JOBS

In a modern democratic society, people have the right to a decent job at decent pay. There are enormous needs in this country that must be addressed. Let's put the unemployed and underemployed to work transforming America. Let's create a full-employment economy.

A job is more than a "job." It is more than just making an income. A job is, in an important sense, how we relate to the world in which we live. Being a productive member of society, a contributor to the well-being of our neighbors and our community, gives our lives meaning, dignity, and satisfaction. In 1944, in his second-to-last State of the Union speech, President Franklin Delano Roosevelt stated, "We have come to a clear realization of the fact that true individual freedom cannot exist without economic security and independence." He talked about the need to establish a second Bill of Rights, an economic bill of rights for the American people, a set of principles as important as the political freedoms guaranteed by our Constitution.

The very first right that Roosevelt listed was: *"the right to a useful and remunerative job in the industries or shops or farms or mines of the nation."* That profound principle was true in 1944. It is true today. We must create a full-employment economy.

Today, as mentioned earlier, *real* unemployment is not 5 percent. It is almost 10 percent, if one includes those who have given up looking for work, or who are working part-time when they want to work full-time. In many communities around the country, the unemployment rate is even higher than that. And it is tragically high among young people who are not college graduates. Today it is estimated that about 20 million Americans are unemployed or underemployed and that less than 63 percent of the adult population has a job.

If we are serious about reversing the decline of the middle class, we need a major federal jobs program that puts millions of Americans to work at decent-paying jobs. A full-employment economy will not only improve the standard of living of millions of Americans, it will create a more efficient and productive society.

We're not talking about "make-work" projects that keep people busy to justify a paycheck. We are talking about putting millions of people to work building an economy that addresses the enormous unmet needs we face, and creating the kind of country we can and must become.

- We need workers to rebuild our crumbling infrastructure—our roads, bridges, water systems, wastewater plants, airports, railways, levees, and dams.

- We need workers to help us lead the world in combating climate change—making our homes and buildings more energy-efficient and transforming our energy system away from fossil fuel and into sustainable energy. We will also need a twenty-first-century grid capable of transmitting that energy.
- We need workers to help us address the crisis in affordable housing—making certain that every family in America lives in safe and affordable housing. This means not only building millions of units of new housing, but rebuilding the older housing stock in communities throughout the country.
- We need workers to create a modern Pre-K and child-care system worthy of the youngest Americans and their parents.
- We need workers to make certain that our children attend modern, well-constructed schools. And we need the best and brightest of our young people to enter the teaching profession so that our kids get a world-class education.
- We need workers to build, in every community in America, urban and rural, a high-quality broadband system. In the modern world, broadband is a necessity, not a luxury.
- We need more doctors, nurses, dentists, and other medical personnel in order to provide quality health care to all as a right. There are medically underserved areas in large cities and small towns where millions of Americans, even those with insurance, are unable to access the health care that they need.
- We need to make it easier for the entrepreneurial spirit to flourish. That means providing help to those businesses that really need it, not to large

and profitable corporations that are shipping our jobs abroad.

- We need to experiment with new economic models. In more and more work sites throughout the country, workers now own and control their own businesses through employee-owned enterprises. This approach often results in increased productivity and greater job satisfaction. It is a concept that should be expanded.

REBUILDING OUR CRUMBLING INFRASTRUCTURE

At a time when our roads, bridges, water systems, rail and airports, levees, dams, schools, and housing stock are decaying, the most effective way to rapidly create meaningful jobs is to rebuild our crumbling infrastructure. That's why I've introduced legislation that would invest $1 trillion over five years to modernize our country's physical infrastructure. This legislation would create and maintain at least 13 million good-paying jobs, while making our country more productive, efficient, and safe. It would be paid for by eliminating tax loopholes that allow multinational corporations to stash their profits in tax havens around the world to avoid about $100 billion a year in federal taxes.

The American people understand that our infrastructure is collapsing all around us. Every day, we drive across bridges that are in disrepair and on roads with unforgiving potholes. We get trapped in never-ending traffic jams that tax our nerves, and ride in overcrowded railroad and subway trains that often get us to work late. We travel through antiquated airports where planes are often canceled or delayed for preventable reasons. In many parts of the country people worry that local levees could give way in a storm, flooding towns and cities.

These worries are very real, as we saw when Hurricane Katrina hit New Orleans.

In hundreds of communities all over our country, officials are now struggling with toxic and polluted drinking water. We've seen what happened in Flint, Michigan, but communities all across the country, from southern Vermont to West Virginia to California, also have serious problems with the quality of their water.

I understand that infrastructure is not exactly the most exciting issue out there. Last time I checked, infrastructure activists were not turning out tens of thousands of people to protest the sorry state of our nation's culverts. But let's be clear: The state of our infrastructure is of enormous importance to our country. It greatly impacts the quality of our lives, our economy, and the environment.

It makes a real difference in people's lives if they can drive to work on noncongested roads. It matters that people can travel safely and efficiently on trains and subways. The quality of life for millions of Americans will be improved if they are living in safe and affordable homes rather than overpriced and dilapidated apartments. We have the right to know that the water we are drinking is safe, and that our children are attending high-quality schools.

These are not radical demands. This is what America should be about. This is the kind of America we can create.

For most of our history, the United States proudly led the world in building innovative infrastructure, from a network of canals, to the transcontinental railroad, to airport construction, to the interstate highway system. We launched an ambitious rural electrification program, massive flood control projects, and more. These innovations grew our economy, gave our businesses a competitive advantage, provided our workers a decent standard of living, and were the envy of the world. Sadly, that is no longer the case.

The American Society of Civil Engineers gave our infrastructure an overall grade of D-plus in its most recent report card. How can it be that the United States, the richest and most powerful nation in the history of the planet, has let its infrastructure slip into such disrepair that it is at a "strong risk of failure"? The answer, it turns out, is quite simple.

For decades, we have significantly underfunded the maintenance and improvement of the physical infrastructure that our country depends on. We have given tax breaks to the wealthy rather than investing in our future. The United States now spends just 2.4 percent of gross domestic product on infrastructure, less than at any point in the last twenty years. Meanwhile, Europe spends more than twice our gross share of GDP on infrastructure, and China spends close to four times our rate. Today, the United States' overall infrastructure ranks thirteenth in the world, down from seventh just a decade ago.

Almost one-third of our nation's roads are in poor or mediocre condition, while more than 40 percent of urban highways are considered congested. We spend 6.9 billion hours stuck in traffic each year, wasting 3.8 billion gallons of fuel, costing $160 billion, and causing significant frustration and even rage. And that does not include the environmental costs of the carbon emissions from unnecessarily burning that extra 3.8 billion gallons of fuel. Every driver spends, on average, an extra $325 each year in vehicle repairs due to our bad roads. And while there is no national database of deaths and injuries caused by deficient transportation infrastructure, the U.S. Department of Transportation estimates that highway deaths from obsolete and poor roads could be as high as 14,000 per year.

Nearly a quarter of our nation's bridges are rated as "functionally obsolete," and an astounding one of every nine is considered "structurally deficient." One such bridge was the I-35 bridge in Minneapolis. On August 1, 2007—on the very same day that a bipartisan group of U.S. senators held a largely ignored press conference in Washington about the deteriorating condition of our nation's infrastructure—the westbound I-35 bridge collapsed, killing 13 people and injuring 145.

Light rail and bus transit systems across the country, because of a lack of funding, are postponing billions of dollars in needed repairs and upgrades, even as more people take buses, trains, and subways to get to work. Obviously, when mass transit options aren't good, more people choose to ride in cars—which creates more wear and tear on our roads and more congestion. It's a lose-lose situation.

Meanwhile, 45 percent of American households lack any meaningful access to transit at all, which continues to be a significant issue in rural areas such as my state of Vermont. People in rural areas should have options for getting to work other than their cars.

Our nation's passenger and freight rail networks are antiquated, in spite of the fact that Amtrak's ridership has never been higher and our energy-efficient railroads move more freight than ever. While we have partisan debates in Congress about the merits of high-speed rail, countries across Europe and Asia have gone ahead and built networks where trains travel at two hundred miles per hour and faster. High-speed rail relieves congestion on highways and at airports, and whisks people around quickly and efficiently in dozens of countries. In contrast the Acela, Amtrak's fastest train, travels at an average speed of just sixty-five miles per hour.

Anyone who flies regularly knows that many of America's airports are bursting at the seams, and that there are too many non-weather-related delays and cancellations. The cost of airport delays is approaching $25 billion a year, and the FAA estimates it will reach $34 billion a year by 2020 unless we improve airport capacity and efficiency. Our airports need almost $76 billion over the next five years to accommodate growth in passenger and cargo activity and to rehabilitate existing facilities. Are we facing this situation? No. And, maybe even worse, many of our airports still rely on outdated 1960s radar technology, because Congress chronically underfunds deployment of a new satellite-based air traffic control system.

According to the American Water Works Association, we need to increase attention to the serious water problems that we have: "Much of our drinking water infrastructure, the more than 1 million miles of pipes beneath our streets, is nearing the end of its useful life and approaching the age in which it needs to be replaced. Delaying the investment we need—nearly $1 trillion—can result in degrading water service, increasing water service disruptions, and increasing expenditures for emergency repairs."

In February 2016, I visited Flint, Michigan, and saw firsthand a tragic example of the human cost of a crumbling water system, which left the city's drinking water poisoned with toxic lead.

In their reckless zeal to slash spending, public officials jeopardized the health and well-being of the residents they are entrusted with keeping safe. Rather than wait three years for a new water pipe that would bring water from Lake Huron to Flint, a revolving door of "emergency managers" appointed by Michigan governor Rick Snyder decided to save a few dollars by taking water from the highly polluted Flint River.

In April of 2014, with the blessing of Michigan environmental officials, water from the squalid Flint River

At a difficult town meeting in Flint, Michigan. (Fred Guerrier, Revolution Messaging)

started to flow into homes and businesses. Residents immediately complained about the foul smell, awful taste, and brown color of the water, and some became ill with E. coli infections and other maladies. But an even bigger, invisible problem was lurking. The polluted river water and the harsh chemicals added to make it "drinkable" corroded Flint's aging water pipes, and leached highly toxic lead into the water supply.

When ingested, even small amounts of lead can cause serious health problems—especially for children under the age of six, who can experience severe behavior problems and learning disabilities. At very high levels, lead poisoning can be fatal.

A practicing pediatrician, Dr. Mona Hanna-Attisha, helped bring the problem to the public's attention, even though state agencies dismissed her concerns for months. She believes all of Flint's 8,657 children under six years old are at significant risk of "damning lifelong and generational consequences," and will likely need substantial resources to manage the long-term effects on their health and educational attainment.

Flint is a wake-up call to the fragile nature of our public water supply but, unfortunately, Flint is not alone.

The water in Hannibal, Missouri, has been undrinkable for three years, having been found to harm the liver, kidneys, and central nervous system. Water mismanagement in Tyler, Texas, has led to an increased cancer risk. The water in Gardena, California, turned brown and green last year. Toxic algae in Lake Erie, fed by unchecked phosphorus runoff, made the water undrinkable for half a million residents of Toledo, Ohio, in 2014.

Even regarding lead, Flint is not alone. According to the Natural Resources Defense Council (NRDC), about one thousand systems serving nearly 4 million people reported exceeding the EPA's "action level" of 15 parts per billion of lead in their drinking water between 2013 and 2015. Not surprisingly, these environmental crises tend to disproportionally affect poor and minority communities—people without a lot of political clout.

Let me say it once more: We live in the richest country in the history of the world. It is absurd that, increasingly, we are unable to drink the water that comes out of the faucets in our homes. If we addressed this problem, we would reduce health risks and save substantial sums of money. (It is projected that in 2017 we will spend more money for bottled water than we do for soda.) We would also create a significant number of jobs.

Our wastewater treatment plants are not in much better shape. Each year, tens and sometimes hundreds of billions of gallons of untreated sewage is discharged into our nation's waterways when plants fail or pipes burst, often during heavy rains. The cost of cleaning up after these failures runs into the billions of dollars a year, and causes long-term environmental damage to our rivers and lakes.

More than four thousand of our dams are rated as "deficient," and nearly 9 percent of our levees are "likely to fail" during a major flood. As we have seen, this is a life-and-death issue. Major recent disasters—and there have been many—pale in comparison to the damages caused in the wake of Hurricane Katrina. Katrina was a massive storm when it hit New Orleans in August 2005, causing widespread destruction and loss of life. However, the bulk of the tragedy began when levees in New Orleans failed, *after* the storm had passed. And we should never forget how it ended: with 1,500 dead, close to $100 billion in damage, and whole neighborhoods wiped out in one of America's most historic cities.

When we talk about a deteriorating infrastructure, we are talking about human life at risk, human health at risk—and major economic losses. Bottlenecks at our marine seaports, which handle 95 percent of all overseas imports and exports, cause delays that prevent goods from getting to their destinations on time. The same is true for our inland waterways, which carry the equivalent of 50 million truck trips of goods each year. American businesses are increasingly being put at a competitive disadvantage in the global economy because they can't easily transport their goods and services to market, and because their employees find it hard to get to work affordably. It is estimated that American businesses lose $27 billion a year in delays and extra shipping costs, which are invariably passed along to consumers.

One of the things we take for granted is electricity. In the 1930s the federal government made it possible for everyone, even those in very rural areas, to have electric power at their homes. But today America's aging electrical grid consists of an antiquated patchwork system of interconnected power generation, transmission, and distribution facilities, some of which date back to the early 1900s. Our grid suffers from hundreds of major power failures each year, many of which are avoidable. Our grid simply is not up to twenty-first-century challenges, including possible cyberattacks and resiliency after ever-more-common extreme weather events. The World Economic Forum ranks our electric grid at twenty-fourth in the world in terms of reliability, just behind Barbados. Yes, behind Barbados.

We invented and developed the Internet in the United States, but today we are falling behind many other countries in access and speed. We are, sad to say, sixteenth in the world in terms of broadband access, and we are only marginally better in terms of average broadband speed. How can it be that businesses, schools, and families in Bucharest, Romania, have access to much faster and less expensive Internet service than does most of the United States? How can it be that in the year 2016, in rural areas all over this country, Internet service remains nonexistent or extremely slow? What the Rural Electrification Act did in the 1930s for electric service, the Congress must do today for universal and affordable broadband.

It should be abundantly clear to any reasonable person that the economic status quo is not working. We have to think big and act boldly. A $1 trillion investment in rebuilding our physical and human infrastructure would go a long way toward transforming our country and moving to a full-employment economy.

In fact, investing in infrastructure would give the economy a bigger bang for the buck than any other federal investment. The International Monetary Fund (IMF)—hardly a bastion of radical economic theory—recently reported that well-designed infrastructure projects, including those paid for with borrowed money, effectively pay for themselves, because the projects spur almost $3 in economic output for each dollar spent.

If spending $1 trillion over five years to improve our infrastructure and create jobs is a lot of money, consider for a moment the cost of *not* acting. As I have noted, the sad state of our infrastructure is a significant drag on our economy. The total cost likely already exceeds $200 billion in lost productivity per year—which, incidentally, is exactly the amount I propose to spend each year to fix the problem. And that doesn't count the human cost of not acting.

I was a mayor for eight years, and one thing I learned very quickly was that deteriorating infrastructure does not magically get better by ignoring it. It just gets worse, and more expensive to fix. It is easier to maintain roads and bridges than to rebuild them. The most cost-effective way to deal with infrastructure is through a strong and consistent maintenance program. And not building strong new systems today will leave our communities weaker later on, and our businesses less able to compete on a global scale.

There is no reason on earth why the richest country in history can't deliver a sound infrastructure to its people. And, no surprise, there is no question that this is what the American people want. A 2013 Gallup poll found that 72 percent of the American people support *increasing government spending* on infrastructure projects that put people to work.

The good news is that it is not too late to get back on track. Our political revolution demands that we improve the physical infrastructure our economy and our society depends on, and in the process create the millions of jobs we so desperately need.

CREATING JOBS IN CLEAN ENERGY

When we talk about rebuilding America and making our country more efficient, productive, and safe, there is no issue more important, in my mind, than combating climate change and transforming our energy system away from fossil fuels and into energy efficiency and sustainable energy. When we do that, we not only help lead the world in saving the planet, but we create an extraordinary number of good-paying jobs.

The scientific community is virtually unanimous in telling us that to avoid truly catastrophic consequences, we have a short window of time to dramatically cut the greenhouse gases that cause global warming. I have laid out a plan to cut U.S. carbon pollution by at least 40 percent by 2030 and 80 percent by 2050 from 1990 levels by establishing a tax on carbon, aggressively implementing energy efficiency efforts, quickly moving away from fossil fuels, and deploying historic levels of new renewable energy like wind, solar, and geothermal. This is an absolutely and necessarily achievable goal. It is also a huge opportunity in terms of strengthening our economy and creating needed jobs.

Let's start with energy efficiency. Homes, office buildings, factories, schools, libraries, and other buildings can all be made significantly more efficient with state-of-the-art insulation, LED lighting, and modern heating and cooling systems. For every dollar invested in efficiency upgrades, families and businesses can enjoy up to $4 in energy savings, and for every billion dollars spent, we can create up to eight thousand new jobs, roughly ten times as many as the same investment in the coal industry would create. It is no wonder that small businesses are popping up all around the country to do this kind of work. Now our job is to drive demand by providing incentives for building owners to make the improvements. Energy efficiency truly is a win-win-win in the fight against climate change, in terms of reducing energy use, saving consumers money, and creating jobs.

Likewise, transitioning to domestically produced clean energy will create hundreds of thousands of jobs, and if we do it right, stimulate domestic manufacturing. The solar industry is adding workers at a rate nearly twenty times faster than the overall economy, and solar employment has grown by 86 percent in the past five years, adding nearly 80,000 domestic living-wage jobs in the manufacture and installation of solar panels. Moreover, the roughly 210,000 Americans currently employed in solar is expected to double by the end of 2020, helping to spur $140 billion in economic activity. And if anyone still doubts that solar power works, my state of Vermont—with its northern, snowy climate— leads the nation in solar jobs per capita, according to the Solar Foundation, a top industry research group. If Vermont can do it, it can be done virtually anywhere in America.

Similarly, jobs in the wind energy sector are growing rapidly, with federal incentives attracting more than $100 billion in private investment to the U.S. economy since 2008. According to the U.S. Department of Energy, there are more than five hundred wind energy manufacturing facilities of various sizes in the country, and the sector already employs about 50,000 people in manufacturing, installation, and maintenance. Of course, we have just begun to tap the enormous potential of wind energy. In fact, the same DOE report says the wind energy sector could grow to as many as 650,000 jobs by the year 2050.

Still other jobs will be created in an area where the U.S. historically has excelled: technology research and development. Affordable electric vehicles and recharg-

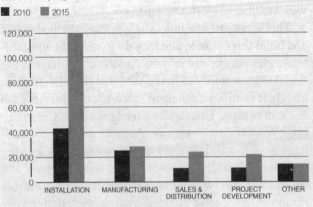

Solar Employment Growth by Sector, 2010 and 2015

■ 2010   ■ 2015

Data Source: The Solar Foundation's *National Solar Jobs Census 2015*

ing stations, more efficient solar panels, advanced battery systems to store wind and solar energy, and innovative controls to seamlessly integrate renewables into our power grid will all require cutting-edge research. This is the stuff we do so well when challenged as a nation, whether by putting a man on the moon, eradicating diseases, or developing the Internet. The U.S. can and must dedicate our engineering know-how to a clean energy revolution, in our universities, in our national energy labs, and in businesses and communities all across the country.

Of course, there will be some job displacement as we move away from fossil fuels. When I was in McDowell County, West Virginia, I saw firsthand what happened in terms of poverty and unemployment when the coal industry disappeared. In my view, it is absolutely imperative that workers in those industries do not get left behind, and that they receive the education, training, and access to new jobs they will need to succeed in a changing economy. These workers must also receive help to maintain wage support, health care, and pensions until they are able to start new jobs.

This is not just idle talk. These workers helped power and build this country, and they do some of the most difficult and dangerous jobs in America. We have a national responsibility to make sure that their livelihoods and their families are helped, not hurt, by the transition to clean energy. That is why I introduced the Clean Energy Worker Just Transition Act—to provide comprehensive job training and benefits to workers as they transition to making the solar panels, wind turbines, and batteries of the twenty-first century. It will also direct resources to the most affected communities, particularly in Appalachian coal country, to clean up the disastrous environmental legacy of coal mining, and to build the infrastructure needed to attract new investment and revitalize local economies.

CREATING JOBS BY HOUSING FAMILIES

Another significant challenge that similarly has an upside in terms of creating jobs is addressing the affordable housing crisis in our country. From the time I was elected mayor of Burlington, Vermont, in 1981, I have made affordable housing a top priority, and one of my proudest achievements as mayor was creating the first municipally funded community housing trust in the nation. Today, the Champlain Housing Trust that we pioneered in northern Vermont thirty years ago is not only the largest and most successful housing trust in the United States, it is also the model for similar efforts all over the world.

As I traveled the country during the campaign, I heard, over and over again, about the affordable housing crisis that we face as a nation. Public housing in New York City, which houses more people than the entire city of Boston, has a $17 billion maintenance backlog. Yes, that's right—17 billion dollars. Much of that housing, built decades ago, is now deteriorating, leaving poor and elderly people in unsafe, unhealthy, and substandard high-rise apartments. In San Francisco, Seattle, and elsewhere, I heard about the crisis of gentrification and how working people can no longer afford to remain in the communities they have lived in for their entire lives, and that they want to stay in.

In rural areas, low-income people are paying outrageously high prices and fuel bills living in trailer parks. While most homes, especially homes of decent quality, appreciate over the years, that is not the case with mobile homes. They deteriorate in value. While the ownership of housing is often a means of increasing wealth for the middle class, it is often the very opposite for poor people in rural areas.

When I was a kid, the expectation was that no family should spend more than 25 percent of its income on housing. My family, which lived in a rent-controlled apartment in Brooklyn, spent a much smaller percentage than that. According to the National Low Income Housing Coalition (NLIHC), that reality has changed. Today, more than a quarter of the nation's 43.2 million renter households are "severely rent-burdened," using more than half their income to pay rent.

Of course, the situation is direst for families with the lowest incomes, with 6.6 million families below the poverty line paying at least *half* of their very limited incomes just to put a roof over their heads, leaving precious little for other necessities like food, health care, and transportation.

NLIHC calculates that the nation faces an immediate shortage of 7.2 million affordable apartments for extremely low-income families. Meanwhile, more than half a million people—families with children, veterans, the mentally ill, and runaway youth—are living in their cars, in homeless shelters, or on the streets.

Access to safe, decent, and affordable housing is critically important for families and healthy communities. Study after study has shown that without stable housing, it is much harder for working people to hold down jobs and get the health care they need, and children are put at a profound disadvantage in terms of intellectual and emotional development and school performance. The very idea that everyone has equal opportunity to succeed evaporates in the absence of stable and affordable housing. We have to level the playing field. We have to build millions of units of affordable housing.

In 2001, I authored and then helped lead a fifteen-year effort to pass and secure funding for the National Housing Trust Fund, the first new federal housing construction program in almost three decades and the first ever aimed at building affordable rental housing for extremely low-income households. While the Obama administration has begun to fund the program, the level of funding is totally inadequate. We should fund the NHTF at no less than $5 billion every year over at least a decade.

Decent-quality, affordable housing should be a right of all Americans. This is important in order for family members to have good relationships with one another, that kids grow up in a healthy environment, and that seniors be able to retire with security and dignity.

Clearly, that is not what we see today.

We need to create millions of units of affordable housing in larger cities, in smaller towns, and in almost every part of the country. And when we do that we also create jobs, a whole lot of good-paying jobs—construction jobs, service jobs, and jobs in building materials and supplies businesses. Jobs we need.

CREATING CHILD-CARE AND PRESCHOOL JOBS

When I talk about rebuilding America, I am not just talking about our physical infrastructure, about bricks and mortar—as important as that is. I also mean our *human* infrastructure, and meeting the needs of some of the most vulnerable people in our country. The truth is that, as a nation, we do a disgraceful job in providing for our children. We not only have the highest rate of childhood poverty of almost any major nation on earth, but we have a dysfunctional child-care and Pre-K system that has completely ignored the radical changes that have taken place in our economy over the last forty years.

In my view, there is no more important job in America than taking care of, nurturing, and educating our youngest children. Today's infants, toddlers, and preschoolers are the future of our country. They have the potential to grow up to be our future doctors, nurses, scientists, engineers, astronauts, farmers, and political leaders. But without the right kind of education, love, and nourishment, particularly at a young age, they also have the potential to become drug dealers, criminals, and people who engage in self-destructive activities that will land them in jail and/or a life of poverty.

Every psychologist who has studied the issue agrees that the most formative years of a human being's life are from zero to four. In fact, according to the most recent research, approximately 90 percent of brain development occurs before the age of five. Yet we have millions of young children who are in inadequate child-care facilities with adults who lack the training and expertise to effectively nurture them. And it says a lot about our attitude toward young children when many of our child-care workers earn the minimum wage with minimal benefits.

According to the Bureau of Labor Statistics, the average child-care worker in 2015 had only a high school diploma, received short-term on-the-job training, and made just $9.77 an hour, less than the typical parking lot attendant or janitor.

At a time when nearly 60 percent of women are now in the workforce, we need a revolution in this country in terms of how we provide child care and Pre-K education. The bottom line is that we have got to make sure every family in America has the opportunity to send their kids to a high-quality child-care and Pre-K program. We must invest in our young people today, because by doing so we invest in the potential of our nation. And by making high-quality child care a priority and enacting other family-friendly policies, we could allow an additional 5.5 million women to enter the workforce and generate some $500 billion a year in economic growth—about 3.5 percent of gross domestic product.

According to the most recent federal study, only 10 percent of our nation's child-care programs are considered to be of high quality. Too many child-care facilities and preschools are run-down. They are not open long enough to meet the demands of parents who work the late shift or odd hours. They do not provide for the nutritional needs of children. They don't provide health care services to kids who get sick. They don't have the ability to take care of kids with disabilities or special needs. And too many of them are often staffed with poorly trained and poorly paid workers.

For the future of America and for the long-term health of our economy, we must recognize that providing high-quality child-care and Pre-K programs costs a hell of a lot less than locking up young adults later in life because they were neglected when they were toddlers, got a bad start in school, and got into trouble as they grew up.

The child-care crisis in this country is something that is far too rarely discussed. But it is something that must be addressed, and addressed now. And when we do, we will not only improve the lives of our youngest children, we will create millions of jobs and improve the economy now and into the future.

This is not just my opinion. According to a 2007 report by the Federal Reserve Bank of Minneapolis, "The most efficient means to boost the productivity of the workforce 15 to 20 years down the road is to invest in today's youngest children. . . . Research shows that investments in high-quality early education appear to reduce future crime and are more cost effective than additional spending on police or incarceration. . . . We don't pretend to have all the answers to economic development, but we're quite certain that investing in early-childhood education is more likely to create a vibrant economy than using public funds to lure a sports team by building a new stadium or attracting an automaker by providing tax breaks."

Unfortunately, compared with other countries, the U.S. ranks near the bottom when it comes to spending on child care and preschool. Unlike the U.S., dozens of countries around the world have recognized the importance of investing in early care and education. Across the member nations of the Organization for Economic Co-operation and Development, 84 percent of four-year-olds are enrolled in early education, versus just 69 percent in the U.S. Moreover, just 51 percent of three-year-olds in the U.S. are enrolled in publicly funded early education, compared with more than 90 percent in the United Kingdom, Germany, Belgium, Denmark, Iceland, Norway, Spain, and Sweden. Even poorer countries like Slovenia, Argentina, Hungary, Mexico, Chile, and Poland invest more of their GDP in child care and preschool than we do. We have got to do a lot better than that.

How do we get there?

First, we have got to make child care and preschool affordable and available to all. The best child-care centers and preschools in America are simply out of reach for most families. Today, it costs an average of about $18,000 a year to provide an infant with high-quality child care in America. That's $3,000 more than a full-time minimum-wage worker makes. In most states, child care costs more than a college education and the average rent. And 85 percent of children who are eligible to receive child-care assistance don't get the care they need because of a lack of funding.

In my view, we need to provide free, full-day, high-quality child care from infancy to age three for the 75 percent of families making $100,000 a year or less. For families making between $100,000 and $150,000, we need to cap child-care expenses at no more than 10 percent of income. And we need to make sure that every child, starting at age three, will be guaranteed a prekindergarten education regardless of family income.

By making this investment, we will provide over 16 million children with the financial assistance they need to enroll in child-care and preschool programs in America, up from about 1.5 million today. And, in the process, we will double the number of early-childhood educators in this country from about 1.3 million today to more than 2.6 million.

Second, we have got to make sure that every child-care and preschool facility in America provides high-quality care. That means substantially smaller class sizes. It means offering care at least ten hours a day to meet the needs of parents who work nontraditional hours. It means providing children with healthy and nutritious meals, making sure they have access to health and wellness services, and hiring experts to provide care to kids with disabilities and special needs.

Moreover, improving the quality of child care means requiring child-care workers and preschool teachers to have the appropriate level of education and training. At a minimum, all child-care workers should have a Child Development Associate's (CDA) credential, all caregivers should have an associate's degree, and all preschool teachers should have a bachelor's degree. These enhanced educational requirements will increase the quality of child-care and preschool programs, and will also create new jobs on college campuses in early-childhood education.

And it means paying child-care workers and preschool teachers a living wage. Child-care workers should be paid a minimum of $15 an hour and preschool teachers should be paid no less than similarly qualified kindergarten teachers. Today, the typical kindergarten teacher makes almost twice as much as a preschool teacher. It's time to end that arbitrary disparity.

Greatly expanding access for early care and education also means that children will need new learning environments that they can thrive in. The American Academy of Pediatrics (AAP) and the American Public Health Association (APHA) have recommended that each child in a high-quality facility should have at least seventy-five square feet of indoor space. Based on these recommendations, we would need to construct, renovate, or rehabilitate over 180,000 child-care facilities and preschools throughout the country, creating an additional 1.1 million new construction jobs in the process.

The U.S. actually had universal child care from 1943 to 1946, when child care was virtually free. During those years, more than 100,000 children from families of all incomes received the care they needed, which allowed women to enter the workplace at a time when men were leaving in droves to fight in the war. In the 1940s, universal child care was considered a national security priority. In the twenty-first century, when having both parents in the workforce is an economic necessity for the vast majority of families, we need affordable, high-quality child care more than ever.

Taking good care of the youngest children in America, and allowing parents to access high-quality affordable child care, will have a profound impact on the future of our country. It will enable millions of children to be better prepared for school, bring more women into the workforce, and make our economy much more productive.

It will also create millions of good-paying jobs as a bonus.

TURNING WORKERS INTO OWNERS

While we create millions of good-paying jobs rebuilding our physical and human infrastructure and transforming our country, there is another economic step forward that we must take. We need to take a hard look at new business ownership models in the country. To my mind, we need to significantly expand employee ownership.

Over the last fifteen years, large multinational corporations have shut down some 60,000 factories in America and moved millions of decent-paying jobs abroad in search of cheap labor. The only thing that matters to these corporations are short-term profits, strong dividends, and high compensation packages for the CEOs. What happens to the employees, what happens to the environment, what happens to the community in which they function matters very little. These are not *American* companies—

they are companies currently *located* in America. Tomorrow, if the economics made sense to them, they could be located in China. Their only allegiance is to the bottom line.

It is time, as a nation, that we stop worshipping corporate greed and businessmen like Jack Welch, the former head of General Electric. While in corporate circles, and in the corporate media, Jack Welch is regarded as a brilliant and successful businessman, the truth is that he represents almost everything that is wrong with contemporary capitalism. As the CEO of General Electric, Welch moved dozens of GE factories abroad, outsourced hundreds of thousands of jobs, and slashed benefits for many of his employees. To add insult to injury, after destroying the retirement dreams of so many of his workers, he received a $400 million golden parachute for himself. This type of greed and ruthless capitalism is not an economic model we should be embracing. We can do better; we must do better.

The economic establishment tells us that there is no alternative to this type of rapacious, cutthroat capitalism, that this is how the system and globalization works, and that there's no turning back. They are dead wrong.

The truth is that we can and we must develop new economic models to create jobs and increase wages and productivity. Instead of giving huge tax breaks to corporations that ship our jobs to China and other low-wage countries, we need to provide assistance to workers who want to purchase their own businesses by establishing worker-owned cooperatives and majority-owned employee stock ownership plans (ESOPs). Study after study has shown that employee ownership increases employment, increases productivity, increases sales, and increases wages in the United States.

In fact, according to a survey by Georgetown University and American University, during the Great

Recession in 2008, while corporations were slashing jobs, employee-owned firms increased jobs by 2 percent. Amazingly, while the construction industry slashed 10 percent of its jobs in 2008 after the housing market collapsed, many worker-owned construction firms actually added jobs.

Unlike large corporations that have been shipping jobs overseas, employee-owned businesses, by and large, are not shutting down and moving their businesses to China, Bangladesh, or other low-wage countries. Further, employee-owned businesses boost morale, because workers share in profits and have more control over their work lives. The employees are not simply cogs in a machine owned by someone else. They have a say in how the company is run.

One of the great things about living in Vermont is that you don't need a study to understand the benefits of employee ownership. All you need to do is ask the worker-owners at Chroma Technology in Bellows Falls; Gardener's Supply in Burlington; King Arthur Flour in Norwich; or Carris Reels in Rutland. I have had the honor of meeting with many of these employees. Never in my life have I seen workers who have more pride in the work that they do—from senior executives and managers all the way down to the cashier and the store clerk. Today, there are more than thirty-six worker-owned companies in Vermont.

And Vermont is certainly not alone. Nationally, there are about seven thousand worker-owned businesses throughout the country, with over 14 million employees.

In New York City, Cooperative Home Care Associates in the Bronx is the nation's largest worker-owned cooperative, employing over two thousand people—largely African-American and Latin-American women. This company has a turnover rate of just 15 percent—far less than the prevailing rates of 40 to 60 percent for the rest of the home-care industry. Job stability for the co-operative's worker-owners translates into better care for the clients who depend on them.

In Cleveland, the Evergreen Cooperatives, a network of worker-owned businesses created in conjunction with local universities and hospitals, is creating living-wage jobs for residents of neighborhoods that have suffered from decades of disinvestment.

In Oakland, California, a group of black women opened the Mandela Food Cooperative as a worker-owned solution to the lack of healthy food in their own community. In Morganton, North Carolina, the worker-owned Opportunity Threads cooperative is a leading force in revitalizing a local textile industry decimated by globalization.

The workers in these operations understand that when employees own their companies, when they work for themselves, when they are involved in the decision-making that impacts their jobs, they are no longer just punching a time clock. They become more motivated, absenteeism goes down, worker productivity goes up, and people stay on the job for a longer period of time.

And these ventures don't need to be small, niche companies. The 74,000 employees at the Mondragon cooperatives in Spain is a model for worker ownership worldwide. At a time when the rest of Spain continues to experience a serious recession, the worker-owned businesses in Mondragon have been able to manage the economic crisis exceptionally well. And the executives of these worker cooperatives cannot make more than eight times as much as their average worker. (CEOs in the U.S. earn nearly three hundred times as much as their average employee.)

Unfortunately, despite the important role that worker ownership can play in revitalizing our economy, the federal government has failed to commit the resources needed to allow employee ownership to realize its true potential.

During the next Congress, I will be introducing a bill to create a U.S. Employee Ownership Bank to provide low-interest loans, grants, and technical assistance to help workers purchase businesses through a majority-owned employee stock ownership plan or a worker-owned cooperative.

I will also be introducing a bill to establish and expand employee ownership centers that provide training and technical support to promote employee ownership and participation throughout the country.

By providing low-interest federal loans, by educating business owners and employees about the benefits of worker ownership, and by providing them with the tools to succeed, we can allow the employee ownership model to realize its true potential, and create and save millions of jobs in the process.

There are also other opportunities to encourage worker ownership of businesses. As thousands of Baby Boomer business owners begin to plan for retirement, existing federal law provides tax benefits to retiring owners who sell to their workers. With federal assistance, an estimated 150,000 to 300,000 small- and medium-sized businesses could be sold to the workers who helped build them.

For many years, worker ownership enjoyed the support of both Republicans and Democrats. As Ronald Reagan said in 1987, "I can't help but believe that in the future we will see in the United States and throughout the Western world an increasing trend toward the next logical step: employee ownership. It is a path that befits a free people."

REAL TAX REFORM

For the past forty years, Wall Street banks, large profitable corporations, and the billionaire class have rigged the tax code to redistribute wealth and income to the richest and most powerful people in this country. At a time of massive wealth and income inequality, when major corporation after major corporation pays nothing in federal income taxes and many CEOs enjoy an effective tax rate that is lower than their secretaries', we need progressive income tax reform based on the ability to pay.

On December 10, 2010, I spoke on the floor of the Senate for eight and a half hours. Some called it a filibuster. Others said it was just a very long speech. It doesn't really matter. The reason I took to the Senate floor for such a long period of time was to express outrage at the proposed two-year extension of the Bush tax breaks for the top 2 percent. I thought it was profoundly unfair, economically unwise, and politically wrong to provide hundreds of billions in additional tax breaks to the wealthiest people in this country, especially while the overwhelming majority of Americans were still suffering through the Great Recession.

Almost every Republican, and far too many Democrats, claimed that if the Bush tax breaks for the wealthy expired, the economy would suffer and unemployment would increase. After decades of evidence that unequivocally refuted trickle-down economics, the Republican establishment was just not giving up. When the superwealthy get more tax breaks, they don't spend more, they don't invest more in the economy, they don't create more jobs. They just look for new ways to reduce their remaining taxes.

The Bush tax breaks were in place for more than a decade, and they did not create a single net new private-sector job. In fact, under the eight years of President Bush, the private sector lost nearly half a million jobs and the deficit exploded. On the other hand, in 1993, when President Bill Clinton increased taxes on the top 2 percent and used that revenue to reinvest in America and reduce the deficit, more than 22 million jobs were created, and we had a $236 billion budget surplus.

Had Congress let the Bush tax cuts expire in 2010, the top marginal income tax rate would have gone back to 39.6 percent—where it was when President Clinton was in office. That is not very high for someone earning millions of dollars a year, in my opinion. But apparently, it would have been too big a sacrifice for the people on top, despite the great wealth and political power they already had. So the tax cuts stayed in place, a $186 billion gift to the top 2 percent.

Delivering the filibuster on the Senate floor. (C-SPAN)

The bill that I was filibustering also extended the 15 percent rate for capital gains and dividends, which meant we would continue to tax income from passive investments at a lower rate than we tax work. And that meant some millionaires and billionaires could continue paying a lower tax rate than firefighters, nurses, and teachers. As recently as 1978, the maximum capital gains rate was almost 50 percent, but that was steadily reduced over the next fifteen years, until George W. Bush pushed through the 15 percent rate in 2003. Extending that rate was another gift to the wealthy, this one priced at $53 billion.

The bill reduced the estate tax to 35 percent—and raised the minimum inheritance to which it was applied to $5 million—a gift to the top two-tenths of 1 percent. As recently as the 1990s, the estate tax was 55 percent and applied to all estates worth more than $1 million. Bush actually succeeded in eliminating the estate tax entirely for a year, but he was unable to keep the income inequality clock turned back to pre-1916, when there was no tax on inheritances, no matter how big the estate. The wealthy had to "settle" for reduced rates and a fivefold increase in the minimum amount before the tax kicks in—a $68 billion tax break for the economic elite.

To this day, I still cannot believe that Congress's response to the worst economic crisis since the 1930s was more tax cuts for the wealthy. In December 2010, millions of middle-class Americans who had lost their jobs were still searching for work. Millions had lost their homes to foreclosure and many had become homeless, including tens of thousands of veterans—men and women who served in uniform to defend this country. A growing number of children across the country were going hungry, and many seniors couldn't afford the prescription drugs they needed. But pass more tax cuts for the wealthy was exactly what Congress did, despite my protestations on the Senate floor and my best efforts to rally the American people.

At the time, I predicted that as soon as the wealthy got their tax cuts, Republicans (and many Democrats) would flip a switch and start yammering on about the urgent need to reduce the deficit. Do you think they even once suggested raising more revenue to balance the budget? Of course not. They demanded budget cuts. That's right—deep budget cuts in the middle of a recession, to reduce a deficit that had grown out of control because George W. Bush gave the wealthiest people in this country massive tax cuts while waging disastrous and costly wars in Iraq and Afghanistan.

Sure enough, the budget cuts went through. Over the next decade, Congress cut trillions of dollars from education, health care, and vitally important programs that help the children, the elderly, the sick, and the poor.

In the past decade, how many times have you heard the refrain, "America is broke"? How many times have we heard politicians say that they would like to expand Social Security, provide health care to all or make college affordable, but those goals are just not feasible when we have a $19.4 trillion national debt?

Baloney. The establishment wants you to believe America is broke, indeed they *need* you to believe America is broke. But in reality, we are the richest country in the world, and we are richer than at any other time in history. The U.S. has a record-breaking $88 trillion in total wealth, twice the amount of just fifteen years ago and almost four times greater than the next wealthiest country.

And yet every year the federal budget gets squeezed more and more, and the deficit grows. The problem is not that we're broke. The problem is that way too much of that extraordinary wealth is owned by the top 1 percent, who, instead of paying their fair share in taxes, have been receiving huge tax breaks for years.

If we taxed the wealthy in a progressive manner, we could begin to address the most urgent needs facing our country. But we don't. According to Citizens for Tax Justice, the richest 1 percent of Americans, who took in an astounding 21.6 percent of all income in the U.S. last year, paid just 23.6 percent of all federal, state, and local taxes. That is not the kind of tax system we need in America.

It's not just the marginal tax rates that benefit the rich, it's also the loopholes. As Warren Buffett, the multibillionaire investor, has often reminded us, he pays a lower effective tax rate than his own secretary. This is because capital gains and dividends are, quite incredibly, taxed at a lower rate than wages and salaries.

And then there is the carried-interest loophole, a tax break that allows Wall Street hedge fund managers to treat most of their earnings as long-term capital gains instead of payments for services rendered. Although it makes no rational sense, this loophole cuts the tax rate in half for a small group of incredibly wealthy people—costing the U.S. Treasury as much as $180 billion over a ten-year period.

Add in a whole slew of other credits and deductions that advantage the wealthy, and a billionaire hedge fund manager can pay a lower effective tax rate than a truck driver, teacher, or nurse. The old adage "It takes money to make money" is alive and well. The tax code is helping the very rich get insanely richer, while the middle class is disappearing and the poor are getting poorer. It is the Robin Hood principle in reverse.

In my view, we have got to send a message to the billionaire class: "You can't have it all." You can't get huge tax breaks while children in this country go hungry. You can't continue getting tax breaks by shipping American jobs to China. You can't hide your profits in the Cayman Islands and other tax havens while there are massive unmet needs in every corner of this nation. Your greed has got to end. You cannot take advantage of all the benefits of America if you refuse to accept your responsibilities as Americans. We need a tax system that is fair and progressive.

The good news is that the overwhelming majority of Americans agree. A June 2016 survey by the Brookings Institution and the Public Religion Research Institute found that almost 70 percent of Americans support increasing taxes for people earning $250,000 or more per year. And what should send shivers down the spine of the billionaire class is that 54 percent of Republicans agree. "Over the last four years," the survey noted, "there has been a sea change in opinion among Republicans with regard to taxing the wealthy," noting an astounding 18-point increase in Republican support for increasing taxes on the rich just since 2012.

That is remarkable, and it shows that the American people are catching on to how unfair the tax system is.

And the Brookings survey was not an outlier. An April 2016 Gallup poll found 61 percent of Americans believe upper-income individuals pay too little in taxes. And to the conservative pundits who insist redistributing wealth is fundamentally un-American, the American people respectfully disagree, 52 percent believing "that our government should *redistribute wealth by heavy taxes on the rich*."

CORPORATE TAXES

According to conservative groups like the Heritage Foundation, Cato Institute, and U.S. Chamber of Commerce, and their many allies in Congress, corporations in the United States are the highest-taxed in the world. That is a lie. Yes, technically the top statutory corporate income tax rate of 35 percent is the third highest, but, in reality, most corporations don't pay anywhere close to the statutory rate.

An April 2016 Government Accountability Office study found that large corporations actually paid just 14 percent of their profits in federal income taxes from 2008 to 2012. Not 35 percent, but 14 percent.

And rather incredibly, one of every five large, profitable corporations paid no federal income taxes at all in 2012. Not 35 percent, but *zero* percent.

The reality is that for decades, corporations have been paying a smaller and smaller share of overall federal tax revenues. In 1952, corporate income taxes accounted for 32 percent of all federal revenue. By 2015, that number had been reduced by two-thirds, to just 10.6 percent. In other words, a much greater share of paying for the basic government services the American people enjoy and demand—national defense, education, health care, the social safety net, caring for our veterans, running the national parks, and so much more—falls on the backs of working families instead of profitable corporations.

And yet, according to a March 2016 article in *The Economist*, U.S. corporate profits are at all-time highs. How can that be? It should come as no surprise that just as our tax code benefits wealthy individuals, it also benefits some of the largest and most profitable corporations in the world with myriad tax breaks, deductions, credits, and tax avoidance loopholes. Our tax code has essentially legalized tax dodging for large corporations.

Take, for example, legal tax avoidance schemes, like stashing cash in offshore tax havens. The Cayman Islands and Bermuda are two of the favorite countries for corporations to stash their cash, since they have secretive banking laws and no corporate taxes at all. None. All you need to do is set up a post office box in one of those countries, and voilà—you now have a foreign company, with no tax liabilities! The practice has become so absurd that a single five-story office building in the Cayman Islands is now the official legal "home" to more than 18,000 corporations. Incredibly, this one tax avoidance scheme alone allows corporations to avoid paying more than $100 billion in U.S. taxes each and every year.

These companies benefit in innumerable ways from being based in America, by using taxpayer-funded infrastructure, accessing the most highly trained and productive workforce in the world, using numerous government services (and sometimes, grants and contracts), and so much more. They are proud to be American companies. That is, until it's time to pay their fair share of taxes.

And some of the worst offenders are the big Wall Street banks.

After the greed, recklessness, and illegal behavior on Wall Street drove this country into the deepest recession since the 1930s, the largest banks in the United States took every advantage of being American. They loved America and everything that taxpayers could do for them. In 2008, Congress passed a $700 billion bailout, paid for by American taxpayers. And the Federal Reserve gave the financial institutions $16 trillion in virtually zero-interest loans. America. What a great country!

But just two years later, as soon as these behemoths started making record-breaking profits again, they suddenly lost their love for their native country. At a time when the nation was suffering from a huge deficit—largely created by the recession that Wall Street caused—the major financial institutions did everything they

This Cayman Islands office building is home to more than 18,000 corporations. (AP Photo/David McFadden)

could to avoid paying American taxes by, among other things, establishing shell corporations in the Cayman Islands and other tax havens.

In 2010, Bank of America set up more than two hundred subsidiaries in the Caymans. Not only did it pay no federal income taxes that year, it received a tax refund for $1.9 billion. Apparently Bank of America thought stiffing the American treasury was the appropriate way to thank taxpayers for the more than $1.3 trillion it received through the bailout and the Federal Reserve.

In 2013, JPMorgan Chase made a profit of more than $17 billion, but received a $1.3 billion tax refund, thanks in large part to its four subsidiaries incorporated in offshore tax havens. I guess JPMorgan Chase thought that was the right thing to do after receiving a bailout of more than $400 billion.

In 2013, Citigroup made a profit of more than $6.3 billion, but received a tax refund of $260 million. During the financial crisis, Citigroup received $2.5 trillion in financial assistance from the Federal Reserve that kept it from going under.

And in 2014, Goldman Sachs had twenty subsidiaries in offshore tax havens, which allowed it to avoid an estimated $4.6 billion in U.S. taxes. What a nice way to say thanks for the more than $800 billion in assistance Goldman received during the financial crisis.

On and on it goes. Wall Street banks and large companies love America when they need corporate welfare. But when it comes to paying American taxes, they want nothing to do with this country.

And let's be clear: Offshore tax abuse is not just limited to Wall Street.

Pharmaceutical companies like Eli Lilly and Pfizer have fought to make it illegal for the American people to get cheaper prescription drugs from Canada and Europe. But, during tax season, Eli Lilly and Pfizer shift drug patents and profits to the Netherlands and other offshore tax havens to avoid paying U.S. taxes.

One of the most popular tax avoidance schemes that the pharmaceutical industry has exploited is called a "corporate inversion"—which allows American corporations to merge with foreign companies in low-tax countries to save billions in taxes.

Some of the highest-profile inversions—attempted or successful—have involved pharmaceutical companies like Pfizer, Eli Lilly, Mylan (the manufacturer of the EpiPen), Amgen, Merck, Actavis, AbbVie, and others. These are all U.S. companies, but many have more than 80 percent of their cash overseas, sheltered from U.S. taxes.

Gilead Sciences is perhaps the most egregious example of a pharmaceutical company stiffing American taxpayers. Here is the backstory. In 2014, Gilead came out with a game-changing new drug to treat the chronic liver disease Hepatitis C. If left untreated, this disease can end in what one nurse-practitioner called "some of the worst deaths I've ever seen. . . . You die not knowing who you are, your belly looks twelve months pregnant, you're malnourished, and you're bleeding to death." Fortunately, the new drug—Sovaldi—works extraordinarily well, is successful nearly 90 percent of the time, and has few side effects.

Like many new drugs, Sovaldi was developed with grants from the National Institutes of Health to help spur innovation and develop important breakthrough medicines and therapies. Gilead bought the small company that discovered the drug for $11 billion, and got fast-track approval from the FDA in December 2013 to begin selling it. And that's where the feel-good part of the story ends.

Gilead set the price for Sovaldi at $1,000 *per pill*, or $84,000 for a twelve-week course of treatment, even though analysts believe it could cost Gilead as little as $100 to manufacture the eighty-four pills. Public and private insurers spent more on Sovaldi in 2014—its first year on the market—than on any other prescription drug. But the astronomical cost put it out of reach for many Hep C patients, who are disproportionately low-income or veterans. The budgets of Medicare Part D and Medicaid strained under the costs, and the VA struggled to provide it to all veterans with the disease.

According to a July 2016 Americans for Tax Fairness report, Gilead made back its initial investment in less than a year. The company rewarded its CEO with $200 million in compensation, which is, even at Sovaldi's insanely inflated price, enough to treat three thousand Hep C patients. In two years, Gilead's profits soared more than fivefold, from $4 billion in 2013 to $22 billion in

2015. Yet, its overall effective tax rate plummeted from 27.3 percent to 16.4 percent over the same period. How did the company do that?

First, Gilead transferred some of its physical assets to Ireland. And then—with a completely straight face—it claimed that while two-thirds of its revenues were generated in America, only one-third of its *profits* were made here, which allowed Gilead to dodge $9.7 billion in U.S. taxes last year alone.

Wonder what that $9.7 billion in lost tax revenue would mean for the United States? According to Americans for Tax Fairness, it would "double to 2 million the number of low-income kids and pregnant women served in a year by the highly successful Head Start program. Or help 7 million households stay warm over three winters through the LIHEAP program. Or ensure one and a half years of nutritional assistance to 8.5 million participants in the Women, Infants and Children (WIC) program."

Remember, American taxpayers helped pay for the initial research. They paid for the government agencies that granted market exclusivity, and that approved Sovaldi on an expedited basis. They subsidized its purchase for countless seniors, low-income patients, and veterans. American taxpayers helped make Gilead the most profitable Fortune 500 prescription drug company in the world in 2015, making over $18 billion in profits. And Gilead's way of thanking the taxpayer is by stiffing the national treasury of nearly $10 billion.

High-tech companies are also very good at gaming the tax system, and no one is better at it than Apple. Apple created some of the most iconic and popular computers, handheld devices, and software with American know-how and all of the benefits and synergies of being located in Silicon Valley. But when it comes time to manufacturing its products, Apple turns to China to avoid paying American wages. And then Apple shifts most of its profits to Ireland, Luxembourg, the British Virgin Islands, and other tax havens to avoid paying U.S. taxes. In fact, Apple has more than $180 billion in profits offshore—more than any other American company. Without such maneuvers, Apple would owe an estimated $59 billion in federal taxes.

In late August 2016, after benefiting from years of dubious tax breaks even by tax haven standards, the European Commission ordered Ireland to collect $14.5 billion in back taxes from Apple. Just two days later, CEO Tim Cook said Apple *might* be ready to move the company's money again, maybe even to the United States. "We provisioned several billion dollars for the U.S. for payment as soon as we repatriate it, and right now I would forecast that repatriation to occur next year," Cook said. Of course, "several billion" is a lot less than the $59 billion Apple owes the American people, which is why you can bet Cook has a small army of lobbyists furiously working the halls of Congress to pass some sort of "tax holiday."

Over and over, profitable corporations take advantage of the many benefits of being American companies, but when it comes time to pay their taxes, they suddenly abandon their allegiances to this country.

A 2008 Government Accountability Office report found 83 of the Fortune 100 companies use at least one offshore tax scheme to lower their taxes, and that number is undoubtedly higher today. In 2015 alone, American corporations held a total of $2.4 trillion in offshore profits in tax haven countries, deferring payment of some $700 billion in U.S. taxes. *Seven hundred billion dollars.*

America is *not* broke. The very wealthy and hugely profitable corporations just aren't paying the taxes that, in the words of Supreme Court Justice Oliver Wendell

Holmes more than a century ago, "are the price we pay for a civilized society."

Quite simply, the tax avoidance schemes they use rob our national coffers of the revenue we need to provide quality health care for all, care for the men and women who served in the military, make higher education affordable, allow seniors to retire in dignity, rebuild our roads and bridges, make sure no child goes to bed hungry, protect the environment, and much more.

And the crazy thing is that the tax code—*our* tax code—allows this kind of tax dodging—it is all legal. How the code got that way is no surprise: Corporations have spent billions over the years in campaign contributions and lobbying to make sure Congress creates and maintains the many loopholes they benefit from.

Here's a not-so-radical idea: Instead of just listening to the rich and powerful few, maybe Congress should start listening to the majority of the American people who want a fair tax system.

Ending Corporate Tax Dodging

Corporate tax reform must start by preventing profitable companies from sheltering profits in tax haven countries like the Cayman Islands. In 2015, I introduced legislation with Senator Brian Schatz of Hawaii and Representative Jan Schakowsky of Illinois to do just that.

The Corporate Tax Dodging Prevention Act would end the loophole that allows corporations to defer paying taxes on overseas profits. Instead, it would require corporations to pay U.S. taxes on offshore profits as they are earned. This bill would take away the tax incentives for corporations to shift profits and move jobs and factories offshore, by taxing their profits no matter where they are generated. American corporations would continue to get a credit against their U.S. tax liability for foreign taxes they pay, but they would have to pay the federal government the difference between the foreign rate and the U.S. rate.

The bill would also prevent corporations from establishing completely fictitious foreign shell companies to avoid paying U.S. taxes. True, this may have a deleterious effect on that building on Grand Cayman Island, with its more than 18,000 corporate "residents," but it would go a long way toward collecting the $100 billion a year in taxes that are lost when companies stash profits overseas.

Further, the legislation would eliminate a tax loophole that allows big oil companies—some of the most profitable corporations ever—to pay less in taxes. Currently, oil companies can treat royalty payments to foreign governments as if they are foreign tax payments, deducting one dollar in U.S. taxes owed for every dollar paid in royalties. That's crazy. Oil royalties are *not taxes*. They are a cost of doing business. My bill would close this loophole, which is really just an American taxpayer subsidy for big oil.

This legislation will raise an estimated $1 trillion in new revenue over the next decade—revenue that I think we should use to create 13 million new jobs rebuilding our roads and bridges, public transportation and intercity rail, drinking and wastewater facilities, and addressing other pressing infrastructure needs.

Here's the simple truth: You can't be an American company only when it benefits you—you also have to be an American company when it comes to paying your fair share of taxes. If Wall Street and big corporations don't agree, the next time they need a bailout or some other kind of public assistance, let them go to the Cayman Islands, Bermuda, or Panama and ask those countries for corporate welfare.

Top Ten Corporate Tax Avoiders

Here are some of the worst corporate tax dodgers in America. Not coincidentally, the CEO of every company listed belongs to the Business Roundtable—an organization that lobbies Congress to slash corporate taxes. But that's not all. The Roundtable also wants to raise the eligibility age for Social Security and Medicare to seventy, and to cut cost-of-living adjustments for seniors and disabled veterans. These CEOs callously promote the idea that increasing their corporate profits is more important than their fellow Americans receiving the benefits they have earned by working or by serving in the military.

1. **Johnson Controls.** In 2015, this auto parts and HVAC manufacturer outsourced hundreds of good-paying jobs from Milwaukee to China, Mexico, and Slovakia. A year later, the company—which ranks 67 on the Fortune 500 list—announced it would acquire an Irish company to save $150 million in taxes. It's hard to understand why. Although Johnson Controls made a $1 billion profit in 2015, it not only paid no federal income taxes, it received a $477 million tax refund.

2. **IBM.** Big Blue has a long record of outsourcing good-paying jobs, slashing pensions, and cutting retiree health benefits. In 2015, IBM made nearly $6 billion in profits in the U.S. Not only did IBM pay nothing

in federal income taxes that year, it received a $321 million tax refund from the IRS, while also receiving $1.35 billion in government contracts. And from 2008 to 2012 IBM avoided $13.2 billion in U.S. taxes by operating subsidiaries in fifteen offshore tax havens.

3. **Xerox.** Xerox has established at least fifty-two subsidiaries in offshore tax havens, including eight in Bermuda, to avoid U.S. taxes. Last year, it made a $547 million profit, but received a tax refund of $23 million. In 2016, it eliminated over five thousand jobs.

4. **American Airlines.** In 2016, American Airlines was ranked dead last in on-time flights, but when it comes to tax dodging this airline is one of the best. In 2015, while making a profit of more than $4.6 billion, American Airlines received a tax refund of nearly $3 billion.

5. **Pacific Gas & Electric.** In 2016, this huge utility company was convicted of obstructing a federal investigation into a gas pipeline explosion that killed eight people and destroyed thirty-eight homes. The maximum fine for this felony is $3 million, which shouldn't be hard for PG&E to pay. While PG&E made a profit of $847 million in 2015, it received a $27 million tax refund.

6. **Boeing.** Since 1994, Boeing has shipped almost 60,000 jobs overseas. In 2014, shortly after forcing U.S. workers to accept

an end to the company's defined-benefit pension plan, Boeing's CEO—who made $23.5 million in compensation that year—callously explained his decision to put off retirement: "The heart will still be beating, the employees will still be cowering, I'll be working hard." When it comes to avoiding taxes, no company works harder than Boeing. From 2001 through 2014, Boeing made $52.5 billion in U.S. profits, but received a net federal tax refund of $757 million and state tax refunds totaling $55 million.

7. **General Electric.** When it comes to dodging taxes, GE brings good things to life. From 2008 through 2013, while GE made nearly $34 billion in profits, it received tax refunds of nearly $3 billion. Meanwhile, during the financial crisis, GE received a $16 billion bailout from the Federal Reserve while its CEO, Jeffrey Immelt, served as a director of the New York Fed.

8. **Citigroup.** The third-largest bank in America, with over $1.8 trillion in assets, Citigroup needed a $2.5 trillion bailout in 2008. When it returned to profitability in 2013, earning $6.4 billion, not only did it pay nothing in federal income taxes, it received a tax refund of $260 million. A year later, it established 427 subsidiaries in offshore tax havens, including 90 in the Cayman Islands, to avoid paying $11.7 billion in taxes.

9. **Pfizer.** One of the largest and most lucrative prescription drug companies in Amer-

ica, Pfizer made $43 billion in profits worldwide from 2010 to 2012, but instead of owing federal income taxes, it received $2.2 billion in tax refunds.

10. **Verizon.** Not only did this telecommunications giant avoid paying federal income taxes on $42.5 billion in U.S. profits from 2008 through 2013, it received a tax rebate of $732 million. And Verizon isn't just good at avoiding U.S. taxes. In 2009, it used a Dutch subsidiary to convert $1 billion of equity into debt to escape paying virtually any taxes in Europe.

REFORMING THE PERSONAL INCOME TAX

The ideas that all Americans are created equal and that all of us are entitled to life, liberty, and the pursuit of happiness were, according to the founders, supposed to be "self-evident truths." But those foundational notions about what this country is supposed to be all about are seriously imperiled by the grotesque level of wealth and income inequality that exists in America today.

If American justice means anything, it means ending tax breaks to the rich and powerful so that we can rebuild the middle class, raise wages, reduce poverty, and create millions of good-paying jobs. It also means implementing a fair and progressive tax code.

During the campaign, I proposed raising taxes on the wealthiest 2.1 percent of American households making over $250,000, and individuals with incomes above $200,000. Under this plan, 97.9 percent of Americans would not see their taxes go up. However, within the top

2.1 percent, the rates get progressively higher at the top income levels. The top marginal rates would be:

- 37 percent on income between $250,000 and $500,000.
- 43 percent on income between $500,000 and $2 million.
- 48 percent on income between $2 million and $10 million (in 2013, only 113,000 households, the top 0.08 percent, had income between $2 million and $10 million).
- 52 percent on income above $10 million (in 2013, only 13,000 households, just 0.01 percent of taxpayers, had income exceeding $10 million).

During the campaign I proposed that the new revenue being generated by creating a progressive personal income tax be used to fund a Medicare for All single-payer health care system.

A Progressive Estate Tax

More than 240 years ago, the founders of our country declared their independence from what they viewed as a tyrannical aristocracy in England. But today's tyrannical aristocracy is no longer a foreign power. It's an American billionaire class that has unprecedented economic and political influence over all of our lives. Unless we reduce skyrocketing wealth and income inequality, unless we end the ability of the superrich to buy elections, the United States will be well on its way to becoming an oligarchic form of society where almost all power rests with the billionaire class.

More than a century ago, President Theodore Roosevelt recognized the danger of massive wealth and income inequality and what it meant to the economic and political well-being of the country. In addition to busting up the big trusts of his time, he fought for the creation of a progressive estate tax to reduce the enormous concentration of wealth that existed during the Gilded Age.

"The absence of effective state, and, especially, national, restraint upon unfair money-getting has tended to create a small class of enormously wealthy and economically powerful men, whose chief object is to hold and increase their power," the Republican president said. "The really big fortune, the swollen fortune, by the mere fact of its size acquires qualities which differentiate it in kind as well as in degree from what is passed by men of relatively small means. Therefore, I believe in . . . a graduated inheritance tax on big fortunes, properly safeguarded against evasion and increasing rapidly in amount with the size of the estate."

Roosevelt spoke those words on August 31, 1910. They are even more relevant today.

Since 1916, the estate tax has been a bulwark against an oligarchic form of society. However, as we have seen, the estate tax has been weakened over the years. Strengthening it is one of the fairest ways to reduce wealth inequality, while at the same time raising significant new revenues that the country needs to rebuild the middle class.

During the campaign, I proposed restoring the minimum estate size subject to the tax from $5 million to $3.5 million, where it was in 2009. This would only impact the estates of the wealthiest 0.3 percent of Americans who inherit more than $3.5 million. And along the lines of what Teddy Roosevelt suggested, we should make it graduated to target the biggest estates:

- 45 percent for the value of an estate between $3.5 million and $10 million.

- 50 percent for the value of an estate between $10 million and $50 million.
- 55 percent for the value of an estate in excess of $50 million.

We should also implement a 10 percent surtax on the value of estates above $1 billion to break up the extreme wealth of the 540 billionaires in the United States—the wealthiest 0.0002 percent of America—and end tax breaks for dynasty trusts. This includes eliminating the so-called "grantor retained annuity trust," and the "generation-skipping tax," whose loopholes have allowed billionaires like Sheldon Adelson and the Walton family, the owners of Wal-Mart, to legally manipulate the rules for trusts passed on from one generation to the next without paying estate or gift taxes, resulting in savings of $100 billion in taxes since 2000.

Look, I know estate tax minutiae are not exactly sexy, but the point is this: There are all sorts of loopholes that help the wealthiest families avoid paying estate and gift taxes. We must close each and every one of them, including gift tax exclusions and valuation discounts.

I come from an agricultural state, so let me dismiss the argument that "the estate tax is bad for family farmers." When challenged to find a family farmer who was subject to the estate tax, the conservative Farm Bureau couldn't. Of course, that doesn't keep it from repeating the myth. In any case, my proposal would protect family farmers by allowing them to lower the value of their farmland by up to $3 million for estate tax purposes, through the use of agricultural easements. It would also increase the maximum exclusion for conservation easements to $2 million.

TREAT CAPITAL GAINS AND DIVIDENDS THE SAME AS WORK

Capital gains and corporate stock dividends are taxed at lower rates than the wages and salaries most of us live on. The Congressional Budget Office (CBO) estimated that 68 percent of this tax break went to the richest 1 percent of Americans in 2013. This is why someone like Warren Buffett, the second-wealthiest American, is able to pay an effective tax rate that is lower than his secretary's. To his credit, Buffett says this is profoundly wrong.

We need to enact a real "Buffett Rule" by repealing the low income tax rates on capital gains and stock dividends for those who make more than $250,000 a year. We should also repeal the exclusion of capital gains on bequests and gifts from taxable income. This exclusion in effect subsidizes wealthy families who hold on to assets in order to pass them on to the next generation, increasing the sort of dynastic wealth that is a feature of economic inequality.

LIMIT TAX DEDUCTIONS OF THE TOP 2 PERCENT

Our tax code has several complex provisions to limit the benefits of tax breaks for the wealthy, including the alternative minimum tax (AMT), the personal exemption phaseout (PEP), and the limit on itemized deductions. I proposed replacing these provisions with a simpler one limiting the tax savings for each dollar of deductions to just 28 cents for high-income households.

A NEW TRADE POLICY

We need a new trade policy that creates decent-paying jobs in America and ends the race to the bottom. Corporate America cannot continue to throw American workers out on the street while they outsource our jobs and enjoy record-breaking profits.

One of the major reasons the middle class has been in a forty-year decline, poverty has been increasing, and the gap between the very rich and everyone else has been growing wider is because we have been losing millions of jobs as a direct result of our disastrous trade policies. We must do everything possible to stop companies from outsourcing American jobs.

The reality is that over the last thirty-five years, so-called free trade policies have been unrelentingly bad for American workers. Written by corporate America, these rigged agreements have made it far easier for companies to shut down manufacturing plants in the U.S., throw workers out on the street, and move to Mexico, China, and other countries where workers are paid a fraction of what they are in the U.S.

You do not need a Ph.D. in economics to understand that while our trade agreements have worked extremely well for huge corporations, they have miserably failed working people. Since 2001, nearly 60,000 manufacturing plants in this country have been shut down and boarded up, and we have lost more than 4.8 million decent-paying manufacturing jobs. Not all of these factories and jobs were lost due to our trade policies, but many of them were.

To fully understand what these trade agreements are all about, we should remember what Jack Welch, the former CEO of General Electric, said back in 1998. "Ideally," he said, "you'd have every plant you own on a barge to move with currencies and changes in the economy."

What Mr. Welch was saying is that in the CEO's perfect world, companies like his would effortlessly move from country to country, wherever labor was cheapest, taxes were lowest, and environmental protections were weakest. In other words, if the U.S. increased its minimum wage, a company could simply pull up anchor and ship its jobs to Mexico. If Mexico strengthened its environmental laws, no problem, that company would simply move to China. If China banned sweatshops, then the company could just move to Vietnam. Until Vietnam decided to increase taxes, in which case . . . Well, you get the idea. This is the essence of what the "race to the bottom" is all about, and why millions of Americans are rejecting unfettered free trade.

Mr. Welch's analogy of a company on a barge was brutally honest. In this era of free trade, he basically acknowledged that corporations have absolutely no loyalty to the countries where they are based or to the workers they employ. That's exactly what these corporate-backed, corporate-written free trade deals are all about. They really aren't about trade at all. Trade, when structured in a fair manner, can be a driver of increased wages and widely shared prosperity. But free trade agreements aren't fair. Rather, they are all about increasing the profits of multinational corporations that have allegiance only to their bottom line.

During the presidential campaign, I met with Americans all over this country who have had their lives torn apart as a result of job-killing trade deals. And I did my best to give voice to these struggling Americans whom the corporate-owned media, one of the biggest cheerleaders of "free" trade, almost completely ignores.

Unbelievably, while trade agreements have an enormous impact on the lives of millions of Americans, they are virtually never discussed on television and rarely discussed in newspapers. According to Media Matters, a nonpartisan media watchdog, as the debate on the disastrous Trans-Pacific Partnership was heating up, not one of the major networks chose to mention this trade agreement on its evening broadcast news programs from August 1, 2013, through May 10, 2015. This includes *ABC World News Tonight*, *CBS Evening News*, and *NBC Nightly News*. And with the exception of Ed Schultz of MSNBC, who has since been taken off the air, the cable news networks barely mentioned the TPP—a trade agreement that encompasses 40 percent of the global economy. But the workers impacted by trade deals certainly know all about them.

In Michigan, I held a press conference with Kim Ward, whose job at American Axle in Lansing was shipped to Mexico along with 1,900 others. As Ms. Ward told me, "I loved my job. I was able to provide for my family and put a roof over their heads. We had a good thing going. We raised our family together. Then the company wanted to slash pay in half and cut benefits. The workers went on strike but eventually made concessions. Still, the company moved the plant to Mexico. A lot of lives were destroyed by what happened, and it's not fair." Kim is right. It is not fair.

Unfortunately, Kim's story is hardly unique. In fact, it is a recurring theme all throughout the Wolverine State. In 1960, Detroit was the richest city in America and General Motors was the nation's largest private employer, paying union workers a living wage with affordable health care and a secure retirement. But, as a result of our destructive trade rules and other unfair policies, half of Detroit's autoworkers lost their jobs from 1998 to 2011 as GM and Ford moved factory after factory to Mexico. Today, the Motor City is a shell of its former self and is one of the poorest cities in America.

No city in America has suffered more than Flint, Michigan. Long before Flint's children were poisoned by contaminated drinking water, the city was poisoned by disastrous trade policies. Unfettered free trade and corporate tax loopholes allowed General Motors to eliminate more than 72,000 jobs in Flint when it moved several manufacturing plants to Mexico. Free trade turned this once-prosperous middle-class city, where residents could own a home, raise a family, and retire in dignity and with security, into a place where good jobs are scarce and extreme poverty is high. Today, one quarter of Flint residents have an annual income of less than $15,000 and 65 percent of its children live in poverty.

Of course, Michigan is not alone. In Wisconsin, I visited town after town devastated by major manufacturing plant closures. In Janesville, General Motors shut down its manufacturing plant in 2008, eliminated over 2,800 good-paying jobs, and moved the facility to Silao, Mexico, where workers are paid one-tenth of what the workers in Janesville made. Another eight hundred people lost their jobs when Chrysler shut down its engine plant in Kenosha and moved it to Saltillo, Mexico.

In Indiana, I saw once vibrant and strong manufacturing towns like Gary, South Bend, Muncie, Bloomington, Indianapolis, and Evansville all littered with abandoned factories and steel mills, sky-high poverty rates, and foreclosed homes. I met with workers manufacturing furnaces for United Technologies who were told that 2,100 of their jobs would soon be shipped to Mexico, where workers are paid just $3 an hour. It turns out the announcement to the workers that they would be losing their jobs was caught on video, and when that video went viral, people from all walks of life caught a glimpse of the callousness by which corporate America shuts down plants and destroys lives.

On the video, an executive tells the workers: "It became clear that the best way to stay competitive and protect the business for the long term is to move production from our facility in Indianapolis to Monterrey, Mexico. . . . I want to be clear, this is strictly a business decision. We still have a job to do; we have to take care of what needs to be done every day and do it well, just like we always do."

You can't make this stuff up. The people running this company have no shame. United Technologies made a $7 billion profit in 2015 thanks to the hard work of its employees, who were rewarded with the announcement that they would soon lose their jobs because the company had to cut costs to remain competitive. Of course, United Technologies had plenty of money in 2014 to provide its retiring CEO, Louis Schenevert, with a golden parachute worth $172 million. This is the kind of corporate greed that is destroying the middle class of this country—a $172 million severance package for the boss, while workers are thrown out on the street. And it is happening all over America.

In Pennsylvania, I learned about a thousand workers in Dunmore who lost their jobs in 2001 when Thomson Consumer Electronics moved its television manufacturing plant to Mexicali, Mexico, where workers are paid $4.40 an hour in wages and benefits—less than a third of what the workers in Pennsylvania made. In 2008, Sony shut down the last television factory plant in America, in Westmoreland, Pennsylvania, and moved production to a facility in Baja, Mexico. In 2014, Americans purchased over 34 million television sets. Not a single one of them was made in the U.S.

In Chicago, we learned that Nabisco was shutting down its manufacturing plant at 73rd and Kedzie and shipping six hundred jobs to Mexico, where workers make in one week what the workers on the South Side of Chicago made in just a couple of hours. In June 2016, the Democratic National Committee's Platform Committee heard heart-wrenching testimony from Michael Smith, a proud father of four children and one of the hundreds of workers who had lost jobs at this plant.

Here is what Mr. Smith said: "Nabisco built the largest cookie and cracker production facility in the world in Mexico. They then asked people like me in Chicago to compete with workers in Mexico, where the general minimum wage is just 73 pesos per day, or $4.19 per day. We were asked to take a wage and benefit reduction of sixty percent. . . . But even with this sacrifice . . . there are six hundred less of us working in Chicago as our jobs are moved to a new workforce in Central Mexico, a workforce they hired at the factory that they built with the profits we and our families for generations have made for Nabisco. I am not a number, nor are my family, nor my neighbors, nor my coworkers merely numbers. We are, however, victims of this ongoing global snatch-and-grab that has gutted our community, denied our children a bright future, and made our communities less safe as a result of homelessness and the inability to provide important public services."

We owe it to Michael Smith, Kim Ward, the GM workers in Flint, the United Technologies workers, and the millions of others like them who have lost their jobs, to develop trade policies that create jobs in America, not in Mexico and other low-wage countries.

And, let's be clear: This is a problem that is not limited to the Midwest. It is hitting every corner of our country.

When I visited North Carolina, I saw how our trade policies have battered the Tar Heel State, which was a worldwide leader in the manufacturing of furniture, textiles, and apparel. Jobs in these industries once allowed North Carolinians with little education to make a middle-class income at textile mills, furniture factories, and garment shops. That is no longer true today. Since the World Trade Organization (WTO) began phasing out quotas for textile imports, North Carolina has lost over 70 percent of its textile jobs and 63 percent of its apparel workers. And since NAFTA, the Tar Heel State has seen half of its manufacturing workforce disappear.

In 2008, hundreds of workers making $15 an hour in the small town of Lenoir lost their jobs when Broyhill Furniture moved factories to China, where workers are paid just 70 cents an hour. Median income in Wilkes County, another area hard-hit by the closure of textile mills, has plummeted by 30 percent since 2000. Mount Airy, the hometown of Andy Griffith, has lost more than three thousand textile and apparel jobs since 1999. Former textile workers in this town of ten thousand are now lucky if they get a job paying a fraction of the wages they previously earned.

Leviton's light switch factory in Ashe County shipped 211 jobs to Mexico in 2009. While you will rarely hear about this on ABC, CBS, NBC, and Fox News, unfettered free trade has decimated North Carolina, resulting in the loss of almost 360,000 good-paying jobs.

In Kentucky, Mattel shuttered its last U.S. toy manufacturing plant in 2001, shipping 980 jobs to Mexico, China, and other countries in Asia. Thirteen years later, Fruit of the Loom (owned by Warren Buffett, the second-richest person in the U.S., worth more than $68 billion) closed its last U.S. manufacturing plant, in Jamestown, outsourcing six hundred jobs to Honduras. This one really stung local officials, who had just approved a $12 million taxpayer-funded water plant, primarily to benefit Fruit of the Loom.

"How can you reconcile destroying the livelihoods of six hundred families," a local county judge wrote to Mr. Buffett at the time. "Surely greater profits can't be more important than the lives of these people," he wrote, pleading with Mr. Buffett to keep the plant open. Mr. Buffett never responded, and the factory was closed just a few months later.

In 1991, Fruit of the Loom was the second-largest manufacturing employer in Kentucky, with eleven thousand workers. Today, this iconic American company no longer employs a single factory worker in the U.S. Not one.

Out on the West Coast, I visited Anaheim, California, the home of Disneyland, most of whose popular toys are made in sweatshops in China. And, by the way, I learned that many of its theme park employees earn wages so low that they are forced to sleep in motels. Of course, not everyone is hurting at Disney. In 2015, the company made $8.4 billion in profits and paid its CEO almost $45 million in total compensation. If you want to know what a rigged economy and corporate greed look like, look no further than this Fortune 500 company.

After Anaheim, I visited the Port of Los Angeles, where huge container and cargo ships arrive filled to capacity with televisions, computers, bicycles, toys, and other products, all made in China. Sadly, many of these ships return to Asia empty. This situation has become so bad that even *The Wall Street Journal*, one of the most ardent pro–free trade publications on the planet, reported on October 13, 2015, "One of the fastest-growing U.S. exports right now is air," after a surge in container ships left U.S. ports without a single American-made product to be exported abroad.

To understand the absurdity of our unfettered free trade policies, just take a trip to one of the many gift shops at our national parks and museums. A few years ago, long before I had considered running for president, I visited the Smithsonian's National Museum of American History to do some holiday shopping for my grandkids. What I discovered is that in the gift shop of the premier museum dedicated to celebrating the history of the United States, most of the products offered for sale were not even made in America!

It was reflective of where we were as a nation when bronze-colored busts of U.S. presidents, from George Washington to Barack Obama, were marked "Made in China."

Unfortunately, this situation was not unique to the National Museum of American History. The same was true in gift shops at the Jefferson Memorial, the Washington Monument, the FDR Memorial, and the Lincoln Memorial. Product after product at these stores were made in China, or Honduras, or Mexico. The good news is that today, after I raised the issue, those bronze presidential busts are made in America.

As a member of Congress and as a senator, not only have I opposed every one of these job-killing free trade agreements, but I am proud to have stood with workers on picket lines to protest them. And as someone who has been all over this country as part of a presidential campaign, and has seen the job destruction that trade deals have caused, I am more committed than ever to reversing these policies.

When we talk about unfettered free trade, it is important to understand that these policies have been developed in a bipartisan manner, with the support of both Republican and Democratic presidents. Corporate America spoke, the leaders of both parties responded to their needs, and American workers suffered. These agreements have also been supported by virtually the entire corporate media. Check the editorial pages of *every major newspaper* in America and you will find them all pro–free trade.

It is astounding how wrong proponents of unfettered free trade have always been. Recall what they have said year after year, trade agreement after trade agreement.

In 1993, during the debate over NAFTA, President Bill Clinton promised us that the trade agreement with Mexico and Canada would "create a million jobs in the first five years."

Kentucky's Senator Mitch McConnell, later to become the Republican Senate majority leader, promised: "American firms will not move to Mexico just for lower wages."

The ultraconservative Heritage Foundation told us: "Virtually all economists agree that NAFTA will produce a net increase of U.S. jobs over the next decade."

Unfortunately, President Clinton, Senator McConnell, the Heritage Foundation, and many, many others were way off the mark. Instead of creating a million American jobs, the Economic Policy Institute found, NAFTA destroyed more than 850,000 American jobs. In fact, every state in the nation has lost jobs as a result of NAFTA.

In 1993, the year before NAFTA was implemented, the United States actually had a trade surplus with Mexico of more than $1.6 billion. Since NAFTA was implemented in 1994, the United States has run up a cumulative trade deficit with Mexico of nearly $1 trillion. Last year alone, the trade deficit with Mexico was more than $60 billion, as we imported a record-breaking $296 billion in Mexican-made products. By any objective measure, NAFTA has been a complete failure.

Yet, in 2000, less than six years after NAFTA was implemented, most Republicans, too many Democrats, and editorial boards all across the country told us that what we really needed was another unfettered free trade deal, this time with China, an authoritarian Communist country almost four times our size. They told us that this trade agreement would create a thriving middle class in China that would purchase all kinds of American-made goods and products. And we were told that this trade deal was not NAFTA. This one would be much different and much better.

In fact, President Clinton said that granting China permanent normal trade relations (PNTR) status would be "a hundred-to-nothing deal for America when it comes to the economic consequences."

A few months later, Jerry Jasinowski, then head of the National Association of Manufacturers (representing the largest multinational corporations in the world, including ExxonMobil, Intel, Xerox, Dow Chemical, and Procter & Gamble), told us that Chinese consumers were "hungry for the opportunity to buy more American products" and that normalizing trade with China would "create hundreds of thousands of good-paying jobs for U.S. workers."

A Republican member of Congress from Connecticut assured us that PNTR with China would be "the bargain of the century" that would "bring down the curtain of Chinese protectionism."

They could not have been more wrong. PNTR with China has led to the loss of 3.2 million jobs, as American workers have been forced to compete with some of the most desperate workers in the world. Since normalized trade with China was enacted, the U.S. has racked up a cumulative trade deficit with China of more than $3.7 trillion, and our annual trade deficit with that country has more than quadrupled.

How could the proponents of free trade have been so wrong, again? Maybe, just maybe, they were purposely misleading us, or perhaps some of them were misled by corporate America. But, in terms of PNTR with China,

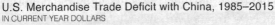

U.S. Merchandise Trade Deficit with China, 1985–2015
IN CURRENT YEAR DOLLARS

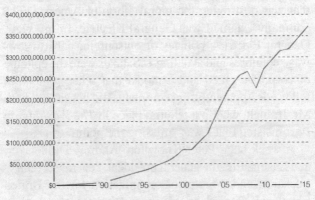

Data Source: U.S. Census Bureau and the Bureau of Economic Analysis

it is interesting to see what those in favor of free trade said *before* the deal passed Congress and what they said *after* PNTR was signed into law in 2000.

On December 6, 2002, Jeffrey Immelt, then-CEO of General Electric, said at an investor meeting: "When I am talking to GE managers, I talk China, China, China, China, China. You need to be there. You need to change the way people talk about it and how they get there. I am a nut on China. Outsourcing from China is going to grow to 5 billion dollars. We are building a tech center in China. Every discussion today has to center on China. The cost basis is extremely attractive. You can take an eighteen-cubic-foot refrigerator, make it in China, land it in the United States, and land it for less than we can make an eighteen-cubic-foot refrigerator today, ourselves."

That's what PNTR with China was really all about. It was not about creating American jobs. It was about allowing companies like General Electric to ship decent-paying American jobs to China.

During the campaign, I was asked by the editorial board of New York's *Daily News* to name a corporation that was destroying the moral fabric of America. The company I named was General Electric. In my view, General Electric's policies of outsourcing jobs to low-wage countries and avoiding U.S. taxes were the epitome of corporate greed and a model that other companies followed. Apparently, my comments did not sit well with Mr. Immelt, who in a rebuttal piece in *The Washington Post* insisted that I was "missing the point."

A week later, Peter Knowlton, Andrew Dinkelaker, and Eugene Elk, the general president, general secretary-treasurer, and director of organization for the United Electrical, Radio and Machine Workers of America (UE), responded to Mr. Immelt in a letter to the editor.

Here is what they wrote: "As officers of a national union that has represented GE workers for 80 years, we can affirm, from our union's experience and knowledge of GE, that Mr. Sanders is right. Since 1999, GE has reduced its U.S. workforce by 37 percent, and since 2008 the company has closed more than 50 factories and facilities in the United States. In 1995, 68 percent of GE's total employment was in the United States; by 2015 it was 38 percent. For a decade, GE has pursued a policy it calls the 'competitive wage,' aimed at cutting the wage rates of its manufacturing workers in half, even as the pay of Mr. Immelt and other executives soars higher into the stratosphere. . . . Mr. Immelt claims that GE is 'in the business of building real things and generating real growth' for our country. We fail to see how destroying communities, turning good jobs into poverty jobs and depriving your retired employees of health-care benefits generates 'real growth' in anything but the company's profits and executives' pay."

General Electric is hardly alone. Just three years after the PNTR deal, and two years after China was admitted into the WTO, the National Labor Committee documented grievous labor conditions in that country. They found that Wal-Mart had nearly 4,500 factories in China where workers were paid as little as 13 cents an hour and worked as many as sixteen hours a day, seven days a week. While I expect that these labor conditions are better now than they were in 2003, the reality is that there are millions of Chinese workers who are still being exploited making products for Wal-Mart.

So here's the bottom line. Wal-Mart does virtually all of its manufacturing in China. In the United States, they pay their employees starvation wages, forcing many of them to go on government programs like food stamps and Medicaid in order to survive. And, then, not surprisingly, it turns out that the Walton family, now worth over $130 billion, is the wealthiest family in America.

And let's be clear: Blue-collar workers aren't the only ones who have been hurt by "free" trade. One of the things free trade supporters have told us is that while we may lose some blue-collar jobs, PNTR with China and other trade agreements will create millions of high-paying white-collar technology and computer jobs— the jobs of the future. Well, that also turned out to be wrong, and again, the CEOs knew it.

On October 10, 2003, *The Wall Street Journal* reported: "Andy Grove, the founder of Intel, predicted . . . that the U.S. will lose the bulk of its information technology jobs to China and India over the next decade. . . . Given cost and productivity pressures, the Santa Clara–based semiconductor maker reluctantly 'has no choice' but to continue sending work abroad, Grove said."

Of course, Mr. Grove was right. Since 1997, we have lost over 43 percent of computer jobs—ranging from the production of semiconductors to medical equipment. That's more than the 31 percent loss in our overall manufacturing employment.

And just think about all of the innovations U.S. companies have made in technology. The iPad, the iPhone, the iPod, IBM computers, Dell Computers, the Microsoft Xbox, big-screen TVs. None of these American inventions are manufactured in the U.S. Most of them are manufactured in China. In fact, according to a December 15, 2010, article in *The Wall Street Journal*, Apple's iPhone—one of the bestselling U.S. technology products—actually added $1.9 billion to the U.S. trade deficit with China in 2009.

Michael Marks, then-CEO of Flextronics, a company that manufactures Xbox consoles for Microsoft and computer hardware, told *Businessweek* in 2003: "All electronics hardware manufacturing is going to China. . . . Our employment base is actually at a record high: about 100,000. We've done this by cutting the workforce in high-cost locations and adding in low-cost places. We put a lot of consumer products in Asia, where they belong in the first place. China has been the hottest location. We have 35,000 there. For example, we moved all of the production of Microsoft's Xbox consoles from Mexico to China."

On October 21, 2004, John Chambers, the CEO of Cisco, said, "What we're trying to do is outline an entire strategy of becoming a Chinese company."

All of these comments were made just within a few years of the PNTR trade deal with China. The reality is that PNTR had nothing to do with creating high-tech jobs in America, any more than it did with creating blue-collar jobs here. Rather, it just made it easier to ship both high-tech and blue-collar jobs abroad.

Twelve years after the passage of PNTR with China, there was a Democratic president in the White House who had campaigned on rewriting NAFTA and opposing trade agreements negotiated by George W. Bush.

Here is what then-candidate Barack Obama told the AFL-CIO in Philadelphia on April 2, 2008:

> *What I refuse to accept is that we have to sign trade deals like the South Korea Agreement that are bad for American workers. What I oppose, and what I have always opposed, are trade deals that put the interests of multinational corporations ahead of the interests of American workers—like NAFTA, and CAFTA, and permanent normal trade relations with China. And I'll also oppose the Colombia Free Trade Agreement if President Bush insists on sending it to Congress, because the violence against unions in Colombia would make a mockery of the very labor protections that we have insisted be included in these kinds of agreements. So you can trust me when I say that whatever trade deals we negotiate when I'm president will be good for American workers, and that they'll have strong labor and environmental protections that we'll enforce.*

Unfortunately, once in office, President Obama urged Congress to approve the exact same deals that he opposed as a candidate. In 2012, he insisted that the South Korea Free Trade Agreement would create at least 70,000 American jobs and reduce the trade deficit. The U.S. Chamber of Commerce went even further by saying it would create some 280,000 jobs. They were both wrong. Since its implementation, we have lost over 100,000 jobs to South Korea, and our trade deficit with that country has gone up by about 115 percent.

President Obama promised that mechanisms in the Colombia Free Trade Agreement would prevent the assassinations, murders, and horrific violence against trade unionists that had gone on for so long in that country. Yet, according to the AFL-CIO, since the agreement was signed, "workers attempting to exercise their rights have suffered at least 1,466 threats and acts of violence, including 955 death threats and 99 assassinations."

Just think about that for a moment. If we found out that ninety-nine CEOs had been assassinated in Colombia, do you think we would continue to have a free trade agreement with that country? I don't think so.

President Obama is a friend of mine. I have worked with him on many issues. But on the issue of trade he has been dead wrong. And today he is wrong again, for working with corporate America and advocating for the passage of the Trans-Pacific Partnership.

The simple reality is that the TPP is based on the same flawed trade model as NAFTA. The TPP should be called what it is: NAFTA on steroids. One recent study estimates that TPP would mean pay cuts for all but the wealthiest 10 percent of Americans, making the growing problem of income inequality even worse. Another study estimates the TPP would lead to the elimination of nearly half a million American jobs and a significant reduction in economic growth.

Albert Einstein once said, "The definition of insanity is doing the same thing over and over again and expecting different results."

Passing the TPP would be insane. Unfettered free trade has failed us in the past, and it will fail us in the future. But this time, with the TPP, the consequences could be even direr.

The TPP continues an approach toward trade that forces Americans to compete against desperate workers overseas. In Vietnam, the minimum wage is just 65 cents an hour. Even worse, the TPP would give Malaysia privileged access to the U.S. market. This is a country where migrant workers in the electronics industry are working as modern-day slaves—some have even had their passports and wages confiscated and are unable to return to their own countries. It is bad enough to force U.S. workers to compete with low-wage labor; they should not have to compete with no-wage labor.

When analyzing a free trade agreement like the TPP, it's important to take a look at who is for it and who is against it. Large, multinational corporations that have already outsourced millions of good-paying American jobs to China, Mexico, Bangladesh, and other low-wage countries are among TPP's biggest supporters. They think TPP is a great idea because they understand it will allow them to accelerate efforts to hire cheap labor abroad. Wall Street investors and large pharmaceutical companies also love the TPP, because their global profits will increase dramatically if this agreement is passed.

On the other hand, every union in this country, representing more than 12 million American workers, is opposed to the TPP, because they all understand it will lead to the loss of decent-paying jobs and will depress wages. Virtually every major environmental organization also opposes TPP, understanding that it will make it easier for multinational corporations to pollute and degrade the environment.

Many major religious groups oppose TPP because they know it would reward some of the worst violators of human rights in the world.

The TPP, like other free trade agreements, advances a very dangerous provision that undermines democracy and allows multinational corporations to override governmental decisions designed to protect public health, labor rights, and the environment.

This provision, called the "investor-state dispute settlement system," allows a foreign corporation to sue a government if it believes that its expected future profits would be threatened. This is no small issue. It is a major step toward the complete corporatization of the world economy, where corporate profits are explicitly made more important than the health and well-being of the people of the world.

As an example of how this investor-state dispute resolution works, thanks to NAFTA, TransCanada is suing the U.S. in an international tribunal for $15 billion in damages because President Obama did the right thing by rejecting the Keystone XL Pipeline. The president's decision, made in the interest of the nation, was based on his concern that the pipeline would accelerate climate change.

However, according to the investor-state dispute resolution system within NAFTA, TransCanada's "right" to make a profit might just supersede President Obama's desire to protect the planet.

As the Sierra Club cowrote along with other environmental groups, "The Obama Administration's rejection of the Keystone XL pipeline was an execution of its legal right, done amidst widespread evidence that the project would hurt communities and the environment. It is therefore egregious that, under NAFTA, TransCanada can demand billions of dollars for a sound policy decision that is squarely within the U.S. law."

And TransCanada isn't the first company to use the investor-state dispute settlement system to extort money from countries that had the temerity to pass laws or regulations impacting corporate profits. In 2012, a World Bank tribunal ordered the country of Ecuador to pay a $1.7 billion fine to Occidental Petroleum for canceling an oil contract in the Amazon for environmental reasons. This penalty was later reduced to $980 million, which is still more than 1 percent of Ecuador's entire GDP.

A French waste management firm, Veolia, has used the investor-state dispute settlement process to sue Egypt for $110 million because it increased the minimum wage and improved labor laws. In other words, Egypt's "crime" was trying to improve life for its low-wage workers.

Vattenfall, a Swedish energy company, sued Germany for $5 billion over its decision to phase out nuclear power after the Fukushima disaster.

Do we really want to tell governments all around the world, including ours, that if they pass legislation protecting the well-being of their citizens or protecting their environment they could be subject to substantial fines? Of course not. But that's exactly what is happening today. And TPP would only make it worse.

Moreover, the TPP would substantially raise the price of prescription drugs for some of the most desperate people in the world. Pharmaceutical companies are doing everything they can to extend their monopoly and market-exclusivity rights to make it harder for people to access lower-cost generic drugs, even if it means that thousands will die because they cannot afford the drugs they need.

According to Oxfam International, more than half of HIV/AIDS patients in Vietnam—over 125,000 people—could lose access to the medications they need to survive if the TPP is implemented. Doctors Without Borders has said, "The TPP agreement is on track to become the most harmful trade pact ever for access to medicines in developing countries."

Enough is enough. We need to do everything we can to reject TPP. To do otherwise would be insanity.

The goal of U.S. trade policy must be to create good-paying jobs in this country and to lift living standards around the world. We can no longer continue with an approach that leads to a race to the bottom for American workers and huge profits for multinational corporations.

Over the past thirty-five years, trade agreement after trade agreement has not only failed to create jobs, but has instead contributed to unprecedented and unsustainable trade deficits, the net loss of nearly 5 million U.S. manufacturing jobs, millions of lost service-sector jobs, and flat or declining median wages.

Economists across the political spectrum—including the pro-NAFTA Peterson Institute for International Economics, which estimated that 39 percent of the growth in U.S. wage inequality is attributable to our disastrous trade deals—agree that "free" trade has contributed to rising U.S. income inequality. U.S. manufacturing workers who lose jobs to trade and find new employment are typically forced to take significant pay cuts. Three out of every five displaced manufacturing workers who were rehired in 2014 took home smaller paychecks, and one out of three lost more than 20 percent of his or her income.

We have got to turn this around. American jobs must no longer be our number one export. We must not only defeat the TPP, we must fundamentally renegotiate our failed trade agreements—including NAFTA, PNTR with China, and other existing trade pacts.

As part of a new trade policy, we must eliminate the incentives baked into our current trade and tax agreements that make it easier for multinational corporations to ship jobs overseas. Corporations should not be able to get a tax deduction for the expenses involved in moving their factories abroad—and throwing American workers out on the street.

Instead of providing federal tax breaks, contracts, grants, and loans to corporations that outsource jobs, we need to support the small businesses that are creating good jobs in America. The backbone of a growing economy is made up of small businesses on "Main Street" all over America, not giant corporations and huge financial institutions on Wall Street. As big multinational corporations have downsized and outsourced millions of jobs overseas, small businesses have been doing the exact opposite. We need to help those companies that are creating jobs in this country, not in China.

It is clear to me that the American people want their tax dollars used to put their fellow Americans back to work. They want government contracts going to American companies, not companies abroad. That's the way it's done in every other country, and there's no reason why it can't be done that way here as well. We must expand, not eviscerate, "Buy American," "Buy Local," and other government policies that will increase jobs in the U.S. This includes service-sector contracts that will stop the offshoring of government call centers and data processing facilities to the Philippines and other countries.

Moreover, we need to make sure that strong and binding labor, environmental, and human rights standards are written into the core text of all trade agreements. At a minimum, this means that all countries must comply with the standards of the International Labor Organization, the Multilateral Environmental Agreements, and the United Nations Covenant on Civil and Political Rights.

We must add to the core text of every U.S. trade agreement enforceable rules against currency cheating, which allows countries to unfairly dump their products in this country and makes our exports more expensive abroad. And we need to establish a simple rule that food may be imported into the United States only if it meets or exceeds U.S. standards with respect to safety, pesticide use, inspections, packaging, and labeling.

We must also take a hard look at the concept of a "social tariff." It is inherently unfair for American workers to have to compete against countries with abysmally low wages, minimal environmental standards, and poor records on human rights.

REFORMING WALL STREET

Today, the six major financial institutions in this country have almost $10 trillion in assets, equivalent to nearly 60 percent of our entire GDP. They issue more than two-thirds of all credit cards, underwrite more than 35 percent of all mortgages, hold 95 percent of all financial derivatives, and control more than 40 percent of all bank deposits. Meanwhile, their business model is based on fraud. It's time for real Wall Street reform.

Greed, fraud, dishonesty, and arrogance. These are the words that best describe the reality of Wall Street today.

Fortunately, the American people are catching on. They understand that there is something profoundly wrong when a handful of billionaires on Wall Street wield extraordinary power and influence over the political and economic life of our country. They understand that Congress does not regulate Wall Street—it is Wall Street that regulates Congress.

And the reason for that is simple: Not a single industry in America has contributed more to congressional campaigns and political parties than the financial sector. None. Since the 1990s, the financial services industry has spent billions of dollars on lobbying and campaign contributions to get Congress to deregulate Wall Street, repeal the Glass-Steagall Act, and eliminate consumer protection laws.

They spent this money to get the government "off their backs," promising to show the American people

Press interest after a speech about Wall Street in New York.
(Arun Chaudhary, Revolution Messaging)

how much more innovative and efficient a deregulated financial sector would be. Well, they sure showed the American people. In 2008, Wall Street, the largest unregulated gambling casino in the history of the world, crashed and precipitated the worst financial crisis since the Great Depression. This crash caused incalculable harm to tens of millions of Americans and people throughout the world. In fact, Wall Street greed nearly destroyed the U.S. and global economies.

THE 2008 CRASH

As a result of the financial meltdown of 2008, more than 9 million American jobs were destroyed. Real unemployment skyrocketed to more than 17 percent, as more than 27 million workers were unemployed, underemployed, or had stopped looking for work altogether.

The American dream of homeownership turned into a nightmare of foreclosure for millions of households, as more and more people could not afford to pay their

mortgages. This was bound to happen. For years, financial predators received fat commissions from lenders
for steering Americans into the riskiest subprime
mortgages imaginable—no documentation, no job, no
income . . . no problem. And then, the banks bundled
those mortgages, over and over again, into almost worthless and unregulated derivatives, until the house of cards
collapsed.

By the time the dust settled, the housing meltdown
had led to 15 million foreclosures and a huge spike in
homelessness. And a third of the remaining homeowners were underwater—owing more on their mortgages
than their homes were worth. It got so bad that thousands of Americans set up tent cities in Sacramento,
Fresno, Tampa Bay, and Reno because they had no place
else to live. Millions more lived in cars or on a friend's
couch.

As a result of the Wall Street crash, Americans lost
more than $13 trillion in personal wealth—shattering
retirement dreams, wiping out life savings, and making
it impossible for families to afford to send their kids to
college. And while the crisis caused enormous economic
pain in every corner of the country, African-American
and Latino families were hardest hit, because they were
disproportionately targeted with subprime mortgages,
many of which were designed to fail. It is no accident
that minorities were 70 percent more likely to lose their
homes to foreclosure than were white Americans. The
ugly stain of racism manifests itself in many different
ways in twenty-first-century America.

And because African-Americans and Latinos tended
to have most of their wealth tied up in their homes, the
total net worth of African-American households fell by
more than 50 percent and by more than 65 percent for
Latino families.

Today, nine years after the housing crisis began, 4.3

million homeowners still owe more than their houses are worth. Further, as a result of the ongoing housing crisis, more than a quarter of the nation's 43 million renter households pay at least half their incomes for housing, leaving precious little for other necessities like food and medicine.

WHAT A RIGGED FINANCIAL SYSTEM LOOKS LIKE

Wall Street is the most powerful institution in this country, and the financial leaders there wield that power ferociously to protect their interests. As a result of the "revolving door" between Wall Street and the federal government, the needs and interests of the giant banks become converted into government policy. Not only does Wall Street have an endless supply of powerful people to lobby government, they hold key positions *within* the government—including two recent secretaries of the treasury from Goldman Sachs.

No matter how irresponsible their actions are, the financial titans always end up on top. Millions still suffer as a result of the Wall Street crash, but not the people in power who helped cause that disaster. While middle-class Americans lost their jobs, their homes, and their life savings, the people on top are doing phenomenally well. Here are just a few examples of people who were operating the levers of government and pushed policies that helped to create the Great Recession of 2008:

Robert Rubin. Robert Rubin stands out as the poster child for the revolving door that exists between Wall Street and Washington. Rubin started his career by making a fortune at Goldman Sachs, where he worked for twenty-six years, including two years as its co-chairman. In 1993, President Clinton appointed him head of the National Economic Council, and in 1995 he became treasury secretary. While in government he spearheaded financial deregulation, including the repeal of Glass-Steagall. He also prevented the regulation of derivatives.

In 1999, Rubin returned to Wall Street, and after brokering a deal with Republicans to legalize the $70 billion merger between Citicorp and Travelers Group, he was hired by the newly formed Citigroup and received about $15 million a year for his services.

Less than a decade later—a decade in which Rubin earned more than $126 million at Citigroup—taxpayers bailed out his megabank because of the enormous risks Rubin and others encouraged it to take. In 2010, the bipartisan Financial Crisis Inquiry Commission (FCIC) voted unanimously to refer Rubin to the Justice Department for "potential fraud" for misleading investors about Citigroup's exposure to subprime mortgages.

When DOJ declined to act, Phil Angelides, chair of the FCIC, said, "It's been a disappointment to me and others that the Justice Department has not pursued the potential wrongdoing by individuals identified in the matters we referred to them. At the very least, they owe the American people the reassurance that they conducted a thorough investigation of individuals who engaged in misconduct." I couldn't agree more.

Henry "Hank" Paulson. Like Rubin, a Democrat, Hank Paulson, who is a Republican, was a leader at Goldman Sachs. He was the CEO there from 1999 to 2006. While there he accumulated 4.5 million shares of Goldman stock, and in his last year he received a $45 million bonus. Under Paulson's leadership, Goldman engaged in the kinds of reckless schemes that led to the financial crisis just a few years later.

After George W. Bush nominated Paulson to become treasury secretary in 2006, he had to sell his stocks to avoid a conflict of interest, netting about $600 million. As treasury secretary, Paulson repeatedly defended the deregulation of Wall Street, assuring Congress and the world that the markets were strong and the financial system stable. That is, until one day when he came before the Senate Democratic and Republican caucuses, handed us a three-page bill, and said that if we did not give him a $700 *billion* blank check within a few days, the entire financial system would collapse. The great defender of free market capitalism came to Congress for a bailout—and the largest welfare check in the history of the country.

At the meeting of the Democratic Caucus, I suggested to Paulson that he ask his banker and billionaire friends who benefited from the excesses of Wall Street, rather than middle-class taxpayers, to pick up the tab. Needless to say, Paulson disagreed.

Hank Paulson is now worth an estimated $700 million.

Tim Geithner. A Robert Rubin acolyte, Geithner was president of the New York Federal Reserve between 2003 and 2009. In this position, he failed to ensure the safety and soundness of financial institutions before, during, and after the financial crisis. Instead of losing his job, Geithner was promoted by President Obama to treasury secretary, in which capacity he opposed strong efforts to regulate Wall Street, break up the banks, claw back executive bonuses, and protect underwater homeowners.

After leaving Treasury, Geithner landed a job as president of a multibillion-dollar hedge fund, where he received a generous line of credit from JPMorgan Chase, a bank that received over $400 billion in financial assistance from—you guessed it—the New York Fed and the Treasury Department.

Alan Greenspan. In my view, Alan Greenspan will go down in history as one of the worst chairmen of the Federal Reserve. Future textbooks will refer to Greenspan as an example of how *not* to run a central bank. In order to underline the bipartisan support that Wall Street has in Congress, during his time of leadership at the Fed he was hailed not only by Republicans but also by most Democrats as "the Maestro." This, despite his extremely conservative views, which called for, among other reactionary policies, the elimination of the minimum wage.

In 2000, at a House Financial Services Committee hearing on bank mergers, I asked Greenspan, "Aren't you concerned that with such a growing concentration of wealth, if one of these huge institutions fails it will have a horrendous impact on the national and global economy?" Greenspan replied, "No, I'm not. I believe that the general growth in large institutions has occurred in the context of an underlying structure of markets in which many of the larger risks are dramatically—I should say, fully—hedged."

Greenspan could not have been more wrong. Yet after leaving the Fed, he was hired to advise some of the biggest banks and wealthiest hedge fund managers in the world. He now has an estimated net worth of at least $10 million.

And on and on it goes.

AND THE RICH GET RICHER

Median household income has gone down by $1,400 since 1999, but banks made a record-breaking profit of $164 billion in 2015 alone. The top twenty-five hedge fund managers made more in 2015 than the combined salaries of every kindergarten teacher in America, while paying a lower tax rate than most truck drivers or nurses.

Millions of Americans lost their homes and much of their wealth during the foreclosure crisis, but one hedge fund manager alone made almost $4 billion on their economic pain by betting that the housing market would collapse.

While taxpayers provided over a trillion dollars in financial assistance to bail out Goldman Sachs and JPMorgan Chase, today the CEOs of these financial institutions are worth over $1 billion each. The reality is that Wall Street executives continue to receive huge compensation packages and bonuses, as if the financial crisis they created never happened.

THE BUSINESS MODEL ON WALL STREET IS FRAUD

It seems like every few weeks we read about a giant financial institution that has been fined or that has reached a settlement for illegal behavior. Some people believe this is an aberration—that we have an honest financial system in which, every now and then, a major institution does something wrong and gets caught. Unfortunately, the overwhelming evidence suggests otherwise.

The reality is that fraud *is* the business model on Wall Street. It is not the *exception* to the rule—it *is* the rule. And in the weak regulatory climate we have, Wall Street likely gets away with a lot more illegal behavior than we even know about.

How many times have we heard the myth that what Wall Street did may have been wrong but it wasn't illegal? It is time to shatter that myth once and for all. Since 2009, major banks have been fined more than $200 billion for reckless, unfair, and deceptive activities.

Here are just a few examples:

- In August 2014, Bank of America paid more than $16 billion to settle charges that it lied to investors about the riskiness of the mortgage-backed securities it sold during the run-up to the crisis.
- In April 2016, Goldman Sachs reached a $5 billion settlement for marketing and selling fraudulent mortgage-backed securities that were the foundation of the housing crisis. This is in addition to the $550 million Goldman paid to settle another 2010 fraudulent mortgage case.
- In April 2016, Wells Fargo reached a $1.2 billion settlement with the Department of Justice (DOJ) for "reckless" and "shoddy" underwriting on thousands of home loans from 2001 to 2008.
- In February 2016, Morgan Stanley reached a $3.2 billion settlement with the DOJ and several states for misleading investors about the quality of the mortgage bonds it was selling.
- In February 2016, HSBC reached a $601 million settlement with the DOJ and other federal and state agencies for abusive mortgage lending practices.
- In July 2014, Citigroup reached a $7 billion settlement for mortgage fraud. Then–attorney general Eric Holder said Citigroup's "activities contributed mightily to the financial crisis that devastated our

economy in 2008. . . . The bank's misconduct was egregious. As a result of their assurances that toxic financial products were sound, Citigroup was able to expand its market share and increase profits." Richard Bowen, a former Citigroup executive turned whistle-blower, added, "In July of 2008, I gave the SEC a thousand pages documenting fraud and the false representations given to investors in many securitizations. . . . In light of the huge losses this behavior caused our country, it is out-rageous that, six years later, a settlement of only civil fraud charges would be announced, with no individuals being held accountable and no real admission of wrongdoing or true penalties as-sessed."

- In November 2013, JPMorgan Chase settled for $13 billion for lying to Fannie Mae and Freddie Mac about the quality of mortgage-backed secu-rities it sold them. Settlement documents revealed how every large bank in the U.S. committed mort-gage fraud. In 2011, JPMorgan also admitted to wrongly foreclosing on some military families and overcharging 4,500 more for their mortgages. "We failed to comply with aspects of the law," admit-ted an executive vice president.
- In 2011, the Justice Department fined Bank of America (which had purchased Countrywide) $335 million because Countrywide charged 200,000 minority homeowners more for their mortgages than they did whites and steered them into risky subprime loans designed to fail.
- In 2012, Wells Fargo was fined $175 million to settle similar claims of discriminatory and preda-tory subprime lending in black and Hispanic neighborhoods. According to sworn affidavits,

Wells Fargo loan officers referred to black customers as "mud people" and called their subprime mortgages "ghetto loans."

Maybe you are thinking that the illegal behavior of the executives at these huge financial institutions was limited to the housing crisis. That it was a onetime thing. I'm afraid not. Fraud is their business model, through and through:

- In July 2016, State Street Bank reached a $382 million settlement with DOJ for rigging foreign currency exchanges.
- In June 2014, the French bank BNP Paribas was ordered to pay $8.9 billion in penalties by a U.S. district judge after pleading guilty to charges of violating U.S. money laundering laws by conducting business in Sudan, Iran, and Cuba.
- In July 2016, HSBC was fined $1.9 billion, after senior DOJ officials overruled the recommendation by prosecutors to pursue criminal charges, for laundering Mexican drug trafficking money, because it "could result in a global financial disaster."
- In May 2015, five banks, including JPMorgan Chase and Citigroup, paid a $5.4 billion fine after pleading guilty to "a brazen display of collusion and foreign exchange rate market manipulation," according to Attorney General Loretta Lynch.
- In February 2015, ten banks, including Goldman Sachs and JPMorgan Chase, were investigated for tampering with the process of setting the price of precious metals for global markets.
- In March 2014, the FDIC accused sixteen big banks—including Bank of America, Citigroup, and JPMorgan Chase—of fraud and conspiracy in an "epic plot" to manipulate bank-to-bank inter-

est rates that underpin at least $350 trillion *(tril-lion!)* in global financial transactions.

- In April 2011, Wachovia (since acquired by Wells Fargo) was fined for laundering billions of dollars in illegal drug money. The federal prosecutor said, "Wachovia's blatant disregard for our banking laws gave international cocaine cartels a virtual carte blanche to finance their operations." The fine was less than 2 percent of the bank's $12.3 billion profit in 2009.

- In July 2016, JPMorgan Chase paid $200 million to settle criminal and civil charges related to bribing foreign officials.

Of course, these are just a few examples that demonstrate what I mean when I say that the business model of Wall Street is fraud. Money laundering, currency manipulation, bribery, conspiracy, rate tampering, collusion: These are the routine practices of Wall Street. And, this is not just my opinion. This is what a number of financial executives themselves have acknowledged.

In a 2015 University of Notre Dame survey on ethics in the financial services industry, 51 percent of Wall Street executives thought it was likely that their competitors engage in unethical or illegal activity to gain an edge. More than one-third have either witnessed or have firsthand knowledge of wrongdoing. Nearly one in five believe they must engage in illegal or unethical activity to be successful. And a quarter have signed or been asked to sign confidentiality agreements that prohibit reporting illegal or unethical activities to the authorities.

When a banker from Barclays was caught trying to rig the $5 trillion-per-day currency market in 2010, he said blithely, "If you ain't cheating, you ain't trying."

And in 2008, an analyst from Standard & Poor's, a credit-rating agency that consistently and knowingly gave AAA ratings to near-worthless mortgage-backed securities, said, "Let's hope we are all wealthy and retired by the time this house of cards falters."

Our country can no longer afford to tolerate the culture of fraud and corruption on Wall Street. The people responsible for illegal behavior must be held accountable. Unfortunately, that has not been the case so far.

ENDING "TOO BIG TO JAIL"

It is no secret that millions of Americans have become disillusioned with our political process. They don't vote. They don't believe much of what comes out of Washington. They have concluded that the system is rigged.

In my view, one of the reasons for that deep cynicism is that people see different rules for the rich and powerful than for everyone else. They see kids arrested and sometimes even jailed for possessing marijuana or for other minor crimes. But when it comes to Wall Street executives, whose illegal behavior hurts millions of Americans, they see that somehow there are no arrests, no police records, and no jail time.

We are supposed to be a country of laws and equal justice. There is not supposed to be one standard for Wall Street executives and another for everybody else. Wall Street caused incalculable harm to our country, and the people who were responsible must be held to account.

That is why, in 2013, I was stunned when our country's top law enforcement official suggested it might be difficult to prosecute executives of major financial institutions who commit crimes because it could destabilize the financial system of our country and the world. Since when did that become a criterion for deciding whether or not to prosecute the law?

Then–attorney general Eric Holder told the Senate

Judiciary Committee: "I am concerned that the size of some of these institutions becomes so large that it does become difficult for us to prosecute them when we are hit with indications that if we do prosecute—if we do bring a criminal charge—it will have a negative impact on the national economy, perhaps even the world economy."

In other words, not only are Wall Street banks too big to fail, their executives are too big to jail. After leaving his job as attorney general, Holder returned to the giant law firm where he previously worked, Covington & Burling, whose clients just so happen to include JPMorgan Chase, Bank of America, Citigroup, and Wells Fargo—some of the largest financial institutions in America.

There is something fundamentally wrong with our criminal justice system when not one major Wall Street executive has been prosecuted for causing the near collapse of our entire economy. That has got to change. "Equal Justice Under Law" cannot just be words engraved on the entrance of the Supreme Court. It must be the standard that applies to all Americans, including Wall Street executives.

WHERE DO WE GO FROM HERE?

The time is long overdue for real financial reform in this country. It will not be easy given the enormous power of Wall Street and its political supporters, but it is absolutely necessary if we are to have the kind of strong and stable economy that we need to rebuild the shrinking middle class.

The "heads, bankers win/tails, everyone else loses" system must come to an end. We need to create a financial system that works for ordinary Americans, not just those on top. Here are just some of the steps forward that will help us achieve that goal.

Ending "Too Big to Fail"

To create an economy that works for all Americans and not just a handful of billionaires, we have got to address the ever-increasing size of the megabanks. And we must end, once and for all, the scheme that is nothing more than a free insurance policy for Wall Street: the policy of "too big to fail."

We need a banking system that is part of a productive economy—making loans at affordable rates to small- and medium-sized businesses so that we create a growing economy with decent-paying jobs. We need a banking system that encourages homeownership by offering affordable mortgage products that are designed to work for both the lender and the borrower. We need a banking system that is transparent and accountable, and that adheres to the highest ethical standards as well as to the spirit and the letter of the law.

This is not the banking system we have today. Wall Street cannot continue to be an island unto itself, gambling trillions of other people's money on risky derivatives, acting illegally, and making huge profits, all the while assured that if its schemes fail, the taxpayers will be there to bail them out.

Of course, that is precisely what happened in 2008, when taxpayers bailed out Wall Street. Financial institutions received a $700 billion gift from Congress. And, thanks to an amendment I offered in 2010, we were able to learn that the Federal Reserve provided $16 trillion in secret loans to some of the largest financial institutions and corporations in the U.S. and throughout the world. We were told these unprecedented actions were necessary because the financial institutions involved were simply "too big to fail." In other words, they were so large and intertwined with all aspects of the economy that if they collapsed, the U.S. economy and maybe the entire global economy would go down with them.

One might have thought that, as part of the bailout, these huge banks would have been reduced in size to make certain that we never experience a recurrence of what happened in 2008. Well, that's not exactly what happened. In fact, the very opposite occurred. Today, three out of the four largest financial institutions—JPMorgan Chase, Bank of America, and Wells Fargo—are about 80 percent bigger than they were before we bailed them out.

Today the six largest banks issue more than two-thirds of all credit cards and more than 35 percent of all mortgages. They control more than 95 percent of financial derivatives and hold more than 40 percent of all bank deposits. Their assets have almost quadrupled since the mid-1990s and are now equivalent to nearly 60 percent of our GDP.

If these banks were too big to fail in 2008, what would happen if any of them were to fail today? The taxpayers would be on the hook again, and almost certainly for more money than in the last bailout. We cannot allow that to happen. No financial institution should be so large that its failure would cause catastrophic risk to millions of Americans or to our nation's economic well-being. No financial institution should have holdings so extensive that its failure would send the world economy into crisis.

If a bank is too big to fail, it is too big to exist. When it comes to Wall Street reform, that must be our bottom line. This is true not just because of the risk to our economy of another collapse and another bailout; it is also true because the current extreme concentration of ownership in the financial industry allows a very small number of huge financial institutions to have far too much economic and political power over this country.

If Teddy Roosevelt, the Republican trustbuster, were alive today, he would say, "Break 'em up." And he would be right.

Here's how we can do it.

We must pass legislation to cap the size of the largest financial institutions in this country so that their assets are no more than 2 percent of GDP—which is equal to about $350 billion today. This would break up the ten biggest banks in the country: JPMorgan Chase, Bank of America, Citigroup, Wells Fargo, Goldman Sachs, Morgan Stanley, U.S. Bancorp, PNC, Bank of New York Mellon, and HSBC North America.

This is not a radical idea. Under this plan, the size of JPMorgan Chase would simply go back to where it was in 1997. Bank of America would shrink to where it was in 1998. Wells Fargo would go down to where it was in 2002. And Citigroup would shrink to where it was during the second term of Bill Clinton's administration.

Breaking up the big banks would reduce systemic risk in our financial system. It would also mean increased competition. Oligopolies—where the market is dominated by just a few economic actors—are never good for consumers. Smaller banks are more likely to offer affordable financial products that Americans actually want and need, and consumers would have more banking products to choose from.

The idea of breaking up the too-big-to-fail banks is supported not only by a number of progressive economists, but also by some leading figures in the financial community.

The Independent Community Bankers of America, representing six thousand community banks, supports the idea because they understand that the function of banking should not be about speculation in derivatives and other esoteric financial instruments. Rather, it should be about providing affordable loans to businesses to create jobs in a productive economy, and providing Americans with loans they can afford to purchase homes, cars, and other consumer needs. In other words, the function of banking should be boring.

Past and present presidents of Federal Reserve banks in Dallas, St. Louis, Kansas City, and Minneapolis also support breaking up these behemoth banks. While these individuals are much more conservative than I am, all of them understand how dangerous too-big-to-fail banks are to our economy.

And I am proud that for the first time, the Democratic Party is on record as supporting this concept as well, thanks to an agreement our campaign worked out with Hillary Clinton's campaign. The 2016 Democratic National Committee platform declares: "Banks should not be able to gamble with taxpayers' deposits or pose an undue risk to Main Street. Democrats support a variety of ways to stop this from happening, including . . . breaking up too-big-to-fail financial institutions that pose a systemic risk to the stability of our economy."

This is a very important political step forward. Now it is our job to make sure the next president and Congress turn that platform statement into reality.

Enacting a Twenty-First-Century Glass-Steagall Act

In 1933, President Franklin Roosevelt signed the Glass-Steagall Act as an emergency response to the failure of nearly five thousand banks during the Great Depression. The law protected the deposits of ordinary people by creating a firewall between taxpayer-insured commercial banks on one side, and investment banks and insurance services on the other. It effectively kept Wall Street speculators from gambling with other people's money, and prevented another banking meltdown for more than five decades. That is, until Wall Street got

Congress to dilute it under President Reagan and kill it under President Bill Clinton.

In 1999, I was proud to lead the fight in the House of Representatives against repealing Glass-Steagall. During the floor debate, I warned that repealing the law "will lead to fewer banks and financial service providers; increased charges and fees for individual consumers and small businesses; diminished credit for rural America; and taxpayer exposure to potential losses should a financial conglomerate fail. It will lead to more mega-mergers; a small number of corporations dominating the financial service industry; and further concentration of economic power in our country."

I wish that I had been wrong but, unfortunately, what actually happened in 2008 was even worse than I predicted. Allowing commercial banks to merge with investment banks and insurance companies in 1999 was a huge mistake. It precipitated the largest taxpayer bailout in the history of the world. It substantially increased wealth and income inequality and further concentrated economic power in this country.

It is time again to separate everyday banking functions from the far riskier activities of investment banking and insurance services. Wall Street should not be able to gamble with your bank deposits. It is time to pass a twenty-first-century Glass-Steagall Act—legislation that Senator Elizabeth Warren, I, and others have worked on.

Regulating Risky Derivatives

We must also provide greater stability and transparency to the financial system by prohibiting taxpayer-insured banks from holding derivatives contracts on their balance sheets. Derivatives, like credit default swaps and synthetic collateralized debt obligations, are the risky financial products that nearly destroyed the economy. They are basically insurance policies on future events that may or may not happen, like a corporate bankruptcy or a drop in oil prices or the collapse of the housing market.

Their value is based on the performance of an underlying asset, but as we saw during the financial crisis, the underlying assets are sometimes worthless. Yet that doesn't keep Wall Street from speculating on these complex financial instruments. In fact, today, commercial banks still have over $190 trillion of derivatives contracts on their books. That is insane. And I'm not alone in thinking that.

As far back as 1992, Felix Rohatyn, the investment banker who helped New York out of its financial crisis in the 1970s, described derivatives as the equivalent of "financial hydrogen bombs." The billionaire financier George Soros has said that he doesn't dabble in derivatives "because we don't really understand how they work." And five years before the Wall Street crash, Warren Buffett, the Oracle of Omaha, warned his investors that derivatives were "financial weapons of mass destruction, carrying dangers that, while now latent, are potentially lethal."

Rohatyn, Soros, and Buffett were all correct in their assessments of derivatives. That is why we must make sure derivatives that are held in investment banks, hedge funds, and private equity funds are strongly regulated. Right now, state insurance commissioners and gambling authorities are banned from regulating them. We must lift that ban. They should be treated and regulated like the high-stakes wagers they are.

In addition, all derivatives trading should be done in an open, transparent exchange, similar to the stock market, without exceptions. As it stands now, these already complex and mysterious instruments are mostly traded in the shadows. It's time to bring them into the sunlight and see if they can withstand the scrutiny.

Finally, financial regulators must ensure that all of the participants in the derivatives market have enough capital to pay up if they lose their bets. Remember, derivatives are essentially insurance policies. Can you imagine paying for fire insurance on your house for twenty years, but when the house burns down the insurer says it doesn't actually have any money to pay your claim? Without sufficient capital levels, derivatives are the equivalent of selling an arsonist a fire insurance policy on *your* house. It makes no sense, and the incentives are all backward.

A Tax on Wall Street Speculation

As was brilliantly documented in Michael Lewis's book *Flash Boys*, Wall Street makes billions by buying huge quantities of stocks and bonds and then selling them shortly thereafter. The big investment houses and hedge funds have invested hundreds of millions of dollars in super-high-speed computers that detect the slightest price movements, then execute trades in mere fractions of a second. Once the price goes up—sometimes by just a fraction of a penny per share, and after just a few seconds or even less—the traders dump the securities. When repeated tens of millions of times, the practice reaps an unbelievably enormous profit for Wall Street.

Needless to say, this game of high-speed speculation adds absolutely nothing to a productive economy. What it does is make buying and selling securities more expensive for the vast majority of investors, including your pension fund or 401(k) administrator. And, because it is largely computer-driven, it adds yet another destabilizing force to the financial markets.

If we are serious about reforming our financial sys-

tem, we have got to establish a tax on Wall Street speculators. We have got to discourage reckless gambling on
Wall Street and encourage productive investments in a
job-creating economy.

By imposing a small financial transaction tax of just
0.5 percent on stock trades (that's just 50 cents for every
$100 worth of stock), a 0.1 percent fee on bonds, and a
0.005 percent fee on derivatives, we would help tap the
brakes on high-frequency speculative trading. And we
would raise up to $300 billion a year, which I have pro-
posed using to make public colleges and universities
tuition-free. During the financial crisis, the middle class
bailed out Wall Street. Now it's Wall Street's turn to help
the middle class.

Reforming Credit-Rating Agencies

We cannot have a safe and sound financial system if we
are unable to trust the credit-rating agencies to accu-
rately rate the creditworthiness of financial products.
And the only way we can have that trust is to make sure
that credit-rating agencies cannot make a profit from
Wall Street.

Leading up to the Great Recession, the three major
credit agencies—Moody's, Standard & Poor's, and
Fitch—would routinely give inflated AAA ratings to
risky and sometimes worthless mortgage-backed securities and derivatives, even though the agencies knew
the ratings were bogus. Without those AAA ratings, it
is highly doubtful many investors—again, including
pension funds and 401(k) administrators—would have
ever bought them.

The reason these risky financial schemes were given
such favorable ratings is simple: Wall Street paid for
them. Rather than providing useful risk information to
investors (which is the reason they exist in the first

place), the credit-rating agencies were colluding with Wall Street, because that's where the money was.

The rating agencies' role in the Wall Street meltdown was extremely significant. By 2010, hundreds of billions of dollars of supposedly AAA mortgage-backed securities had been downgraded to "junk" status—where they should have been all along. But because they were purchased with the inflated credit ratings that commanded a premium price, more than half a trillion dollars in value simply disappeared, almost overnight. And that was before a single house was foreclosed on.

Unfortunately, the ethical underpinnings and financial incentives within these agencies are fundamentally askew. When employees of Moody's were asked in an internal survey what their four highest job goals were, the top three were (1) generating more revenue, (2) increasing market share, and (3) fostering good relationships with customers. Fourth on the list was performing high-quality analytical work. At least they were being honest.

In my view, we need to turn for-profit credit-rating agencies into transparent nonprofit institutions, independent from Wall Street and accountable to a board of directors that represents the public interest. Wall Street must no longer be able to pick and choose which credit agency will rate their products.

Ending Usury

Having a financial system that works for all Americans means stopping financial institutions from ripping us off by charging sky-high interest rates and outrageous fees. To my mind, it is unacceptable that people all over this country pay a $3, $4, or $5 fee each time they go to the ATM. It is unconscionable that millions of Americans are paying credit card interest rates of 20 or 30 percent.

The Bible, and virtually every major religion on earth, has a term for this practice. It's called usury. In *The Divine Comedy*, Dante reserved a special place in the Seventh Circle of Hell for people who charged usurious interest rates. Today we don't need the hellfire, the pitchforks, or the rivers of boiling blood, but we do need a national usury law that caps interest rates on credit cards and consumer loans at 15 percent.

In 1980, Congress passed legislation requiring credit unions to cap interest rates on their loans, with some exceptions, at no more than 15 percent. And that law has worked very well. But unfortunately, it included only credit unions, and not banks. That makes no sense to me.

Unlike big banks, credit unions are member-owned and democratically controlled cooperatives that exist solely to provide affordable banking services to their members. Unlike big banks, credit unions didn't engage in risky behavior that caused the financial collapse. And, unlike big banks, credit unions did not receive a huge bailout from the taxpayers of this country.

Average ATM Surcharge

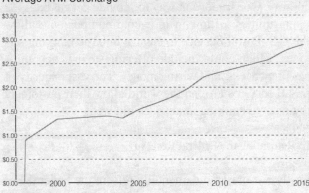

Data Source: Bankrate.com 2015 Checking Survey

Credit unions are the good guys. While I support capping interest rates charged on the loans they make, we must extend this cap to every lender in America.

Moreover, we must cap all ATM fees at $2. People should not have to pay a 10 percent fee for withdrawing $40 of their own money. Big banks need to stop acting like loan sharks and start acting like responsible lenders.

Allow Post Offices to Offer Banking Services

Today, rather unbelievably, there are millions of Americans who live in communities that are not served by regular banking services, places in which the giant banks don't think it's worth their time to invest. Well, what do you do if you live in such a neighborhood and need to cash a check? Where do you go?

You go to a payday lender, who will likely charge an interest rate of over 300 percent and trap you into a vicious cycle of debt. That should not be allowed within the American financial system. We need to stop payday lenders from exploiting millions of Americans and making the poor even poorer.

Post offices exist in almost every community in our country. One important way to provide decent banking opportunities for low-income communities is to allow the U.S. Postal Service to engage in basic banking services, which could include offering savings accounts, cashing checks, and wiring money. The vast majority of postal services around the world allow their customers to do some banking, and so should we.

Reforming the Federal Reserve

Lastly, we must fundamentally reform the Federal Reserve to make it responsive to the needs of ordinary Americans and not just billionaires on Wall Street.

When the financial system was on the verge of collapse, the Federal Reserve acted with a fierce sense of urgency, offering $16 trillion in virtually zero-interest loans to banks and corporations throughout the world. The Fed helped save Wall Street. However, it did little to save Main Street. And, as a result, millions of families saw a decline in their standard of living and a dimming of their hope for the future.

The decisions that the Federal Reserve made during the crisis sent a very clear message: While the rich and powerful are "too big to fail" and are worthy of an endless supply of cheap credit, ordinary Americans must fend for themselves. This was a clear case of socialism for the rich and rugged individualism for everyone else. But it doesn't need to be this way. The Fed was never supposed to be concerned just about Wall Street.

Americans deserve a central bank that works for them and not just for the big banks. We must reform the Fed to make sure it acts with the same sense of urgency to fulfill its full-employment mandate, increase wages, and rebuild the middle class as it did when it saved Wall Street. Let me outline how I believe we can do just that.

First, we must strengthen, not weaken, the Volcker Rule, which prohibits commercial banks from gambling with the bank deposits of the American people. The Fed has got to make it crystal clear to large financial institutions that the era of excessive speculation is over.

Second, the Fed must stop providing incentives for banks to keep money out of the economy. Since 2008, the Fed has been paying financial institutions interest rates on excess reserves parked at the central bank—reserves that have grown to an unprecedented $2.2 trillion. Instead of paying banks interest on these reserves, the Fed should charge a fee that the Small Business Administration could use to provide direct loans and loan guarantees to small businesses.

Third, as a condition of receiving financial assistance from the Fed, banks must commit to increased lending to creditworthy small businesses and manufacturers in a job-creating productive economy, reducing credit card interest rates and fees, and helping underwater and struggling homeowners. Just think of all of the productive short- and long-term investments that could be made in our country right now if Wall Street used the money it received from the Federal Reserve wisely. Instead of casino-style speculation, Wall Street could and should invest in helping to restore our infrastructure, build affordable housing, and transform our energy system. Those are the types of investments that the Fed must encourage.

Fourth, we must eliminate the blatant conflicts of interest at the Fed. The reality is that the Federal Reserve has been hijacked by the very bankers it is in charge of regulating. I think most people would be shocked to learn that Jamie Dimon, CEO of JPMorgan Chase, served on the board of the New York Fed at the same time that his bank received a $391 billion Fed bailout. And he is not the only example. At least eighteen current and former Fed board members were affiliated with banks and companies that received emergency loans from the Fed during the financial crisis. We can no longer allow the foxes to guard the henhouse at the Federal Reserve.

Fifth, we must make the Federal Reserve more transparent. Too much of the Fed's business is conducted in secret, known only to the bankers on its various boards and committees. The only reason we even know about the Fed's jaw-dropping $16 trillion in secret emergency lending during the financial crisis is because I inserted an amendment in the 2010 Dodd-Frank Wall Street Reform and Consumer Protection Act to audit the Fed. We must require the Government Accountability Office to conduct a full and independent audit of the Fed, each and every year.

Currently, the Federal Open Market Committee does not release full and unredacted transcripts of its meetings to the public for five years. We must require the committee to release those transcripts within six months or less. If we had made this reform in 2004, the American people would have learned about the housing bubble well in advance of the financial crisis.

The bottom line is that we need a Federal Reserve that works for all Americans, not just the CEOs of large financial institutions.

FOUR

HEALTH CARE FOR ALL

Health care is a right, not a privilege. The United States must join the rest of the industrialized world and guarantee health care to every man, woman, and child through a Medicare for All single-payer system.

I have, for as far back as I can remember, always believed that health care is a *right* of all people, not a privilege. Health care is a basic human need. We all get born, we all get sick or have accidents, we all need care and die at the end of our lives. Everyone *needs* health care. Everyone should *have* health care.

It has never made sense to me that the quality of care a person receives—indeed, whether that person receives *any* care—should be dependent upon the job that he or she has or the wealth of their family. It has never made sense to me that Americans should be forced into bankruptcy because of a serious illness. It has never made sense to me that some people will live and some people will die because of their health insurance status.

Most important, it has never made sense to me that our health care system is primarily designed to make huge profits for multibillion-dollar insurance companies, drug companies, hospitals, and medical equipment suppliers. Health care is not a commodity. It is a human right. The goal of a sane health care system should be to keep people well, not to make stockholders rich.

Let's be clear: While Republicans and representatives of the insurance and pharmaceutical industries tell us that we have the "greatest" health care system in the world, that is nonsense. Our current system is the most expensive, bureaucratic, wasteful, and ineffective in the world. While the health care industry makes hundreds of billions a year in profit, tens of millions of Americans have totally inadequate coverage, and many of our people suffer and die unnecessarily.

The bottom line is that in the United States we spend an enormous amount of money for a health care system that performs poorly. It's time for a change—a real change.

Needless to say, the idea of universal health care is not a particularly radical idea. It exists fifty miles north of where I live in Burlington, Vermont. Canada guarantees health care for all its citizens through a single-payer health care system, and has done so for the past thirty years under governments with very different ideologies. In fact, universal health care exists in *every* major country on earth, except the United States. The national health systems may vary in each of these countries, but all of them guarantee health care for all their citizens and none of them allow private health insurance companies to profit off human illness.

Despite the gains of the Affordable Care Act, which I strongly supported, the health care situation in the

United States remains dire. Over 28 million Americans lack any health insurance and some 30 million are under-insured because of high deductibles and copayments. And these high deductibles and copayments are no joke. I have talked to people throughout the country who the official statistics say are "insured," but it doesn't do them any good because they can't afford to go to the doctor due to those high deductibles and copayments. I have talked to seniors who cut their prescription drug pills in half because they can't afford the outrageously high cost of their medicine. In America, you can be "covered," but that doesn't necessarily mean that you are getting the health care you need.

In Vermont and around the country, doctors have told me about patients who have died unnecessarily because they put off their medical visits until it was too late. These were people who had no insurance or lacked the out-of-pocket cash their insurance plans required them to pay. It is not talked about much, but thousands of people die each year in our country because they don't get to the doctor when they should. What an outrage!

Further, there are millions of Americans with decent insurance coverage who can't find a medical home because we have a disastrous primary health care system, and many regions of the country are medically underserved. The goal of any rational health care system is to enable people to get medical care when they *need* that care. Obviously, that approach eases human pain and suffering; if people cannot find a doctor when they need medical care, they will only get sicker. It is also cost-effective. It is much more expensive to pay for extended hospital stays and the long-term treatment of chronic illness than to successfully treat medical conditions in their early stages.

Today, in wealthy communities all across the country, there is an abundance of doctors, dentists, and other medical personnel. That is not the case in low-income areas—urban or rural. When I visited Mississippi I found that there were entire (largely black) counties in that state that had no doctors—no doctors at all. But it's not just a racial issue. There's a dire shortage of doctors in rural areas of the largely white state of Kansas as well, and in many other regions in America.

What do these millions of people do when they need medical care and don't have a doctor? Some of them simply delay treatment and get sicker. Others die. Most, however, go to the emergency room at the local hospital. Instead of a having a doctor of their own who knows their family and their medical history, they get triage-style care in an emergency room. Not only is this an inadequate form of care, it is enormously expensive. An emergency room visit is the most expensive form of primary care in the country.

As part of the Affordable Care Act, in order to address the crisis in primary health care, I helped lead the effort to greatly expand funding for the Federally Qualified Health Center (FQHC) program.

Majority Leader Harry Reid, Congressman Jim Clyburn, and I, with the support of President Obama, were able to put an additional $11 billion into the program. This resulted in 6 million more Americans in medically underserved areas gaining access to primary health care, dental care, mental health counseling, and low-cost prescription drugs. Twenty-four million Americans are now served by FQHCs across the country, and in the state of Vermont almost 25 percent of our people now get their primary health care through these community health centers.

We also tripled funding for the National Health Service Corps, the federal program that provides debt forgiveness for those medical, dental, and nursing school graduates prepared to practice in medically underserved areas. One of the many manifestations of an irrational health care system is that while we overpay certain types of providers, we grossly underpay those in primary care—who are the backbone of any rational system. The National Health Service Corps helps to address that crisis.

At the end of the campaign, I worked with Secretary Clinton to reach an agreement that calls for a doubling of funds for community health centers and a massive increase in funding for the National Health Service Corps. This proposal, if adopted, would go a long way toward providing universal primary care in this country. It would save lives, ease suffering, and save billions of taxpayer dollars. As a member of the U.S. Senate Committee on Health, Education, Labor and Pensions, I will do everything in my power to see that that proposal gets passed.

Today the United States spends far more per capita on health care than any other nation. According to the latest information, we spend $3.2 trillion a year on health care—about $10,000 for every man, woman, and child. In 2013, we spent 17.1 percent of our GDP on health care. This was almost 50 percent more than the next highest spender, France, and double what the United Kingdom spent.

The goal of a sane and efficient health care system is to invest in the provision of health care and disease prevention. We should be spending money on doctors, nurses, mental health specialists, dentists, nurse-practitioners, social workers, and other personnel who provide *real* services to people and improve their lives. We should be investing in the research and development of new drugs and technologies that can cure disease and alleviate pain.

We should *not* be wasting hundreds of billions of dollars a year on profiteering, on huge executive compen-

Health Care Spending as a Percentage of GDP, 1980–2013

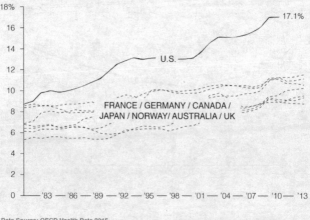

Data Source: OECD Health Data 2015

sation packages, and on outrageous administrative costs. The waste and bureaucracy of the current system is almost unimaginable.

Think, for a moment, about how much time and money is spent in this country as people argue with their insurance companies as to whether or not a particular procedure is covered—and understand that *not* paying claims is exactly what insurance companies do. Think about the many billions of dollars drug companies spend each year on television advertising telling us what drugs we need to buy, and the amount of money they spend trying to influence doctors to use their particular brand. Think about all the people working in the basements of hospitals throughout the country who are not treating patients or improving their lives, but rather billing them and in some cases hounding them for back payments they cannot afford.

This waste and bureaucracy not only impacts patients and their relationship to insurance companies and

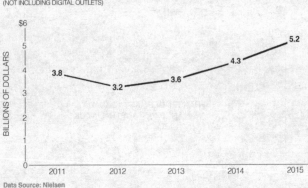

Spending on Prescription Drug Advertising
TELEVISION, MAGAZINES, NEWSPAPERS, RADIO, OUTDOOR, CINEMA
(NOT INCLUDING DIGITAL OUTLETS)

Data Source: Nielsen

hospitals, it is also doing incredible damage to health care professionals. Just as patients are affected by our profit-driven system, so are health care providers—the doctors, nurses, and trained professionals whose job it is to care for the sick and injured and to prevent disease.

The vast majority of health care professionals in this country are men and women who sought out healing professions because they wanted to care for people, wanted to make a difference in the lives of their neighbors and their community. These are not people who sought out careers where they would be forced to spend countless hours in front of a computer screen filling out forms, or on the phone arguing with insurance companies on behalf of a patient.

But that is the demoralizing reality in our current system as the provision of health care in America becomes more and more corporatized, more and more geared toward profit making. Health care providers today spend less and less time treating their patients, and more and more time justifying what they do and fighting to be paid by the insurance company for the services they render. As a result of this bureaucracy and insurance company interference, too many doctors and other medical professionals are giving up on the profession they love.

Every day they must consider a host of questions completely unrelated to the needs of their patients. They must determine whether the services they render and the amount of time they spend will be paid for by the insurance company, whether the facility where they work will think they are working efficiently enough, whether their patients will be able to receive any follow-up care.

In a doctor's office today that accepts Medicare, Medicaid, and private insurance—especially offices participating in various demonstration programs aimed at improving quality—there can easily be over a hundred different measures to verify what office personnel are doing. And only a few of these measures have anything to do with the actual outcome of the visit, little to do with whether the patient was any better off having come in for the appointment.

Lost in all of this—for the patient and the provider—is the simple notion that a patient should be able to go to the doctor when needed, and that the doctor should be able to provide the best-quality care he or she can. A visit to the doctor's office should not be a bureaucratic nightmare. It should not be about filling out forms. It should not be a struggle with the insurance company to get it to cover a particular procedure. A doctor/patient relationship should be about the needs of the patient, not the profits of the insurance company.

The irrationality of the current system can thus be seen not just in the profit margins and outrageously high compensation packages of CEOs in the insurance and pharmaceutical industries, but, more significantly, in the huge amount of waste and inefficiencies inherent in an enormously complicated system designed to maximize profit rather than provide high-quality and cost-effective health care.

The United States has thousands of different health insurance plans, all of which set different reimbursement rates across different networks for providers and procedures. This results in extremely high administrative costs. According to a recent report drafted by thirty-nine physicians from the Physicians for a National Health Program (PNHP) and endorsed by some 2,500 medical doctors, a movement to "a single payer system would trim administration, reduce incentives to over-treat, lower drug prices, minimize wasteful investments in redundant facilities, and eliminate almost all marketing and investor profits. These measures would yield the substantial savings needed to fund universal care and new investments in currently under-funded services and public health activities—without any net increase in national health spending."

In other words, eliminating the hundreds of billions of dollars in wasteful and unnecessary administrative costs we now spend would free up all the funds we need to provide health care to *every* American. We don't need to spend more money on health care. We just need to spend our health-care dollars more efficiently.

According to the PNHP, "Private insurers' overhead currently averages 12 percent, as compared with only 2.1 percent for fee-for-service Medicare. The complexity of reimbursement systems also forces physicians and hospitals to waste substantial resources on documentation, billing, and collections. As a result, U.S. healthcare administration costs are about double those in Canada, where the single-payer system pays hospitals global budgets and positions via simplified fee schedules. Reducing U.S. administrative costs to Canadian levels would save over $400 billion annually."

Our dysfunctional health care system impacts not

only patients and medical professionals, but our entire economy. Given that employer-based health care is the way most Americans get their coverage, small- and medium-sized businesses are forced to spend an enormous amount of time and energy determining how they can get the most cost-effective coverage for their employees. It is not uncommon for employers to spend weeks every year negotiating with insurance companies, and switching carriers every year or two to get the best deal they can.

When we talk about our current health care system, what is often overlooked is the negative impact it has on our entrepreneurial spirit. Millions of Americans remain on their jobs today not because they want to be there, not because they enjoy their work, but because their present employer provides decent health care benefits for them and their family.

Think about the extraordinary impact it would have on our economy if every American had the freedom to follow his or her dreams, and not have to worry about whether the family had health insurance. Universal health care would provide a major boon to our economy, unleashing the entrepreneurial spirit of millions of people.

A for-profit health care system distorts medical priorities. Its main priority is to make as much money as possible, not necessarily to protect human health. The result is that we spend too much on high-tech procedures, which are very profitable, and too little on disease prevention. We spend more than we should on unnecessary surgeries, and too little on primary care and social work. We spend more money per capita than any other country on prescription drugs, too little on nutrition education.

As an example of the complete irrationality of the current system, I have talked to hospital administrators who describe how public and private insurance companies will spend tens of thousands of dollars on major surgery for a low-income person, but provide no coverage to make certain that when that person leaves the hospital and returns home, there is enough food for them to eat or the apartment is warm enough. Surprise, surprise: Some of those people, especially seniors, return to the hospital within a few days.

If we weren't so accustomed to it, the waste and misplaced priorities of the current system would shock every American to the core. Despite the fact that we spend far, far more per capita on health care than any other country, we have fewer practicing physicians than the median Organization for Economic Co-operation and Development (OECD) country. Because of the cost, we also hesitate to visit the doctor's office when we should. In fact, the average Canadian goes to their physician almost twice as often as we do.

Medical procedures are very profitable. It should not be surprising, therefore, that the United States spends far more for medical procedures than any other country. According to a study by the International Federation of Health Plans, the average price of bypass surgery is $73,345 in the U.S. This is more than $30,000 higher than in the next-highest-spending country, Australia.

While health care costs soar, and millions of Americans are unable to afford health insurance or prescription drugs, the health care industry reaps huge profits and pays its CEOs outrageously high compensation packages. In 2015, Leonard S. Schleifer, CEO of Regeneron Pharmaceuticals, made $47 million; Jeffrey M. Leiden, CEO of Vertex Pharmaceuticals, $28 million; Alex Gorsky, CEO of Johnson & Johnson, $21 million; Alan B. Miller, CEO of Universal Health Services, $20 million; Kenneth C. Frazier, CEO of Merck, nearly $20 million; David M. Cordani, CEO of Cigna, $17.3 million;

and Mark T. Bertolini, CEO of Aetna, over $17.2 million. Yes. The priorities of the current system dictate that we have more than enough money to pay out fat executive salaries in the health care industry. We just don't have enough money to make sure that working people can get the health care they need.

PRESCRIPTION DRUGS

When we talk about the high cost of health care in the United States, and the inability of so many people to secure the care they need, we cannot ignore the crisis of the outrageously high cost of prescription drugs. In America, people get much sicker than they should, and sometimes die because they cannot afford the medicine that they need. Sometimes, in order to pay for their medicine, they end up lacking the money they need to provide for other basic needs.

Today in the United States we pay, by far, the highest price in the world for prescription drugs. A 2010 study showed that the United States paid, on average, double what Canada, Australia, and the United Kingdom do. A 2013 report from the International Federation of Health Plans listed the comparative cost of the same drug sold in different countries. Here are a few examples of the different prices charged for widely used drugs in the U.S. and Canada. (In some instances, drug prices are cheaper in other countries than they are in Canada.)

In Canada, Embrel sold for $1,646 while in the U.S. it sold for $3,000. In Canada, Celebrex sold for $51 while in the U.S. it sold for $330. In Canada, Copaxone sold for $1,400 while in the U.S. it sold for $3,900. In Canada, Nexium sold for $30 while in the U.S. it sold for $305. And on and on it goes.

While the five largest drug companies made a combined $50 billion in profits last year, one out of five Americans between the ages of nineteen and sixty-four were unable to fill the prescriptions their doctors wrote. In other words, people go to the doctor because they are sick, they get a diagnosis from their doctor, but they can't afford the treatment. Then they get sicker. Does this make any sense to anyone?

One of the reasons the pharmaceutical industry makes huge profits is pretty simple: Unlike every other major country on earth, all of which negotiate prices with the pharmaceutical industry, here in the U.S. drug companies can charge any price they want. And so they do. You can walk into your pharmacy tomorrow to get a refill of the same medicine that you have used for twenty years, and the price could be double what it was when you got your last refill six months before. And there is not a thing you can do about it.

The best-known example of the rapaciousness of drug companies is a corporate profit machine called Valeant. In June 2015, Valeant raised the price of Glumetza, its diabetes drug, to $3,432 from $572. About a month later, Valeant hiked Glumetza's price again, to $5,148. Later in 2015 Valeant raised the price of its acid reflux drug Zegerid from $421 to $3,034. Valeant increased the price of Cuprimine, a treatment for Wilson's disease, from $6,547 to $26,189.

When I was chairman of the Senate Committee on Veterans' Affairs, I encountered a major example of a drug company rip-off. The VA, the largest integrated health care system in the country, spends billions on prescription drugs. It also has many patients who suffer from Hepatitis C, a very serious disease. Several years ago, a new Hepatitis C drug, Sovaldi, was created. This medication was developed with federal funding by a company named Pharmasset. (In fact, one of the drug's developers was actually employed by the VA.)

After successfully developing Sovaldi, Pharmasset was purchased by Gilead Sciences, a large drug company. Upon purchasing Pharmasset, Gilead brought Sovaldi to market for the unbelievable cost of $84,000 for a twelve-week course of treatment, or $1,000 per pill.

This outrageous price means that, through the VA, the taxpayers of this country are subsidizing huge profits for Gilead Sciences in order to treat the men and women who have put their lives on the line to defend our country. It also means that in the private world thousands of people with Hepatitis C—many of whom have suffered for years—won't be able to get a medication that could cure them in a short period of time. They suffer. A drug company makes huge profits.

Do you want to know why we pay the highest prices in the world for prescription drugs, and why there are no regulations preventing the drug companies from selling their products for any price they want?

It might have something to do with the fact that the pharmaceutical industry is one of the most politically powerful industries in the country and spends endless amounts of money on lobbying and campaign contributions. The pharmaceutical industry has spent more than $3 billion on lobbying since 1998. This is $1 billion more than the insurance industry, which came in second place in lobbying expenditures.

The pharmaceutical industry, because of its great power, rarely loses legislative fights. It has effectively purchased the Congress, and there are Republican and Democratic leaders who support its every effort.

However, in July 1999, while I was in the House, I did set the industry back a bit when I put together what turned out to be the very first bus trip over the Canadian border to buy lower-cost prescription drugs. It is a day I will always cherish. We took a busload of Vermonters, mostly working-class women struggling with breast cancer, from St. Albans, Vermont, to Montreal. I will never forget the look on the faces of those women, who were fighting for their lives, when they were able to buy the breast cancer medicine tamoxifen at 10 percent of what they were paying in Vermont.

The result of that well-publicized trip, and other trips taken by members of Congress with their constituents, was that the American people caught on to the fact that prescription drugs were substantially less expensive in Canada. Today, in one way or another, millions of Americans purchase their prescription drugs from Canada and other countries where the cost is a fraction of what it is here.

After that bus trip to Canada, I took to the floor of the House and asked a very simple question: "How do you have a drug manufactured by a company, manufactured in the same factory, put in the same bottles, sold in Canada for one-tenth of the price that that same medicine is sold for in the United States of America? How can that happen?"

The answer has everything to do with the power and greed of the pharmaceutical industry, and a health care system more concerned about profits than about the needs of the American people.

DENTAL CARE

When people talk about "health care," they are usually referring to the medical care we receive when we go to a doctor for one or another problem with our body. But health care is more than that. Largely ignored is the reality that we have a major dental crisis in this country. Tens of millions of Americans are unable to afford the dental care they need. They suffer with painful toothaches. They get teeth extracted because it's cheaper than getting the tooth properly treated, a plight I suffered when I was a young man. Without good teeth, people are unable to properly digest the food they eat, which can lead to other medical problems.

Bad teeth can not only lead to pain and illness, but it has an economic consequence. Try applying for a job when your front teeth are missing and you can't smile. Having bad or missing teeth makes it clear to the world that you are poor, which makes it harder for you to find employment, which perpetuates the cycle of poverty. And for kids, toothaches are one of the major causes of school absenteeism.

Once a year in southern Virginia, doctors, dentists, and other medical personnel donate a few days of their time to treat the uninsured and underinsured. People without insurance sleep in their cars the night before the medical personnel arrive in order to make sure they get treated. The field where the doctors and dentists set up their temporary facilities looks like a Third World country, with poor people in pain spread throughout waiting to get medical or dental care.

In Vermont, community health centers are a major provider of dental care for low- and moderate-income people. One of the more creative innovations in dental care in recent years, these centers bring dentists and dental practitioners right into schools throughout the state; in Burlington, a modern dental *office* was established in a low-income school. This approach has been very effective in treating kids throughout Burlington, and has been effective in several other areas of the state as well.

MENTAL HEALTH

And then there is the extraordinary crisis that we face in terms of mental health care. As I traveled around the country, it became clear to me that people were deeply concerned about this issue. Whenever I talked about the need for a revolution in mental health treatment, it would get a strong response. People often knew someone—maybe themselves—struggling with drug addiction or a serious mental disorder and unable to find help.

The crisis in mental health impacts every area of our lives.

In my Senate office—and, I suspect, in every Senate office—the calls come in. "I am worried about my brother, what he might do to himself or someone else. But we can't find the mental health treatment he needs at a cost that we can afford." In our country today there are thousands of people walking the streets, many of them owning guns, who are suicidal and/or homicidal. And we are doing virtually nothing to address this crisis.

Further, in schools throughout this country, teachers are finding themselves increasingly overwhelmed with special-needs kids who are disrupting their classes, and there is often very little help available for them. There is a massive shortage of pediatric psychiatrists and psychologists.

Every police chief in the country will tell you about the connection between mental illness, addiction, and crime. Thousands of mentally unstable people cannot stay on a job or earn a steady income, many of them alienated from their families. In order to survive, some of them will steal. People who are addicted to opiates or heroin need to feed their habits. They will commit crimes to get the drugs they require. Instead of providing the care and treatment these people need, we are putting them in jails. This does nothing to address the underlying causes of their problems, and ends up wasting billions in taxpayer dollars.

According to an excellent special report in *USA Today*:

> More than half a million Americans with serious mental illness are falling through the cracks of a system in tatters. The mentally ill who have nowhere to go and find little sympathy from those around them often land hard in emergency rooms, county jails and city streets. The lucky ones find homes with family. The unlucky ones show up in the morgue. . . .
>
> States looking to save money have pared away both the community mental health services designed to keep people healthy, as well as the hospital care needed to help them heal after a crisis.
>
> States have been reducing hospital beds for decades, because of insurance pressures as well as a desire to provide more care outside institutions. Tight budgets during the recession forced some of the most devastating cuts in recent memory, says Robert Glover, executive director of the National Association of State Mental Health Program Directors. States cut $5 billion in mental health services from 2009 to 2012. In the same period, the country eliminated at least 4,500 public psychiatric hospital beds—nearly 10% of the total supply, he says.
>
> The result is that, all too often, people with mental illness get no care at all. Nearly 40% of adults with "severe" mental illness—such as schizophrenia or bipolar disorder—received no treatment in the previous year, according to the 2012 National Survey on Drug Use and Health.

Among adults with any mental illness, 60% were untreated.

In the year 2016, the time is long overdue for us to understand that a mental health problem should be treated like any other health-related issue. People must be able to get the mental health treatment they need, when they need it—not six months from now or, even worse, maybe never.

In America today, we need a revolution in mental health treatment.

HEALTH CARE OUTCOMES

One might reasonably think that, given the fact that we spend far more per capita on health care than any other country on earth, our health care outcomes would be as good as or better than other countries'. Surely, with all the money we spend, we must be living longer and healthier lives, our infant mortality rates must be lower than they are in other countries, and our people must be suffering fewer illnesses.

Well, that might be a reasonable thought, but it is wrong. Dead wrong. Let me quote from a press release from the Commonwealth Fund, a private foundation that studies international health care systems, describing the results of a major 2014 study it did on health care systems around the world:

Despite having the most expensive health care system, the United States ranks last overall among 11 industrialized countries on measures of health system quality, efficiency, access to care, equity, and healthy lives, according to a new Commonwealth Fund report. The other countries included *in the study were Australia, Canada, France, Germany, the Netherlands, New Zealand, Norway, Sweden, Switzerland, and the United Kingdom. While there is room for improvement in every country, the U.S. stands out for having the highest costs and lowest performance—the U.S. spent $8,508 per person on health care in 2011, compared with $3,406 in the United Kingdom, which ranked first overall.*

That report indicated that the U.S. had the lowest life expectancy at birth of the countries studied, and the highest infant mortality rate. The prevalence of chronic diseases also appeared to be higher in the U.S. The study found that 68 percent of U.S. adults age sixty-five or older had at least two chronic conditions. In other countries, this figure ranged from 33 percent in the United Kingdom to 56 percent in Canada.

A HEALTHY SOCIETY CREATES GOOD HEALTH

Let me conclude this chapter by stating that we must create a high-quality, universal health care system guaranteeing health care for every man, woman, and child—but we must do even more than that. We must create a healthy society.

Most people understand that being in good health, physically and emotionally, is more than just a function of the care you receive—no matter how high-quality that care may be.

If you are poor and struggling every day with the stress of putting food on the table and a roof over your head, your health suffers. Several years ago I chaired a Senate hearing entitled "Poverty as a Death Sentence," and that title is absolutely correct. The life expectancy for poor people is much lower than it is for wealthy people, and there are parts of the country now where Americans are actually dying at a younger age than their parents did. This is often the result of economic despair and an increase in drug addiction, alcoholism, and suicide.

If you go to work every day hating your job, there's no question that your frustration and anger will impact your health. People cannot spend forty or fifty hours a week doing something that they dislike without suffering serious health consequences. People cannot fight their way through traffic jams every day, or experience delays in crowded airports, without paying a health-related price.

If you are a senior citizen, living alone and isolated, as many are, your health will suffer. Too many seniors in our country suffer from depression and alcohol-related problems. Friends, family, and community help us stay healthy.

If you are a child breathing filthy air from a coal-burning plant or some other source of pollution, your health will suffer. In low-income communities throughout this country, children suffer from high rates of asthma and other preventable diseases. Clean air, clean water, and decent food are necessary if we are to stay healthy.

The bottom line is that everything is connected to everything. Our political task is nothing less than the transformation of our nation. Health care for all, absolutely. But in order to create a healthy society, we also need to end poverty and provide decent-paying jobs for all people. We need a strong educational system, a clean environment, and equal opportunity for everyone regardless of their race, gender, sexual orientation, or nationality. These, in fact, are all health-related issues.

THE CHOICE IS NOW

At a time when tens of millions of Americans are uninsured or underinsured, when we have major crises in primary health care, the cost of prescription drugs, dental care, and mental health treatment, this country has got to make two very fundamental decisions. First, do we join the rest of the industrialized world and guarantee comprehensive health care to all people as a right, or do we stay with the current dysfunctional system that we have? Second, if we choose to move toward universal health care, what is the best and most cost-effective approach?

To me, the answer is pretty simple. From both a moral and economic perspective, the United States must guarantee health care for every man, woman, and child as a right. And the best way to do that is through a Medicare for All single-payer system.

Here is an outline of the single-payer plan I introduced during my presidential campaign.

MEDICARE FOR ALL: LEAVING NO ONE BEHIND

Coverage

A federally administered single-payer health care program means comprehensive coverage for all Americans. This plan will cover the entire continuum of health care, from inpatient to outpatient care; preventive to emergency care; primary to specialty care, including long-term and palliative care; vision, hearing, and oral health care; mental health and substance abuse services; as well as prescription medications, medical equipment, supplies, diagnostics, and treatments. Patients will be able to choose a health care provider without worrying about whether that provider is in-network and will be able to get the care they need without having to read any fine print or trying to figure out how they can afford the out-of-pocket costs.

What It Means for Patients

As a patient, all you need to do is go to the doctor and show your insurance card. A single-payer plan means no more copays, no more deductibles, and no more fighting with insurance companies when they fail to pay for charges.

Getting Health Care Spending
Under Control

We outspend all other countries on our health, and our medical spending continues to grow faster than the rate of inflation. Creating a single, public insurance system will go a long way toward getting health care spending under control. The United States has thousands of different health insurance plans, all of which set different reimbursement rates across different networks for providers and procedures. This results in an enormous amount of paperwork and high administrative costs. Two patients with the same condition may get very different care depending on where they live, the health insurance they have, and what their insurance covers. A patient may pay different amounts for the same prescription drug depending solely on where the prescription is filled. Health care providers and patients must navigate this complex and bewildering system, wasting precious time and resources.

By moving to an integrated system, the government will finally have the ability to stand up to drug companies and negotiate fair prices for the American people collectively. The government will also be able to track access to various providers and make smart investments to avoid provider shortages and ensure that communities have the providers they need.

Major Savings for Families and Businesses

The United States currently spends $3.2 trillion on health care each year—about $10,000 per person. Reforming our system, simplifying our payment structure, and incentivizing new ways to make sure patients are actually getting better care will generate massive savings. This plan has been estimated to save the American people and businesses more than $6 trillion over the next decade.

The Typical Middle-Class Family Would Save Over $5,000 Under This Plan

Last year, the average working family paid $4,955 in premiums and $1,318 in deductibles to private health insurance companies. Under this plan, a family of four earning $50,000 would pay just $466 per year to the single-payer program, amounting to a savings of over $5,800 for that family each year.

Businesses Would Save Over $9,400 a Year in Health Care Costs for the Average Employee

The average annual cost to the employer for a worker with a family who makes $50,000 a year would go from $12,591 to just $3,100.

How Much Will It Cost?

This plan has been estimated to cost $1.38 trillion per year.

How Would It Be Paid For?

- A 6.2 percent income-based health care premium paid by employers. Revenue raised: $630 billion per year.
- A 2.2 percent income-based premium paid by households. Revenue raised: $210 billion per year. A family of four taking the standard deduction can have income up to $28,800 and not pay this tax.

Progressive Income Tax Rates

- Revenue raised: $110 billion a year. Under this plan the marginal income tax rate would be:

- 37 percent on income between $250,000 and $500,000.
- 43 percent on income between $500,000 and $2 million.
- 48 percent on income between $2 million and $10 million. (In 2013, only 113,000 households, the top 0.08 percent of taxpayers, had income between $2 million and $10 million.)
- 52 percent on income above $10 million. (In 2013, only 13,000 households, just 0.01 percent of taxpayers, had income exceeding $10 million.)

- Taxing capital gains and dividends the same as income from work. Revenue raised: $92 billion per year. Warren Buffett, the second-wealthiest person in the country, has said that he pays a lower effective tax rate than his secretary. The reason is that he receives most of his income from capital gains and dividends, which are taxed at a much lower rate than income from work. This plan will end the special tax break for capital gains and dividends on household income above $250,000.

- Limit tax deductions for the rich. Revenue raised: $15 billion per year. Under this plan, households making over $250,000 would no longer be able to save more than 28 cents in taxes from every dollar in tax deductions. This limit would replace more complicated and less effective limits on tax breaks for the rich, including the alternative minimum tax, the personal exemption phaseout, and the limit on itemized deductions.

- The Responsible Estate Tax. Revenue raised: $21 billion per year. This provision would tax the estates of the wealthiest 0.3 percent (three-tenths of 1 percent) of Americans who inherit over $3.5 million at progressive rates and would close loopholes in the estate tax.
- Savings from health tax expenditures. Revenue raised: $310 billion per year. Several tax breaks that subsidize health care (health-related "tax expenditures") would become obsolete and disappear under a single-payer health care system, saving $310 billion per year.

Most important, health care provided by employers is compensation that is not subject to payroll taxes or income taxes under current law. This is a significant tax break that would effectively disappear under this plan, because all Americans would receive health care through the new single-payer, rather than employer-based, program.

FIVE

MAKING HIGHER EDUCATION AFFORDABLE

I n the twenty-first century, a public education system that goes from kindergarten through high school is no longer good enough. The world is changing, technology is changing, our economy is changing. If we are to succeed in the highly competitive global economy and have the best-educated workforce in the world, public colleges and universities must become tuition-free.

In May 2014, a year before I began my campaign for president, I held a press conference in my Burlington Senate office to discuss the crisis of college affordability and student debt. I invited a group of university students who were graduating that month to join me, and many arrived wearing simple white placards hanging from their necks showing the amount of student debt they had. One sign had a precise number: $24,547. Another read $30,000, another $40,000. A young physician who had recently graduated medical school had a debt of $300,000.

What struck me was that these were all bright young adults who should have been looking forward to building independent lives and careers. But instead, they were weighed down by the reality that they were deeply in debt before they'd even completed their first job application. Graduation should mark a joyous new beginning, not the start of an anxiety-ridden, decades-long financial bind.

One of the truly remarkable aspects of the campaign that I would launch a year later—and quite frankly, one that took me by surprise—was how much the campaign resonated with young people. In state after state, they joined our campaign in droves. They were motivated by a sense of youthful optimism, but they were also deeply concerned about the state of our country and the world. Some were alarmed by climate change. Others were worried about the availability of jobs and the stagnant economy. In communities of color, many were outraged that the very people entrusted to protect them were instead targeting and harassing them. Some were worried they could be sent off to fight yet another ill-conceived war in the Middle East, or be deported even though this was the only country they had ever known.

But the issue that was so often uppermost in the minds of the countless young people I met all across the country was the ever-escalating cost of college and the scourge of student debt. Whether they were thinking about attending college, were currently enrolled, or had already graduated, they were deeply worried that they would be saddled with an unsustainable amount of debt for years to come. Unfortunately, they were right to worry.

The high cost of college and student debt impacts not only those who are in college and their families, but low-income and working-class families who are simply not able to send their kids to college. Today in America, hundreds of thousands of bright young people who have the desire and the ability to get a college education will not be able to do so because their families lack the money. This is a tragedy for those young people and their families, but it is also a tragedy for our nation. How many scientists, engineers, businesspeople, teachers, doctors, and nurses are we losing because higher education in this country is unaffordable for so many?

This year, nearly 70 percent of all students graduating with a bachelor's degree will leave school with some debt, with the average amount exceeding $35,000. One in eight graduates will graduate with more than $50,000 in outstanding student loans. And that's not including the mountains of credit card debt that some students incur trying to make ends meet while in school. Obviously, for those going to medical school, dental school, nursing school, or graduate school in general, the debt is much higher.

Unlike other types of personal debt that have been decreasing in recent years, student debt has been steadily increasing. In all, 43.3 million people—current students, graduates, and those who left college before graduating—now owe more than $1.3 trillion in student loans. This is more than triple the amount of student debt in 2004, and more than all credit card and auto loan debt in the United States combined. And an increasing portion of those 43.3 million people will carry their student debt their entire lives. According to the Government Accountability Office, Americans *nearing retirement* have the fastest-growing student loan debt of any age group, having soared from $2.8 billion in 2005 to $18.2 billion by 2013.

I remember well a gentleman I met during a town meeting in Nevada. Fifty-five years of age, he told us that he had been paying off his student loan for twenty-five years but was more in debt today than when he first took out the loan. He's worried now that his Social Security

Student Debt, 1993–2015
AVERAGE INDIVIDUAL DEBT IN EACH YEAR'S GRADUATING CLASS

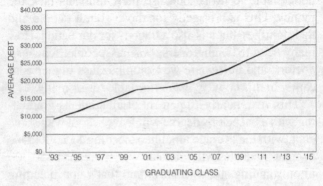

GRADUATING CLASS

Data Source: Mark Kantrowitz, WSJ.com

checks will be garnished in order to pay off that debt. How crazy is that?

In my view, it is profoundly wrong that so many talented, hardworking young people are starting their adult lives under such a crushing mountain of debt—debt that will weigh them down and hold them back for much or even most of their lives. And it is profoundly unfair that other students, simply because they had the good fortune to be born into wealthy families, can graduate college without a cent of debt. If we are a country that truly believes in equal opportunity, shouldn't we level the playing field for all young Americans? I certainly think so.

Here is a simple question: Instead of encouraging young people to get a higher education, why are we punishing them for doing so? Why are we making it so hard? That seems pretty crazy to me.

It is crazy not just for the individuals impacted, but for the future of our economy and our economic competitiveness. The United States used to lead the world in the percentage of people who graduated college, which is one of the reasons that we have the strongest economy in the world. Today, that is no longer the case.

In 2011 CNN reported:

> The U.S. once led the world in college gradu- ates. As an example of this, Americans age fifty- five to sixty-four still lead their peers in other nations in the portion with college degrees (41 percent). But this number has flatlined for Ameri- cans. In 2008, the same percentage of Americans age twenty-five to thirty-four and age fifty-five to sixty-four were college graduates.
>
> Meanwhile, other nations have caught up, and some have pulled ahead. Among this younger age group from twenty-five to thirty-four, all of the fol- lowing nations now have a larger percent of college graduates than the U.S.: Australia, Belgium, Can- ada, Denmark, France, Ireland, Israel, Japan, South Korea, Luxembourg, New Zealand, Norway, Sweden, and the United Kingdom.

And *Education Week* wrote about a recent report from the Organization for Economic Co-operation and Development that shows: "Since 1995, higher education in the United States has become increasingly more ex- pensive. The nation's college-graduation rate has not grown at the same speed, and as that slowed, other coun- tries have caught up and even surpassed the United States in their supply of college graduates."

Frankly, this is very frightening. We used to lead the world in terms of the percentage of all people who are college graduates, but now among the younger genera- tion we are in fifteenth place, and falling further and further behind. Does anyone not believe that this will have severe economic consequences for the future of our economy and our way of life?

That is why I ran for president on a program of making public colleges and universities tuition-free. I believe that higher education in America should be a right for all, not a privilege for the few. That means that everyone, regardless of their station in life, should be able to get all of the education they need.

This is a revolutionary and transformative concept that goes well beyond the impact it will have on higher education. All across the country today there are low-income children in the fourth or fifth grade who already understand, instinctively, that they are never going to make it into the middle class. Their parents are poor, they are poor, and they will be poor in the future. And that's the way it is.

They and their parents live in communities where very few people go to college. Hanging around with college-educated families is not their world. For those children, the idea of getting a college education and making it into the middle class is as likely as going to the moon. And many of those kids, at a very early age, give up on school and learning. They may not officially drop out of school until they are sixteen, but they intellectually drop out at much younger ages.

Our mission must be to give hope to those young people. If every parent in this country, every teacher in this country, and every student in this country understands that if kids study hard and do well in school they *will* be able to go to college, regardless of the income of their family, that will have a radical impact on primary and secondary education in the United States—and on the lives of millions of families. That's what we can accomplish by making public colleges and universities tuition-free and making certain that every American, no matter his or her economic status, has the opportunity for a higher education.

Education has always been—perhaps more than any

other institution in our society—the great equalizer. Education, especially in a rapidly evolving economy, is how people qualify for better jobs, and do well at them. It is the key to solving many of the serious problems of economic, racial, and gender inequality plaguing our society.

But as college becomes less affordable, and as working families take on increasing amounts of debt, higher education may actually be increasing social and economic inequality, rather than alleviating it. Making higher education universally available will not only create a better-educated society, it will allow us to be a more just society.

In 1877, Rutherford B. Hayes was the first president to make a strong case for universally available public education. "Universal suffrage should rest upon universal education," he said in his inaugural address, adding, "Liberal and permanent provision should be made for the support of free schools." For Hayes, a Republican, education was the basis for full economic and political participation, and the basis for prosperity. I agree.

There used to be a time, forty or fifty years ago, when many people could graduate from high school and move right into a decent-paying job with good benefits. Strong unions offered apprenticeships, and a large manufacturing sector provided opportunities for those without an advanced degree. A couple with a sole breadwinner could buy a home, raise a family, and send their kids to college. That was the American dream. Those days are pretty much over. With the loss of some 60,000 factories in the last fifteen years, and the decline of the trade union movement, it is harder and harder for workers to make it into the middle class.

Today, perhaps the most important pathway to the middle class runs through higher education. While not all middle-class jobs in today's economy require a college degree, an increasing number do. People need a higher education to make it into the middle class and successfully compete in a global economy.

But the fact of the matter is that rising costs are making it harder and harder for ordinary Americans to get the college education they want. Since 1970, average inflation-adjusted tuition at a four-year public university has almost quadrupled. In the last ten years alone, tuition has increased by almost 60 percent.

Meanwhile, in the midst of this crisis, government has been doing exactly the wrong thing. While the cost of attending college is going up and up, per-student public funding for higher education has been going down. While this has been going on for decades, the Great Recession accelerated this trend, as state governments around the country began the process of making draconian cuts to funding for public colleges. For many governors, whose campaign contributions came from the wealthy and large corporations, giving tax breaks to the rich was a higher priority than enabling working-class students to get a college education. In 1980, state governments contributed close to 80 percent of the cost of instruction; today, it is less than half. What exactly does this mean for the more than three-quarters of college students in the United States who attend *public* colleges?

It means that students and their parents, even though wages have been stagnant for decades, must bear a higher percentage of the soaring costs of a college degree. The cost of a public-college education accounted for 4 percent of the average family's annual income forty years ago; today it is 15 percent. In 1978 it was possible to earn enough money to pay for a year of college tuition just by working a full-time summer job that paid minimum wage. Today, it would take a minimum-wage worker an entire year to earn enough to cover the average annual in-state tuition at a public university—if that worker had no other expenses at all for that year. But we all know that a person cannot live on, much less save any money on, a minimum-wage job.

It is no wonder many students from low-income families are forced to work while attending college, sometimes holding down more than one job in addition to attending classes, studying, and working unpaid internships. Try working the late shift at McDonald's while you are preparing for finals. Not easy. I have talked to too many students who are trying hard to focus on their education while working thirty to forty hours a week.

Some students concoct elaborate cost-saving schemes, taking courses at less expensive schools and transferring credits, only to find that not all schools will accept the credits. And as we've seen, most take on unsustainable amounts of debt.

Why do we put them through this? Why are we making it so difficult for these students to succeed?

While it is my view that all students in this country, regardless of income, have the right to get a higher education if they have the ability and desire, it is important to take a hard look at why the cost of college is rising so rapidly. And it is also important to point out that the reason the cost of higher education is increasing is *not* that colleges are spending any more per student. Other factors are driving the steep cost curve.

One of them is the increasing costs of health insurance for staff and faculty. The fact that we have the most expensive health care system in the world significantly impacts college costs, just as it does any large business. Another major cost driver is the proliferation of administrative positions in higher education. Just between 1993 and 2009, administrative positions grew by more than 60 percent, more than ten times the growth rate of tenured professors, and at many times the salary. As colleges and universities become more corporatized and bureaucratic, colleges need more bureaucrats to run them. Exactly how much do students benefit by having, in some cases, dozens of vice presidents of this or that, each earning hundreds of thousands of dollars or more? Not very much.

Another reason college educations are becoming so expensive is that colleges are increasingly being run as businesses competing for market share. To become more attractive to prospective students, they spend huge amounts of money on fancy student centers and dorms, state-of-the-art gyms and sports stadiums, and countless other campus amenities. While this trend is certainly more exaggerated at private schools, public colleges and universities are not immune to big spending on "bells and whistles" that drive up tuition while providing little or no academic benefit to students.

Now, I know that I'm a bit old-fashioned, but I still believe that the function of a college or university is to provide the best-quality education possible. And I suspect students can survive without fancy dormitory suites, gourmet food, and football coaches who make $5 million a year.

Further, the cost of college textbooks has risen tenfold since 1977. The average full-time university student in the United States now pays more than $1,200 each year just for books and supplies. This exorbitant increase is driven by stranglehold contracts with book publishers that restrict digital access to their products and that release newer and more expensive editions every few years that prevent students from using less expensive used books. Let's call it what it is: a racket. My Senate colleague Richard Durbin of Illinois introduced a bill to move toward open-source digital content as an alternative to traditional textbooks. I think that makes a lot of sense, but unfortunately the bill has not even been given a hearing in Congress.

The high cost of college isn't just bad for students and their families, it's bad for our economy, too. While a college education will eventually pay off for many people, the large amount of debt incurred for that education has a real and immediate impact on the standard of living of millions, and on our national economy. Growing student debt is one of the major reasons young people are delaying getting married and having kids, and why families are putting off buying homes, starting businesses, and saving for retirement. This, in turn, is slowing overall economic growth. And less growth means fewer jobs and less tax revenue to pay for the services Americans want and deserve.

Further, ballooning student debt is introducing an element of risk into our financial system that is eerily reminiscent of the housing mortgage crisis. Some financial analysts even believe that student loan debt could be the next debt bubble to burst, as the total amount of outstanding debt grows at an alarming rate while more and more students lack the income to repay their loans.

Already, more than one in four student loan borrowers is delinquent or in default. And more than 40 percent of those who borrowed from the government's main loan program are either in default or delinquency on the more than $200 billion they owe the government. If the $1.3 trillion in debt owed collectively by 43 million Americans goes bad for whatever reason, it would put an extreme strain on our financial system and could even precipitate another crisis.

You would think—for the sake of the overall economy, at least, if not for the students themselves—that government policy would allow people to get out from under unsustainable student debt by refinancing at lower interest rates. You would think that Americans carrying student debt would be able to refinance that debt like they can with their home mortgages, right? Wrong. Incredibly, most student debt in this country cannot be refinanced, even if the loan was originally made at very high interest rates.

Further, unlike other forms of debt, student loans are very difficult to discharge, even in bankruptcy. In fact, it is much easier for a big bank or corporation to declare insolvency and be forgiven for outstanding debts than it is for an individual going through personal bankruptcy to discharge a student loan.

So what happens if a borrower can't pay a student loan? Some borrowers have had their tax refunds withheld, and some seniors have had their Social Security benefits garnished. Some student loans end up with aggressive collection agencies, who hound borrowers to the point of harassment. And some borrowers have even been arrested. In Texas—where tuition increases led to higher rates of borrowing, and with it, more defaults—marshals have arrested people for not paying student loans. America rightfully outlawed debtors' prisons in the mid-nineteenth century, but some cities and states are issuing contempt-of-court warrants that get around those rules.

Education and learning is an inherent part of what being a human being is all about. In my view, we should be creating opportunities for Americans to continue learning, formally and informally, until the day they die. Further, at a time of exploding technology and a rapidly changing economy, the United States needs a well-educated population if we are to compete effectively in the global economy. I have already heard from many employers who tell me that they are unable to find the high-skilled employees they need for the good-paying new jobs being created.

The United States should not be falling behind other

countries in terms of making public colleges and universities accessible to all, regardless of income. We should be leading the way. We should be understanding that investing in our young people's education is not only the right thing to do for them, it's the right thing to do for the future of our economy and our country.

MAKING PUBLIC COLLEGES AND UNIVERSITIES TUITION-FREE

During the presidential campaign I outlined a simple and straightforward proposal that would make public colleges and universities tuition-free. This plan, the College for All Act, would allow all Americans, if they had the ability and the desire, to go to college regardless of the income of their families. It would also prevent them from going deeply into debt as a result of their education. The College for All Act would create a partnership between the U.S. government and states that would provide $2 in federal funding for every dollar a state spends on making public colleges and universities tuition-free for undergraduate students. The plan would also cover 100 percent of the cost of books and room and board for low-income students.

The College for All Act would more than triple the federal work-study program to build a valuable career experience that would help students after they graduate. And it would expand Pell Grants, which used to cover three-quarters of the cost of a college education for many low-income students, but now cover only a third of it on average.

The College for All Act would open the door to a middle-class life for millions of young Americans and make our economy stronger and more productive. Yes, it's that simple.

Free college tuition is not a radical idea. In Finland, Denmark, Ireland, Iceland, Norway, Sweden, and Mexico, public colleges and universities are free. In Denmark, not only is college tuition-free, but people who go to college in that country actually get paid. In Germany the public colleges are free not only for Germans, but also for international students, which is why every year more than 4,500 students from the United States enroll in German universities. For a token fee of about $200 per year, an American student can earn a degree in math or engineering from one of the premier universities in Europe.

Governments in those countries understand the value of investing in their young people. They know that these students will acquire the knowledge and skills to strengthen their countries and become the teachers, architects, engineers, scientists, and entrepreneurs of the future. They realize that by allowing all qualified students—regardless of income—to achieve a higher education, they are making a down payment on their countries' economic prosperity.

It may seem hard to believe, but there was a time in the not-too-distant past when higher education was pretty close to being free in this country. In 1965, average tuition at a four-year public university was just $243, and many of the best colleges, such as the City University of New York (CUNY), did not charge any tuition at all. Hundreds of thousands of students received a free education from CUNY, and many of them came from working-class backgrounds and were the first in their families to attend college. Likewise, the University of California system, considered by many to be the crown jewel of public higher education in this country, did not begin charging tuition until the 1980s.

And for many years, we made a much greater effort to make attending any college—public or private—

more affordable. In 1944, the United States government thanked the millions of soldiers who won the war against fascism by allowing them the opportunity of getting a higher education. Under the Servicemen's Readjustment Act of 1944, the federal government covered tuition, lab fees, books, health insurance, and supplies for veterans returning from World War II. This "GI Bill" helped propel countless veterans into the middle class, and many economists believe that it was a major reason for the high productivity and economic growth our nation enjoyed during the postwar years.

In 1988 a congressional report concluded that for every dollar the federal government spent on the GI Bill, the return on investment was $6.90 in additional tax revenues. This is a lesson that we cannot afford to forget. Investing in educational opportunities for our people improves their standard of living and improves the economic well-being of the entire country. And we should be making that investment today.

So, maybe free tuition at public colleges and universities for qualified students is a good idea, but how do we pay for my plan? Again, simple. By imposing a small speculation fee on Wall Street investment houses and hedge funds. A financial transaction tax of just 0.5 percent on stock trades (that's 50 cents for every $100 worth of stock), a 0.1 percent fee on bonds, and a 0.005 percent fee on derivatives would raise up to $300 billion a year, significantly more revenue than my college plan would require. And in addition to paying for tuition-free college and driving down student debt, this tax would help tap the brakes on the exceptionally dubious practice of computer-driven, high-speed trading that is destabilizing the financial markets.

More than a thousand economists have endorsed a tax on Wall Street speculation, and today some forty countries throughout the world have imposed a financial transactions tax, including Britain, Germany, France, Switzerland, China, India, South Korea, Hong Kong, Singapore, Taiwan, and Brazil. The taxpayers of this country bailed out Wall Street in 2008; as I said earlier, now it's time for Wall Street to start helping the middle class of this country—by making public colleges and universities throughout the country tuition-free.

DEALING WITH THE STUDENT DEBT CRISIS

In 2010, President Obama signed a law making it easier for borrowers to repay their student loans and avoid default through income-based repayment. It also included some limited loan forgiveness for public servants and long-term debtors. These were important steps, but they do not go nearly far enough in addressing the oppressive burden of crushing student loan debt.

It makes absolutely no sense that Americans can refinance their homes when interest rates are low, but millions of college graduates are stuck with interest rates of 5, 6, or 7 percent for the life of their student loans. That is why, under the College for All Act, people would be able to refinance their outstanding student loans to take advantage of favorable interest rates, which happen now to be at historic lows. Depending on the terms of the original loan, many borrowers would see immediate savings of more than a hundred dollars every month for the duration of their loan repayment period.

Further, it makes no sense that Americans can purchase a car with a 2 percent loan, but the interest rate for a new student loan is more than twice that amount. Under the College for All Act, the formula for setting new student loan interest rates would go back to where it was in 2006. If this plan were in effect today, interest rates on new loans would be slashed on average by more than half: from 4.29 percent to 2.32 percent for undergraduate loans; from 5.84 percent to 2.32 percent for graduate Direct Loans; and from 6.84 percent to 3.12 percent for Direct PLUS Loans. Again, this could mean, depending on the size of the loan, monthly savings of a hundred dollars or more.

The College for All Act will also put an end to the offensive reality that the federal government makes a profit off student loans. In fact, over the next decade, the federal government stands to make a profit of more than $81 billion on student loan payments. To my mind, this is morally wrong, bad economics, and completely backward. It is absurd that the federal government makes a profit on the backs of low-income and working-class young Americans pursuing a college degree. As a matter of public policy, we should be doing everything possible to make college more affordable—not more expensive. This has got to stop; we have to end the practice of the federal government's profiting from student loans, and my plan would do just that.

CRACKING DOWN ON FOR-PROFIT SCHOOLS

Another problematic student loan practice is being perpetrated by the growing number of for-profit "career" schools that effectively see federal student aid as a profit center to exploit, without regard to the quality of the education they provide.

There is no question that some career colleges do a fine job preparing students for employment in specialty fields. However, far too often, these for-profit businesses lure students based on confusing or misleading information and exaggerated claims, and then charge excessive tuition and fees for poor-quality training in occupations that are either low-paying or offer few jobs. Trump University, which scammed thousands of people seeking to learn the inside secrets of real estate deals, is just the tip of the iceberg.

The Senate Committee on Health, Education, Labor and Pensions, of which I have long been a member, found that these for-profit schools spend, on average, 30 percent more per student on marketing and recruiting than on actual instruction. It should not be surprising that students graduating from these for-profit schools have significantly lower rates of employment in their fields of study and higher rates of student loan default compared with their peers graduating from public and nonprofit schools.

But many of these schools don't care one lick whether the students fail after they graduate—because their chief concern is making a profit off taxpayer-funded student loans.

The U.S. Department of Education has begun to crack down on the most egregious and predatory practices of for-profit schools. New federal regulations require career colleges to be much more transparent in their marketing and to make real efforts to improve employment outcomes for students, or else risk losing access to federal student aid. These "gainful employment" regulations, while not perfect, will increase accountability at for-profit career colleges and help students avoid becoming unreasonably burdened by student loan debt they cannot repay.

That's a good start, but we can and should go much further in terms of cracking down on these colleges that too often prey on students while making an outrageous profit off taxpayer money.

SUPPORTING FIRST-TIME AND
LOW-INCOME STUDENTS

In addition to opening the door for kids from low-income and working-class backgrounds to attend college, we also have to do a much better job supporting these students before they go to college, and once they are there. Too many young people who begin college do not graduate.

That is why I am a strong supporter of commonsense programs like the federal TRIO program, which provides important services for students who have a higher-than-average likelihood of either not going to college at all or of dropping out before graduating. These include low-income students, students from families where neither parent ever went to college, returning veterans, students with disabilities, and working adult learners. TRIO helps these young people believe they can succeed at college, it helps them to apply, and it gives them support once they are enrolled. TRIO has an incredibly strong track record of success.

Several years ago, when I addressed a group of Vermont TRIO students, I mentioned that I wished there had been a similar program in my day. My father dropped out of high school, and my mother never went to college. I know how difficult it can be to figure out what college to go to, how to apply, what to study, and how to pay for it. I remember being in classes with kids whose parents were lawyers, doctors, and businessmen and feeling like I was an outsider in an entirely new world. The truth of the matter is that this whole experience can be very daunting if you are the first in the family to attend college.

Maybe that's why I am always so moved when I visit with TRIO participants. Or maybe it's because it is endlessly inspiring to see young adults succeed in spite of the many challenges life throws at them. Just because they don't come from families with a lot of money doesn't mean they aren't as smart as other kids, or have any less potential. TRIO does a really excellent job at tapping that potential, by giving these students a little extra attention, providing the tools they need to succeed, and reinforcing the notion that if they work hard they can graduate from college and improve their lives.

And yet, like clockwork, Republicans propose cuts to TRIO almost every year. It never ceases to amaze me that some in Congress will go to the mat to protect massive tax breaks for millionaires and billionaires, but will so easily cut funding for an inexpensive and cost-effective program that helps working-class kids succeed.

BETTER PREPARING STUDENTS TO GO TO COLLEGE

We also have to better prepare students before they go to college, by improving our primary and secondary schools, which too often are failing our youth, especially in low-income and minority communities. Elsewhere in this book I address the urgent need to modernize the physical schools our children attend, and to support their dedicated teachers and staff. Let me briefly touch on how we educate our youth.

Thankfully, we have finally begun to move away from No Child Left Behind's system of test-based sanctions and the blame-and-shame approach to school accountability, which for the past fourteen years got in the way of providing every child with access to a quality education. NCLB didn't improve education, it simply forced teachers to "teach to the test."

This past December, President Obama signed the Every Student Succeeds Act, which kept in place federal accountability guidelines while giving states and schools flexibility to develop approaches that work best for their students and their communities. The new law includes language I authored to allow states to develop alternatives to national standardized tests. While not perfect, ESSA is a step toward providing a quality education to all of our children, which will in turn help prepare our youth to succeed in college.

Not everybody wants to go to college, and not everybody needs to go to college. This country needs a large supply of carpenters, plumbers, welders, bricklayers, ironworkers, mechanics, and many other professions that pay workers, especially those with unions, good wages for doing very important, skilled work. As part of a new approach to higher education and vocational training, we must provide those students with the education and training they need, regardless of the incomes of their families.

There are many other issues affecting primary and secondary education that are beyond the scope of this book. These include the effects of intergenerational poverty that disadvantage low-income children, massive disinvestment in minority communities, lack of adequate afterschool and summer programming, the opioid crisis that is ripping apart both urban and rural communities, and the chronic underfunding of schools. Suffice it to say that as a society, we are failing far too many of our children. These young people are the very future of our country. To my mind, we have both a moral obligation and an economic imperative to do better. Much better.

SIX

COMBATING CLIMATE CHANGE

The debate is over. The vast majority of the scientific community has spoken. Climate change is real, it is caused by human activity, and it is already causing devastating harm here in the United States and all around the globe. It is absolutely imperative that we boldly transform our energy system away from fossil fuel to energy efficiency and sustainable energy. The future of the planet is at stake.

On January 7, 2015, I took to the floor of the U.S. Senate to express my strong opposition to the Keystone XL Pipeline, a project that would result in the increased excavation and transportation across our country of some of the dirtiest fuel on the planet. As the grandfather of seven beautiful children, this is what I said: "I believe that decades from now our kids and our grandchildren will scratch their heads and they will say, 'What world were these people—members of Congress—living in in 2015 when they voted for this Keystone Pipeline? How did it happen that they did not listen to the overwhelming majority of scientists who told us we have to cut greenhouse gas emissions, not increase them?' I think our kids and our grandchildren will be saying to us, 'Why did you do that to us? Why did you leave this planet less habitable than it could have been?'"

To my mind, global climate change is the single greatest threat facing the planet. It poses an actual existential threat to our country and our world. We are the custodians of the earth, and it would be a moral disgrace if we left to future generations a planet that was unhealthy, dangerous, and increasingly uninhabitable. We must transform our energy system and drastically reduce greenhouse gas emissions. There is no alternative.

Ever since the Industrial Revolution began two hundred years ago, we have been burning increasing amounts of carbon-based fossil fuels—principally oil, natural gas, and coal—to heat our factories and homes, generate electricity, and power our vehicles. And for most of that time, we have been dumping the by-products of that combustion, some of which are highly toxic, into our atmosphere, our soil, and our waterways. Over the years, we have become better at scrubbing out certain pollutants, including sulfur oxides and particulates that contribute to acid rain and smog, but an incontrovertible fact remains: When we burn carbon-based fossil fuels, we release significant amounts of carbon dioxide into the atmosphere. In fact, today, humans release between 35 and 40 billion tons of carbon dioxide into the atmosphere every year.

According to NASA scientists, in the past 650,000 years the concentration of carbon dioxide in the atmosphere has never exceeded 300 ppm (parts per million). At the beginning of the Industrial Revolution, carbon levels were less than 270 ppm. Ever since, atmospheric carbon dioxide levels have risen, slowly at first, but at increasing rates as we burned more and more fossil fuels. According to the Mauna Loa Observatory in

Hawaii, carbon dioxide levels crossed the 400 ppm threshold for the first time in 2013, and continue to rise by an average of 2 ppm every year. So what does this mean?

Carbon dioxide is a "greenhouse gas" that traps heat from the sun and earth in the atmosphere. The more carbon dioxide in the atmosphere, the greater the greenhouse gas effect, and the more the atmosphere and the oceans warm. This is hardly a new idea. Nor is it, as some would have you believe, a theory. In fact, scientists started connecting carbon emissions to atmospheric warming in the mid-1800s, and in 1917 Alexander Graham Bell coined the now popular term when he warned that "the unchecked burning of fossil fuels . . . would have a sort of greenhouse effect," turning the atmosphere into "a sort of hot-house."

My good friend and fellow Vermonter Bill McKibben named his climate change advocacy group 350.org, because 350 ppm of atmospheric carbon dioxide is what Dr. James Hansen, former head of the Goddard Institute for Space Studies and one of the most respected climatologists in the world, says is the maximum level to "preserve a planet similar to that on which civilization developed and to which life on Earth is adapted." Tragically, we have now exceeded 400 ppm.

And while carbon dioxide accounts for 81 percent of all U.S. greenhouse gas emissions, it is not the sole problem. Methane, which is released during the extraction, transportation, and combustion of natural gas, oil, and coal, accounts for 11 percent of greenhouse gas emissions. But while it is a smaller slice of the overall greenhouse gas emissions pie pound for pound, methane traps eighty-five times more heat than carbon dioxide does. Similarly, while nitrous oxide—also a by-product of fossil fuel combustion—accounts for just 6 percent of all greenhouse gas emission, it traps almost three hundred times more heat than carbon dioxide. And certain synthetic fluorinated gases, like hydrofluorocarbons and chlorofluorocarbons, account for just 3 percent of the pie, but are tens of thousands times more powerful than carbon dioxide.

The results of dumping these heat-trapping gases into the atmosphere year after year are frighteningly clear. The year 2015 was the hottest year on record, and 2016 is on pace to be hotter still. July 2016 was the hottest month ever recorded on the planet. Thirteen of the fifteen hottest years have occurred since the year 2000.

Extreme heat waves have gripped large swaths of the planet, often with catastrophic results, especially for the elderly, the sick, and the poor. The deadliest heat wave ever recorded killed more than 71,000 people in Europe in 2003. A 2010 heat wave in Russia killed 55,700 people. In 2015, temperatures in India and Pakistan topped 120 degrees Fahrenheit and killed more than 1,820 people. In July of 2016, the city of Basra, Iraq, reached 129 degrees—the highest temperature ever recorded in the Eastern Hemisphere, and the second-highest temperature ever recorded on the planet.

The U.S. has been hit with what used to be considered "unusual" heat waves almost every year since 2012. In June 2015, record heat seared parts of Arizona, Nevada, and California, with temperatures reaching 120 degrees Fahrenheit in Yuma, Arizona; 115 in Las Vegas; and 125 in Needles, California. Later in the summer, we were introduced to a new term, as a "heat dome" settled over much of the country, and for several consecutive days every state in the lower forty-eight recorded temperatures in excess of 95, with many registering in the triple digits.

In recent years, as temperatures rise, we have seen significant shrinking of the ice sheets in Greenland and

Antarctica. In Antarctica alone, NASA estimates that more than 100 billion tons of ice is melting each and every year, which is equivalent to a quarter of all the water in massive Lake Erie. But that is nothing compared with Greenland, which is losing more than 300 billion tons of ice a year. Alaska and Canada are each losing another 75 billion tons a year from melting glaciers. Where is all that melted ice going?

The oceans have already risen by about eight inches since the beginning of the last century. That might not sound like much, but the National Oceanic and Atmospheric Administration (NOAA) predicts they will rise by as much as three feet by the end of this century. More than 150 million Americans live along the coasts, and eleven of the world's fifteen largest cities are found in coastal areas. An August 2016 report by the online real estate sales company Zillow said that rising sea levels could claim up to 1.9 million homes by 2100, worth a combined $882 billion.

Rising oceans are already creating the world's first "climate refugees." Residents from the Republic of Maldives, a tiny nation made up of more than a thousand islands southeast of India, are abandoning some of the lower-lying islands as the ocean rises. Closer to home, residents of Isle de Jean Charles in southeastern Louisiana, most of whom are Biloxi-Chitimacha-Choctaw Native Americans, are preparing to leave the only place they have ever called home as their land becomes flooded. In August 2016, the six hundred Inupiat villagers of Shishmaref voted to relocate their four-hundred-year-old Native Alaskan village, one of thirty-one Alaskan villages facing an "imminent threat of destruction" from climate change that has caused erosion and flooding, according to the Arctic Institute.

Meanwhile, the oceans themselves are warming and becoming more acidified as they absorb carbon dioxide from the atmosphere. These changes are disrupting important fisheries, threatening the food supply for millions of people, and endangering fragile and important ecosystems like coral reefs that are becoming "bleached" in the warm acidic waters.

And all across the world, extreme weather disturbances are becoming more common, including hurricanes, torrential rainfalls, and severe flooding. In October of 2015, Hurricane Patricia became the most powerful tropical cyclone ever measured in the Western Hemisphere, with maximum sustained winds of 215 miles per hour and gusts up to 247 miles per hour. This was just a few years after Hurricane Sandy killed 233 people and caused more than $75 billion in damages and lost economic output. Sandy was such an intense storm that NOAA had to come up with a new term: "superstorm."

Nor has my home state of Vermont been immune. In August 2011, Tropical Storm Irene ripped through Vermont, causing the deaths of six people and washing away hundreds of bridges and dozens of miles of road. If you had told me even a few days before Irene struck that Vermont, nestled in rolling green mountains on the border with Canada, would be devastated by a tropical storm, I would have surely thought you were crazy. But what is truly crazy is how these storms are becoming more and more commonplace.

As I write this book, a massive storm has dumped more than twenty inches of rain in two days on southeast Louisiana, causing widespread flooding that has already killed eleven people and forced thirty thousand from their homes. According to an official with the NOAA's Center for Environmental Information, the extraordinarily heavy rain in Louisiana—which in some areas topped thirty-one inches over seven days—"is consistent with what we expect to see in the future if you look at climate models."

Bill McKibben summed up the phenomenon succinctly. "The basic physics are simple: Warm air holds more water vapor, something that is turning out to be one of the most important facts of the twenty-first century." In other words, warmer air means more superstorms.

I spent quite a bit of time traveling through California in May and June of 2016 in the lead-up to the second-to-last Democratic primary, and it struck me just how much climate change has impacted that beautiful state. The past five years have been the driest on record in California, forcing many towns to reduce water consumption by more than 30 percent. In 2015, more than half a million acres, or more than 5 percent of the state's agricultural land, was left uncultivated because of the drought, robbing the state of $1.8 billion in economic activity and more than ten thousand jobs. Historic wildfires scorched 118,000 acres of land last year, more than double the five-year average. Extreme heat has sent dozens of people, mostly in low-income communities without air-conditioning, to an early death. And along their 840-mile coastline, Californians watch cautiously as the ocean rises, threatening communities and businesses.

Meanwhile, there is another aspect to climate change that should concern us all. During the first Democratic presidential debate, in October 2015, I said, in response to a question posed by CNN moderator Anderson Cooper, that I considered climate change to be our nation's greatest national security threat. That clearly was not the answer most people expected to hear, but it is the opinion of a growing number of leading national security experts, including many in the CIA and the Department of Defense.

Of course, there is no shortage of national security concerns, including international terrorism, ISIS, global poverty, health pandemics, and the belligerent actions of individual countries like Russia, North Korea, and China. But unlike these other threats, climate change cannot be thwarted by good intelligence work, or stopped at a border, or negotiated with, or contained by economic sanctions. It cannot be beaten on a battlefield or bombed from the air. It has no vaccine or treatment. And yet, unless we act boldly, and within this very short window of opportunity, it will likely wreak havoc and destabilize whole nations and regions, with serious security ramifications for many countries, including the United States.

The Intergovernmental Panel on Climate Change (IPCC), which includes more than 1,300 scientists from around the world, says that unless we drastically change course in terms of greenhouse gas emissions, temperatures will continue to rise by as much as five or ten degrees Fahrenheit over the next century. Some scientists believe that number is on the low side. What will this mean?

What this significant temperature increase will mean is more drought, more crop failures, and more famine. Drinking water, already a precious commodity in many areas, will become even scarcer. Millions of people will be displaced by rising sea levels, extreme weather events, and flooding. Tropical diseases like malaria, dengue, and yellow fever will spread into parts of the world where they don't currently exist. All of this will likely lead to increased human suffering and death, but the results will be even direr than that.

The growing scarcity of basic human needs could well lead to perpetual warfare in regions around the world, as people fight over limited supplies of water, farmland, and other natural resources. A world in which we see mass migrations of people in search of food, water, and other basic needs is not going to be a safe or stable world. That's not just my opinion—that is the opinion of leading national security experts in our country and throughout the world. Yes: Climate change is our nation's great national security threat.

And the sad truth is that the effects of climate change will fall especially hard upon the most vulnerable people in our country and throughout the world—people who have the fewest resources to protect themselves and the fewest options when disaster strikes. According to the U.N. Institute for Environment and Human Security and the International Organization for Migration, up to 200 million people could be displaced by 2050 as a result of the effects of climate change. That is more than three times the total number of refugees in the world today who have fled for any reason, including dire poverty, war, and famine. Think about it. We have a major refugee crisis today. That crisis could become much, much worse in the coming decades as a result of climate change.

I do not mean to paint a helpless picture of a dystopian future over which we have no control, but Pope Francis was absolutely right when he said, "The world is on a suicidal course with regard to climate change." Of course, we must not, we cannot, and we will not allow that to happen. We have got to address this global crisis before it's too late.

While the global challenge of climate change is huge, there is no question in my mind that it can be addressed and effectively combated. There is also no question in my mind that the United States can and should lead the international effort. As a nation, we have the knowledge and the technology, which is growing more effective and affordable every day. With millions of people in our country unemployed, we certainly have the manpower. What we are lacking now is the political will—the failure to acknowledge the severity of the crisis and to act accordingly.

Under President Obama there is no question that we have made some progress in moving forward in transforming our energy system, and I'm proud that I've been active in that effort. Drive around my state of Vermont and you will see far more solar panels and wind turbines than you saw ten years ago, and we have been aggressive in terms of energy efficiency. The municipally owned electric department of my home city of Burlington, Vermont, now runs almost entirely on sustainable energy, and because of efficiency efforts started when I was mayor in the 1980s, the city uses less electricity today than it did in 1989, despite significant growth. There is a small electric co-op in Vermont that provides cheap electricity to its members by sourcing the majority of its electricity from the methane gas that comes from an old landfill, and many Vermont dairy farmers are converting cow manure to electricity.

These kinds of initiatives are taking place all over the country and in many parts of the world. In Iowa, more than 30 percent of electricity is generated by wind turbines. In Texas, wind is producing some of the cheapest electricity in the country. In California, there are utility-scale solar facilities that supply electricity to hundreds of thousands of homes. The potential for energy production from geothermal, biomass, radiant energy, and tidal power and other technologies is almost boundless. We are making progress, but much, much more needs to be done. After all, the future of the planet is at stake.

One of the more profound lessons that I've learned in politics is that everything is related to everything else. Nothing exists in a vacuum. There is no clearer example of that than our failure to boldly address the crisis of climate change and how that relates to a corrupt political and campaign finance system.

On one hand, the scientists tell us in an almost unanimous voice that bold action is needed to transform our energy system and prevent horrific damage to our planet. Further, poll after poll tells us that a significant majority of Americans believes we should be more aggressive in moving to energy efficiency and sustainable energy, not only to combat climate change, but to improve our ability to provide clean air and clean water. One *might* think that, in a rational and democratic society, if the people want something to happen, and science tells them that they are right in wanting it, it would happen.

Well, in today's world, that's not quite the way it works. In opposition to science and what the people want are enormously powerful forces who want to maintain the status quo. They are more interested in short-term profits for fossil fuel companies than in the future of the planet. They have a lot of power, they have a lot of money, and they know how to make a corrupt political and campaign finance system work for them.

In recent years the major energy companies have thrown unprecedented amounts of money at elected officials to buy their loyalty. Since 1999 they have spent a staggering $2.2 *billion* in federal lobbying, and another $330 million in direct federal campaign contributions. But that's just the part we know about. Thanks to the disastrous Citizens United Supreme Court decision, the fossil fuel industry can pour unlimited amounts of money into the political system without having to disclose how much they've given or whom they've given it to.

Moreover, elements of the fossil fuel industry have intentionally lied about the impact of climate change and have funded organizations that have waged major campaigns of obfuscation and distortion. For many years the corporate media, especially television, heavily funded by fossil fuel ads, have either downplayed the significance of climate change or ignored the issue.

Excellent investigative journalism has recently revealed that Exxon did pioneering research on the impacts of climate change in the *1970s,* but that Exxon executives hid the findings and instead spread disinformation and confusion to protect its bottom line.

The Koch brothers, the extreme right-wing family who have made most of their money in fossil fuels, have funded numerous "think tanks" to obfuscate the issue. According to Greenpeace, the Koch brothers have given over $80 million to climate denial front groups that are working to delay policies and regulations aimed at stopping global warming.

All of this is eerily reminiscent of the fight over regulating tobacco, when representatives of the tobacco industry repeatedly testified before Congress that cigarettes don't cause cancer, emphysema, and other illnesses. As a result of their lies, how many millions of people throughout the world unnecessarily died? Over the years, how many trillions of dollars have been spent to treat tobacco-caused illnesses?

And here's a scary thought: It is very likely that the damage done to human life by the lies of the tobacco industry will be minimal compared with the damage done by the lies of the fossil fuel industry. Cigarettes and tobacco products cause many individual cases of cancer and other diseases. Climate change has the potential to destroy whole communities and regions and lead to terrible wars.

Let's be clear: The reason we haven't solved climate change isn't because the science isn't clear, or that people don't want to address the crisis. It's because a small subsection of the 1 percent are hell-bent on doing everything in their power to block action. Sadly, they have deliberately chosen to put their profits ahead of the health of our people and planet.

One of the most remarkable aspects of modern-day American politics is that we now have virtually an entire political party, the Republican Party, that has rejected science in regard to climate change. This is no small thing. How do we, in general, develop rational public policy if we reject science? How can the findings of the worldwide scientific community be ignored with regard to the greatest environmental crisis ever to have faced the planet?

Unbelievably, almost none of the many candidates who competed in the Republican presidential primary process admitted to believing that climate change is real or that we need to take action to move away from fossil fuel. Donald Trump, in fact, said he believes that climate change is a hoax, developed by the Chinese. This is all rather extraordinary, but not surprising—if you follow the money and the campaign contributions. Here is the pathetic truth: The moment any candidate acknowledges the reality of climate change, and wants to do something about it, that candidate loses campaign funding from major corporate donors.

Notwithstanding consistent and resolute opposition from most Republicans and some Democrats in Congress, President Obama has taken some important executive actions to reduce greenhouse gas emissions. For instance, the EPA's Clean Power Plan will reduce carbon emissions from some of the most polluting sources of energy, and new fuel-efficiency goals for cars and light trucks will almost double fuel efficiency by 2025. These are good steps, but the best available science says they will make but a small dent in carbon levels in the atmosphere, and that we must go much further to avoid the worst consequences of climate change.

Our goal should be to cut U.S. carbon pollution by at

least 40 percent by 2030 and 80 percent by 2050, compared with where we were in 1990. These are not some unachievable, utopian goals. We can make it happen, by dramatically increasing energy efficiency, aggressively moving away from fossil fuels, and deploying historic levels of new renewable energy like wind, solar, and geothermal. And we must help lead an international mobilization to make sure other countries take similar efforts. We can, and must, do this, for our children and our planet. Let me briefly address the steps we need to take to get there.

PROMOTING ENERGY EFFICIENCY

Energy efficiency is the low-hanging fruit in the battle against climate change. It is easy, it is relatively inexpensive, and every kilowatt we save through efficiency measures is one kilowatt that we do not have to produce. Pretty straightforward.

Forty percent of the energy used in this country is used to heat, cool, and light buildings. Making our homes, office buildings, schools, and factories more energy-efficient will reduce energy demand, save money on fuel bills, cut carbon emissions, and create good-paying jobs. This is not rocket science. We are talking about making sure every new building is built to the highest efficiency standards and that old buildings are retrofitted to incorporate, to the extent possible, state-of-the-art insulation, efficient LED lighting, and modern heating and cooling systems.

It never ceases to amaze me that in my state of Vermont, where we still have some very cold winters, many people, particularly low-income families, live in poorly insulated homes. The reason is simple: They do not have the money to pay for the up-front costs to weatherize their homes. This is an issue I have encountered over and over; the cost of an energy project—whether weatherizing a house, installing energy-efficient lighting, replacing an old heating system for a more efficient one, or installing solar panels—is often a barrier to implementing the project, even though these efficiency improvements can return as much as three or four dollars in savings over the life of the improvement for every dollar invested.

That is why innovative financing mechanisms, like on-bill financing and Property Assessed Clean Energy (PACE) districts, are so important, for homeowners and business owners alike. These programs allow a utility or a municipality to lend customers money to make efficiency improvements. The consumers then pay off the loan directly on their utility or property tax bill as their energy costs decline. If this is not a win-win situation, I'm not sure what is. The barrier to up-front costs is removed and the consumer uses less energy. It is totally absurd that people today are paying far more for fuel than they should, while emitting unnecessary amounts of carbon, because they lack the up-front costs to weatherize their homes. Every homeowner and building owner in America should be able to get the assistance they need to weatherize their homes and buildings.

We must also take a hard look at increasing efficiency in the transportation sector, which produces 28 percent of all greenhouse gas emissions and half of all toxic emissions. The new efficiency standards that I strongly supported will reduce gasoline consumption by 12 billion barrels over ten years. However, even then, the U.S. will lag behind the more aggressive efficiency standards in Japan, Canada, South Korea, and most European nations. Instead of the current goal of reaching 54.5 mpg, we should, at the very least, set the goal at 65 mpg. If Europe can do it, so can we.

We must make hybrid cars and electric vehicles much more affordable and build the infrastructure consumers will need. The potential reduction in carbon emissions from electric cars is enormous, especially as we transition to an electric grid powered increasingly by renewable energy. We should be funding cutting-edge electric car research—especially advanced battery storage—incentivizing the purchase of EVs, and building the quickly recharging infrastructure necessary for widespread adoption.

Lastly, increasing transportation efficiency means making major improvements to our intercity rail and public transit systems. Modern rail and transit systems would take significant numbers of trucks and cars off the roads, move people and cargo in a far more energy-efficient manner, and significantly reduce carbon emissions.

ENDING SUBSIDIES TO FOSSIL FUEL COMPANIES

The great irony of climate change is that American taxpayers are subsidizing the most profitable industry in history, whose products are quite literally killing us, to the tune of more than $10 billion every single year. For decades, we have given the oil, gas, and coal companies myriad tax breaks, direct subsidies, and fantastically lucrative leases and royalty agreements to extract oil, gas, and coal from our public lands and off our shores. It makes absolutely no sense, and it has to stop.

According to the Office of Management and Budget, federal taxpayer incentives for fossil fuel extraction alone cost $5 billion every year—and that doesn't include the $49 billion in federal research and development subsidies since 1948. All told, in an example of completely upside-down priorities, for every dollar of taxpayer funds invested in renewable energy over the past fifteen years, fossil fuels have received eighty dollars! That is utterly absurd, especially when you consider that the five largest oil companies—ExxonMobil, Shell, Chevron, BP, and ConocoPhillips—had combined profits of $93 billion in 2013, and yet got combined tax breaks of $2.4 billion that year.

The first step to weaning ourselves off fossil fuels is to end the huge subsidies from which fossil fuel companies have long benefited, and that energy companies have spent billions in lobbying costs and campaign contributions to preserve. That is why, as a U.S. senator, I introduced the End Polluter Welfare Act, which would save American taxpayers $130 billion over the next decade, money that could be directed instead toward transitioning to a clean energy economy.

TAXING CARBON AND METHANE POLLUTION

Another important step in dramatically reducing greenhouse emissions is to start charging fossil fuel companies for the pollution they create. Quite simply, these companies make money hand over fist while the costs of the harm they cause to the environment and public health are borne by the taxpayer. We must flip that equation on its head and make energy companies pay for the true costs of burning fossil fuels, by putting a price on carbon and methane. In economic terms, taxing carbon and methane would require fossil fuel companies to internalize the costs of the negative externalities the companies cause. Not only is this fair, but it would be a game changer in terms of reducing greenhouse gas emissions.

In 2015, I introduced the Climate Protection and Justice Act, which would tax the emissions of the largest fossil fuel producers and importers in this country at the source of production. Most of the proceeds gained from this pollution fee would be returned to the bottom 80 percent of Americans, to offset any rate hikes imposed by the fossil fuel companies. For an average family of four, this would amount to a rebate of roughly $900 in 2017, and would grow to an annual rebate of $1,900 in 2030. Some of the revenue would also be invested in more energy-efficient homes and buildings, renewable energy production, clean energy research, climate resiliency projects in low-income and minority communities that are disproportionately impacted by climate change, and low-carbon practices like the use of non-petroleum-based fertilizers on farms. Once fossil fuel energy reflects its true environmental costs, renewable energy sources like solar and wind will become even more attractive and competitive, which is precisely the point.

BANNING FRACKING

In the short term, we should put an end to the most environmentally egregious methods of extracting fossil fuels, and to my mind, that begins with banning fracking. Hydraulic fracturing involves injecting a high-pressure mixture of water, sand, and chemicals to release otherwise inaccessible oil and natural gas deposits trapped deep in underground rock formations. While innovative from an engineering perspective, fracking is highly problematic, for several reasons.

As was documented in Josh Fox's excellent documentary *Gasland*, the chemicals injected into the ground pose serious health and environmental risks to drinking water, air quality, and wildlife. However, the full extent of the risk is not known, because the gas industry isn't required to disclose what chemicals are used, or in what quantities. If that complete lack of transparency sounds outrageous, it is. We have Dick Cheney to thank for the "Halliburton loophole," which exempts fracking companies from many of the disclosures normally required under the Safe Drinking Water Act.

Moreover, the process of fracking leaks considerable amounts of methane into the atmosphere and groundwater—some studies suggest as much as 15 to 20 percent higher than conventional natural gas drilling methods. And let us not forget, methane is eighty-five times more potent than carbon dioxide in terms of trapping heat.

Fracking is one of the main reasons I reject the notion that natural gas is a "bridge fuel" that can help us transition from oil and coal to clean sustainable energy. While it is true that natural gas burns cleaner than oil or coal, it still releases significant amounts of carbon dioxide when combusted. To my mind, being the best of three bad fossil fuel options does not make it a "good" option. Fracking simply increases the supply of and reliance on a fossil fuel that is contributing to global warming, while doing irreparable damage to the areas where it is extracted. It's time to put an end to fracking.

LET'S JUST KEEP IT IN THE GROUND

There are other extraction practices that should not be allowed, and there are environmentally sensitive areas that should be off-limits to exploration. To my mind, a no-brainer is the need to permanently ban oil extraction in the Arctic National Wildlife Refuge, which spans 19.6 million acres in Alaska and boasts the most biodiversity of any protected area north of the Arctic Circle. It is too precious a natural resource to put at risk from the detrimental consequences of oil production and extraction.

We should also end all new federal leases for oil, gas, or coal extraction on public lands and waters. Public lands and water are for the public to enjoy for generations to come—not for the oil companies to exploit for profit in the short term. This includes prohibiting offshore drilling in the Arctic and the Atlantic, stopping new leases, and ending nonproducing leases for offshore drilling in the Pacific and Gulf of Mexico. If there is a lesson to be learned from the disastrous 2010 BP oil spill disaster, it is that there is no such thing as safe offshore oil drilling.

We must also ban the practice of mountaintop removal in the Appalachian Mountains, where coal companies are blowing up entire mountaintops to get at the thin seams of coal below. The communities in the region are paying a huge price for this destructive practice in their health, culture, and environment. Let's invest in Appalachian communities to help them transition to a clean, prosperous, and healthy future.

NO MORE KEYSTONES

President Obama was right to kill the Keystone XL Pipeline, but we must not let future administrations resurrect the project, or to ever allow anything else like it. If the goal is to turn away from fossil fuels, it would have been very wrong to let a Canadian oil company ship some of the dirtiest oil on the planet across the United States to the Gulf of Mexico. It astounds me that anyone could think that a pipeline transporting highly toxic tar sands over our rivers and fragile aquifers, only to be exported to other countries, was somehow in the national interest.

I was proud to be the first national politician to publicly oppose Keystone XL; the first to oppose the Bakken oil pipeline, which would cross Iowa; and the first to oppose the Northeast Energy Direct Pipeline, which would bring fracked natural gas through New Hampshire. We need to invest in clean energy, not lock ourselves into new long-term commitments to fossil fuels.

INVESTING IN RENEWABLE ENERGY

Up to now, I have outlined various steps we need to take to move away from fossil fuels and dramatically lower the greenhouse gas emissions that cause global warming. We must concurrently make a massive and sustained investment in sustainable energy like wind, solar, and geothermal to make a seamless transition from dirty fossil fuels to a clean energy future.

One of the best ways to incentivize the development of renewable energy is by expanding federal investment and production tax incentives for building new energy-generation projects. The solar investment tax credit (ITC) is an up-front credit equal to 30 percent of the cost of building a commercial or residential solar project, and the production tax credit (PTC) is a $0.023/kWh credit taken over ten years by wind, geothermal, and closed-loop biomass projects based on the amount of energy actually produced.

The ITC is a huge reason why over the last decade, solar power has experienced an annual growth rate of nearly 60 percent and the cost of solar panels has been driven down by more than 75 percent since 2008, according to the Solar Energy Industries Association (SEIA). Our national solar capacity is now almost 27 gigawatts—enough energy to power more than 5 million homes. However, it is clear we have just begun to tap solar power's enormous potential; SEIA expects our national capacity to reach nearly 100 GW by the end of 2020.

Similarly, the PTC has made possible the development of wind farms, which now have a generating capacity of 75 gigawatts, enough to power 17 million American homes. In fact, wind provided almost 30 percent of all new domestic power capacity in the last five years, and with proper federal support could generate 20 percent or more of our nation's electricity by 2030. This is not a pipe dream—it can be done. Last year, just over 30 percent of the electricity used in Iowa came from the wind.

However, the long-term unpredictability of the PTC and ITC has stunted investment in clean energy projects, which often take five or more years to plan. Congress did recently extend the credits for a few years, which according to Bloomberg New Energy Finance could result in 37 gigawatts of new wind and solar capacity over the next five years, enough to power 8 million more households. However, efforts to make the tax incentives permanent are met on Capitol Hill by that familiar refrain: We simply don't have the money. And other opponents, mostly captive fans of the oil lobby, insist that the ITC and PTC distort the energy market by hiding the real costs of renewable energy. What a load of crap.

The hypocrisy of those who argue that the PTC and ITC are too expensive or are no longer needed because the solar and wind industries should be able to stand on their own is stunning. Taxpayers have been subsidizing fossil fuel companies through tax credits for more than one hundred years, and Congress long ago made those incentives permanent features of the federal tax code. And those who argue that renewable energy has hidden costs conveniently turn a blind eye to the fact that fossil fuels are cooking our planet—talk about hidden costs! It is time to end the hypocrisy, and make the ITC and PTC permanent.

GRID MODERNIZATION AND ADVANCED BATTERY STORAGE

It is not uncommon to hear some commentator on Fox News gleefully declaring that solar and wind can't possibly work because the sun doesn't always shine and the wind doesn't always blow. While we have made huge advances in the research and production of wind and solar energy in recent years, it is obviously true that there are currently real limitations to the full utilization of these sustainable technologies. The intermittent nature of solar and wind power requires the development of advanced battery solutions and improved weather forecasting and modeling so the managers of the electrical grid can better plan for when and how much energy will be flowing into the grid from wind and solar. These are hardly insurmountable challenges, and great progress is already being made.

There have been significant developments in advanced battery storage technologies that help balance energy supply with demand by capturing energy at times when there is excess on the system for use during hours of high demand. These are happening both on the commercial and homeowner level—for instance, with Tesla's Powerwall units. These types of battery systems will only become more affordable for utilities and families as they become more common and efficient.

Likewise, we are making progress on capturing the full capacity of solar and wind power. My state of Vermont was the first in the nation to deploy a statewide "smart grid," which is helping utilities more effectively use intermittently available renewable energy sources, as well as respond to outages more quickly. Working with Sandia National Labs, scientists are studying how to better forecast when solar and wind energy will be available, to maximize the integration of these clean energy sources into the grid. They are also testing the viability of a first-in-the-nation, neighborhood-scale "micro-grid," powered entirely by the sun, with dedicated backup battery storage.

The reality is that the U.S. government has always played a critically important role in funding research and development for almost every major source of energy, from hydro to fossil fuels to nuclear energy. The federal government has spent hundreds of billions on nuclear power research over decades, and still hasn't figured out how to make it safe. The least we can do to ensure our energy supply is clean, reliable, and affordable is to spend a fraction of that amount to help better integrate solar and wind power into the grid and figure out how to affordably store energy when the sun isn't shining and the wind isn't blowing.

CLIMATE JUSTICE

It is important to acknowledge that while the impacts of climate change will touch us all, its impacts will not be felt equally. As is so often the case, disenfranchised minority and poor communities will undoubtedly be hardest hit. Just take a look at the disproportionate impact of Hurricane Katrina on poor and African-American neighborhoods in New Orleans. Do you really think a wealthier neighborhood would have had such substandard levees? Not likely. Which is why, as we develop plans to address climate resiliency, we must recognize the heightened public health risks faced by low-income and minority communities.

Of course, this is not a problem unique to the United States. In November 2015, the World Bank issued a report highlighting how the effects of global warming are being disproportionately borne by poor communities around the world, and that trend will only worsen, because those communities are least prepared to deal with such "climate shocks" as rising seas, extreme weather, or severe droughts. The report estimated that as many as 100 million people could be pushed into extreme poverty by 2030 because of disrupted agriculture and the spread of malaria and other diseases. This is why funding resiliency efforts in poor communities and mitigating the disproportionate impacts of climate change on the most vulnerable must be a part of any international climate negotiations.

We must also make sure that poor and minority communities share in the benefits of the clean energy revolution. From access to new green jobs to energy efficiency and renewable energy efforts, we have to make sure no one is left behind. That is why, in 2015, I introduced legislation to make solar energy more accessible to low-income families. While the cost of solar panels has gone down significantly, it is still out of reach for millions of low-income families that need it the most—families that struggle to pay electricity bills. This effort would also help build solar arrays on community facilities and public housing, and target set-asides for projects in Appalachia, Native American tribal areas, and Alaskan native communities.

LEADING AT HOME AND ABROAD

Climate change is truly a global problem. The decisions individual countries, especially the advanced industrialized countries, make about their energy systems affect everyone else on this planet. The carbon dioxide released into the atmosphere in the United States, China, or Spain has no nationality and respects no borders, nor does the heat wave, hurricane, or drought caused by global warming. Moreover, even if the U.S. were to successfully transform its energy system to 100 percent renewables, it would not likely be enough to avoid the worst consequences of climate change. The fact of the matter is, we are all in the same boat, together, and solving this unprecedented global challenge will require an unprecedented level of international cooperation. As the most powerful country in the history of the planet, the United States must help lead that effort.

The December 2015 Paris Climate Conference (COP21) was an important step in that direction, in that, for the first time, 195 countries adopted a universal, legally binding global climate deal. I applaud President Obama for his unwavering leadership in Paris, and for standing up to the powerful interests in this country who opposed his efforts. However, while the agreement sets out a global action plan to limit global warming, many climate scientists believe the accord goes nowhere near far enough in terms of reducing global carbon emissions. The good news is there is a framework in place. Our goal now must be to strengthen the accord by setting more aggressive carbon reduction goals.

We cannot leave it up to our government to carry the water for us. We all know that the fossil fuel industry has enormous power, and enormous influence over governmental decisions throughout the world. What has to happen is that the United States must help lead an international mobilization on a scale not seen since World War II to address this planetary environmental crisis. If we could save our way of life by leading an international coalition in that massive and terrible war, we must now endeavor to save the planet through a similar effort.

Further, while we cannot solve this problem alone, the United States can and should lead by example. Our country has contributed greatly to climate change, but we also have the largest stage and the greatest know-how to lead in implementing climate change solutions. Part of our challenge should be to show that the transition to a clean energy future can work, that we can produce affordable clean energy and strengthen our economy. Right now, the template developing countries have for industrialization is based on burning fossil fuels. We are uniquely positioned, with the largest economy in the world, to demonstrate there is a viable alternative.

Unless we take bold action to reverse climate change, our children, grandchildren, and great-grandchildren are going to look back on this period in history and ask a very simple question: Where were they? Why didn't the United States of America, the most powerful nation on earth, lead the international community in cutting greenhouse gas emissions and preventing the devastating damage that the scientific community was sure would come?

SEVEN

REAL CRIMINAL JUSTICE REFORM

In the United States today we have more people in jail than any other country on earth. We are spending $80 billion a year to lock up 2.2 million Americans, disproportionately African-American, Latino, and Native American. To my mind, it makes a lot more sense to invest in education and jobs than in jails and incarceration. It's time for real criminal justice reform.

If my campaign for president stood for anything, it was about all of us standing together, as one nation, to demand a better life for all. Black, white, Latino, Asian-American, and Native American. Standing together, and not allowing demagogues to scapegoat minorities and divide us up. Standing together, to create the kind of America we know we can become.

If we are to be successful in that goal, we must confront one of the most contentious and intractable issues facing our country—the same issue that I protested in Chicago fifty years ago—the ugly stain of racism.

The sad reality is that racism has plagued the United States since before its founding. The atrocities committed against the Native Americans who inhabited this land long before Europeans arrived are beyond appalling, as is the abomination of slavery perpetrated against Africans (and their descendants) brought to this continent to labor in servitude. Racism has impacted people who immigrated to this country from Latin America and Asia. It has impacted the Irish, the Italians, and the Jews. Racism has afflicted our nation for centuries, and it continues to afflict our nation today.

Ironically, after Barack Obama became the first African-American president, some people triumphantly declared an end to racism, that we had finally moved beyond the color line. Unfortunately, they were completely wrong. In fact, the past eight years have shown just how open the wounds of racism remain in our country, and the many ways they manifest.

This was brought to light even more during the presidential campaign, thanks to a major party candidate who, instead of bringing the American people together, seemed intent on doing everything possible to divide us up. Donald Trump threatened to deport 11 million Latinos, restrict immigration based on religion, and create a national database of Muslim citizens. And his relationship to the African-American community featured his role as one of the leaders of the "birther movement," a disgusting effort to undermine the legitimacy of our first African-American president by suggesting that he was not born in the United States.

There is no question that in recent decades we have made significant progress in creating a country where we judge people, as Dr. Martin Luther King Jr. urged, not by the color of their skin, not by the language they speak, not by the country they came from, but by the content of their character and their qualities as human beings.

Make no mistake about it. While we have come a long way, there is still a long distance to go before we fulfill Dr. King's dream.

POLICE DEPARTMENT REFORM

Among many other struggles we must engage in to combat racism in this country, we must stop police brutality and the killing of unarmed African-Americans. This has emerged as one of the great civil rights issues of the early twenty-first century.

The names and the incidents are all too familiar to us. Innocent people who should be alive today, but who died while being arrested or in the custody of the police. Sandra Bland, Michael Brown, Rekia Boyd, Eric Garner, Walter Scott, Freddie Gray, Jessica Hernandez, Tamir Rice, Jonathan Ferrell, Philando Castile, Alton Sterling, Oscar Grant, Antonio Zambrano-Montes, Laquan McDonald, Samuel DuBose, and Anastacio Hernandez-Rojas—and many others. We know their names. Each of them died unarmed at the hands of police officers or in police custody.

Eric Garner was choked to death in New York City because he was selling single cigarettes. Alton Sterling was shot while pinned on the ground by Baton Rouge police, who were called because Sterling was selling CDs outside a store. Freddie Gray died of a spinal cord injury while in Baltimore police custody. Twelve-year-old Tamir Rice was killed by Cleveland police officers within two seconds of their arrival on the scene.

Sandra Bland was pulled from her car, thrown to the ground, and handcuffed. Three days later, she was found dead in her Texas jail cell. Samuel DuBose was fatally shot in Cincinnati during a traffic stop for a missing front license plate. Philando Castile was killed by police

Leaving the desolate neighborhood where Freddie Gray was killed in Baltimore. (Mark Wilson/Getty Images)

in Minneapolis during a traffic stop for a busted tail-light. Walter Scott was pulled over for a broken brake light in South Carolina, and was shot in the back by an officer. And on and on it goes.

Across the nation, too many African-Americans and other minorities find themselves subjected to a system that treats citizens who have not committed crimes like criminals. Because of overpolicing in minority communities and racial profiling, African-Americans are twice as likely to be arrested and almost four times as likely to experience the use of force during encounters with the police than whites. Although there is no national database of police shootings, one group that tracks these cases says that in 2015, police officers killed at least 102 unarmed black people, five times the rate at which they killed unarmed whites.

Violence and brutality of any kind at the hands of the police is unacceptable and must not be tolerated. It is no wonder that a growing number of communities of color do not trust the police, and why the influence of the Black Lives Matter movement is growing.

I was a mayor for eight years and in that capacity worked closely with my police department and police officers throughout Vermont. As a congressman and senator I have worked with law enforcement officials throughout the country. And here's the truth: Being a police officer is an extremely difficult and stressful job. Many officers are underpaid and undertrained and have irregular schedules that negatively impact their family lives. The vast majority of those who serve in law enforcement are decent, hardworking people who are motivated to make their communities better places to live, and many have sacrificed much to do their jobs.

To my mind, that is all the more reason we must stand up and denounce acts of illegal behavior when they are perpetrated by the police. Police officers must be held accountable. In a society based on law, nobody can be above the law, especially those who are charged with enforcing the law.

WE MUST END THE "WAR ON DRUGS"

Of course, the intersection of racism and criminal justice is not limited to police violence. To my mind, an even bigger issue is the failed "War on Drugs," which has over the decades harmed millions of lives through the arrest and jailing of people for nonviolent crimes. The number of incarcerated drug offenders has increased *twelvefold* since 1980, and this "war" has disproportionately targeted people of color.

According to the Substance Abuse and Mental Health Services Administration, blacks and whites use drugs at roughly the same overall rates. However, blacks are arrested for drug use at far greater rates than whites, largely because of overpolicing, racial profiling, and—according to the Department of Justice—the fact that blacks are three times more likely to be searched during a traffic stop compared with white motorists.

Take marijuana use. How many encounters between young people and the police begin with officers detecting the odor of marijuana? According to the best research, blacks smoke marijuana at a slightly higher rate than whites. According to the American Civil Liberties Union (ACLU), however, they are four times more likely to be arrested for marijuana possession. Think about it: Does anyone doubt for a second that an upper-middle-class white kid in Greenwich, Connecticut, has a much lower chance of being arrested for smoking marijuana than a lower-income black kid in Chicago or Baltimore?

And marijuana is inexplicably a "Schedule I" drug—the designation reserved for highly dangerous and addictive drugs such as heroin—under the federal Controlled Substances Act. Now, people can argue about the pros and cons of legalizing marijuana, just as we can argue the merits of the legality of tobacco, which causes cancer and other terrible diseases. But no sane person thinks that marijuana is equivalent to heroin, a killer drug, in terms of its health impact. That is absurd. But that is the way it's treated.

To fully grasp how this impacts our criminal justice system, consider that in 2014 there were 620,000 total marijuana possession arrests. That's more than one every minute. There were more than 7 million marijuana possession arrests in the U.S. from 2001 to 2010. And that's a major reason why African-Americans account for 37 percent of those arrested for drug offenses when they only comprise 14 percent of regular drug users.

Overall, blacks are imprisoned at seven times the rate of whites. In fact, according to the most recent statistics, one of every fifteen African-American men is incarcerated, compared with one in every one hundred six white men. If current trends continue, one in four black males born today can expect to spend time in prison during his lifetime. This is an outrage. This is the destruction of a generation. This must change. Sadly, the situation is not that much better for African-American women, who are three times more likely than white women to be incarcerated.

Moreover, African-Americans face more serious consequences when sentenced. Even when convicted for the exact same crimes, black offenders receive sentences that were on average 10 percent longer than those received by white offenders. And for decades, racially biased mandatory minimums have unfairly punished people of color. For instance, for years powdered cocaine (used more frequently by whites than blacks) required a hundred times the weight to trigger the same mandatory penalty as crack cocaine (used almost three times more frequently by blacks).

These statistics, needless to say, raise serious doubts about equal treatment under the law. Just look at the outcomes: African-Americans and Latinos together comprised 57 percent of all prisoners in 2014, even though neither of these two groups make up even one-quarter of the U.S. population. Meanwhile, African-American youth alone make up two-fifths of all confined youth today.

Further, what has to be understood is that, according to the Bureau of Justice Statistics, just 6 percent of African-American arrests in 2014 were for violent crimes and another 14 percent were for property crimes. What is driving the incarceration of blacks is nonviolent drug-related crimes. In fact, according to the Federal Bureau of Prisons, half of all federal prisoners are locked up for nonviolent drug offenses. This is expensive.

It is a waste of human potential. It is, in a word, stupid. We must end the overincarceration of nonviolent young Americans who do not pose a serious threat to our society.

By the way, if anyone thinks that a criminal record regarding a marijuana arrest is some small matter, think again. There are a lot of people out there who apply for jobs and don't get them because of that record. And if you don't get a job, and you don't have any income, bad things happen.

Further, we have been putting far too little emphasis on prevention, like good education, after-school programming, and meaningful job opportunities that give young people healthy alternatives to drifting into a life of drug use. I have been to urban communities that have major drug addiction issues. Meanwhile, their after-school and mentoring programs have been shut down for lack of funds. That's brilliant. Leave kids on the streets with nothing to do, and then become shocked and appalled when they become involved with drugs.

My Republican colleagues are proud that they have saved taxpayer money by eliminating funding for summer job programs. Really? Do they not understand that a kid who earns a paycheck and learns a skill is far less likely to end up in jail, at far greater cost to the taxpayer?

DEALING WITH MENTAL HEALTH

In addition, the time is long overdue for this country to understand that we cannot jail our way out of health problems like mental illness and drug addiction. Our country is facing an opioid crisis, both in terms of prescription pain medicine abuse and heroin addiction. People are dying every day from overdoses. But the solution is not to lock up addicts. We have to treat substance abuse as a serious public health issue rather than a criminal issue, so that all people—regardless of their income—can get the help they need.

In addition, in terms of treating addiction, we put far too little emphasis on coordinated treatment and support programs that combine medication-assisted therapies, such as methadone and buprenorphine, with counseling and behavioral therapies.

We must also understand that we have a mental health crisis in this country, and that many mentally ill people are ending up in jail because there is no place else for them to go. Over the last several decades we have made a bad situation even worse by cutting back on the programs and support systems that mentally ill people need in order to survive and improve. Once again, we are being penny-wise and pound-foolish. We save money by cutting back on housing and treatment for the mentally ill. We spend far, far more by having vulnerable people end up in jail.

Of the 44 million adults with a mental illness, fewer than half received the mental health services they needed in the past year. Instead of making mental health services more affordable and accessible for all Americans, we dump people in jail—where they get little or no treatment—at far greater cost.

The end result of the "war on drugs" and our failure to treat mental illness in a rational way is that the United States of America has more people in jails and prisons than any other country on earth. We have less than 5 percent of the world's population, yet we have a quarter of all prisoners. We now have more people in jails and prisons than does the Communist totalitarian state of China, which has a population four times our own.

It is a national tragedy that the number of incarcerated Americans has more than quadrupled since Ronald Reagan first ran on a "get tough on crime" platform—from

International Rates of Incarceration

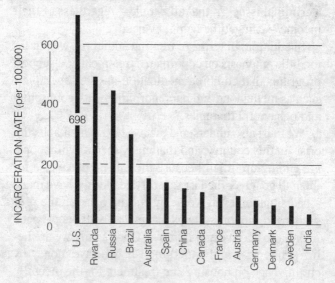

Data Source: International Centre for Prison Studies

about 500,000 in 1980 to more than 2.2 million today. And we spend $80 billion a year in federal, state, and local taxpayer dollars to lock them up. Eighty billion dollars a year! I can think of an awful lot of real needs that can be met with $80 billion a year.

ENDING PRIVATE PRISONS

Private corporations should not be making profits off the incarceration of human beings. But that is exactly what is happening today in our country, big-time. According to the ACLU, as part of the movement toward privatization that we are seeing in sector after sector, the number of adult prisoners housed in private prisons has jumped almost 1,600 percent since 1990. Last year, there were about 130,000 federal and state prisoners in private facilities.

According to a February 2016 report by In the Public Interest, the two largest private prison operators in the United States made a combined $361 million housing them. The Corrections Corporation of America, the nation's largest private prison operator, collected $3,356 a year in profit for each prisoner, while GEO Group, the country's second largest, made $2,135 a year in profit per prisoner.

That is unacceptable. Study after study has shown that private prisons are not cheaper, they're not safer, and they do not provide better outcomes for either the prisoners or the state. What they do provide is an incentive to keep prison beds full. They interfere with the administration of justice. No one, in my view, should be allowed to profit from putting more people behind bars.

The private prison racket extends to the Department of Homeland Security, too. More than 60 percent of all immigration detention beds are in prisons operated by for-profit prison corporations. These include two of the country's three family detention centers that house unaccompanied minors and mothers with babies, where there have been reports of inadequate food and medical treatment, sexual abuse, and other serious human rights abuses.

In September 2015, I introduced the Justice Is Not for Sale Act, to bar the federal government from contracting with private prison companies. I also made abolishing private prisons a plank in my presidential campaign. I was very pleased, therefore, when, in August 2016, the Department of Justice said it would phase out the use of private prisons. Just two weeks later the Department of Homeland Security announced it might follow suit. We have got to end the private prison racket in America as quickly as possible. Our focus should be on keeping people out of jail and making sure they stay out when they are released.

ENDING THE DEATH PENALTY

Let me say one last thing about fixing our broken criminal justice system. It is long past time for the United States of America to join almost every other advanced country on earth in abolishing the death penalty. The death penalty is cruel and unusual punishment. It is applied disproportionately to people of color. It has been proven to not deter violent crime. The inevitable endless judicial appeals tie up the courts for years, at the taxpayer's expense. And far too many people are now thought, after they were put to death by the state, to have been innocent.

We are all shocked and disgusted by some of the horrific murders that we see in this country. When people commit horrendous crimes, we should lock them up and throw away the key. But the state, in a democratic and civilized society, should not itself be involved in murder.

Frankly, we should not be in the company of China (the world's leader in use of the death penalty), Saudi Arabia, Iran, Iraq, Sudan, Yemen, Egypt, and Somalia. Rather, we should be in the company of virtually every other major democratic society that understands that even when confronted with unspeakable violence, we must move beyond ancient concepts of revenge. We must recognize, as Mohandas Gandhi did, that, in the end, an "eye for an eye" simply makes everybody blind.

THE IMPACTS OF INSTITUTIONAL AND STRUCTURAL RACISM

Just weeks before his death, Dr. Martin Luther King Jr. spoke to a union group in New York about what he called "The other America." He said: "One America is flowing with the milk of prosperity and the honey of equality. That America is the habitat of millions of people who have food and material necessities for their bodies, culture and education for their minds, freedom and human dignity for their spirits. . . . But as we assemble here tonight, I'm sure that each of us is painfully aware of the fact that there is another America, and that other America has a daily ugliness about it that transforms the buoyancy of hope into the fatigue of despair."

The problem was structural, King said: "This country has socialism for the rich, rugged individualism for the poor."

What he saw in 1968, and what we all should recognize today, is that we must simultaneously address the structural and institutional racism that exists in this country while creating an economy that works for all and not just the people on top. This is especially true in minority communities, where poverty, unemployment, and inadequate schools are rampant.

According to the U.S. Census Bureau, African-American median household income in 2014 was $35,398, compared with $60,256 for non-Hispanic white households. While African-Americans account for 12.2 percent of our nation's population, they make up just 5.7 percent of income earners in the top quintile (the top 20 percent of all households). On the other end of the spectrum, African-Americans are heavily overrepresented in the lowest quintile of earners. In fact, more than 26 percent of African-Americans were living at or below the poverty level in comparison with about 10 percent of non-Hispanic whites.

Most black and Latino households have less than $350 in savings. According to the Pew Research Center, the average African-American household has a total net worth—the value of all assets minus debts—of just $11,000. Meanwhile, the average white family has a net worth of $141,900. And to make things even worse, when Wall Street nearly drove the economy off a cliff, minority households and communities were hardest hit.

Even in good times, the black unemployment rate has remained almost twice as high as the white rate over the last forty years. But during the Great Recession, African-Americans lost jobs at twice the rate of white workers, and in pockets of the country it was even worse. According to the Economic Policy Institute, the black unemployment rate in Miami went from 6.7 percent before the recession to 17.2 percent in 2010. In greater Los Angeles, it rose from 8.6 percent to 19.3 percent. In Las Vegas, it soared from 8.2 percent to 20.1 percent. And in Detroit, black unemployment reached Depression-era levels of 25.7 percent. Real African-American youth unemployment broke 50 percent.

Even in April 2011, more than three years after the recession began and in the midst of what was supposed to be the recovery, the official black unemployment rate stood at 16.1 percent, twice the official white unemployment rate of 8.0 percent. And the jobs weren't just slower to come back—many never came back at all. And that's been going on for a while.

Against that backdrop of rising unemployment and declining wages, black and Latino households were disproportionately steered into expensive subprime mortgages for years leading up to the housing crash. African-Americans were three times more likely to receive a subprime loan than whites, and many of those loans were *designed* to fail. Which is why, when the housing bubble burst, minority households were 70 percent more likely to lose their homes to foreclosure than white households. And because African-Americans and Latinos tended to have most of their wealth tied up in their homes, total net worth fell by more than 50 percent for African-American households and by more than 65 percent for Latino families.

Can you imagine what that does to families that have spent their entire lives working hard, struggling to get ahead? Can you imagine what that does to entire neighborhoods—like Freddie Gray's West Baltimore— where the poverty rate now exceeds 35 percent, where less than half of the residents have jobs, where more than a third of the homes are vacant or abandoned, and where less than 5 percent of the population has a college degree?

In this country, we treat our children shamefully. We have the highest rate of childhood poverty of almost any major country on earth, and we maintain a dysfunctional child-care system. But as bad as the situation is for kids in our country as a whole, it is far worse in minority communities.

Black children, who make up just 18 percent of preschoolers, account for 48 percent of all out-of-school suspensions before kindergarten. We are failing our black children before they even start kindergarten. Even though we know that 90 percent of brain development occurs between birth and five years of age, we allow early-childhood education in minority communities to remain a total disgrace.

Black elementary and high school students are more than three times as likely as whites to attend schools where fewer than 60 percent of teachers meet all state certification and licensure requirements. They are more likely to attend schools with higher concentrations of

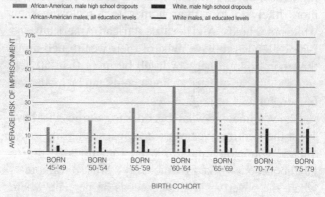

Average Risk of Imprisonment by Age 30–34 for Men Born Between 1945–1949 and 1975–1979, by Race and Education

Data Source: Western and Wildeman 2009

first-year teachers. They are expelled at three times the rate of white students. According to the Department of Education, African-American students are more likely to suffer harsh punishments—suspensions and arrests—at school.

African-American kids are five times more likely than white children to have lead poisoning, and one in six has asthma. Indigenous peoples are disproportionately impacted by destructive mining practices and the dumping of hazardous materials on their lands. Low-income Latinos are more likely to live in areas with high levels of hazardous air pollution than anyone else.

There is a pipeline from school to jail that we have to turn into a pipeline from school to a promising future. If current trends continue, an estimated 69 percent of African-American men who drop out of high school will end up in jail. We have to make certain they do not.

REFORMING A BROKEN CRIMINAL JUSTICE SYSTEM

We must come together with a sense of shared purpose and demand policies to transform this country into a nation that affirms the value of all our people, regardless of race, income, or national origin. We need a criminal justice system that not only protects our people from crime, but is based on justice for all, nondiscriminatory policies, and the understanding that the prevention of crime is a much worthier approach than punishment.

We must reexamine honestly how we police America, and the federal government can play an important role in establishing a new model police training program that reorients us in the way we do law enforcement. First and foremost, we must develop new rules on the allowable use of force. Police officers need to be trained to de-escalate confrontations and to humanely interact with people, especially people who have mental illnesses. Lethal force should be the last response, not the first.

Every effort should be made to have police forces reflect the diversity of the communities they work in. And that must include positions of leadership and in training departments. We must demand greater civilian oversight of police departments and ongoing and meaningful community engagement.

We must demilitarize our police forces so that they don't look and act like invading armies. Police departments must be part of the community they serve, and trusted by the community. Too often, we see local police forces with military-style vehicles and weapons that make them look like occupying armies trying to conquer some faraway country.

We should federally fund and require body cameras for law enforcement officers to make it easier to hold everyone accountable for their actions, while establishing standards to protect the privacy of innocent people.

We must ensure that police departments do not shield bad actors from accountability and that they instead show zero tolerance for abuses of police power. All employees deserve due process protections, but departments must vigorously investigate, and if necessary prosecute, allegations of wrongdoing, especially those involving the use of force. Every death that occurs during an arrest or while someone is in police custody should be investigated by the U.S. Department of Justice.

We must stop cash-starved communities from using their police forces as revenue generators. In many cities, the incentives for policing are upside down. Police departments are bringing in substantial revenue by ticketing poor people for minor offenses and by seizing the personal property of people who are suspected of criminal involvement. When policing becomes a source of revenue, officers are often pressured to meet goals that can lead to unnecessary or unlawful traffic stops and citations. And civil asset forfeiture laws allow police to take property from people even before they are charged with a crime. Even worse, it is often difficult and expensive for an innocent person to get his or her property back. We must end these practices.

The time is long overdue for us to take marijuana off the federal government's list of outlawed drugs under the Controlled Substances Act. Four states and the District of Columbia have already legalized the personal use of marijuana, and the federal government shouldn't stand in the way of other states deciding to regulate it the same way they do alcohol and tobacco. That means, too, that businesses in states that have legalized marijuana should be fully able to use the banking system, without fear of federal prosecution.

We must invest in drug courts and interventions so people end up in treatment rather than prison. We must end mandatory minimum sentencing and give judges the discretion to better tailor sentences to the specific facts of a given case. The federal system of parole needs to be reinstated, because people who are serving long sentences need incentives to make productive choices and earn their way to shorter sentences.

We must make it easier, not harder, for people who have served sentences to reintegrate into society. They need a path back from prison that will allow them to lead productive lives rather than returning to a life of crime, and to jail. I recall a town meeting I had in Iowa on criminal justice where one of our speakers, a former inmate, recounted that he learned he was being released one day before he was let out. On the next day he was given a check for $75 and sent on his way. That was it. We can and must do better than that. People who leave jail need jobs, housing, education, and a real chance to make it in civil society.

Giving former inmates a real chance means "banning the box" to prohibit employers from discriminating against job applicants because of a prior conviction. Individuals reentering the workforce should be able to apply for work based on their current merits rather than on past wrongdoings.

And once someone gets out of jail, their full voting rights should be restored. As many as 6 million Americans, largely poor and minority, who have served their time in jail were not able to vote in the 2016 election. This has nothing to do with criminal justice. It is a partisan political decision. When people do their time, their rights as citizens in a democratic society should be reinstated.

EIGHT

IMMIGRATION REFORM NOW

Our immigration system is broken. We need comprehensive immigration reform that provides a pathway to citizenship for undocumented immigrants living in the shadows, keeps families together, and promotes civil, human, and labor rights for all.

I am proud to be the son of an immigrant. My father came to this country from Poland at the age of seventeen without a nickel in his pocket. Several years ago, my brother, Larry, and I visited the tiny town where he was born and raised. While we were there, I was struck by the unbelievable courage of that young man who—with no money, little education, and not knowing one word of English—traveled across the ocean in 1921 in search of a better life.

His story, my story, our story is the story of America: hardworking people and families coming to the United States to create a brighter future for themselves and their children. It is a story rooted in family and fueled by hope.

There is a reason the Statue of Liberty is one of our most iconic images. Since the nation's founding, untold numbers of people have come to our shores to improve their lives, escape oppression or violence, or flee desperate poverty. More than any other country in the history of the modern world, the United States has been shaped in its identity and character by the process of immigration and the contributions of those immigrants.

But at the same time, the history of immigration in our country has often been difficult and contentious; to suggest otherwise is to forget about some of the great struggles of our past. In the 1850s, the once dominant Whig Party was splintered by the virulently anti-immigrant Know Nothing movement. Whipped up by nativist politicians fanning fear of foreigners and blaming immigrants for all sorts of domestic problems, Know Nothing Party rallies routinely devolved into shouting and even violence.

For more than a year, I traveled throughout this country and talked to immigrant families—particularly Latino families—and I was deeply moved by their stories of struggle, their victories and defeats, and their extraordinary aspirations. I was also moved by the fear and the sadness that grips so many of them because of the increasingly dark tenor of today's immigration debate.

This mood existed, of course, largely because Donald Trump engaged in a level of unabashed xenophobia and immigrant bashing not seen in our country for a very long time. It is hard to believe that in the year 2016, we had a major party candidate for president who made bigotry the cornerstone of his campaign. But an unintended consequence of his vitriol is that immigration reform has been brought into the spotlight, where it belongs. After all, Trump is correct in saying that our immigration system is broken; he is just dead wrong about both the causes and the solutions.

Today there are more than 11 million undocumented immigrants in this country living in the shadows. More than 85 percent have resided in the United States for at least five years, and many have been here for decades. The vast majority are law-abiding. They have come from many countries, and for many reasons.

Undocumented immigrants are woven into the fabric of our society and our economy. They work in some of the hardest and lowest-paid jobs. Without undocumented workers, it is likely that the agricultural system in the United States would collapse, with rapidly rising food prices and limitations on the variety of foods we consume. The undocumented are also integral parts of the communities in which they live, as they volunteer at local libraries, serve on school PTAs, and coach their kids on baseball and soccer teams.

Today these families are forced to live in fear that their immigration status will be found out. The threat of deportation is never far from their minds, and I will never forget hearing their stories while on the campaign trail.

In Phoenix, Arizona, a group of high school students, some with tears running down their cheeks, recounted how they worry that when they get home from school they might find out that their mom or dad was arrested and about to be deported. Never mind that the students were all born here and are American citizens—their parents are not. These kids live every day knowing that their families could be torn apart. No child, no teenager, no adult should have to go through that. Yet today in America, millions do.

I talked to a young man serving in the United States military, and he told me that while he was deployed on active duty, his wife was deported. That is one hell of a way to thank someone willing to die defending his country. Our country.

I talked to a twelve-year-old boy, born in Arizona, who was being raised on this side of the Mexican border after his mother was deported. He told me about being torn between going to live with his mother in Mexico or staying here in the only country he has ever known.

The vast majority of undocumented immigrants have come to the United States to work and improve their stations in life. They are highly motivated to be productive members of society. And the reality is, they contribute significantly to our economy.

According to Pew's Hispanic Trends Project, an estimated 8.4 million unauthorized immigrants work in the U.S.: about 5.2 percent of the entire labor force. Collectively, they pay an estimated $11.6 billion each year in state and local taxes, according to the Institute on Taxation and Economic Policy (ITEP). This includes state and local income taxes, property taxes on homes they own or rent, gas taxes at the pumps, and sales and excise taxes on the goods they buy. Moreover, ITEP estimates they pay an average of 8 percent of their incomes in state and local taxes—which, by the way, is 48 percent higher than the 5.4 percent paid by the top 1 percent of taxpayers.

If all undocumented immigrants in the country today were granted legal status, their state and local tax contributions would increase by $2.1 billion a year.

About half of undocumented workers also pay federal income taxes, but since their work is often under the table and off the books, they can't collect on their end of the social contract. It is estimated that these undocumented workers have contributed close to $300 billion to the Social Security Trust Fund—for benefits they will not receive. And that doesn't include federal income or payroll taxes.

Meanwhile, undocumented workers are not protected by many of the labor laws and regulations that cover other workers. If undocumented workers experience unsafe working conditions, they often will not speak up for fear of being fired or exposed to the authorities. If they are harassed on the job, they have no recourse. If they are forced to work unreasonably long hours or cheated out of pay, they have nowhere to turn. And for the most part, they can forget about forming a union to press for better conditions.

Now, who do you think really benefits *most* from illegal immigration?

As University of California economics professor Gordon Hanson noted, the "benefits go primarily to one group of individuals, and that is employers in industries that hire illegal immigrants intensively: construction, agriculture, hospitality, and tourism." The reality is that many businesses, large and small, have long used undocumented workers to pad their bottom lines.

Just consider the agricultural workforce. In California alone—where the $45 billion-a-year agricultural sector supplies more than half the produce consumed in the United States—between 40 and 50 percent of the workforce is made up of undocumented workers. No wonder California has been the site of some of the most important immigrant labor struggles, brought to the consciousness of many Americans in the 1960s and 1970s by the great United Farm Workers leader, Cesar Chavez.

That struggle continues today. In May, I met with a group of Latino leaders in Bakersfield, including David Villarino-Gonzalez, Cesar Chavez's son-in-law, to discuss the plight of farmworkers in the San Joaquin Valley. The next day, I visited Forty Acres in Delano, where Chavez organized for better labor conditions in the 1960s. I was honored to be led on the tour by Federico Chavez, a nephew of the late organizer and an active volunteer for my campaign.

We discussed the fact that all too often, farmworkers are still paid horrendously low wages, exposed to pesticides, and deprived of the most basic decent living conditions. Many of their homes lack clean drinking water. Just as when Cesar Chavez led the UFW, today's struggle is aimed at providing decent wages and working conditions for farmworkers, and demanding that the corporations that own the farms treat their employees with dignity.

Of course, this issue isn't limited to just California. In 2008, I traveled to southern Florida to meet with the Coalition of Immokalee Workers (CIW), which does heroic work standing up for migrant workers who are paid starvation wages for backbreaking work. Most of these farmworkers grow and harvest tomatoes that are bought by fast-food giants and supermarket chains. The working and living conditions in Immokalee were unimaginable. In fact, several labor contractors there had been prosecuted for holding farmworkers against their will. In other words, they were engaged in involuntary slavery, chaining workers inside U-Haul trucks at night and beating them during the day.

I invited some CIW leaders to testify at a Senate hearing on abusive labor practices, which helped bring increased scrutiny to the issue. Because of the tremendous grassroots effort of CIW, supported by Oxfam America and dozens of other organizations, working conditions in Immokalee began to improve, and workers received a small wage increase when Burger King, Subway, Taco Bell, Whole Foods, and many others agreed to pay higher prices for the tomatoes. But this struggle also continues, with CIW launching a national boycott of Wendy's earlier this year. Moreover, how many more Immokalees are out there? How many thousands of undocumented workers are being ruthlessly exploited every day, with few people knowing about it?

Exploitation of undocumented workers is certainly not limited to the agricultural sector. A 2013 report by NPR's *Marketplace* exposed how the Chicago doll manufacturing company Ty used several layers of shadowy labor brokers to find undocumented workers for its factories. Since the workers weren't direct employees of the company, Ty had plausible deniability about their immigration status. These workers labored long hours at the minimum wage, and then had to pay the brokers out of their own pockets for the privilege of being selected to work that day or week. And sometimes they weren't paid at all. Of course, they had no legal recourse, no one to complain to. *Marketplace* found similar practices at Fresh Express, Sony, Frito-Lay, and Smirnoff.

Wal-Mart has employed undocumented workers to clean their stores. Tyson Foods has used them to process chickens (amid many violations of laws on workplace conditions and allegations of human smuggling). Many American families, including at least two nominees for attorney general, have employed undocumented workers to care for their children. Undocumented workers cut lawns, clean hotel rooms, work in oil fields, and staff nursing homes. In my state of Vermont, they work on a growing number of dairy farms. They work on construction crews, and many helped rebuild entire neighborhoods in New Orleans after Katrina.

If we are serious about increasing wages in this country for all workers, immigrant and native-born alike, we must extend labor protections to undocumented workers and stop allowing employers to pay them starvation wages. If we start giving undocumented workers legal protections, we can slow down the "race to the bottom." Wages for the lowest-paid workers in the country will rise and, with legal status, they will be able to join unions and negotiate decent pay and working conditions. A rising tide lifts all boats.

But that would impact big business's bottom line, and therein lies the rub. After all, the political and business establishment in this country is really not all that concerned about immigration's impact on native-born, low-skill workers—but they are *very* concerned about profit margins. Let me give you an example.

During the campaign, I was criticized by Secretary Clinton for opposing a 2007 immigration bill. The truth is, while I supported much of the bill, I could not bring myself to vote for it, because it included a massive expansion of temporary guest worker programs. I was not alone in opposition. The bill was also opposed by other progressive members of Congress, by the AFL-CIO, and by the League of United Latin American Citizens (LULAC), the nation's largest and oldest Hispanic organization.

Over the years, corporate America has successfully pushed for the creation of federal programs that allow employers to bring temporary "guest workers" into the country, supposedly because there is no one here who can do the jobs. Of course, that threshold is very squishy and has been exploited by the business community. When employers report that there is no one in this country able to do the jobs they want filled, and that they need to bring in foreign labor, what is really going on is that there is no one here willing to do the job for the low wages being offered. Too often, guest worker programs are used not to help employers hire labor they couldn't find locally, but to drive down wages with cheap labor from abroad. Instead of a rising tide lifting all boats, it is a leaky boat sinking slowly to the bottom. But, it gets worse.

The Southern Poverty Law Center and the AFL-CIO have documented many cases of employers cheating guest workers out of wages, seizing their passports, forcing them to live in substandard conditions, and even denying them medical treatment for on-the-job injuries. Guest workers will understandably hesitate before complaining, because while they are here legally, their temporary visa is tied to a specific company. Their fate is effectively controlled by the employer, no less than the Kentucky coal miner in Merle Travis's song "Sixteen Tons" who "pretty near owes his soul to the company store."

There is a lot of discussion and demagoguery regarding "illegal immigration." There is too little discussion and legislative action regarding how corporate America and the business community exploit and benefit from the labor of undocumented workers.

When we talk about the "flood" of undocumented people who have come into the United States, we must consider the impact of American policy, especially trade policy and the North American Free Trade Agreement (NAFTA). When NAFTA was passed, its proponents said that liberalized trade with Mexico would increase the standard of living in that country, and thus reduce the flow of undocumented immigrants into the United States. In fact, the exact opposite happened.

After NAFTA went into effect in 1994, inexpensive (and highly subsidized) American corn exports to Mexico increased fivefold, flooding the Mexican market and pushing hundreds of thousands of farmers off their lands. Pork imports rose twenty-five-fold, eliminating 120,000 Mexican jobs. The number of Mexicans living in extreme poverty surged by more than 14 million. And the number of Mexicans entering the U.S. without authorization increased by 185 percent between 1992 and 2011. Free trade didn't stem illegal immigration, it accelerated it.

The nexus between free trade, illegal immigration, and exploitation of undocumented workers was chronicled by David Bacon in a 2012 article in *The Nation*. He recounts the plight of several Mexican farmers and butchers who lost their jobs when U.S. pork flooded the Mexican market after NAFTA. In desperation, they all left their families behind, crossed the border illegally, and carefully made their way to the town of Tar Heel, North Carolina.

There, they got under-the-table jobs at the world's largest meat processing facility, owned by Smithfield, where half of the plant's workers were Hispanic immigrants. Little did they know that their cheap labor was padding the bottom line of the very company that had flooded Mexico with the inexpensive pork that led to the loss of their livelihoods in the first place. You just can't make this stuff up.

In 2005, Human Rights Watch called out Smithfield's Tar Heel plant for a whole slew of unsafe working conditions. Plant managers seemed indifferent to safety problems even though worker injuries—many gruesome, and some even fatal—were common. But then again, they didn't have to worry: Undocumented workers have no rights, and they will think long and hard before complaining or even seeking medical care, because, by doing either, they risk losing their jobs or being deported.

Proponents of the Central America Free Trade Act (CAFTA)—which expanded NAFTA to five Central American nations—similarly argued that the 2004 agreement would stem illegal immigration. But prolonged economic instability, some of the worst gang violence in the world, and widespread drug trafficking in Guatemala, El Salvador, and Honduras have sent a surge of undocumented immigrants to the U.S. since 2014. This includes previously unheard of numbers of mothers with young children, and unaccompanied minors sent by their parents on a perilous trip north in search of safety.

These refugees are fleeing horrific violence in their home countries, and many suffer kidnapping, extortion, human trafficking, and rape as they travel through Mexico. It is deeply distressing to me that so many voices in our country blithely insist that these desperate people, mostly women and young children, should be sent back to the countries they fled. What horrors will they face if they are forced to return?

As a civilized nation, we have a moral obligation to make sure these families and children are humanely cared for while in U.S. custody. But sadly, that is not always the case. The three family detention centers opened since 2014 are overcrowded and lack proper medical facilities. Detainees are treated as criminals, sometimes being woken up every fifteen minutes at night. There have been documented cases of prisoner abuse, including rape. Almost half of all unaccompanied children in custody do not even have a lawyer while in deportation proceedings.

To my mind, the U.S. government should not be in the painful and inhumane business of locking up families who have fled violence. We must put an end to family detention, and treat these families with the compassion and dignity they deserve. That is why I called on President Obama to extend Temporary Protected Status for families who fled violence in Central America.

And that is why, in April 2016, I proudly stood with immigration activists in Reading, Pennsylvania—including actress Rosario Dawson, Mayor Valentin Rodriguez of West Reading, and Adanjesús Marin of Working Families PA—to call for the closing of the Berks County Family Detention Center. As I write, several mothers with young children at the Berks Center are on a hunger strike, protesting living conditions and cursory asylum hearings. Many are waiting to be deported, and are terrified about the future that awaits them and their children.

And while Berks is a government-run facility, the other two family detention centers, both located in Texas, are operated by private companies. They are making a profit off the anguish of asylum seekers, paid for with taxpayer money. This is so profoundly wrong. As my good friend and colleague Representative Raul Grijalva noted, "Allowing corporations to profit by locking up desperate adults and children undermines our decency as a nation."

America has always been a haven for the oppressed. We cannot and must not shirk our historic role as a protector of vulnerable people fleeing persecution. We must, as President Lincoln urged in his first inaugural address, appeal to the better angels of our nature. We must treat others as we would like to be treated.

Sadly, in 2016, we had a major party candidate for president spending endless hours doing the exact opposite, appealing to our worst human traits—bigotry and racism. It is way past time to stop peddling hatred for political gain. We need real solutions to the real problems facing our country, including immigration.

We cannot, should not, and will not sweep up 11 million people and throw them out of the country. Tearing apart families and disrupting whole communities is not only inhumane, it isn't close to being feasible. Can you imagine the size and cost of the "deportation force" that would be needed to track down, arrest, and process 11 million people? Or the number of prison cells needed to temporarily house them? Or the number of planes or buses needed to deport them? Not to mention the incredible economic dislocation that action would have. Really, the whole idea is beyond absurd.

We need to get serious. We need comprehensive

immigration reform. And for a short while in 2013, it looked like we might make some real progress.

After considerable debate, the Senate passed an immigration reform bill that would have given legal status to millions of aspiring Americans. As with any complicated legislation, there were aspects of that bill that I strongly supported and parts that I disagreed with. However, while far from perfect, this legislation was an important step toward addressing the immigration crisis facing our country, and I was proud to vote for it.

Unfortunately, after the Senate passed the bill, the Republican-controlled House of Representatives failed to take it up, killing any hope for its passage. The right-wing extremists in the Republican Party prevailed. They preferred to have a politically charged wedge issue to use to divide the country than to forge a real solution to a major American problem.

While Senate Majority Leader Mitch McConnell refused to reconsider immigration reform in the 2015 session, he did find time to debate a proposal by Pennsylvania's Republican senator Pat Toomey to deny federal economic development assistance to "sanctuary cities," where police and other public agencies do not inquire into a person's immigration status during routine business. After all, feeding into concerns about public safety to gin up the Republican base pays far greater political dividends than actually taking meaningful action on immigration reform.

Congress won't even pass the DREAM Act, which offers permanent residency to young people without criminal records if they serve in our armed forces or attend college. Is this not what we want from our youth? To be upstanding citizens, contribute to the national defense, and learn skills to strengthen our economy? Apparently, that's not the Republican perspective.

In light of congressional inaction, President Obama

was absolutely right to issue a series of Executive Orders in November 2014, to accomplish some of what Congress has failed to do. While I would have much preferred that Congress—rather than the President—address our broken immigration system, the sad truth is that Congress has not acted.

President Obama's Executive Orders would allow approximately 4 million undocumented immigrants to stay in the U.S. without fear of deportation. One order expanded the Deferred Action for Childhood Arrivals (DACA) program to include more people, and extended the DACA work authorization period from two years to three years. A second order made it easier for the parents of U.S. citizens and lawful permanent residents to stay in the country, and a third extended the same relief to spouses and children of U.S. citizens and lawful permanent residents. Beneficiaries of all three orders had to pass strict background checks before being granted relief to stay in this country.

I guess it should come as no surprise that a group of Republicans challenged the Executive Orders in court, saying that the president exceeded his constitutional authority. Of course, Obama only resorted to issuing the orders after Congress refused to do its job.

LET'S PASS COMPREHENSIVE IMMIGRATION REFORM

The incoming Congress must do its job, and pass what the majority of Americans demand—a comprehensive and humane immigration reform policy. Let me outline what I think that means.

First and foremost, it means creating a path for the 11 million undocumented people in our country to become lawful permanent residents, and eventually, citizens. It is time to bring these people out of the shadows and give them the full protection of the law. They should be allowed to improve their lives while contributing more fully and fairly to the American economy, including paying their fair share of income, Social Security, and Medicare taxes.

The path to citizenship must be fair in terms of not having overly restrictive eligibility dates and application periods. Financial penalties and fees must likewise be fair—they cannot be so onerous as to be an obstacle for attaining legal residency.

Immigration reform must include the DREAM Act: the granting of conditional residency to people who serve in the military or attend college. It's time to tap the potential of all of our youth.

Immigration reform must allow individuals to apply for relief, even if convicted for nonviolent offenses. A prior nonviolent conviction, like the seventeen-year-old DUI charge that led to last year's deportation of Iowa City pastor Max Villatoro, shouldn't automatically disqualify someone from legal residency. Done correctly, immigration reform will allow the authorities to appropriately focus on violent offenders, instead of hardworking people who want to get right with the law.

Immigration reform must eliminate the three-year, ten-year, and permanent "bars." Every year, thousands of people leave the country to "normalize" their immigration status, which, depending on the circumstances, sometimes has to be done outside the country. However, once outside, they realize that they are barred from reentering for three or ten years, or in some cases permanently, because they were previously here illegally. It makes no sense to bar people—some of whom have been living here for many years—from reentering, only to allow them back in years later. Let's eliminate this Catch-22 many people face when legally applying for a green card.

Immigration reform means ending arbitrary family deportation sweeps. And it means expanding the use of humanitarian parole for unjustly deported immigrants, to hasten the reunification of broken families.

Immigration reform means immediately ending family detention. And it means promoting alternatives to individual detention, which would allow thousands of nonviolent detainees to reunite with their families as they wait for their day in court. A good start would be getting rid of the requirement that Immigration and Customs Enforcement maintain a level of 34,000 detention beds. Eliminating the costly and harmful "bed quota" would allow ICE to use alternatives to detention that could save taxpayers $5 million per day, or $1.4 billion per year.

Immigration reform means ending for-profit, privately run immigration detention facilities. In September 2015, I introduced the Justice Is Not for Sale Act with Reps. Raul Grijalva, Keith Ellison, and Bobby Rush to ban all private prisons, including immigrant detention centers. I was very pleased when, in August, the Department of Justice said it would phase out the use of private prisons. Just two weeks later, Department of Homeland Security Secretary Jeh Johnson announced that DHS might follow suit. We must keep up the pressure to make sure this happens.

Immigration reform means significantly improving conditions inside public-run detention facilities, especially for vulnerable populations, including pregnant women, unaccompanied minors, LGBT individuals, and detainees with disabilities.

Immigration reform means making sure all detained immigrants always have access to legal counsel before and during hearings to ensure due process and equal protection. And it means providing adequate funding to eliminate the backlog in immigration courts, and restoring judicial discretion to allow immigration judges to consider the unique circumstances of each case.

Immigration reform must focus on cracking down on unscrupulous employers that exploit undocumented workers, rather than penalizing workers. And it should establish a whistle-blower visa for undocumented workers who report labor violations—to protect those who currently don't report infractions for fear of deportation, and to hold accountable employers that currently abuse workers with impunity.

Immigration reform must include tough measures to prevent employers from exploiting temporary guest workers, especially those on H-2B, H-1B, and J-1 visas. Binding workers to a specific employer or not allowing their family members to work creates a situation ripe for abuse and exacerbates an already unequal relationship between the employer and the employee. We can't continue to let this go unchecked.

Immigration reform means making sure our borders are modern and secure, especially in this era of nonstate terrorism. Rather than building walls, we must target construction wisely and invest smartly in high-tech equipment and state-of-the-art cameras. We must avoid the overmilitarization of our border communities, and work more closely with local residents and law enforcement.

Immigration reform must create viable and legal channels that match our labor market needs and that promote family cohesion. Family-based visas are at the center of a humane immigration system, which recognizes that workers with families nearby are healthier and more productive, and that their families, particularly children, benefit immensely as well. Prioritizing the unity of families is a time-tested American value.

In light of a historic refugee crisis, immigration reform means reaffirming our commitment to accepting our fair share of refugees. At a time when millions of people have fled unspeakable violence with nothing but the shirts on their backs, we must do our part to offer safe refuge. And we must make a special effort to enhance protections for survivors of gender-based violence and human trafficking.

Until we achieve a single-payer health care system, all immigrants—including undocumented workers and their families—should be able to purchase insurance through Affordable Care Act exchanges. Aspiring Americans represent a large portion of the remaining uninsured in our country, and allowing them to purchase health insurance with their own money is good for them and will reduce overall health care costs.

And lastly, immigration reform means recognizing that inequality across the world is a major driving force behind migration. The truth is, our free trade policies are exacerbating inequality by devastating local economies, pushing millions to migrate. We must rewrite our trade policies to end the race to the bottom, and instead work to lift the living standard of Americans and people throughout the world.

These are just some of the major aspects of what I think immigration reform means. There are certainly others. But what should never get lost in the wonky details of immigration policy is that we are talking about people. We are talking about *families*.

During the campaign, I visited Friendship Park in San Diego, California. Located right on the Pacific Ocean, it is a beautiful location. It is also a very sad location, because it is the place where, every Saturday and Sunday from ten A.M. to two P.M., the U.S. Border Patrol opens a gate, allowing visitors to approach an eighteen-foot-high, tightly woven steel fence that marks the border between San Diego and Tijuana.

Here in Friendship Park, family members on one side of the border come to meet family members from the other side. They cannot hug or kiss, but they can stick a thin finger, perhaps a pinky, through the fence to have some minimal physical contact with their loved ones. While many people visiting the fence smile and laugh, many others weep.

It occurred to me that Friendship Park is a metaphor for our broken immigration system and the challenges before us. Fundamentally, we need immigration policies that bring families together, not policies that divide them.

With strong moral leadership, I believe we can move our nation toward commonsense, humane, and comprehensive immigration reform. And by doing that, we can reverse the decline of our middle class, better prepare the United States to compete in the global economy, and build upon the best parts of our national tradition of embracing diversity and difference and harnessing them for the common good.

NINE

PROTECTING OUR MOST VULNERABLE

A great nation is judged not by how many millionaires and billionaires it has, or by the size of its military budget. It is not judged by the greed of its largest corporations. It is judged by how well it treats its weakest and most vulnerable citizens. A truly great nation is one that is filled with compassion and solidarity.

The United States of America is the richest country in the history of the world. We are a nation of extraordinary wealth. There are now over ten times as many billionaires in this country as there were just sixteen years ago. We have, by far, the highest level of income and wealth inequality of any major country, and the gap between the very rich and everyone else is growing wider and wider.

If we were to judge a nation simply by how many millionaires and billionaires it has, America would be number one—bar none. But that is not how we should judge a nation.

As President Franklin Delano Roosevelt reminded us: "The test of our progress is not whether we add more to the abundance of those who have much, it is whether we provide enough for those who have little."

By that measure, we are not number one. In fact, the United States lags behind virtually every other major country on earth in terms of our social safety net and in how well we provide for the weak and the vulnerable.

In America today, 43.1 million people are living in poverty—13.5 percent of our entire population. The poverty rate is higher today than it was in 1968. And that is the *official* poverty rate, which is based on a formula developed more than fifty years ago that doesn't take into account the cost of child-care or work-related expenses. If the poverty threshold were set to reflect the actual costs of getting by in this country, a lot more people would be considered to be living in poverty. Millions more.

Let's be clear about what living in poverty means. For a household with three people, the official poverty threshold is $18,871. Do you have any idea how hard it is for a family to live on $18,871? Many low-income families spend at least half their incomes on housing. For them, that means about $9,000 a year remains for everything else: food, clothing, transportation, child care, utilities, health care, medicine, a Christmas gift for your kid.

In today's world, a computer, broadband, and cell phone are increasingly becoming a necessity of life. How do you find a job, make appointments for interviews, or connect to the world without a phone? Can you keep a job if your employer can't get ahold of you? And all that stuff is pretty expensive.

If you're in a rural area, you most likely need a car to get to work. Old cars break down, and it's often expensive to fix them. Not to mention the other costs of having a car: registration, insurance, inspection, and the cost of a driver's license. Oh, yes. Cars run on gas, and you have to fill the gas tank to get to work. If you are in an urban area, the cost of a bus or train is not inexpensive.

In terms of the cost of food, it is likely that if you live in a low-income neighborhood you pay more for lower-quality food than middle-class people do, because there may not be a decent supermarket in your neighborhood. Probably not a bank, either, and you may have to pay a substantial sum to get a check cashed.

I remember being at a meeting with clergymen in Baltimore who were telling me that being poor is a very expensive proposition. And they were right.

There is no question that government programs like food stamps, Medicaid, the earned income tax credit, and subsidized housing help. But not enough. The truth is that being poor in America is enormously dispiriting and stressful.

And what is perhaps most disturbing: Under-eighteens are the age group with the highest poverty rate. Fully 19.7 percent of American children are living in poverty—which gives the United States the distinction of having the highest child poverty rate of almost any major country on earth.

How can it be that in a country with $88 trillion in wealth, we allow one in five children to live in poverty? How can it be that in our great country, since the Great Recession of 2008, the number of homeless children in our public schools has doubled, now numbering nearly 1.4 million homeless kids drifting from school to school, as their parents try to find temporary housing in which to live?

At a town hall meeting I held in West Virginia's Mc-Dowell County, one of the poorest counties in the nation, an elementary school teacher there by the name of

Tonya Spinella spoke with eloquence on this subject. Here is what she said:

"Our students have an intellect, a drive, and a thirst for knowledge just as any burgeoning young minds across the nation do. Our students, however, have something else. In many cases they are born into crippling poverty, broken or untraditional family structures, or are, worse yet, born into families with severe and debilitating drug addictions. How can we expect our students to remember their homework or to bring a pencil to class if they have been up crying all night because they have a cavity they cannot treat? How can we expect them to learn multiplication when all they can think about is the ever-present threat of eviction after a parent loses their job? How can we expect them to succeed in life when all they've ever been told is that they cannot succeed because they are from McDowell County?"

Tonya is right, and we should all be grateful for the enormously important work that she does with her students. But it's not just McDowell County, West Virginia. I heard the same message in the Bronx, in Texas, in Arizona, and in Baltimore. I heard it all across the country. I heard it as it applies to white kids, black kids, Latino kids, Native American kids, and Asian-American kids. How can it be that we have enough money to give tax breaks to billionaires and spend more on defense than the next seven countries combined, but we don't have enough to make sure that every American child has a roof over his or her head and enough food to eat?

In New York City I visited with residents in high-rise public housing projects in Brooklyn and the Bronx. At a time when parents there are desperately trying to keep their kids away from drugs and gangs, I saw a community center that was shut down and locked up because of a lack of funds. No mentoring or after-school recreational programs for the children there. I was told by the members of the city council and state legislature who accompanied me about a $17 billion maintenance and construction backlog in housing projects all across the city. Walls are crumbling. Elevators aren't working, and old people can't climb the stairs to go shopping. People are getting sick from mold in the walls.

In May of 2016, I campaigned in Puerto Rico and visited San Juan. The people who live in Puerto Rico—American citizens—are not eligible to vote for president of the United States. (They are, however, able to participate in the Democratic presidential primary.) It is not widely known in the rest of the United States, but Puerto Rico, a U.S. commonwealth, has been in a severe depression for over a decade. Unemployment on the island is more than twice the U.S. average, and almost 60 percent of children live in poverty. A bankrupt government has been shutting down schools and health care facilities and laying off thousands of workers. There are fierce divisions there about the political future of the island. Some Puerto Ricans want statehood, others want Puerto Rico to become an independent nation, while others want changes to the current system.

Yet in the midst of all the squalor and economic pain, I saw extraordinary determination in a remarkable Montessori School sustained by dedicated teachers and parents in one of the poorest neighborhoods in San Juan. The students there, speaking fluent English, participated in a town meeting we held at the school.

I also visited a tenant-run community housing land trust formed to improve the ramshackle homes and community infrastructure where people have lived for decades along the polluted Martín Peña Channel. This community, which is overrun by raw sewage during heavy rains, has long been ignored by the island government, and by our national government.

As a nation, our priorities have become horribly

distorted. Congress listens to the lobbyists from wealthy and powerful corporate interests, and ignores the pain of children who are hungry and homeless.

The corporate media spends a lot of time covering the lifestyles of the rich and the famous, but not all that much time covering the poor and the desperate. To a large degree, these people, the millions of poor people in America, are invisible, living under the radar screen. Their suffering is not seen on our evening news. But it's there.

We have already seen how the link between poverty and poor health impacts African-Americans and other minorities. It affects poor whites, too. A June 2016 study by the Hamilton Project found that between 1999 and 2014, mortality rates for poor, middle-aged whites rose by about 10 percent. That is an extraordinary and frightening development. According to those who have studied the issue, the main causes of the decline in longevity among working-class whites are drug and alcohol abuse and suicide.

Early deaths among young white Americans are rising as well. The Centers for Disease Control and Prevention (CDC) reported that over the last fifteen years there has been a nearly 30 percent increase in the death rate among whites between the ages of twenty-five and thirty-four, driven primarily by drug and alcohol overdoses, suicide, and chronic liver disease. Unable to find decent jobs and decent incomes, living in despair, they are wrecking their lives and dying younger than their parents.

Tragically, when people do not have enough income to support their families, when they live under enormous financial stress and have little hope for the future, when they see their lives and the lives of their children moving in exactly the wrong direction, too many turn to drugs and alcohol to numb the pain. And the downward spiral accelerates. Some then turn to suicide.

For decades, in the United States and around the world, most countries have seen an increase in life expectancy. And yet now, in the United States, we are seeing millions of Americans, working-class white people, living shorter lives than their parents. Life expectancy for too many Americans is going down when it should be going up.

Today in America, poverty is truly a death sentence. There is a growing divide between those who can afford to keep themselves healthy and those who are dying because they are poor. Incredibly, the gap in life expectancy between the very richest Americans and the very poorest Americans is fifteen years for men and ten years for women.

A car trip between McDowell County, West Virginia, and Fairfax County, Virginia, takes about six hours. But these two counties live in different worlds. McDowell County is one of the poorest counties in America and Fairfax County is one of the wealthiest. As *The New York Times* reported: "Residents of Fairfax County are among the longest-lived in the country: Men have an average life expectancy of 82 years and women, 85, about the same as in Sweden. In McDowell, the averages are 64 and 73, about the same as Iraq."

A few years ago we had four cases of Ebola in America—a frightening disease, to be sure—and the country almost came to a halt. Four cases, no deaths. But it dominated the airwaves for weeks, the entire public health apparatus was mobilized, and the American people and their leaders were very, very concerned. In 2011, the *American Journal of Public Health* found that 130,000 people die each and every year as a result of poverty. But no one seems to notice or care. Or as

Pope Francis said more succinctly: "How can it be that it is not a news item when an elderly homeless person dies of exposure, but it is news when the stock market loses two points?"

In January 2016, I held a town meeting with about two hundred people in Iowa Falls, Iowa, a typical small town in rural America. I asked those who attended a very simple question: How were they doing economically and had their lives improved since the Great Recession.

I believed then, and I believe now, that if we do not know the reality of what is going on in our country in terms of the struggles people are facing, it will be impossible for us to develop—and generate public support for—policies that can enable us to go forward and address the great challenges we face. So, I asked the people of Iowa Falls about their struggles, and this is what they told me:

A diabetic man told me he could not afford the insulin that was prescribed to him by his doctor. Another man struggling with diabetes said the price for his medication had skyrocketed from just $3.25 a month to more than $600.

A retired worker said that she was struggling to get by on just $10,000 a year because the plastics company she worked for didn't offer her a pension. Then, I asked the audience how people in Iowa could get by on just $10,000 or $12,000 a year.

There was an awkward pause. I wasn't sure if anyone would speak up. And then, in an extremely moving moment, we heard from Carrie Aldrich. Carrie is a forty-six-year-old single mom from Alden, Iowa. With tears in her eyes, this is what she said:

"I've been living on probably less than that [$12,000] for a long time because of disabilities. It's so hard to do anything to pay your bills, you're ashamed all the time. . . . When you can't buy presents for your children it's really, really, really hard—and I work three, four, five jobs sometimes, always minimum wage. I have a degree, divorced, and it's just I'm waiting for disability to come through so my parents have to support me— it's just hard."

What Carrie did took tremendous courage. It's not easy to stand up in a crowded room with national television cameras rolling to talk about what life is like to raise a family with a disability, trying to live on less than $12,000. And the truth is that Carrie is not alone. There are millions of others just like her.

There are frail senior citizens on fixed incomes who are forced to cut their pills in half because they can't afford the outrageously high cost of the medicine they need.

There are disabled veterans who bravely fought to defend our county but are now living out on the streets as we consistently shortchange the Department of Veterans Affairs.

There are workers in their late fifties who worked for the same employer for thirty years and now find themselves unemployed and unemployable because their jobs have been shipped to China or Mexico.

There are the more than half of our older workers who have no retirement savings and no idea as to how they will ever be able to retire with any shred of dignity or security.

There are babies born to mothers who have not completed high school who are almost twice as likely to die before their first birthday as babies born to college graduates.

We can no longer continue to ignore the tremendous economic pain and anxiety that exists in our country today. These problems will not go away by sweeping them under the rug. We have got to address them forthrightly, or they will only get worse. We can no longer continue to scapegoat the poor and the unemployed. We have got to create jobs, raise wages, and protect the weak and the vulnerable. Instead of turning the middle class against those most in pain, we need to develop a sense of solidarity and stand together against wealthy special interests who get richer and richer while most everybody else gets poorer.

And we cannot allow Republicans to make these problems even worse by cutting Social Security, Medicare, Medicaid, veterans' benefits, education, public housing, and nutrition programs, while giving huge tax breaks to those who need them least.

PROTECTING SENIOR CITIZENS

When people become old, they often become frail and sick. They are unable to work and earn an income. In a civilized society, the older generation—the people who raised us—are entitled, and allowed, to live out their remaining years in dignity and security. For millions of seniors in our country today, that is most certainly not the case. We must change that.

Social Security is the most successful government program in our nation's history. Before Social Security was signed into law, nearly half of our senior citizens lived in poverty. Today, while still much too high, the elderly poverty rate is 8.8 percent.

Yet for decades, Republicans have tried to convince the American people that Social Security is in crisis. They say it's going broke, that it won't be there for our kids and grandchildren, that it's a Ponzi scheme, that it is contributing to the deficit. All of that is nonsense.

Through good economic times and bad, Social Security has paid every nickel owed to every eligible

American—on time and without delay. Today, 59 million seniors, people with disabilities, and children receive benefits from Social Security. Social Security is financially self-sufficient, funded by the payroll tax. Far from being broke, the Social Security retirement trust fund has a $2.8 trillion surplus. And not only hasn't Social Security added a dime to the deficit, it is forbidden by law from doing so. The wars in Iraq and Afghanistan that the Republicans forgot to pay for added trillions to the deficit and national debt, but Social Security didn't.

So why are Republicans always trying to undermine public trust in Social Security? For some, it's ideological—they hate that Social Security is a government program that works very well and is extremely popular with the public. It threatens their bedrock philosophy that government can do no good. For others, privatization of Social Security would be a fantastic new opportunity for their friends and campaign contributors on Wall Street to make huge profits by gambling with the retirement savings of working people.

Despite what you may have heard on TV, Social Security is not in crisis and is not going broke. The Social Security retirement trust fund can pay full benefits to every single retiree for the next eighteen years, and three-quarters of benefits afterward. Why not longer? For one thing, wages for the vast majority of American workers are stagnating, making payroll tax receipts lower than they would be if wages were rising. If we had the same level of economic equality we had in 1983, the retirement trust fund would have another $1.1 trillion on hand—and another twenty more years of solvency. Yes, income inequality is a problem for Social Security, too.

Moreover, payroll taxes are only assessed on the first $118,500 of income. That means a Wall Street CEO who makes $20 million per year pays no more in payroll taxes than someone earning $118,500. That is an extremely regressive approach. America doesn't have a problem with "greedy geezers," to quote one Social Security adversary. It has a problem with the superrich not paying their fair share into the system.

About one out of five senior citizens today are trying to make ends meet on incomes of less than $13,000 a year. Frankly, I don't know how they do it. And the truth is that many of them don't do it. Many of them don't take the medicine they should. Their homes are too cold. They don't get the nutrition they should.

That is why we should "lift the cap" and apply the payroll tax to earned and investment income above $250,000. This would raise taxes only on the wealthiest 1.5 percent of Americans. In other words, 98.5 percent of the American people—including those earning between $118,500 and $250,000—would not see their payroll taxes go up by one dime.

Not only would this simple fix extend Social Security's solvency until at least 2074, it would also provide enough new revenue to expand benefits for seniors making less than $16,000 by about $1,300 a year. I think this is a sensible, practical, and fair approach. It asks those who have benefited most from years of tax cuts and who have the means to pay their fair share of payroll taxes.

Today the average Social Security benefit for retired workers is just $1,341 a month. More than one-third of senior citizens depend on Social Security for almost all of their income. During three out of the last six years, despite the skyrocketing cost of prescription drugs, senior citizens and disabled veterans did not receive a cost-of-living adjustment to keep up with inflation. The number of hungry senior citizens is projected to go up by 50 percent by 2025, and many of them are already on waiting lists for the Meals on Wheels program, putting them at greater risk of congestive heart failure, depression, and asthma.

Our job must be to expand benefits, not cut them. Our job must be to strengthen Social Security, not weaken it.

STANDING WITH THE DISABLED

Moreover, let us not forget that Social Security is not just a retirement program. It is an insurance program that protects millions of Americans who become disabled or lose their parents at a young age. Incredibly, the only source of income for about 3 million persons with disabilities is a Social Security Disability Insurance (SSDI) benefit that averages just $35 a day.

In 2015, a CDC report said a stunning 53 million Americans—one of every five adults in our country—has a disability. CDC director Tom Frieden said at the time, "We are all at risk of having a disability at some point in our lifetime." Yet twenty-five years after the historic passage of the Americans With Disabilities Act, we still have miles to go to make sure that everyone who has a disability in this country can live with dignity and respect.

Today, 28.5 percent of disabled Americans are living in poverty. About 6 million persons with disabilities have trouble finding adequate transportation, and half a million have reported that they do not leave their homes because of a lack of transportation. Over 2.4 million Americans with disabilities pay more than half of their limited incomes on housing, and 43 percent of Americans living in homeless shelters have a disability. We have got to do a lot better than that.

For one thing, far too many Americans with disabilities are unable to get the Social Security disability benefits they have earned and deserve. And the average benefit that the 11 million Americans who do receive SSDI get is just $1,166 a month—hardly enough to survive on. Of course, that didn't stop Republicans in Congress from trying to cut disability insurance benefits by 19 percent in 2015, which would have cut the average yearly benefit from $13,980 to just $11,324.

Let's be clear: These are our neighbors who are unable to work because of a disability. Many of them are paralyzed, many have had their legs amputated, and many of them woke up one day and found out that they had only a short time left to live because of a terminal illness. And the Republicans wanted to cut their already inadequate benefits by $2,656 a year. Fortunately, we won that battle, but it sickens me that we even had to wage the fight.

Of course, there are many other ways we fail people with disabilities, beginning with inadequate enforcement of civil rights laws to prevent discrimination in employment, public services, and public accommodations. But we also fail to provide sufficient funding for special education in our schools, and for meaningful job training and employment opportunities for people with disabilities. And there are a host of health care–related issues that we must address, including the dearth of long-term home care options. Clearly, we have a long way to go in terms of being a society that values the contributions of the 53 million people in this country living with disabilities.

CARING FOR OUR VETERANS

While serious people can have legitimate differences of opinion about when our country should go to war, there should never be a debate as to whether we fulfill the promises made to the men and women who served this country in the military. As a nation, we have a moral obligation to provide the best-quality care to those who have put their lives on the line to defend us. But we have often fallen short of that obligation.

What we can never forget is that the cost of war is more than the 6,800 service members who died in Iraq and Afghanistan. The cost of war is more than the hundreds of billions we spend on planes, aircraft carriers, and enormously expensive weapons systems.

The cost of war includes taking care of the men and women we sent off to fight the war, including the hundreds of thousands of veterans with amputations, loss of eyesight, post-traumatic stress disorder, and traumatic brain injury. It includes caring for the spouses and children who have to rebuild their lives after the loss of a loved one. It includes veterans who are having difficulty keeping jobs in order to pay their bills, their high divorce rates, and the terrible tragedy of veterans committing suicide.

The bottom line is that if we are going to send people off to battle, we must do everything we can to make them whole when they return. If we can't do that, we shouldn't be sending them into war in the first place. That's the sacred contract we have with the people who put their lives on the line to defend us. And that is why as the former chairman and a current member of the Senate Veterans' Affairs Committee, I consider it one of my highest priorities in Congress to ensure that our veterans receive the care and benefits they have earned.

Amid reports of unacceptable wait times at a number of VA medical facilities, many Republicans wanted to denigrate the VA and its employees, and use the very real problems in the system as an excuse to privatize VA health care. Many Americans don't realize this, but the VA operates the largest integrated health care system in the nation, treating nearly 6.5 million patients each year. And according to veterans' service organizations, which represent millions of veterans, and the many veterans with whom I have spoken over the years, the quality of care provided by the VA is strong. It needs to get better, but most veterans have a high regard for the VA health care they receive.

So, instead of undermining the system, I spearheaded a bipartisan effort to pass the most comprehensive veterans legislation in decades to increase accountability within the VA and ensure that all veterans have access to timely health care. We strengthened the health system by authorizing twenty-seven new medical facilities and by providing $5 billion to hire more doctors and nurses to care for the surging number of veterans returning from the wars in Iraq and Afghanistan. We provided incentives to attract young doctors to the VA, and made it easier for some veterans to see private doctors or go to community health centers. We expanded VA educational benefits and improved care for veterans who experienced sexual trauma while serving in the military. That is how we honor our veterans—not by paying them lip service and shuttering the VA, but by strengthening the services and care they receive.

But more work remains to be done. Much more. We must improve and streamline the VA disability claims process. We must make comprehensive dental care available at all VA medical centers, and expand caregiver provisions. The number of veterans battling mental health disorders continues to rise, and the number of veterans who commit suicide remains unacceptably high. Some twenty-two veterans take their own lives each and every day. We must make sure that all veterans have the mental health care they need.

We must expand the VA Caregivers Program to provide home care to veterans who need intensive attention. And

Paying attention to our veterans. (Christopher Dilts, Revolution Messaging)

we must fully undo the cuts to military pensions that were insisted upon by Republicans in the last budget deal.

Lastly, we must end the travesty of veterans' homelessness. While significant gains have been made over the past six years, the fact that on any given night there are some 50,000 homeless veterans on the street is a national disgrace.

The sad truth is that war is an extremely expensive proposition—in terms of human life, human suffering, and financial cost. Taking care of veterans is a cost of war. And it is a cost that we can no longer shirk. It's that simple.

EMPOWERING NATIVE AMERICANS

When we speak about people whose needs are often ignored or dismissed, we are surely speaking about the Native American community.

Native Americans are the first Americans, yet they have for far too long been treated as third-class citizens. Time and time again, our Native American brothers and sisters have seen the federal government break solemn promises, abrogate treaties, and allow corporations to put profits ahead of the sovereign rights of tribal communities. Our treatment of Native Americans is a stain on our collective moral conscience.

It is unconscionable that today, many Native Americans still do not have the right to decide some of the most important and basic issues that affect their communities. The United States must not just honor Native American treaty rights and tribal sovereignty, it must also move away from a relationship of paternalism and control and toward one of deference and support. The United States has a duty to ensure equal opportunities and justice for all of its citizens, including the 2.5 million Native Americans who share this land. It is no secret that we are shirking that duty.

Native Americans face appalling levels of inequality, unemployment, poverty, and systemic injustice. One in four Native Americans are living in poverty, and the high school graduation rate is 67 percent, the lowest of any racial demographic group. They have a much lower life expectancy and higher uninsured rates than the population at large, and even those who have health insurance often have difficulty accessing the care they need. The second-leading cause of death for Native Americans between the ages of fifteen and twenty-four is suicide. One in three Native women will be raped in her lifetime, and most of the offenders are non-Native.

The United States has greatly exacerbated the struggles of Indian Country because of its failure to support basic principles of self-determination. Today, Native American land is being taken away and given to multinational corporations for mineral extraction. Native Americans are more likely to be killed by police than any other racial group, and the rate of violent crime against them is twice the national average. Yet, because the federal courts have chipped away at tribal sovereignty, tribal nations are often unable to prosecute criminal offenders for crimes that occur within tribal borders. Tribal governments must have the autonomy and authority to control their land and protect their own people.

In May 2016, I visited the Pine Ridge Reservation in South Dakota, the home of the Oglala Sioux Tribe, and heard from the people there. In Pine Ridge, there is massive poverty, incredibly high unemployment, and high levels of alcoholism and drug addiction. Over 60 percent of children are poor and more than 80 percent of the working-age population do not have a job. The schools and the health care system there are inadequate. Life expectancy on the reservation is just forty-eight years for men and fifty-two for women, the equivalent of that of a poor, Third World country. Despair is rampant, with high rates of youth suicide.

These statistics are not a secret. They have been known for years. But the decades come and go, and nothing happens. The misery continues.

One of the promises I made during the campaign is that I would fight to make sure that the 2016 Democratic Party platform would include the strongest language in support of improving the lives of Native Americans in the history of our country. To accomplish that goal, I appointed Deborah Parker, a Native American leader from the Tulalip Tribes, to the Democratic Platform Committee. Deborah accomplished wonders on that committee, and thanks to her hard work, the platform addresses issues ranging from honoring and strengthening the trust relationship to dealing with economic development, housing, health care, education, women's rights, environmental protection, and much more.

Now, we must make sure that the language in that platform is implemented. We owe the First Americans a debt of gratitude that can never be fully repaid. It's time we started trying. It's time for a new federal relationship with the Native American people.

A BETTER DAY

In his inaugural remarks in January 1937, in the midst of the Great Depression, President Franklin Delano Roosevelt looked out at the nation, and this is what he saw.

He saw tens of millions of its citizens denied the basic necessities of life.

He saw millions of families trying to live on incomes so meager that the pall of family disaster hung over them day by day.

He saw millions denied education, recreation, and the opportunity to better their lot and the lot of their children.

He saw millions lacking the means to buy the products they needed, and by their poverty and lack of disposable income denying opportunities for employment to many other millions.

He saw one-third of a nation ill-housed, ill-clad, ill-nourished.

And he acted. That is exactly what we, as a nation, need to do today. That, and even more.

This is not 1937. Despite the Wall Street Crash of 2008, we are much better off economically in 2016 than we were during the Great Depression. But we must be honest and recognize that millions of Americans in every corner of this country are experiencing significant economic pain and suffering.

We must end the incredible despair that drives too many of our youth to drugs, alcohol, and suicide, and confront the reality that far too many of them are now dying at a younger age than their parents did or will.

We must end the disgrace of having the highest level of childhood poverty of almost any major country on earth and having public school systems in inner cities that are totally failing our children—where kids now stand a greater chance of ending up in jail than ending up with a college degree.

We must no longer abide the reality of tens of thousands of Americans dying every year from preventable deaths because they either lack health insurance, have high deductibles, or cannot afford the outrageously high cost of the prescription drugs they need.

We must end the current situation in which hundreds of thousands of bright young people are unable to go to college because their families are poor or working class, while millions more struggle with suffocating levels of student debt.

We must alleviate the pain of single mothers and families who cannot feed their children because they are working at starvation wages.

We must never again poison entire cities with lead-tainted water because we have allowed our infrastructure to crumble and decay before our eyes.

We must end the disgrace of tens of thousands of veterans sleeping out on the streets.

We must make certain that the elderly and the disabled live with dignity and security.

In other words, we must create a responsive government that works for all the people, and not just the few at the top.

TEN

CORPORATE MEDIA AND THE THREAT TO OUR DEMOCRACY

As A. J. Liebling wrote: "Freedom of the press is guaranteed only to those who own one." Today, a handful of multinational corporations own much of the media and control what the American people see, hear, and read. This is a direct threat to American democracy. It is an issue we cannot continue to ignore.

Media shapes our very lives. It tells us what products we *need* to buy and, by the quantity and nature of coverage, what is "important" and what is "unimportant." Media shapes our political consciousness, and informs us as to the scope of what is "realistic" and "possible."

When we see constant coverage of murders and brutality on television, corporate media is telling us that crime and violence are important issues that we should be concerned about. When there is round-the-clock coverage of the Super Bowl, we are being informed that football and the NFL deserve our rapt attention. When there is very little coverage of the suffering of the 43 million Americans living in poverty, or the thousands of Americans without health insurance who die each year because they can't get to a doctor when they should, corporately owned media is telling us that these are not issues of major concern. For years, major crises like climate change, the impact of trade agreements on our economy, the role of big money in politics, and youth unemployment have received scant media coverage. Trade union leaders, environmentalists, low-income activists, people prepared to challenge the corporate ideology, rarely appear on our TV screens.

Media is not just about what is covered and how it is covered. More importantly, it is about what is *not* covered. And those decisions, of what is and is not covered, are not made in the heavens. They are made by human beings who often have major conflicts of interest.

Every serious presidential campaign spends a great deal of time developing media strategy and we were no exception. While our campaign was largely focused on grassroots activities, we paid a great deal of attention to television, radio, newspapers, and magazines and how, through them, we could best get our ideas out to the public.

In my life as a mayor, congressman, and United States senator from Vermont, I had a lot of involvement with local media. I would hold Vermont press conferences fairly frequently and speak to reporters via telephone many times a week. I also did something that I believe was unique in Congress. For many years I conducted an hour-long national radio town hall meeting with an old friend, the progressive radio talk show host Thom Hartmann. Thom and I would chat for a half hour or so about current issues and I would then take questions from all across the country. It was a lot of fun and, I believe, informative for the listeners.

Running for president, however, exposed me to a whole different level of media coverage. Over the course of the campaign I spoke to hundreds of national and local reporters, and very few days went by when I was not interacting with someone from the mainstream media.

What I learned from that experience was that, as a general rule of thumb, the more important the issue is to large numbers of working people, the less interesting it is to corporate media. The less significant it is to ordinary people, the more attention the media pays. Further, issues being pushed by the top 1 percent get a lot of attention. Issues advocated by representatives of working families, not so much. This was, to be honest, not a new revelation to me. I had seen it for years as a congressman and senator.

Before I relate some of my media experiences on the campaign trail, let me give you one example of the nature of media coverage that I will never forget which took place in the Senate.

In 2013 there was a lot of clamoring in Congress about the need to cut Social Security. Wall Street, corporate lobbyists, virtually all Republicans and a few Democrats were arguing, falsely, that Social Security was "going broke," was adding to the deficit, and that benefits would need to be scaled back. These attacks against Social Security had received an enormous amount of media coverage. They were becoming "accepted wisdom."

Senator Sheldon Whitehouse and I worked together to fight back. We knew that these cuts would be a disaster for millions of seniors and disabled veterans trying to survive on $12,000 or $13,000 a year. We also knew that there were ways to protect and extend Social Security benefits without hurting some of the most vulnerable people in our country.

As part of our strategy, we brought together organizations that represented tens of millions of Americans who were strongly opposed to these cuts. Our coalition included the AARP and virtually every senior group in the country, the American Legion and every major veterans' organization, the AFL-CIO representing more than 13 million workers, the largest disability organizations in America, and the National Organization for Women (NOW).

On January 31, 2013, we held a press conference with the leadership of these organizations. I had never, in my political life, been part of an event where organizations had come together representing so many people from all walks of life—more than 50 million Americans in total. And together they were telling Congress, "Do not cut Social Security." Together, they were speaking out on one of the most important issues facing ordinary Americans.

Guess what?

That event received almost no coverage. It was not of interest to the corporately owned media. And that was not unusual. Time and time again, issues of enormous consequence to working families get relatively little attention.

Needless to say, running for president changed my media profile. As a result of the success of our campaign, I found myself getting far more attention from the national media. I was on *Meet the Press*, *This Week with George Stephanopoulos*, *State of the Union*, *Face the Nation*, and *Fox News Sunday* multiple times. In fact, there were more than a few mornings when I appeared on three or four of the Sunday shows on the same day.

I also appeared on virtually every late night show— often more than once. Stephen Colbert had me on his show frequently, and I appeared with Jimmy Kimmel, Jimmy Fallon, Larry Wilmore, and Seth Meyers, as well as returning to Bill Maher's show.

I even found myself doing a routine on *Saturday*

Night Live with my impersonator Larry David, who did Bernie Sanders better than I did. If you want to know about the impact of television, go on *Saturday Night Live*, or, better yet, have a brilliant comic imitate you on the program. For a while, Larry was getting more attention than I was.

When I was in New York I appeared frequently on the ABC, CBS, and NBC morning shows. On PBS I made several appearances with Tavis Smiley and Judy Woodruff. I even chatted on several occasions with Joy Behar, Whoopi Goldberg, and the other ladies of *The View*, and I showed the world how bad a dancer I am with Ellen DeGeneres on her show.

My kids were impressed that I made the cover of *Rolling Stone*, as well as *Time* and a number of other magazines.

When you run a serious campaign for president you get a lot of attention, and I did. Before I announced for president I doubt that 15 percent of the American population knew who I was. By the time the campaign ended I was, more or less, nationally known. That was the good news for my campaign, and it tells you what a lot of hard work and a good communications director, Michael Briggs, can accomplish.

Here was the bad news.

In terms of my campaign's relationship to the national corporate media, we were at a distinct disadvantage, for a number of reasons.

First, when the campaign began I was considered by the "pundits" to be a "fringe" candidate—not serious, not someone who had a chance to win. Mainstream media does not spend a lot of time covering candidates they believe cannot win, and that was certainly reflected both in the amount and the kind of coverage we received. In *The New York Times*, my opening announcement made page 19, and there wasn't much more coverage on the national networks.

Second, corporate media, owned by large multi-national corporations, are not all that sympathetic to ideas that attack the corporate establishment. In fact, in the very first set of speeches that I gave, I talked about the need for a political revolution that would take on the economic, political, and *media* establishment. That's probably not the best way to ingratiate yourself with those who cover you. Issues like the need to reform our failed trade policies, the need for a Medicare for All single-payer health care system, climate change, and the need for progressive tax reform, issues that I focused on during the campaign and which challenge the wealthy and powerful, are not the kind of subjects that the corporate media gravitates toward.

Third, the nature of media coverage today, especially on television, mostly calls for short sound bites on what the media establishment determines is the "issue of the day." They decide what's important and you make a brief comment in response. While I can and do play that game, it's not easy for me and I don't do particularly well at it. In a complicated world, I find it hard to respond to the issue of the day in twenty seconds or less.

Fourth, and most important, we were at a major disadvantage in that our campaign attempted to offer a serious analysis of the problems facing the country and to provide real solutions to those problems. And that is *definitely* not where the mainstream media is coming from.

For the corporate media, the *real* issues facing the American people—poverty, the decline of the middle class, income and wealth inequality, trade, health care, climate change, etc.—are fairly irrelevant. For them, politics is largely presented as entertainment. In fact, there was a popular program on Showtime called *The Circus*. It was not about clowns, acrobats, and performing animals, it was about the political campaign. With some notable exceptions, reporters are trained to see a campaign as if it were a game show, a baseball game, a soap opera, or a series of conflicts.

Turn on CNN or other networks covering politics and what you will find is that the overwhelming amount of coverage is dedicated to personality, gossip, campaign strategy, scandals, conflicts, polls and who appears to be winning or losing, fund-raising, the ups and downs of the campaign trail, and the dumb things a candidate may say or do. Political coverage is the drama of what happens on the campaign trail. It has very little to do with the needs of the American people and the ideas or programs a candidate offers to address the problems facing the country. Most of the media coverage is about the candidate. Relatively little is about the enormous crises facing the country.

According to a study of media coverage of the 2016 primaries by the Shorenstein Center on Media, Politics and Public Policy, only 11 percent of coverage focused on candidates' policy positions, leadership abilities, and professional histories. I find that hard to believe. My personal sense is that number is much too high.

The "politics as entertainment" approach works very well for someone like Donald Trump, an experienced entertainer. Trump won the Republican primary with a massive amount of media coverage based on his ability to tweet and make sharp personal attacks against his opponents. By late February Trump had, according to figures cited by *The Economist*, enjoyed ten times as much attention on network evening newscasts as Florida Republican senator Marco Rubio. For the corporate media, name-calling and personal attacks are easy to cover, and what it prefers to cover.

That kind of media approach didn't work so well for a campaign like ours, which was determined to focus on the real problems facing our country and what the solutions might be. Many of the speeches I gave at our rallies were an hour or more, and they dealt with substantive issues. Further, I was at a disadvantage, because I have never much been into personal political attacks. In fact, during my entire congressional political career I have never run one negative ad. I don't claim to be a "goody two-shoes," but it has never made sense to me to run a campaign in which you spend most of your time telling your constituents how awful, horrible, and terrible your opponent is. Of course you should articulate how your views and proposals are different from your opponents', but my experience has been that voters much prefer to hear your analysis of the problems they face, and how you would address them. Today's media coverage makes that type of campaign very difficult to run. This became a very, very serious problem for us.

I learned that reality early on. While I was still considering whether or not to run, I did a long interview with a very prominent national newspaper writer. Over and over I stressed that I wanted to talk about my assessment of the major problems facing the country, and how I proposed to address them. And, for forty-five minutes, that's what the discussion was about. The reporter appeared interested in what I had to say, and I thought we had a good conversation. At the very end, as he was leaving, he said: "Oh, by the way, Hillary Clinton said such and such. What's your comment?" I fell for it. Needless to say, that one-minute response became the major part of his story. And that occurred time after time after time.

On a CNN show, an interviewer became visibly angry because I chose not to respond to her questions with

Breaking news! I got a haircut in Lawrence, Kansas. (Hilary Hess, Revolution Messaging)

personal attacks against Secretary Clinton. The interviewer opined that I didn't have "sharp enough elbows" to become a serious candidate, that I wasn't tough enough. Identifying the major problems facing our country, and providing ideas as to how we could address them, was just not good enough.

In fact, I was gently faulted by some for having excessive "message discipline," for spending too much time discussing real issues. Boring. Not what a successful modern campaign was about. The result of all of these factors is that while I was getting coverage, it was far less than what other candidates were getting.

In a December 11, 2015, blog post for *Media Matters for America,* one of the better media watchdogs in the country, Eric Boehlert summarized the situation well. He wrote:

> ABC World News Tonight *has devoted less than one minute to Bernie Sanders' campaign this year. Does that ratio seem out of whack?*

That's the ratio of TV airtime that ABC World
News Tonight *has devoted to Donald Trump's
campaign (81 minutes) versus the amount of TV
time* World News Tonight *has devoted to Bernie
Sanders' campaign this year. And even that one
minute for Sanders is misleading because the actual number is closer to 20 seconds.*

For the entire year.

Boehlert continued:

*The results confirm two media extremes in
play this year, and not just at ABC News. The
network newscasts are wildly overplaying Trump,
who regularly attracts between 20–30 percent of
primary voter support, while at the same time
wildly underplaying Sanders, who regularly attracts between 20–30 percent of primary voter support. (Sanders' supporters have long complained
about the candidate's lack of coverage.)*

*Obviously, Trump is the GOP frontrunner and
it's reasonable that he would get more attention
than Sanders, who's running second for the Democrats. But 234 total network minutes for Trump
compared to just 10 network minutes for Sanders,
as the Tyndall Report found?*

In his article Boehlert also reported that:

- *Trump has received more network coverage than
  all the Democratic candidates combined.*
- *Trump has accounted for 27 percent of all campaign coverage this year.*
- *Republican Jeb Bush received 56 minutes of coverage, followed by Ben Carson's 54 minutes and
  Marco Rubio's 22.*

Boehlert continued:

Did you notice the Bush figure? He's garnered 56 minutes of network news coverage, far outpacing Sanders, even though he is currently wallowing in fifth place in the polls among Republicans. And you know who has also received 56 minutes of network news compared to Sanders' 10? Joe Biden and his decision not to run for president.

Boehlert concluded:

Close observers of trends in network news might also say ABC's paltry Sanders coverage isn't surprising considering the network's flagship news program has recently backed off political coverage, as well as hard news in general.

Look at that ABC number again: 261 minutes devoted to campaign coverage this year, and less than one minute of that has specifically been for Sanders. How does that even happen?

So no, Sanders didn't get virtually ignored this year by World News Tonight because the show's cutting back on campaign coverage. Sanders got virtually ignored by ABC because there was a conscious decision to do so.

John Nichols, a very perceptive journalist for *The Nation* magazine, wrote on March 10, 2016, that the Democratic Party "has a serious race on its hands—as the March 8 upset win for Sanders in Michigan confirmed—between candidates who are engaged in a great debate about who better represents the progressive ideals of the grassroots activists who have forced open the current discussions about inequality, failed trade policies, mass incarceration, and climate change.

Why isn't a contest that features an insurgent candidate mounting a vigorous populist challenge to a former secretary of state with strong support from party leaders and key constituencies attracting more votes than a Republican contest where the candidates argue about the size of their . . . hands?

Anyone who understands how the modern media shape the narrative, as opposed to simply reporting on it, knows the answer. As of late February, the wrangling between Trump and his top two rivals (Rubio and Texas senator Ted Cruz) was given twice as much time on network TV as the Clinton-Sanders contest.

That's especially unfair to Sanders, whose challenge to the billionaire class that owns so much of our media has been dismissed and neglected—even as his poll numbers have risen.

In my view, one of the reasons that so many people are giving up on the political process is that they do not see the reality of their lives reflected in political discourse or on their television screens. They hurt, they struggle to survive, they worry about their children. Is anybody paying attention?

In the United States today, shamefully, we have 43 million people living in poverty, and the highest rate of childhood poverty of almost any major country on earth. Poverty and youth unemployment in minority and rural communities are often off the charts. Homelessness is rampant, and millions of Americans struggle to put food on their table every single day. In Congress and in the media, poverty is an issue that gets very little attention.

Here is an example of how absurd that situation is. On May 25, 2016, *Media Matters for America* discussed the coverage of poverty issues on the major television networks for the first quarter of 2016. This is what was written in a story entitled:

> **Bernie Sanders Left a Mark on Sunday Show Coverage of Inequality and Poverty.** *During the survey period, Sunday political talk shows on ABC, CBS, CNN, Fox Broadcasting, and MSNBC featured 27 segments focused on economic inequality and nine focused specifically on poverty. Interviews with Democratic presidential candidate Sen. Bernie Sanders (I-VT) accounted for 16 of the 27 segments focused on economic inequality and six of the nine segments addressing poverty.*
>
> **Bernie Sanders Is the Only Reason Fox News Sunday Talked About Inequality.** *During the survey period, Fox News Sunday registered a single discussion of economic inequality in the United States—in an interview with Bernie Sanders, who brought the topic up as part of his core remarks. Sanders highlighted the need for job creation, increasing the federal minimum wage, and single-payer health care.*

Think about it for a second. What does it say about corporate media coverage of the major issues facing our country when my candidacy, *alone,* accounted for the majority of attention (limited though it may have been) that network Sunday news shows paid to poverty, one of the great crises facing the nation? The point here is not my role in raising the issue of poverty (and other important issues). The point is how national television coverage doesn't raise it and ignores the reality of important parts of American life.

On the campaign trail, I was determined to raise issues that other candidates were not talking about, and that have long been ignored. One of those issues, of course, was poverty. As I traveled the country I wanted the American people, through the media coverage my campaign was receiving, to get a glimpse of the suffering of their fellow Americans, to get an understanding of what unemployment, low wages, and inadequate housing and health care was doing to the lives of millions. I wanted to let the American people know that these issues were a major priority of mine, and to provide specific ideas as to how, if elected president, I would address them.

In that regard I was not successful.

Throughout the campaign, in rural areas and urban areas, I went to some of the most distressed parts of the states that I was visiting, places where candidates rarely went. While these visits often got good local coverage, they received, with few exceptions, little national attention. The reality that, in the wealthiest country on earth, so many of our people were living in despair and deep poverty was just not something that the national media was particularly interested in.

Some examples:

- After virtually tying Secretary Clinton in the Iowa caucus, and defeating her badly in New Hampshire, I was attracting a lot of national media as I campaigned in South Carolina, the fourth state up in the Democratic nominating process.

  South Carolina is one of the poorest states in the country, and the governor and the legislature there made a bad situation worse by refusing to expand Medicaid as part of the Affordable Care Act. In South Carolina, along with some very brave members of the South Carolina Legislature, I held a press conference focusing on poverty, high unemployment, low wages, the state's inadequate educational system, and the crisis in health insurance. The press conference was very well attended, with virtually all of the national media there.

The legislators, led by Representative Justin Bamberg, had prepared well for the event, were articulate, and gave very forceful comments as to how poverty was impacting the lives of the men, women, and children they represented. Unfortunately, virtually all of the questions we received from the national media were about the campaign. Almost nothing about poverty. There was virtually no national coverage about the issues we had discussed. It was like living in a parallel universe.

- The situation at the Native American reservation in Pine Ridge, South Dakota, is a national disgrace, as is the case in many parts of Indian country, to say the very least. In Pine Ridge, unemployment and poverty are rampant, and the educational and health care systems are totally inadequate. The youth suicide rate is tragically high and life expectancy on the reservation is the equivalent of that of a poor Third World country.

Anyone who has studied American history understands the horrific manner in which the Native American people have been treated from the first days settlers arrived here, long before we even became a country. Throughout our history the Native American people have been lied to and cheated, have seen their land stolen and the treaties they negotiated abrogated. I was determined to call attention to these issues and to help lead the fight for a new relationship between the Native American people and the U.S. government.

The town meeting that I had at the Pine Ridge

reservation brought out hundreds of people. It was an extraordinary afternoon, something that I will never forget. We heard from the tribal elders, and we heard from a lot of young people, who spoke freely about their lives, their dreams, and what they were confronting. I was deeply moved by what I heard. The national media was not.

TrahantReports is a blog written by Mark Trahant, the Charles R. Johnson Professor of Journalism at the University of North Dakota, a member of Idaho's Shoshone-Bannock tribe, a former president of the Native American Journalists Association, and the former editor of the editorial page for the *Seattle Post-Intelligencer.* This is what he wrote on May 14, 2016:

> You have to give Bernie Sanders credit for elevating American Indian and Alaska Native issues. He traveled across Montana, South Dakota, and North Dakota, and at every stop (as he has been doing for months now) he called for a new relationship between the federal government and tribes.
>
> "The reason we are here today is to try to understand what is going on in Pine Ridge and other reservations," Sanders said. "There are a lot of problems here. Poverty is much too high. There are not enough decent jobs in the area. The health care system is inadequate. And we need to fundamentally change the relationship between the U.S. government and the Native American community."
>
> Of course just bringing Native American issues to the surface is a good thing because it forces other candidates to talk

> *about the same issues and come up with possible solutions. Only that's not what's happening. Sanders is getting some press on Native issues, but it's really limited.*
>
> *A quick Google search tells the story. Search Bernie Sanders and Native Americans and there are some 771,000 hits, including videos of his speeches and a few news clips, mostly from regional newspapers. There has not been a major story from any TV network.*

The results were similar with press conferences that I held in New York City on the housing crisis there. Speaking with several members of the state legislature and city council at low-income housing projects in the Bronx and Brooklyn, we held media events that talked about the dilapidated conditions that many tenants faced and the $17 billion maintenance backlog that public housing in New York City faced. We talked about the need to rebuild housing in New York and create jobs. Despite a large group of media following us about, there was almost no coverage of this issue.

One last example. During the campaign in California I held a series of media events with experts and leaders in a number of communities on some of the most important issues facing the state. On one occasion, in San Francisco, with several doctors and nurses at my side, we talked about the health care crisis and why a Medicare for All single-payer program would be important for California. In a Los Angeles community, where fracking had caused health problems, I spoke with local leaders as to why fracking should be banned. At a third meeting, in Modesto, I discussed the crisis of climate change and the need to transform our energy system away from fossil fuels. And in Oakland, I held a press conference on income and wealth inequality with Robert Reich, one of the important economists in our country and a former secretary of labor under Bill Clinton. These events, on issues of enormous consequence, generated almost no national coverage by the large press corps following me daily. With one or two exceptions, these matters were just not something of interest to them.

On the other hand, from the beginning of the campaign to the end, there were major articles and TV coverage on all kinds of stuff that no normal human being was particularly interested in. When was I going to announce my intention to run? When was I going to announce my intention to drop out? When was I was going to endorse Clinton? Why wasn't I spending more time shaking hands and kissing babies? Why did certain staff members leave the campaign? Why were the campaign staffing levels reduced? What did I have for breakfast?

I remember cringing when the car I was traveling in was pulled over in Iowa because we were speeding to an event, with a *New York Times* reporter in the backseat. The state trooper was professional and polite and gave us a warning. Not so the reporter, who, it goes without saying, made it a major part of her coverage.

This is not to say that our campaign did not receive a lot of very positive coverage. We did. And it is not to say that the media was especially negative toward me, or disliked me. That was not the case. It is to say that, generally speaking, the less relevant the issue was to the lives of the American people, the more attention it got.

We had great local and national print and TV coverage about the huge crowds we were drawing at our rallies, about the unprecedented nature of our small-donation fund-raising, about the enthusiasm of our supporters, about our volunteer network, about the outstanding work our social media team was doing, and about the high quality of our television ads. There were also some excellent magazine articles and blog reports that really did understand what our campaign was trying to accomplish.

In terms of good exposure, the best coverage we received was when I was able to communicate with people directly, without the filter of the media. And we were able to do that quite frequently. I was pleasantly surprised that cable TV networks would broadcast parts or occasionally all of the speeches that I gave at our rallies. This would often occur after we had won a caucus or primary.

Further, for me, one of the most effective and enjoyable means of communication was through live TV "forums" or "town meetings." There were a number of them, sponsored by CNN, MSNBC, and Fox. They took place in states where primaries or caucuses were occurring. The format was pretty simple. I would respond to questions from a moderator, and then he or she would open the floor for questions from a live audience. This format gave me the opportunity to provide answers that went beyond a thirty-second sound bite. I also found that almost all of the questions from the audience were about real and relevant issues, not about political gossip or the process. The hosts for these events, who generally did a very good job, were Chris Cuomo, Anderson Cooper, Rachel Maddow, Chris Hayes, Bret Baier, and Chris Matthews.

Why is it that the mainstream media sees politics as entertainment, and largely ignores the major crises facing our country? The answer lies in the fact, which is very rarely discussed (and almost never in the mainstream media), that corporate media is owned by, well, large multinational corporations. And, in case you haven't heard, these corporations have an agenda that serves their bottom line. In fact, that's the reason for their existence.

In other words, it is time for the American people to understand that corporate media in America is not some kind of "objective" entity that sees its function as providing, as best it can, "truth" to its viewers, listeners, and readers. Quite the contrary. Corporate media is made up of businesses, very large businesses, whose primary function is to make as much money as they possibly can. And, in every instance, the largest media corporations are themselves owned by even larger conglomerates that have their own particular set of economic interests. A few examples:

General Electric was, until several years ago, one of the major media conglomerates in the country; until they sold their media interests to Comcast. Before that, they were the owners of the NBC television network and a massive amount of other media. As one of the largest corporations in America, General Electric has extensive interests in areas other than media. It is a major manufacturer, employing a very large number of people. Over the years, GE helped lead the way in taking advantage of trade deals that allowed them to shut down numerous factories in the United States and outsource tens of thousands of American jobs to low-wage countries. In fact, the CEO of GE touted the company's goal of moving facilities to China.

General Electric is also very aggressive in trying to avoid paying U.S. taxes. Despite making billions in profits, they use hundreds of accountants and lawyers to exploit tax laws that their lobbyists helped write so that, in some years, they don't pay anything in federal taxes.

General Electric is a major polluter. According to *The Boston Globe,* the "General Electric Company is sharply objecting to a new federal plan that would force it to spend hundreds of millions of dollars to remove massive amounts of toxic chemicals from the Housatonic River, which the company polluted for nearly 50 years."

Given the economic realities of the General Electric Corporation, what kind of approach do you think NBC had to such issues as outsourcing, taxation, labor relations, and environmental protection? The answer is that for NBC, and other networks with similar types of conflicts, these major issues facing our country were largely ignored. Over the years, for example, trade policy received almost no coverage at all from the major networks. Remember, what is important about media coverage is not just *how* they cover an issue—it is whether they cover it all.

Disney, the owner of ABC, has many thousands of employees in China manufacturing their products at very low wages. In the United States, they have utilized guest worker programs to fire Americans and replace them with low-wage foreign workers. Further, despite making huge profits, they pay the people who work at their theme parks here very low wages. I could be wrong, but I don't expect that you will see programming tonight on ABC discussing the plight of low-wage workers here in the United States or, for that matter, in China. There will also not be much mention of how corporate America is exploiting guest worker programs.

Rupert Murdoch, a right-wing billionaire, is one of the most powerful people on the planet. His News Corporation owns enormous amounts of media throughout the world, including the major newspapers on three continents—North America, Europe, and Australia. In the United States, Murdoch's major holdings include Fox television, *The Wall Street Journal*, the *New York Post, TV Guide*, and *Barron's*. At a time when scientists speak in an increasingly urgent tone about the planetary crisis of climate change, Murdoch works in tandem with the fossil fuel industry in rejecting science. Farron Cousins of the blog DeSmogBlog writes: "When it comes to climate change misinformation, arguably no single person has done more to spread false information or confuse the public than Rupert Murdoch. With his vast media empire that spans the globe, Murdoch has helped misdirect the public, as well as to openly advocate against government policies that would curtail carbon emissions or impose other environmental safeguards."

The scientists tell us, in an almost unanimous voice, that we must transform our energy system away from fossil fuels. Rupert Murdoch disagrees, and hundreds of millions of people are influenced by his ignorance and special interests.

It is not just, however, the inherent conflict of interest between the billionaires who own the media and the "news" their companies convey. There is also the extraordinary power of the multinational corporations that provide billions of dollars a year in advertising revenue to the corporate owners of the media. If you watch TV tonight, check out how many ads come from drug companies, insurance companies, the fossil fuel industry, Wall Street, automobile companies, and the rest of corporate America.

These powerful corporations also have an agenda, and it would be naive not to believe that their views and needs impact coverage of issues important to them. Seen any specials lately as to why we pay the highest prices in the world for our prescription drugs, or why we are the only major country on earth not to have a national health care program? That may have something to do with the hundreds of millions of dollars each year that drug companies and insurance companies spend on advertising.

And let us also not forget that the leading personalities we see on television are themselves, in most cases, multimillionaires with very generous contracts. That does not make them evil or bad people. It just makes them very wealthy, corporate employees who bring to their jobs the perspective that very wealthy corporate employees bring.

No, I don't believe that there is some kind of conspiracy in which corporate bosses get on the phone and tell a journalist what to write or say on television. No, in terms of politics, I don't think that most journalists are right-wingers who have it in for progressives or Democrats. But what I believe very strongly, what the evidence clearly indicates, and what I observed in my campaign is that there is a defined and clear approach in corporate media that determines what is "important" and worthy of coverage and what is not. My experience is that very few journalists cross those boundaries.

Over the course of my political life I cannot recall a mainstream journalist coming up to me and asking what I was going to do to end the scourge of poverty in this country, or how I was going to combat the disgraceful level of income and wealth inequality, or what role I would play in ending the influence of big money in politics. Those, and many similar issues, are just not what corporate media considers important. And my strong guess is that if by mistake, or in some state of confusion, a reporter for the corporate media started asking those types of questions, he or she would not last long with the company.

As I traveled throughout the country I found that local media was often more interested in real issues than was the national media. The local reporters were not as cynical as their national counterparts and, in many instances, had a real understanding and concern about the issues facing their communities. I was especially impressed by the serious coverage provided by reporters in states like Iowa and New Hampshire.

Let me also give a shout-out to some real heroes and heroines. These are people who, with resources far more limited than their corporate competitors, try to inform the American people about the real issues facing our country, issues often ignored or minimized by the corporate media. We received very fair coverage in our campaign from Thom Hartmann, Cenk Uygur of *The Young Turks*, and Amy Goodman of *Democracy Now!* The folks at *The Nation*, *In These Times*, *The Progressive*, and a number of other smaller publications and blogs also worked extremely hard to allow us to convey our message to the American people. Ed Schultz, the Reverend Al Sharpton, Rachel Maddow, and Chris Hayes provided us with the very fair coverage we received on MSNBC. I was also pleased to have been on the Bill Moyers program on PBS on several occasions.

The issue of corporate control over the media, and the degree to which a few large entities can determine what the American people see, hear, and read, has concerned me for many years. In fact, it's hard for me to understand how anyone who cares about the future of this country cannot be concerned.

As a member of the U.S. House, I held several town meetings on this issue in Vermont that had very good turnouts. At a meeting at St. Michael's College in 2003, Michael Copps, who was then a commissioner at the FCC, gave a brilliant discourse on what corporate control means in terms of limiting the points of view that the American people are able to hear. How can we have a vibrant democracy when only one side of an issue gets discussed? Is it an accident that in a nation politically divided, almost all of talk radio is extremely right wing?

He also discussed the impact of media concentration on minority communities and the relatively small amount of media owned by blacks, Latinos, and other minorities. Further, he raised the very important point of what it means when a small community has no locally owned media. Who's going to cover the city council or the school board? How can people become informed about local issues? Commissioner Copps also talked about the impact of corporate and national ownership of media on culture, and how difficult it was for local musicians to get heard when so much of the music piped into the community came from big-name nationally known artists.

I also had town meetings in Vermont with John Nichols and Bob McChesney, who have written extensively about this subject.

In my own political life the issue of big-money ownership of media was, I must confess, also personal. When I was mayor of Burlington I had to withstand horrendous editorials from the local newspaper, the largest in the state, day after day. Their dislike of me and progressive politics was also reflected in their reporting. It was also a little bit weird that, in those days, the owner of the largest TV station in the state was an open financial supporter of the state's Republican Party. And make no mistake about it: That bias was reflected in their reporting.

In my campaign for president, I received 46 percent of the pledged delegates, won twenty-two states, and lost some states by a few votes. In other words, we had a significant amount of support from ordinary people. On the other hand, I did not win 46 percent of the endorsements from the print establishment and the leading newspapers in the country. In fact, I won virtually none. In almost every state, the owners of the establishment newspapers supported Secretary Clinton.

I was very proud to have received the endorsement of *The Seattle Times*. Among all the major newspapers throughout this country, that was it. We received one major newspaper endorsement.

On the other hand, Clinton won the endorsements of *The Des Moines Register*, the *Concord Monitor*, *The Boston Globe*, *The New York Times*, *The Dallas Morning News*, the *Tampa Bay Times*, the *Houston Chronicle*, the *Las Vegas Sun*, the *Star Tribune* of Minneapolis, the *Detroit Free Press*, the *Miami Herald*, the *Omaha World-Herald*, *The Charlotte Observer*, the *Chicago Sun-Times*, the *St. Louis Post-Dispatch*, the *Cincinnati Enquirer*, *The Plain Dealer* of Cleveland, *The Arizona Republic*, the *Idaho Statesman*, New York's *Daily News*, the *Providence Journal*, *The Philadelphia Inquirer*, the *Hartford Courant*, *The Baltimore Sun*, the *Los Angeles Times*, the *Santa Fe New Mexican*, and a number of other publications.

WHO OWNS THE MEDIA?

Most Americans have very little understanding of the degree to which media ownership in America—what we see, hear, and read—is concentrated in the hands of a few giant corporations. In fact, I suspect that when people look at the hundreds of channels they receive on their cable system, or the many hundreds of magazines they can choose from in a good bookstore, they assume that there is a wide diversity of ownership. Unfortunately, that's not the case.

In 1983 the largest fifty corporations controlled 90 percent of the media. That's a high level of concentration. Today, as a result of massive mergers and take-overs, six corporations control 90 percent of what we see, hear, and read. This is outrageous, and a real threat to our democracy. Those six corporations are Comcast, News Corp, Disney, Viacom, Time Warner, and CBS. In 2010, the total revenue of these six corporations was $275 billion. In a recent article in *Forbes* magazine

discussing media ownership, the headline appropriately read: "These 15 Billionaires Own America's News
Media Companies."

Exploding technology is transforming the media
world, and mergers and takeovers are changing the nature of ownership. Freepress.net is one of the best media watchdog organizations in the country, and has been
opposed to the kind of media consolidation that we have
seen in recent years. It has put together a very powerful
description of what media concentration means. Some
examples from Freepress:

COMCAST
2011 Revenue: $55.8 Billion

In 2011, the Federal Communications Commission
approved Comcast's takeover of a majority share of
NBCUniversal from General Electric. This merger
combines the nation's largest cable company and
residential Internet service provider and one of the
world's biggest producers of TV shows and motion
pictures. Comcast's media holdings now reach almost
every home in America. It serves customers in thirty-
nine states and the District of Columbia. In addition
to its vast NBCUniversal holdings, Comcast has 23.6
million cable subscribers, 18 million digital cable
subscribers, 15.9 million high-speed Internet customers, and 7.6 million voice customers. Comcast
recently entered into a partnership with Verizon in
which each company will market and sell the other's
services.

TV: NBCUniversal; twenty-four television stations
and the NBC television network; Telemundo; USA
Network; SyFy; CNBC; MSNBC; Bravo; Oxygen;
Chiller; CNBC World; E!; the Golf Channel; Sleuth;

mun2; Universal HD; VERSUS; Style; G4; Comcast SportsNet (Philadelphia), Comcast SportsNet Mid-Atlantic (Baltimore/Washington, D.C.), Cable Sports Southeast, Comcast SportsNet Chicago, Mountain-West Sports Network, Comcast SportsNet California (Sacramento), Comcast SportsNet New England (Boston), Comcast SportsNet Northwest (Portland, Ore.), Comcast Sports Southwest (Houston), Comcast SportsNet Bay Area (San Francisco), New England Cable News (Boston), Comcast Network Philadelphia, Comcast Network Mid-Atlantic (Baltimore/Washington, D.C.); the Weather Channel (25 percent stake); A&E (16 percent stake); the History Channel (16 percent stake); the Biography Channel (16 percent stake); Lifetime (16 percent stake); the Crime and Investigation Channel (16 percent stake); Pittsburgh Cable News Channel (30 percent stake); FEARnet (31 percent stake); PBS KIDS Sprout (40 percent stake); TV One (34 percent stake); Houston Regional Sports Network (23 percent stake); SportsNet New York (8 percent stake)

Online Holdings: MSNBC.com (50 percent stake); Hulu (32 percent stake); DailyCandy; iVillage; Fandango

Telecom: Clearwire Communications (9 percent stake)

Other: Comcast Interactive Media; Plaxo; Universal Studios Hollywood; Wet 'n Wild theme park; Universal Studios Florida; Universal Islands of Adventure; Philadelphia 76ers; Philadelphia Flyers; Wells Fargo Center; iN DEMAND; Music Choice (12 percent stake), SpectrumCo (64 percent stake)

WALT DISNEY COMPANY
2011 Revenue: $40.1 Billion

The Walt Disney Company owns the ABC television network; cable networks including ESPN, the Disney Channel, SOAPnet, A&E and Lifetime; 277 radio stations, music- and book-publishing companies; film-production companies Touchstone, Miramax and Walt Disney Pictures; Pixar Animation Studios; the cellular service Disney Mobile; and theme parks around the world.

TV: Eight television stations and the ABC television network; ESPN; Disney Channels Worldwide; ABC Family; SOAPnet Networks; A&E (42 percent stake); Lifetime Television (42 percent stake); the History Channel (42 percent stake); Lifetime Movie Network (42 percent stake); the Biography Channel (42 percent stake); History International (42 percent stake); Lifetime Real Women (42 percent stake); Live Well Network (42 percent stake)

Radio: ESPN Radio Network; Radio Disney

Print: *ESPN The Magazine*; Disney Publishing Worldwide; Juvenile Publishing; Digital Publishing; Disney Music Publishing; Marvel Publishing

Entertainment: Marvel Entertainment; ABC Studios; ABC Media Production; Pixar; Walt Disney Pictures; Walt Disney Records; Hollywood Records; Mammoth Records; Buena Vista Records; Lyric Street Records

Other: Buena Vista Concerts; Disney Mobile; Disney Theatrical Productions; the Disney Store; Disney theme parks and water parks; Disney English; Disney Interactive Media Group; Disney Games; Playdom, Inc.

NEWS CORP
2011 Revenue: $33.4 Billion

News Corp's media holdings include the Fox Broadcasting Company; television and cable networks such as Fox, Fox Business Channel, National Geographic, and FX; print publications including *The Wall Street Journal*, the *New York Post*, and *TV Guide*; the magazines *Barron's* and *SmartMoney*; book publisher HarperCollins; film production companies 20th Century Fox, Fox Searchlight Pictures, and Blue Sky Studios; numerous Web sites including MarketWatch .com; and nonmedia holdings including the National Rugby League.

TV: Twenty-seven television stations and Fox Broadcasting Company (Fox Network, MyNetworkTV); Fox News; Fox Business; Fox News Radio Network; Fox News Talk Channel; FSN (12 regional sports networks); FX; SPEED; FUEL TV; Fox College Sports; Fox Movie Channel; Fox Soccer Channel; Fox Soccer Plus; Fox Pan American Sports; Fox Deportes; Big Ten Network; National Geographic U.S.; Nat Geo Adventure; Nat Geo Music; Nat Geo Wild; Fox International Channels; Utilisima; Fox Crime; NEXT; Fox History & Entertainment; the Voyage Channel; STAR World; STAR Movies; NGC Network International; NGC Network Latin America; LAPTV; Movie City; City Mix; City Family; City Stars; City Vibe; the Film Zone; Cinecanal; Elite Sports Limited; BabyTV; STAR India; STAR Taiwan; ESPN STAR Sports; Shine Limited

Online Holdings: Hulu.com (32 percent minority share)

Print: HarperCollins Publishers; the *New York Post*; the *Daily News*; News International (the *Times*; the *Sunday Times*; the *Sun*); News Limited (146 newspapers in Australia); Dow Jones (*The Wall Street Journal*, *Barron's*, *SmartMoney*, Factiva, Dow Jones Newswires, Dow Jones Local Media, Dow Jones VentureSource)

Telecom: Satellite: BSkyB (39 percent minority share); SKY Italia

Entertainment: Fox Filmed Entertainment; Twentieth Century Fox Home Entertainment; Twentieth Century Fox Television; Twentieth Television; Fox Television Studios

Other: Marketing/advertising: News America Marketing Group; News Outdoor; Fox Library; IGN Entertainment, Inc.; Making Fun, Inc.; Wireless Generation

TIME WARNER
2011 Revenue: $29 Billion

Time Warner is the world's second-largest entertainment conglomerate with ownership interests in film, television, and print.

TV: One television station and the Warner Brothers Television Group; Warner Brothers Television; Warner Horizon Television; CW Network (50 percent stake); TBS; TNT; Cartoon Network; truTV; Turner Classic Movies; Boomerang; CNN; HLN; CNN International; HBO; Cinemax; Space; Infinito; I-Sat; Fashion TV; HTV; Much Music; Pogo; Mondo TV; Tabi; CNN Español

Online Holdings: Warner Brothers Digital Distribution; TMZ.com; KidsWB.com

Print: Time, Inc.; 22 magazines including *People*, *Sports Illustrated*, *Time*, *Life*, *InStyle*, *Real Simple*, *Southern Living*, *Entertainment Weekly,* and *Fortune*

Entertainment: Warner Brothers; Warner Brothers Pictures; New Line Cinema; Castle Rock; WB Studio Enterprises, Inc.; Telepictures Productions, Inc.; Warner Brothers Animation, Inc.; Warner Home Video; Warner Premiere; Warner Specialty Films, Inc.; Warner Brothers International Cinemas

Other: Warner Brothers Interactive Entertainment; DC Entertainment; DC Comics

VIACOM
2011 Revenue: $14.9 Billion

Viacom is the world's fourth-largest media conglomerate, with interests primarily in cable television networks, programming production, and distribution. Viacom controls over 160 networks that reach more than 600 million people around the globe.

TV: Viacom Media Networks (160 cable channels including MTV, VH1, CMT, Logo, Nickelodeon, Comedy Central, TV Land, Spike TV, Tr3s, BET, and CENTRIC)

Online Holdings: ParentsConnect.com

Entertainment: Viacom Filmed Entertainment (produces motion pictures under numerous studio brands including Paramount Pictures, Insurge Pictures, MTV Films, and Nickelodeon Movies)

Other: Nickelodeon Games Group

CBS
2011 Revenue: $14.2 Billion

CBS Corporation "has operations in virtually every field of media and entertainment, including broadcast television (CBS and the CW—a joint venture between CBS Corporation and Warner Bros. Entertainment), cable television (Showtime Networks, Smithsonian Networks, and CBS Sports Network), local television (CBS television stations), television production and syndication (CBS Television Studios, CBS Studios International, and CBS Television Distribution), radio (CBS Radio), advertising on out-of-home media (CBS Outdoor), publishing (Simon & Schuster), interactive media (CBS Interactive), music (CBS Records), licensing and merchandising (CBS Consumer Products), video/DVD (CBS Home Entertainment), motion pictures (CBS Films), and socially responsible media (EcoMedia).

TV: Twenty-nine television stations and CBS Television Studios; CBS Entertainment; CBS News; CBS Sports; CBS television stations; CBS Studios International; CBS Television Distribution; the CW; Showtime; CBS College Sports Network; CBS Television Network; Smithsonian Networks

Radio: CBS Radio and 130 radio stations

Online Holdings: CBS Interactive; CNET

Print: Simon & Schuster; *Watch!* magazine; Pocket Books; Scribner; Free Press (publishing house)

Entertainment: CBS Films

Other: CBS Outdoor; CBS Connections; EcoMedia

No sane person denies that the media plays an enormously important role in shaping public consciousness and determining political outcomes. The current media situation in America, where a handful of giant corporations controls the flow of information, is a very serious threat to our democracy.

The very first amendment to our Constitution guarantees freedom of speech and freedom of the press, the right of the people to express their points of view from the rooftops, to allow themselves to be heard. That is something I passionately believe in, because it is the essence of democracy. Unfortunately, as A. J. Liebling wrote back in 1960: "Freedom of the press is guaranteed only to those who own one." And the people who own the press, radio and television stations, and book publishing and movie companies are becoming fewer and fewer, with more and more power. This is a crisis that can no longer be ignored.

CONCLUSION

There were tears and there was disappointment at the Democratic National Convention in Philadelphia when I addressed the delegates there on July 26. For the almost two thousand Sanders supporters who were there that night, and the millions who watched on television, there was the understanding that we had defied the odds, that we had almost pulled off one of the great upsets in American political history, that we had come so very far—just not far enough.

What I said that night, and what I repeat now, is that election days come and go, and our campaign is over. But the political revolution, our revolution, must continue. The fight for economic, social, racial, and environmental justice can never stop. The fight to defeat the greed of the billionaire class must continue.

I hope very much that my campaign for president will not be endlessly discussed from an *historical* perspective, looking back. I hope that my efforts, and the incredibly hard work of hundreds of thousands of grassroots volunteers in every state in our country, will be seen as a turning point in American politics and a blueprint for the future.

For the people who worked in our campaign, I hope that you will stay involved and get your friends involved. Run for the school board, city council, state legislature. Run for governor. Run for Congress. Run for the Senate. Run for president. Hold your elected officials accountable. Know what they're doing and how they're voting—and tell your neighbors.

But transforming America is more than just elections. It's about changing our culture.

Demand that the media focus on the *real* issues facing our nation and the world, not just political gossip. And if corporate media won't change, and they won't, start new media. The Internet offers revolutionary prospects.

This nation treats our children shamefully. We must focus on the needs of the young, especially the many who are disadvantaged. As we change our national priorities, we must prioritize education and will be in desperate need of great educators and child-care workers.

With so many Americans uninsured and underinsured, we need hundreds of thousands of new doctors, dentists, nurses, and other medical personnel. We should not be lagging behind many other countries in life expectancy, especially for lower-income Americans.

We need a radical change in our criminal justice system. We need new law enforcement officials and police officers who understand that our primary goal must be crime prevention, which requires a whole new level of cooperation with educators, social workers, and employers.

In order to combat the global threat of climate change, we need scientists and engineers who will develop clean and inexpensive forms of energy and transportation. There is unbelievable potential in the energy field, and we must not allow the fossil fuel industry to stop us.

We need businesspeople who create and sell new and

innovative products and services, and who treat their employees with respect and dignity, while protecting the environment. Our goal must be to use the exploding technology that we are experiencing to improve life for our people, not to increase unemployment or invade our privacy.

As I've said before, I ended the campaign with far more optimism about the future of this country than when I began. I had the incredible privilege of *seeing* the future in the eyes of well over a million Americans who came out to our town meetings and rallies, many of them young people.

They were white, black, Latino, Native American, and Asian-American. They were men and women, gay and straight. Most were born in this country, some immigrated here. But they all understood that when we stand *together*, when we don't allow demagogues to divide us up, there is nothing we cannot accomplish. They love this country and they know that we can do much, much better.

The great crisis that we face as a nation is not just the objective problems that we face—a rigged economy, a corrupt campaign finance system, a broken criminal justice system, and the extraordinary threat of climate change. The more serious crisis is the limitation of our imaginations. It is falling victim to an incredibly powerful establishment—economic, political, and media— that tells us every day, in a million different ways, that real change is unthinkable and impossible. That we have got to think small, not big. That we must be satisfied with the status quo. That there are no alternatives.

The future of our country and, perhaps, the world requires us to break through those limitations. Humanity is at a crossroads. We can continue down the current path of greed, consumerism, oligarchy, poverty, war, racism, and environmental degradation. Or we can lead the world in moving in a very different direction.

Yes. We can overcome the insatiable greed that now exists and create an economy that ends poverty and provides a decent standard of living for all. Yes. We can create a vibrant democracy where knowledgeable citizens actively debate the great challenges they face. Yes. We can create a health care system that guarantees health care for every man, woman, and child, and that focuses on disease prevention and keeping us healthy, not outrageous profits for insurance companies and the pharmaceutical industry. Yes. We can effectively combat climate change and transform our energy system away from fossil fuel and into energy efficiency and sustainable energy.

No. We will not be able to accomplish those goals if we look at democracy as a spectator sport, assuming others will do it for us. They won't. The future is in *your* hands. Let's get to work.

ACKNOWLEDGMENTS

This book could not have been written in the short timeline that we had without the help of two longtime coworkers of mine, Warren Gunnels and David Weinstein. My wife, Jane, also played an invaluable role. I also want to thank Michael Briggs, Huck Gutman, Shannon Jackson, and Ellyn Heald for their help. Peter Joseph, Thomas Dunne, and the staff at Macmillan were very helpful throughout the entire process, and I much appreciate the support they gave this endeavor.

The success of our campaign was not an accident. It occurred because of the dedication and hard work of hundreds of thousands of volunteers in every state in our country, and because we had a staff that not only worked tirelessly but was prepared to think creatively and outside of the box.

Obviously, I am unable to list the names of all of our supporters, volunteers, or the many hundreds of staff that worked so hard on our campaign. But those are the people who made it all happen. Our supporters contributed financially, they spread the word, and they marched in parades with me. Our volunteers knocked on doors and made phone calls, helped our social media efforts, and organized house parties. Our staff did the difficult advance work that enabled us to have hundreds of rallies and town meetings, pay our bills, and make all the arrangements for the services we contracted. Our media team helped us get the word out.

To all those who helped, in whatever capacity, I say THANK YOU. Together we have made a difference in our country. Together we will carry on.

Bernie Sanders
Burlington, Vermont
September 26, 2016